POLICIES AND PRACTICES IN PUBLIC PERSONNEL
ADMINISTRATION

Report of the Committee on
Position-Classification and Pay Plans in the Public Service
of the
Civil Service Assembly of the United States and Canada

POSITION-CLASSIFICATION
IN THE PUBLIC SERVICE

Committee on

POSITION-CLASSIFICATION AND PAY PLANS IN THE PUBLIC SERVICE

of the

CIVIL SERVICE ASSEMBLY

of the United States and Canada

Chairman: ISMAR BARUCH
United States Civil Service Commission

HARRY ALBERT
San Francisco City and County
Civil Service Commission

GEORGE C. S. BENSON
Northwestern University

C. L. CAMPBELL
New York State Department of
Civil Service

MERRILL J. COLLETT
Public Administration Service

A. E. GAREY
American Federation of State,
County, and Municipal Employees

E. O. GRIFFENHAGEN
Griffenhagen & Associates

ROBERT S. HARE
United States Department of
Agriculture

L. W. HOELSCHER
United States Bureau of the Budget

J. L. JACOBS
J. L. Jacobs & Company

HOWARD P. JONES
New York State Civil Service
Commission

H. ELIOT KAPLAN
National Civil Service Reform League

HARRY W. MARSH
Connecticut State Department of
Personnel

STANLEY OREAR
National Youth Administration

CLARENCE V. PUTMAN
Civil Service Commission of Canada

CARL L. RICHEY
Tennessee Valley Authority

WILLIAM K. SMITH
California State Personnel Board

JOHN STEVEN
Personnel Commission, Los Angeles
City Schools

LUTHER C. STEWARD
National Federation of Federal
Employees

DONALD C. STONE
United States Bureau of the Budget

EMIL WACHTEL
Farm Security Administration

POSITION-CLASSIFICATION IN THE PUBLIC SERVICE

A Report Submitted to the
CIVIL SERVICE ASSEMBLY

By the Committee on
Position-Classification and Pay Plans
in the Public Service

Ismar Baruch, Chairman

CIVIL SERVICE ASSEMBLY
OF THE UNITED STATES AND CANADA

CHICAGO

Public Personnel Association

1313 East 60th Street
Chicago, Illinois   60637

Foreword

THE management of governmental affairs has become increasingly important as the activities of governments have grown in magnitude and broadened in scope, particularly during the last quarter of a century. This has led inevitably to an intensification of interest in problems relating to personnel administration—a function that is an essential and integral part of over-all management. The rapid extension and improvement of merit systems in national, state, and local governments and the renewed interest of many important groups in public personnel problems have marked this development during the last few years. All interested groups, including public personnel workers themselves, have long felt the serious need for a searching review and appraisal of existing personnel policies and practices and the formulation of proposals for the more complete and satisfactory performance of personnel activities. Plans for meeting this need were approved by the Executive Council of the Civil Service Assembly in 1937. The present report is one of a series which, when completed, will bring together for the first time a set of authoritative and forward-looking volumes dealing with the major phases of public personnel administration.

More than sixty outstanding personnel officials, general administrators, technical and research workers, educators, and representatives of civic, professional, and employee groups actively participated in the preliminary planning of this huge undertaking. It was agreed that the final findings and reports resulting from this comprehensive effort would be based upon special field studies of public personnel policies and practices, which would be supplemented by information obtained from existing studies and reports dealing with personnel problems and by the ideas and suggestions of those who were in a position to make helpful contributions because of their training or experience. It was further agreed that the reports should not be the work

v

of one person, or of a small group of persons, professing omniscience in the field. It was felt that the final reports should be the product of group effort and group thinking, which could be realized through the appointment of a series of committees whose members would give their time, energies, and ideas to make the undertaking successful.

To collect and appraise facts regarding present public personnel policies and practices, a specially recruited staff conducted field studies covering twenty-two different public personnel agencies selected because of their differences in size, location, and problems. In each jurisdiction one or more members of this field staff conducted intensive interviews with personnel administrators, technicians, departmental administrators and supervisors, political leaders, and representatives of organized employee associations. Approximately four hundred persons were interviewed during the course of the field studies. Complete notes were made of these interviews. Information and suggestions obtained in this way were supplemented by a careful study and review of other materials, such as: appropriate legislation; annual and special reports of the personnel agencies; special studies and memoranda regarding the work of the personnel agencies which had been prepared by outside organizations and disinterested persons; personnel tests, forms, records, statistics, and methods; and finally, actual observations of the agencies' operations. On many occasions, significant and helpful documentary material not ordinarily available to a researcher was placed at the disposal of the field staff.

As a result of this work, a detailed case history was prepared for each agency covered by the survey. Each case history included statements of fact regarding the personnel policies and practices of the agency; ideas and suggestions obtained from those interviewed, from reports, and from other sources; a critical appraisal of the policies and practices of the agency as they were actually working; and suggestions for changes and improvements which originated with those interviewed or members of the survey staff. The information and suggestions included in each case history were gathered and organized according to a prearranged plan that made it possible to classify the material into broad categories corresponding to certain major aspects of public personnel administration.

The case histories and all other available materials were then placed in the hands of a number of committees for use as basic information in the preparation of final reports. Each committee was given the task of preparing a report dealing with a specified functional subject in the field of public personnel administration. In addition to the case histories, the committees were given access to supplementary descriptive and interpretative material regarding many agencies not covered by the field survey; special reports and theses relating to the work of personnel agencies and to technical and administrative problems in personnel administration; selected bibliographies; and other materials brought together by the Assembly's Headquarters Office in connection with its regular activities as a clearing house in the field of public personnel administration. Committee chairmen and members were encouraged to augment this material by consulting with persons and groups who were in a position to make substantial contributions of ideas and facts and by conducting special investigations and researches. Through the occasional issuance of memoranda and special notes, all committee members were kept currently informed of the progress being made and the problems being faced by participants in the undertaking.

Following a procedure approved by the Assembly's Executive Council regarding each committee, one person was appointed by the President of the Assembly to serve as chairman of an advisory committee to prepare an appropriate report on the particular subject or phase of public personnel administration assigned to it. The members of each committee were chosen because of their interest in, and knowledge of, the matter falling within the committee's general jurisdiction, and because of the diverse viewpoints which they could bring to the committee's work. More than three hundred persons have served on the several committees. About one-half of them are persons actively engaged in public personnel administration. The other half are general administrators, educators, industrial personnel workers, and leading members or representatives of civic and professional groups, governmental research associations, and employee organizations.

It has been the responsibility of each chairman to initiate and coordinate the activities of his committee. The work methods of the several chairmen have naturally differed. Some have used their committees largely as sounding boards on various problems or proposals referred to them and have asked committee members to review outlines and manuscripts and to offer their comments, criticisms, and suggestions for the purpose of injecting the influence of their composite views and experiences into the final reports. Others have asked individual committee members to assume the task of bringing together all necessary material regarding a particular segment of the committee's assignment and to prepare a corresponding section of the final report. It has been the chairman's responsibility, without obtaining formal action by the committee, to reconcile differences of approach and to mold his own ideas and materials and those submitted by his committee members into a final integrated report. This procedure has made it possible for each report to represent the collective contributions of outstanding thinkers and doers in public personnel administration, and of persons engaged in other fields who have the vision, imagination, and freedom from professional introversion to propound the broad principles and objectives that should determine the role of personnel administration in the over-all scheme of public affairs.

At the very inception of the undertaking, it was stressed that each report should represent a synthesis of the most effective and desirable policies and practices on a particular phase of public personnel administration. It was contemplated that each report would be more than a mere tallying of existing practices and malpractices, and that it would thus be qualitative rather than quantitative. It was also agreed that each report would not only carry the story of the effective steps which had been taken by personnel agencies to reach certain objectives, but would go further and project beyond present policies and practices to more desirable or acceptable ones.

Any statement regarding the undertaking would be incomplete without acknowledgment of the contributions which have been received from a number of individuals and organizations. Members of the Assembly's Headquarters Office staff, past and present, have made substantial contributions and rendered effective help throughout the various phases of the project. The broad general outline of the study as a whole was first conceived by G. Lyle Belsley, then Director of the Headquarters Office. He, together with Henry F. Hubbard and Maxwell A. DeVoe, laid the foundation for the study and devised the procedures for its execution. Mr. DeVoe was responsible for the immediate supervision of the special field staff originally engaged in gathering information contained in the case studies and for coordinating the efforts of the several committees participating in the preparation of final reports. John Steven and Doris Haney Jones assisted ably in the gathering of the material contained in the various case studies. With the departure of Mr. DeVoe from the staff, the work of coordinating committee activities and the editorial work involved in preparing the various reports for publication have been the responsibility of Jeremiah Donovan.

Sincere appreciation is hereby tendered to the many public-spirited persons who, without compensation, took an active and helpful part in planning this undertaking and bringing it to its present stage of completion. Great help and much useful information have been made available to the Assembly in connection with this effort by the associations of public agencies and public officials located in the same building with the Assembly's Headquarters Office at 1313 East 60th Street, Chicago, as well as by various other organizations throughout the country. Acknowledgment is made for the assistance rendered by Public Administration Service throughout the process of printing and publishing this report. The Assembly is grateful to the several copyright holders who have permitted the quotations of copyrighted materials in the report. Finally, the entire undertaking was made possible through the finances generously provided by the Spelman Fund of New York. Without this assistance, it would be impossible for the undertaking to achieve the intended goals.

Committee chairmen and members have been able to take only a limited amount of time away from their regular activities for the purpose of carrying forward the undertaking. This fact, together with unforeseeable difficulties encountered by various committees, has made it impossible for all reports of the series to be finished simultaneously or in schematic order. It has therefore been decided to publish the reports, for the most part, in the order of their completion.

This report, *Position-Classification in the Public Service,* like all others in the series, is a document which a committee has prepared and submitted to the Civil Service Assembly. The information and recommendations presented in its pages represent the collective thinking of the chairman and his committee. It is to be stressed, however, that the report was not prepared with a view toward official approval or formal adoption by the Civil Service Assembly, its Executive Council, or its Headquarters staff, and no action of this nature is contemplated. The report is, however, as forward-looking and authoritative as an able chairman and a group of competent associates have been able to make it.

JAMES M. MITCHELL, *Director*
Civil Service Assembly

Preface

Two years ago the Civil Service Assembly's Committee on Position-Classification and Pay Plans endeavored to outline the content of a comprehensive report that would be useful to persons having distinct interests in a wide variety of jurisdictions. We had misgivings that one report on position-classification could adequately take into account the effect of variations in the size and functional complexity of governments at different levels—national, state, and local. We had doubts that one report could adequately satisfy the specific interests of civil service commissioners, directors of personnel, other public personnel administrators, members of their technical staffs, executives and employees in fiscal and operating agencies, legislators, members of professional, civic, and employee organizations, and instructors and students in institutions of learning. The writing of this report on position-classification plans in the public service has not entirely dissipated these misgivings and doubts.

Readers who are familiar with public position-classification will observe that the background of a good part of the report is that of the average-sized jurisdiction. This is particularly true of the chapters on development and continuous administration. Only occasionally has direct reference been made to special problems arising out of extremes in size of jurisdiction. A recent publication of Public Administration Service, *Personnel Programs for Smaller Cities,* indicates that the smaller jurisdictions and their special problems furnish a fruitful field for the preparation and publication of other specialized reports of this type.

Because of the breadth of the subject matter covered and its division into chapters, we hope we have come reasonably close to satisfying the interests of our varied groups of readers. Public personnel administrators and members of their technical staffs will find much on techniques and procedures. Operating executives, legislators, and members of professional, civic, and employee groups will in other chapters find broader discussions of the principles and administrative advantages of position-classification. Technicians will observe the repetition of familiar material. Others may observe that certain parts of the report are too detailed and technical for their use. This, however, is to be expected of a report written for readers who have so many different attitudes and interests.

We have tried to bring together here in one place an adequate discussion of position-classification. This does not mean that all problems are solved and all differences of judgment resolved by some categorical solution upon which the committee has agreed. Generally, most classification workers concur on fundamental principles and on major viewpoints and procedures. There are, however, healthy disagreements on some points. These differences are usually questions of emphasis or practical advantage in a particular situation rather than clashes on fundamentals. It should not be assumed that the committee are in accord as to every statement, suggestion, or conclusion in the report. If agreement on all points were the objective, this report would never have been written. Position-classification is in some respects a still developing art. For example, the precise way in which classes of positions should be arranged to facilitate the development and administration of a pay plan, the form and content of class specifications, even the system of titling classes, are among the several phases of position-classification technique that justify the careful observation and recording of experience in the future. We will be satisfied if this report serves to stimulate the further development and use of position-classification as a facilitating instrument for personnel administration.

The Chairman wishes to record the aid of the members of the committee and others, to whom are due his own grateful acknowledgment and the appreciation of all who find this report useful. The case history studies of personnel administration in twenty-two jurisdictions, prepared by the staff of the Headquarters Office of the Assembly, have constituted a valuable source of reference. Maxwell A. DeVoe, then with the Headquarters Office, prepared many of these reports, outlined initially the scope of this report, and revised portions of the text.

Throughout this project, members of the committee developed the scope of the report, suggested methods of treating various problems, and criticized drafts of text. In some instances, they prepared initial drafts of parts of the text for the chairman's use. Special contributions from members of the committee were as follows: George C. S. Benson prepared a first draft on the history of position-classification in Great Britain; Clarence V. Putman furnished a parallel draft with respect to Canada; Emil Wachtel wrote a first draft of the chapter on basic legal authority. The criticisms and comments of William K. Smith were also exceptionally helpful.

Special acknowledgement is made to Donald C. Stone, and to David L. Robinson Jr., and his associates in Public Administration Service. A similar acknowledgment is made to Carl Richey and his staff members in the Personnel Division of the Tennessee Valley Authority. We are indebted to E. O. Griffenhagen and Frank O. Everett, of Griffenhagen & Associates, and to J. L. Jacobs, of J. L. Jacobs & Co., for advice and criticism drawn from long experience in this field. In particular, we have availed ourselves of the permission of Griffenhagen & Associates to use portions of text from official reports which they prepared.

All members of the Committee except the chairman should be absolved of responsibility for any inadequacies, disproportions, poor judgments, or plain mistakes. Notwithstanding the difficulty encountered by the chairman in attempting to coordinate at long range the views of almost a score of associates, he had the responsibility of weighing their contributions and criticisms and of writing the final report.

The Committee will continue its work on the preparation of a parallel report, to be entitled "Pay Plans in the Public Service."

ISMAR BARUCH

United States Civil Service Commission
Washington, D. C.

Contents

Chapter V. POSITION ANALYSIS FOR CLASSIFICATION PURPOSES

Contents

Chapter VI. BASIC LEGAL AUTHORITY

Chapter VII. DEVELOPMENT AND ADOPTION

Chapter IX. CLASS SPECIFICATIONS

Chapter X. CONTINUOUS ADMINISTRATION OF THE PLAN

Appendices

POSITION-CLASSIFICATION

IN THE PUBLIC SERVICE

Chapter I

Position-Classification and Personnel Administration

INTRODUCTION

THE growth in the magnitude and complexity of governmental services, the importance of personnel in the operations of government, and the unique responsibility of government to the people in general and the taxpayers in particular, are factors which have led to common agreement that matters of personnel administration in government should be conducted on a planned and systematic basis, logically and equitably applied. To do this requires an effective program for public personnel administration in the jurisdiction concerned. Such a program must not only be based on sound policies, objectives, and plans, but must also provide for the use of modern methods and procedures—tools of administration—through which these plans and policies may be executed and their objectives reached.

The soundness of general policies and plans and the effectiveness of procedural methods in personnel work depend, among other things, on knowledge of facts about the service, its organization, work activities, positions, and personnel. A most important part of this factual basis for planning and action consists of facts about the duties and responsibilities of the individual positions in the service. These facts influence personnel processes and individual transactions, including those of recruiting, the establishment and administration of pay scales, promotion, transfer, and the development and conduct of training programs, as well as budgetary and other fiscal operations touching personnel administration. The great mass of factual data coming under this category and its very volume and complexity make the service and its position-content incomprehensible unless such data are properly organized for use.

It is easy to see how futile would be the attempt of any executive, legislator, or civic-minded citizen in a sizable public jurisdiction to remember and mentally arrange the facts about thousands of individual positions every time he was called upon to take a stand on some administrative issue, render a decision on a personnel problem, provide or expend funds for salaries, or vote upon or administer personnel laws or ordinances. In particular, he would find it impossible to know which positions are sufficiently alike to be treated alike so far as his problem or decision is concerned, and which require different treatment. If each of several thousand individual positions has to be studied as a separate item every time a personnel or pay policy must be enunciated, an administrative or budgetary problem solved, a position filled, a personnel procedure or rule applied, or an employee's pay rate fixed, a confused and inefficient situation results, unsatisfactory to legislators, administrators, employees, and the public.

Also, the very nature of governmental jurisdictions places them in a position of peculiar responsibility to the public at large. Individual actions without plan or system and based merely upon the expediency of the moment are undesirable. Public personnel policies and transactions affecting positions and employees should be supportable by facts and logic in the light of broad considerations applicable to the service as a whole. Further, in the management of public personnel affairs, considerations of fairness and equity require uniform action under like circumstances, particularly in the establishment of pay rates. Uniformity, however, is impossible unless it is known in advance what circumstances are sufficiently alike to warrant uniform treatment.

For all these reasons, current facts about the duties and responsibilities of positions need to be maintained in scientifically summarized and correlated fashion: (1) so that the impossible task of understanding readily the myriad details incidental to a mass of individual positions will give way to the comparatively easy task of comprehending a much smaller number of differentiated *classes* of positions; (2) so that positions which should be treated alike when personnel policies, problems, or actions are under consideration can easily be identified and dealt with by groups; and (3) so that, by emphasis on an impartial, scientific approach which utilizes safeguards against favoritism and procedures for equitable treatment, a purely personalized treatment of work and pay problems can be avoided.

Thus, effective personnel administration requires that there be applied to positions the same processes of objective classification and definition that are used to bring order out of a complex array of facts in science, art, and administration generally.

THE MEANING OF "POSITION-CLASSIFICATION"

Reduced to its simplest terms, classification of positions means the process of finding out, by obtaining the facts and analyzing them, what different kinds or "classes" of positions, calling for different treatment in personnel processes, there are in the service; it further includes making a systematic record of the classes found and of the particular positions found to be of each class.[1] The duties and responsibilities of the positions are the basis upon which classes are determined and the individual positions assigned or "allocated" to their appropriate classes.[2]

When every position has been allocated to its appropriate class, each class will consist of all positions, regardless of departmental location, that are sufficiently alike in duties and responsibilities to be called by the same descriptive title, to be accorded the same pay scale under like conditions, and to require substantially the same qualifications on the part of the incumbents. The class in which each individual position has been allocated can be shown simply by giving the position the title of that class which is defined by a written class definition, or "class specification." By such means the nature of each position is determined and identified, and a mass of information concerning the duties and responsibilities of individual positions is reduced in logical fashion to manageable proportions.

Position-classification, like any other service-wide procedure, must be made a definite responsibility of some agency. Moreover, since the structure and functions of government are subject to continual change, the classes, class specifications, and allocations of positions must be changed correspondingly, as current conditions require. Therefore, the administering agency not only applies the classification plan to the service in the first instance, but also operates and amends it currently to keep it adapted to the service. Such an agency is particularly necessary to maintain a unified point of view from department to department.[3]

[1] Griffenhagen & Associates, *Report on Classification and Compensation of Positions in the Service of the Commonwealth of Virginia* (Richmond, 1937), pp. 5, 6, 27, 28.

[2] This is an objective, impersonal basis. Allocations of positions to classes are based on the essential characteristics of the work performed in each position, and not on the education, experience, background, efficiency, or ability that the incumbent employees at the time may happen to possess or lack. The basis of the classification process is discussed more at length in Chapter III.

[3] See pp. 288–91.

Thus, a position-classification plan embraces: (1) a clear-cut scheme of classes and class titles, designed to provide for the positions actually existing; (2) a set of definitions of these classes and class titles in the form of written specifications making clear the factors that should be decisive as to what positions belong in the class and that should distinguish them from those belonging in other classes; and (3) procedures and a code of rules for administering the classification, for allocating all positions in the service to their appropriate classes, for altering classes, class specifications, and allocations to meet changes in organization, methods, and assignments of work and responsibilities, and in general for maintaining conformity between the classification and the service as it exists.[4]

It is not the purpose of position-classification to "standardize the job," i.e., to prescribe the individual operations by which tasks or processes shall be performed, and to establish, by time or motion study, scientific standards of output and workmanship.[5] It accepts the jobs, or positions, as they are; its purpose is to show what they actually are and not what they should be. Position-classification, as carried out in the public service, is, therefore, to be distinguished from some of the aspects or applications of industrial job analysis.[6]

The process of classifying positions on the basis of their duties and responsibilities, and the concept of a "class of positions," as discussed here, should also be distinguished from the use of the words "class," "classified," or "unclassified" in other connections, especially when these terms are used merely to identify positions which are in-

4 "The Classification Plan for the Massachusetts State Service" (Excerpts from report of Griffenhagen & Associates), *Public Personnel Studies*, January 1927, p. 11.

5 Job standardization "establishes mechanical facilities and techniques to be matched with the human element in order not only to effect but to maintain standards of efficiency in this technique with those individuals best qualified to do the work." Gordon S. Watkins and Paul A. Dodd, *The Management of Labor Relations* (McGraw-Hill, 1938), p. 121.

6 Tead and Metcalf state that "job analysis is a scientific study and a statement of all the facts about a job which reveal its contents and the modifying factors which surround it." They outline a job analysis to include information about: A. The job itself (1. general description; 2. machinery; 3. tools and equipment; 4. materials; 5. motions; 6. time; 7. records; 8. pay); B. Qualifications necessary in the worker; C. Standard practice instructions; D. Effect of the job on the worker; and E. Relation of the job to the organization. They point out that "use of time study and motion study technique as methods of precise measurement and observation in connection with the use of job analysis to improve processes is now widely made." *Personnel Administration* (McGraw-Hill, 1926), pp. 250–54. It should be noted, however, that the classification of positions on the basis of their duties and responsibilities is used in private industry, especially some of the larger and more progressive establishments, to accomplish the same purposes as in the public service. See pp. 27–30.

cluded within or excluded from the jurisdiction or authority of the public personnel agency over the selection of appointees, or which are subject to a particular appointment procedure. For example, the term "class" is frequently used in such expressions as "exempt class," "competitive class," "noncompetitive class," "labor class," etc., to distinguish positions according to the legal requirements of the recruiting process.[7] In a good many jurisdictions, the expression "the classified civil service" is used to indicate the positional area under the merit system. Sometimes the "classified civil service" and the position-classification plan happen to be conterminous, but sometimes they are quite different in scope.

To avoid the confusion incident to the use of the same term to apply to two different concepts, it has been suggested that the term "jurisdictional classification" should refer to the classification of positions according to the degree of jurisdiction possessed by the personnel agency over the process of filling them, and that the expression "duties or occupational classification" should refer to the classification of positions on the basis of their duties and responsibilities.[8] However, the preferable term, "position-classification," has come into common use.

VALUE IN PERSONNEL ADMINISTRATION

Position-classification is an administrative instrument of wide usefulness and value in personnel administration. It groups individual positions into classes of positions on a basis that has real meaning in personnel administration. By emphasizing an impartial scientific approach, it helps avoid a purely personalized treatment of work and pay problems. It aids recruiting and testing authorities by making it possible to hold tests for classes of positions instead of a larger number of tests for individual positions having immaterial differences and by furnishing for each class a picture of the work to be performed

[7] "The term 'class' refers to the divisions of the classified service based upon the distinctive methods of appointment to the positions comprehended therein. . . . The positions in the classified service are hereby divided into four classes, to be known as the exempt class, the competitive class, the noncompetitive class, and the labor class." New York State Department of Civil Service, *Model Municipal Civil Service Rules*, 1938, Sec. 5, Rule I (p. 1) and Sec. 1, Rule VIII (p. 5).

[8] "Preliminary Report of the Conference Committee on the Merit System," *Public Personnel Studies*, January 1926, p. 7; "Proposed Rules for a Public Personnel Agency, with Explanatory Comments," *ibid.*, June 1928, pp. 122–23. See also Paul V. Betters, *The Personnel Classification Board* (The Brookings Institution, 1931), pp. 17–18.

and a statement of qualification requirements. In its use as a sound basis for a fairly administered pay plan, it serves the interests of the people, the taxpayers, the operating officials, and the employees. Its system of class titles constitutes a uniform job language defined in class specifications, which in itself provides a base for common understanding among all those agencies and officials having to do with personnel administration. It facilitates the preparation of informative budgets for personal services; clarifies promotion and transfer transactions; aids in developing service rating plans and training programs; aids in planning, clarifying, and improving organization; facilitates the development of good employee-management relations; and makes it possible to keep significant service records and compile meaningful personnel statistics.

In these and many other ways it serves as a facilitating instrument for personnel management and administrative operation, and as a specific tool for conducting many types of transactions involving the public, present and prospective employees, operating officials, accounting, budgeting and appropriating agencies, and the personnel agency of the jurisdiction.[9] It is this broad usefulness which makes a well prepared, currently maintained classification plan for positions the keystone in a sound system of public personnel administration.

[9] For a more detailed description of the principal uses and advantages of a position-classification plan, see Chapter IV.

Chapter II

History of Position-Classification

UNTIL 1908, the concepts underlying position-classification had never been carried to the point of practical application in any jurisdiction in this country, although as ideas they had been recognized, perhaps somewhat inchoately, in official reports prior to that time. It remained for the Civil Service Commission of the City of Chicago and its staff to take the lead in giving practical effect to these concepts and in developing methods and techniques for the purpose.

The Chicago Commission, beginning in 1905, took a definite stand for the "regrading of the service on the basis of the duties performed by the employee, rather than on the basis of the compensation which he receives" and, on the basis of this grading, "the establishment of a salary system which shall have a direct relation to the grade of work in which the employee is engaged."

The program for classifying positions on the new basis of duties and responsibilities was begun by the Civil Service Commission in 1908 and later carried out through its Efficiency Division aided by the Mayor's Municipal Efficiency Commission.

The technical work of the Efficiency Division proceeded according to principles and methods which in their main outlines later became standard as a basis for similar work in other jurisdictions. After some trial and error, the idea was crystallized that the important thing to do was to classify the positions themselves in such a way as to bring together all of those that were sufficiently similar to make it practicable to give them the same treatment. This appears to be the definite origin of what is now known as a "class of positions."

There was thus introduced in municipal personnel administration the methodology of grouping positions into classes on the basis of their duties and responsibilities and the fixing of pay scales on the basis of this classification. This was a most important development because of the emphasis placed on the necessity of allocating to

7

classes the individual positions themselves, as contrasted with the mere preparation of a framework along general occupational lines. The position-classification principles and plan thus developed by the Chicago Commission was adopted by the City Council in 1912.[1]

In the period immediately following the initial activities in the Chicago service, other local jurisdictions, profiting by Chicago's contribution to the technique of public personnel administration, engaged in similar surveys.[2]

In 1911, legislation was enacted by the General Assembly of Illinois, extending the classification and salary standardization ideas, then being worked out in the Chicago service, to the three large Chicago park districts, to Cook County, and the State of Illinois.[3] In 1913 the Bureau of Municipal Research of New York City made a position-classification and salary study of the service in the cities of Milwaukee, Wisconsin,[4] and Portland, Oregon. In the same year, a survey of the Colorado state service was made by the civil service commission to provide a classification plan "on a basis of functions performed."

Other early classification studies were initiated in Pittsburgh and in New York City in 1914-15.[5]

In the New York State service in 1915, agitation for a study looking toward better administration of the state civil service system led to a resolution of the state senate, February 15, 1915, establishing a committee on civil service. A position-classification and a pay plan were developed and definite legislation was proposed in a comprehensive report.[6]

[1] Comprehensive accounts of the early work in Chicago are given in Bureau of Municipal Research, New York City, *Municipal Research*, August 1916, pp. 10–34, and in Edwin O. Griffenhagen, "The Origin of the Modern Occupational Classification in Personnel Administration," *Public Personnel Studies*, September 1924, pp. 184–94. The technical developments thus begun did not long survive in Chicago. See Joseph B. Kingsbury, "The Merit System in Chicago from 1915 to 1923," *ibid.*, November 1926, p. 310.

[2] "The work of the Chicago civil service commission seems to have left its impress more widely than any other single agency in the country. This is due in part to the fact that Chicago was the pioneer in standardization, and partly to the fact of its location which has permitted the Chicago civil service commission easily to effect contacts with cities both in the East and the West, which have looked to it for direction." *Municipal Research*, No. 67, Bureau of Municipal Research (New York City), November 1915, p. 42.

[3] James H. Burdette (President, Illinois Civil Service Commission), "Essentials of a Rational Classification of Service," *Proceedings*, Seventh Meeting of the National Assembly of Civil Service Commissions, June 1914, pp. 43–45.

[4] *Standardization of Salaries of the City of Milwaukee*, November 4, 1913.

[5] *Municipal Research*, August 1916, pp. 35–44, 45–83.

[6] *First Report of the Committee on Civil Service of the Senate of the State of New York*, transmitted to the Legislature March 27, 1916 (Albany: 1916); *Municipal Research*, August 1916, pp. 84–109.

Following this pioneering period, the recognition of position-classification as a necessary base for improved personnel administration spread rapidly. General classification surveys were made in numerous states, cities, and counties, in a large number of which position-classification plans were subsequently established by legislation. Between 1915 and 1920 position-classification plans were officially adopted in several jurisdictions, including Baltimore, Cleveland,[7] Los Angeles, Milwaukee, St. Louis, St. Paul, Seattle, Massachusetts, New Jersey,[8] Ohio, and Milwaukee County. During the next ten years, this group was enlarged by others, including Buffalo, Cincinnati,[9] Columbus, Detroit,[10] Duluth, San Francisco, Toledo, Maryland, Massachusetts (revision),[11] Pennsylvania,[12] Wisconsin,[13] Los Angeles County, St. Louis (Minn.) County, San Francisco County, and most of the Massachusetts counties. The last decade has seen a still greater acceleration in this direction. In this period position-classification plans have been adopted in many additional jurisdictions, including the states of California, New York,[14] Rhode Island, Minnesota, and Alabama; the cities of Minneapolis, Dallas, Bridgeport, Tucson, and Los Angeles; and the counties of Hamilton (Ohio), Suffolk (Mass.), Alameda and San Diego (Calif.).[15] The unprecedented expansion of merit system operations by state or local

[7]"Building up a Municipal Personnel System:—2. Cleveland," *Public Personnel Studies*, July 1928, pp. 161–64.

[8]Charles P. Messick and Fred Telford, "The Development and Administration of Classification and Compensation Plans in the State Service of New Jersey," *ibid.*, April 1925, pp. 122–30.

[9]"Building up a Municipal Personnel System:—1. Cincinnati," *ibid.*, April 1928, pp. 83–86.

[10]Fred Telford and Frank O. Everett, "The Detroit Classification and Salary Standardization Study of 1924," *ibid.*, March 1925, pp. 85–96; "Building up a Municipal Personnel System:—3. Detroit," *ibid.*, January 1929, pp. 2–7.

[11]"The Policies and Procedure Involved in Developing a Compensation Plan for the Massachusetts State Service," *ibid.*, December 1926; "The Classification Plan for the Massachusetts State Service," *ibid.*, January 1927, pp. 11–18.

[12]Clyde L. King and Richard H. Lansburgh, "Pennsylvania Classifies her Employees," *National Municipal Review*, January 1924, pp. 15–19; Lansburgh, "Classification and Standardization in Pennsylvania," *Proceedings*, Seventeenth Annual Meeting of the Assembly of Civil Service Commissions, June 1924, pp. 130–34.

[13]"Classification and Compensation Work in the Wisconsin State Service," *Public Personnel Studies*, July 1927, pp. 138–43.

[14]Frank O. Everett, "The Classification and Compensation of Positions in the Service of the State of New York," *Summary of Proceedings*, Third Eastern States Regional Conference, Civil Service Assembly . . . , 1931, pp. 18–26.

[15]No comprehensive census of jurisdictions having position-classification plans in effect is available. Partial tabulations may be found in Leonard D. White, *Trends in Public Administration* (New York, 1933), p. 257; Mosher and Kingsley, *Public Personnel Administration* (New York, 1936), pp. 356–57; Clay Morris Ross, *A Survey of Public Personnel Legislation and Administrative Regulations* (Bureau of Public Administration, University, Va., 1939), pp. 61–62.

law, or in compliance with federal regulations under the Social Security Act, has included necessarily the development and adoption of position-classification plans as a sound foundation for effective administration.[16]

DOMINION OF CANADA

Following the enactment in 1868 of the first civil service act of the Dominion of Canada,[17] questions relating to the classification and pay of positions occupied the attention of Parliament from time to time. Commissions to investigate and report, among other things, upon the classification of the service, were appointed in 1869, 1875, 1880, and 1891. Some of these commissions recommended the adoption of a plan along the lines of the British civil service. The report of the 1891 Royal Commission is especially significant in that it directed specific attention to the lack of relation of pay to work performed and to inequalities in pay for similar duties. The Commission said:[18]

Finally we come to the very large number of clerks who work entirely under direction and whose duties are of the ordinary character of clerks, such as posting, copying, registering, typewriting, etc. Their salaries range from the minimum of the Third Class, $400, to the maximum of the First Class, $1800. It is to be noted that the higher range of salaries in the latter class is in many cases paid to persons who are doing the same kind of work they did in former years. This is due to the automatic system of the Civil Service by which salaries are steadily increased. It has thus come to pass that there are numbers of persons employed in the same rooms, doing the same work, and having places sometimes at the same desk, whose salaries differ by as wide a range as three hundred per cent. . . .

In the recommendations your commissioners have made in the draft Bill referred to, they have endeavored to guard against the development of this state of things in the future, and to ensure that men who are doing the lower description of work shall be remunerated accordingly, while the higher range of salaries shall be reserved for those who have responsibilities of management, or whose services require a high degree of educational or professional attainments.

[16] With respect to the connection between federal activities under the Social Security Act and personnel administration in state unemployment compensation, public welfare, and health departments, see "National-Local Relationships in Personnel Administration," *Proceedings*, Thirtieth Annual Meeting of the Civil Service Assembly . . . , 1938, pp. 34–35; Albert H. Aronson, "Personnel in a Federal Aid Program," *Personnel Administration*, February 1939, p. 3; *ibid.*, "Merit Systems Under the Social Security Act," *Public Personnel Review*, July 1940, pp. 24–28.

[17] Can. Stat., 31 Vic., c. 34.

[18] *Report of the Royal Commissioners Appointed to Enquire into Certain Matters Relating to the Civil Service of Canada*, 1892, p. xvii.

Another comprehensive investigation of the Canadian civil service was undertaken by a Royal Commission appointed in 1907 to inquire into the operation of the Civil Service Act and into the classification of the service and the salaries paid. The Commission reported that the "uniform idea of classification for all the departments has failed in the working."[19] As a result of this report, Parliament passed the Civil Service Amendment Act of 1908, materially altering the classification structure of the Inside Service at Ottawa and providing that the Outside Service might be classified similarly by Order in Council. Although the principle was recognized that positions should be classified according to the duties and responsibilities involved, no machinery was provided to carry this principle into effect. The lack of uniformity of classification and salaries which resulted from this administrative deficiency was pointed out a few years later by Sir George Murray, who had been appointed by the Prime Minister to inquire into the methods of administration and organization of the public service. He stated in a report of November 30, 1912:[20]

I attribute this mainly to two causes, (a) the principle laid down by the Act of 1908 for classifying the officers then in the service, which . . . paid insufficient regard to the nature of the duties to be performed; and (b) the want of some one coordinating authority with power to deal with all Departments and regulate their staffs on uniform principles.

Notwithstanding the enlightened principles advocated by Sir George Murray, his report produced no legislative results for several years.

It remained for the expansion of the civil service during the World War, coupled with the inadequacies of the Civil Service Act of 1908, to give rise to the enactment of the Civil Service Act of 1918, which extended the jurisdiction of the Civil Service Commission and required the development of a position-classification plan for the service. The Civil Service Commission considered the work of classification and salary standardization the most pressing task imposed on it by the 1918 act, inasmuch as the other work of the Commission was largely dependent upon its completion.[21]

[19] Civil Service Commission, *Report of the Commissioners,* 1908, 7–8 Edward VII, Sess. Pap. 29a.
[20] *Report on the Organization of the Public Service of Canada* by Sir George Murray, 3 George V, Sess. Pap. 57a, p. 21.
[21] The firm of Arthur Young & Company, under the active direction of Edwin O. Griffenhagen, was engaged for the purpose of making the necessary investigations and recommendations.

The following principles were adopted by the Commission and the staff engaged in the work:[22]

1. That the duties and responsibilities appertaining to a position should be the criteria for determining the classification of the position because these attributes constitute the fundamental characteristics that distinguish the position from other positions and because all of the purposes of classification will be served by a grouping that will bring together positions involving substantially the same duties and responsibilities.

2. That positions involving substantially the same duties and responsibilities call for practically the same qualifications as to education, experience, knowledge, and skill in their incumbents and that for this reason such qualification requirements, dependent as they are on the work to be performed, constitute an auxiliary basis for determining the proper classification of a given position.

3. That neither the degree of efficiency with which the duties of a position are being carried out by the person who may be filling it, nor the qualifications such person may possess or lack, nor the pay he may receive, nor any other fact dependent solely on his individuality, shall be considered as having any bearing on the classification of the position in question.

4. That the simplest practical grouping of positions should be adopted that will serve the purposes for which the classification is needed: that in conformity with this principle the unit of classification should be a group (called a "class") embracing all those positions in the service, regardless of departmental lines, that involve duties and responsibilities which are substantially the same.

In accordance with these principles, a comprehensive survey of the duties and responsibilities of all positions in the Canadian civil service was made. The establishment of classes and the actual classification of individual positions were administratively difficult, largely because of concurrent fundamental changes in the control of personnel and organization matters in the service. Departures from tradition gave rise to reactions and oppositions which manifested themselves against the classification activities under way. After considerable cooperative effort a position-classification plan and a pay plan were proposed by the Civil Service Commission and adopted by Parliament on November 10, 1919.

Thus for the first time in the history of the Canadian civil service, a logical and systematic plan of classifying positions for all personnel purposes was put into effect.

The administration of the plan has been a continuous process. The

[22] Civil Service Commission of Canada, *Report of Transmission to Accompany the Classification of the Civil Service of Canada,* Prepared by Arthur Young & Co. (Ottawa, 1919), pp. 7–8. This publication (Appendix B, p. 65 *et seq.*) also summarizes the history of classification in Australia and New Zealand.

1918 act prescribed not only that the organization of the various units in the service should be continuously reviewed in the light of changing conditions of work and procedure, but also that changes in classifications and in the classification plan itself were to be made whenever altered conditions of employment and organization made them necessary or desirable.[23]

From time to time a number of Parliamentary Special Committees have inquired into the operation of the Civil Service Act, and the administration of the service. In 1930, the report of a Royal Commission proposed a change in the grading structure for the technical, scientific, and professional services in the interests of simplicity. Although no action was taken on this report, the idea that the classification could and should be simplified by establishing a limited number of grades, each with a uniform salary range, has been manifested repeatedly in the reports of the special Parliamentary Committees of 1932 (Lawson), 1934 (Bowman), 1938 (Pouliot), and 1939 (Fournier).

For example, the Pouliot Committee suggested:[24]

As the multiplicity of classifications and the discrepancy in salary ranges tend to create jealousy in the Service and have resulted in injustices and dissatisfaction, your Committee suggests that the Service should be divided into five or six broad classes, with a maximum of not more than nine grades in one class, and such division to be set up as soon as possible.

Although such suggestions as these have not given rise to implementing legislation, the Civil Service Commission, nevertheless, in line with evidence adduced and reports made by the special committees, has been working toward the simplification and condensation of the classification plan, with due adherence to the basic policies underlying position-classification.

[23] During the early years of the administration of the plan, changes in the classification of individual positions were dealt with by the Civil Service Commission as requests were received from the departments. In 1929, a procedure was developed of receiving applications for revisions at six-month intervals, all those in one department being investigated at the same time. This practice continued until 1936 when the Treasury Board, on the recommendation of the Civil Service Commission, directed that changes in the classification of individual positions could only be made at a time when all positions in a particular unit were under review, and that these unit reviews or surveys should not be made more often than once a year. This practice has been in operation for more than three years and in this period practically all units of the government service have been reviewed at least once and matters of classification and salary adjusted.

[24] Special Committee on the Operation of the Civil Service Act, *Final Report to the House,* June 27, 1938. By the term "broad classes," the Committee meant classification services, such as clerical, engineering, or scientific.

UNITED STATES GOVERNMENT

From the very beginnings of the federal government, the problem of fixing pay equitably for officers and employees frequently engaged the attention of Congress. It was early and repeatedly recognized that the fair basis for salaries was the work which each employee performed, and over a period of nearly a century Congress sought procedural means for carrying this principle into the everyday administrative operations of the government. Regular and special Congressional and executive committees studied and reported on the problem from time to time, virtually all of them arriving at the conclusion that some means had to be found for classifying or grading positions uniformly and impartially on the basis of the work they involved, in such a way that the same pay scale or salary range, whatever it might be in dollars, could be equitably applied to each position in the same class or grade, and so that the several pay scales would be properly related to the difficulty and responsibility of the work of the positions to which they were made applicable. Time after time, this was stated as a sound and necessary objective in salary administration. However, it was only after long and repeated consideration of the problem that it was perceived that the search for ways and means to accomplish this objective would be ended by agreeing to vest in one central agency the responsibility for the coordination of position-classification in all departments.

The history of appropriation acts and other legislation considered by Congress from 1789 to about 1850 indicates clearly a growing awareness that inadequacy of pay and inequalities of pay in relation to work performed were becoming typical of the salary situation in the service.

In 1836, petitions submitted to Congress by government employees served to focus attention on the need of a systematic method for fixing the salaries of the 336 clerks then employed in the five departments at Washington. Similar petitions were submitted in following years. Specifically, in 1838, the employees asked "that an inquiry be made . . . into the kind and character of the duties of the several clerks in all the departments and subordinate bureaus, and a general law passed, apportioning and fixing salaries to duties, so that all clerks performing like duties shall receive like salaries."[25] In this request they were supported by the heads of the several execu-

25 S.Doc. 71, 25th Cong., 2d sess., Vol. I, January 3, 1838.

tive departments.[26] The Senate, recognizing the need for equalization of salaries in relation to duties, passed a resolution addressed to the heads of departments, which called for reports showing[27]

the classification of the clerks . . . in reference to the character of the labor to be performed, the care and responsibility imposed, the qualifications required, and the relative value to the public of the services of each class as compared with the others . . . .

Thus, 85 years before the passage of the Classification Act of 1923, the Senate set forth a sound basis for position-classification.

In 1851 a number of bills were introduced for the purpose of raising and, at the same time, equalizing clerical salaries, each bill, however, being applicable to only one specified department. Seeing the futility of accomplishing uniformity and equalization throughout the service by enacting the pending uncoordinated bills, Congress in 1853 and 1854 enacted laws which at the time were probably intended to be a reasonably permanent solution of the problem of adjusting and equalizing salaries for the 700 clerical employees in the five departments affected. These laws provided that clerks in the Departments of the Treasury, War, Navy, Interior, and the Post Office "shall be arranged into four classes," and prescribed one salary rate for each class as follows: $1,200 per annum for class one; $1,400 for class two; $1,600 for class three; and $1,800 for class four.[28] Gradually this salary classification was extended to most of the clerical positions in all offices. Until the passage of the Classification Act of 1923, 70 years later, they served to define and limit salary levels in estimating and authorizing appropriations for clerical positions not paid from lump-sum appropriations.

As in the case of its earlier deliberations, Congress again, by enacting these measures in 1853 and 1854, recognized the necessity of equal pay for equal work and coordination of pay schedules among departments. But the 1853 and 1854 acts established no machinery or procedure designed to meet this necessity. They established no central agency, no mandate to ascertain currently the facts about the duties and responsibilities of positions, and no principles for placing positions in the classes enumerated. The 1853 and 1854 acts raised clerical salary rates, but they failed to equalize or coordinate them in relation to work performed.

[26] S.Doc. 239, 25th Cong., 2d sess., Vol. III, February 26, 1838.
[27] S.Res., 25th Cong., 2d sess., March 5, 1838.
[28] Act of March 3, 1853, 10 Stat. 209; Act of April 22, 1854, 10 Stat. 276.

In 1886, the House Committee on Reform in the Civil Service reiterated the familiar principle that "all compensation should be uniform in the several departments and offices for doing work of the same kind." It stated, moreover, that it was "impracticable and inexpedient" for a committee of Congress to prepare a coordinated position-classification plan on the basis of uncoordinated reports from the various departments, and, further that[29]

Neither should Congress act upon the reports of the heads of departments alone, for one of the primary objects is to secure uniformity in all the departments, which was not done by the act of 1853; the reason for which is apparent.

Although the advantages to be gained by a systematic classification of positions were graphically presented to Congress, both in the Committee report and in debate, no action was taken.[30]

Beginning in 1902 the Civil Service Commission frequently urged in its annual reports that steps be taken to "reclassify" positions on the basis of duties performed and to make compensation uniform for work of the same kind.[31]

In 1905, a Committee on Department Methods, appointed by President Theodore Roosevelt upon his own initiative, undertook as one of eighteen projects an investigation dealing with the "Classification of Positions and Gradation of Salaries." In its report to the President, the Committee clearly recognized the necessity and difficulty of classifying like positions uniformly in different bureaus and departments. It stated that[32]

The chief difficulty in the proposed reclassification of employees will be to make sure that the same importance be always given to certain lines of substantially similar work performed in different bureaus and departments. This may be assured by a careful observance of the foregoing schedule in regard to the character of work appropriate to the several grades, or by the determination of a board of equalization appointed by the head of each

---

[29] H.Rept. 1303, (to accompany H.R. 6855) 49th Cong., 1st sess., vol. 5.

[30] *Cong. Record*, 49th Cong., 1st sess., Vol. 17, Part 8, p. 43 of Appendix.

[31] Nineteenth Annual Report (1902), pp. 173–76; 20th Annual Report (1903), p. 17; 23rd Annual Report (1906), p. 8. This had already been referred to briefly in the Commission's Annual Report for 1896, p. 16, in which it said that "a card system is being made which will show certain information regarding every person in the service. . . . The first step toward a classification based on duties, with like pay for like work, will be attained when this information is secured."

[32] Report to the President by the Committee on Department Methods. *Classification of Positions and Gradation of Salaries for Employees of the Executive Departments and Independent Establishments in Washington.* January 4, 1907. A detailed description of the Committee's work is found in G. A. Weber, *Organized Efforts for the Improvement of Methods of Administration* (1919), pp. 74–83. Institute for Government Research, Studies in Administration.

Department for the express purpose of securing uniformity in making the change from the present to the proposed schedule.

Its suggestion that boards of equalization within each department could secure uniformity across departmental lines was unduly optimistic. An interdepartmental committee, called the Committee on Grades and Salaries, composed of one employee named by the head of each establishment, was created by executive order on June 11, 1907. It prepared tables of estimates for positions and salaries in conformity with the recommendations of the Committee on Department Methods. These estimates were submitted to Congress on February 11, 1908,[33] but no general action resulted, notwithstanding the support of President Theodore Roosevelt[34] and President Taft.[35]

It remained for the Congressional Joint Commission on Reclassification of Salaries, appointed by Congress in 1919, to construct the link to connect sound objective with practical everyday operation. In its report to Congress in 1920, it made this recommendation:[36]

The Commission recommends that the future administration of the classification and of the uniform schedules of compensation be delegated by statute to an existing independent agency of the Government, herein referred to as the classification agency, and submits that this agency should logically and preferably be the United States Civil Service Commission.

In explanation of this recommendation, the Congressional Committee said:

It is obvious that if the prime requirements of uniformity and relative equity in the pay for service are to be secured some central independent agency must have the authority—the final authority in every case and in all departments—as to the proper classification of each position. It must ascertain, as the impartial appraiser for the Government and the taxpayers, what the duties of each position are, what responsibilities are involved, what qualifications are required, and into what class and compensation schedule it falls.

Congress almost immediately accepted the principle that an independent central agency should be given the responsibility described by the Congressional Joint Commission. In this respect its questions

---

[33] H.Doc. 648, 60th Cong.
[34] Message of President Roosevelt transmitting estimates for appropriations, S.Doc. 638, 60th Cong., January 6, 1909.
[35] Annual Message of President Taft to the Congress, 61st Cong., 2d sess., December 7, 1909, quoted in *Twenty-sixth Annual Report of the Civil Service Commission* for fiscal year ending June 30, 1909, p. 134.
[36] Congressional Joint Commission on Reclassification of Salaries. *Report*, March 12, 1920. H.Doc. 686, 66th Cong., 2d sess., pp. 67–68.

centered mainly on what agency or type of agency should be established or selected. The Personnel Classification Board, an ex-officio organization, was created by the Classification Act of 1923 as the central classifying agency.

A broad administrative plan for centralized control of the process of fixing pay for positions in the departmental service at Washington was embodied in the Classification Act of 1923.[37] The express requirement that allocations of positions should be so made as to result in "equal compensation for equal work, irrespective of sex," constituted an essential objective of the position-classification plan. This objective was to be accomplished through final allocations by one agency charged with the duty of applying a government-wide viewpoint, of making cross-departmental comparisons, and of determining finally when positions in different agencies and establishments were in fact "equal" in respect to their duties and responsibilities; or if not equal, how they should be ranked in relation to one another.

This plan covered federal departments and agencies in Washington. It also embraced the municipal government of the District of Columbia (with the exception of positions in the police, fire-fighting, and teaching groups), and certain specifically mentioned organizations, including the Botanic Garden, Library of Congress, Library Buildings and Grounds, Government Printing Office, and the Smithsonian Institution.[38] The act excluded mechanical trades and laboring positions, when not in custodial or purely maintenance organizations or scientific or engineering laboratories or shops.

The position-classification plan established in the Classification Act of 1923 did not cover positions in the field service, i.e., outside of the headquarters offices in Washington. Subsequently, the Welch Act of May 28, 1928, directed the Personnel Classification Board to make a comprehensive survey of the field services, including specific recommendations for a classification plan for those services. Pursuant to this authority the Personnel Classification Board conducted a survey (1928–31) covering approximately 104,000 positions in the several field services. The reports submitted by the Board furnished convincing evidence of the need for constructive and consistent poli-

[37] 42 Stat. 1488, U. S. Code, Title 5, secs. 661–74.
[38] Another legislative establishment was brought under the plan by the Act of June 20, 1929, 46 Stat. 38, namely, the Office of the Architect of the Capitol. The number of positions under this position-classification plan was 93,023 on June 30, 1940.

cies and procedures governing the classification and pay of such positions.[39] Following submission of the Board's report, various bills
were introduced at successive sessions of Congress designed to carry
its recommendations substantially into effect. Some of these bills
proposed that the position-classification system would be applied to
all field positions at the same time. Other bills sought a gradual
extension on the premise that a classification survey installation
covering several hundred thousand positions at once would be an
expensive and perhaps cumbersome task. In the 76th Congress, a
bill in the latter group, H.R. 960, commonly known as the Ram-
speck bill, received Congressional approval and was signed by the
President on November 26, 1940. With enumerated exceptions,
Title II of this Act authorizes the President to extend the Classification Act of 1923 to any group of positions in the field or departmental service, not at the time subject to its provisions.

On October 1, 1932, the Personnel Classification Board, created
by the Classification Act of 1923, was abolished, and its duties, powers, and functions transferred to the Civil Service Commission.[40]

Beginning about 1932 many of the statutes creating new or emergency agencies of the government authorized the heads thereof to
fix rates of pay for positions in their organizations without regard to
the Classification Act of 1923. To meet the need for uniformity of
pay scales properly related to work of the same character, difficulty,
and responsibility, the President by executive order promulgated a
salary schedule for positions in the so-called emergency agencies
and those operated in whole or in part from emergency funds, where
the law did not require such agencies to follow the Classification
Act of 1923.[41]

Some of the new agencies of the federal government, including
Home Owners' Loan Corporation, Tennessee Valley Authority, Farm
Credit Administration, Farm Security Administration, Federal De-

[39] *Report of Wage and Personnel Survey*, H.Doc. 602, 70th Cong., 2d sess., Feb.
15, 1929; *Preliminary Class Specifications of Positions in the Field Service*, H.Doc.
772, 71st Cong., 3d sess., 1931; *Closing Report of Wage and Personnel Survey*,
H.Doc. 771, 71st Cong., 3d sess., Feb. 16, 1931; *Salaries for Routine Clerical Work
in Private Industry, 1929* (Government Printing Office, 1931); Herman Feldman,
A Personnel Program for the Federal Civil Service, H.Doc. 773, 71st Cong., 3d
sess. (Government Printing Office, 1931).
[40] Act of June 30, 1932, 47 Stat. 416, Title V, Secs. 505–09.
[41] Executive Order 6440, November 18, 1933, revised by Executive Order 6746,
June 21, 1934. Under the terms of these orders, many of these agencies have
elected to follow the Classification Act of 1923, including acceptance of the
jurisdiction of the Commission. Executive Order 7092, July 3, 1935; Executive
Order 8134, May 15, 1939; 14 Comp. Gen. 867, May 31, 1935.

posit Insurance Corporation, and others, that have the authority to fix rates of pay for positions in their organizations without regard to the Classification Act of 1923 have recognized that a position-classification plan is the proper and necessary basis on which to erect a sound personnel program. These agencies have developed position-classification plans peculiarly adapted to their own needs, have in some instances published class specifications,[42] and have established administrative procedures for the installation and continued administration of such plans.

GREAT BRITAIN

In studying position-classification as it exists in the British civil service and in trying to compare it with prevailing American practice, one is apt to be misled by an oversimplified view, if only the career grades, or "Treasury classes," of clerical, executive, and administrative positions are taken into consideration.[43] The arrangement of these positions and the principles and methods used in recruiting and testing candidates for them are distinctive features of the British civil service. But this should not obscure the fact that the bulk of the service is otherwise arranged. Many classes of positions are established that are in every respect as narrow in position-content as the finest of the American classifications. Many important types of positions, including practically all professional and scientific posi-

[42] The following documents are illustrative: Home Owners' Loan Corporation, *Class Specifications for Positions in State and Other Field Offices,* August 1, 1938; Farm Credit Administration, *Class Specifications for Positions in District Units,* September 1, 1936; Farm Security Administration, *Class Specifications for Positions in the Field Service* (1940).

[43] In England, the authority for personnel administration is divided among the Treasury, the Civil Service Commission, and the operating departments. The Treasury (at the head of which is the Prime Minister) controls the numbers, classification, and pay of civil servants, their conditions and methods of work, and the appropriation estimates of the departments. The Civil Service Commission (which reports directly to the Crown) recruits, examines, and certifies. The departments, under the general oversight of the Treasury, are responsible for day-to-day personnel administration. For a chart of the organization of the British civil service and a description of the functions of the Treasury in personnel management, see Morris B. Lambie, "The British Civil Service," in United States Personnel Classification Board, *Report of Wage and Personnel Survey* (H.Doc. 602, 70th Cong., 2d sess.), pp. 407–12. In addition to the sources cited later, reference may also be made to Maxwell A. DeVoe, "Some Contrasts between the British Civil Service and the Civil Service in this Country," *Summary of Proceedings,* Fourth Eastern Regional Conference, Civil Service Assembly . . . , pp. 68–71; William A. Robson, Ed., *The British Civil Servant* (London: George Allen and Unwin, Ltd., 1937), pp. 29–45, 65–86; Don K. Price, *Civil Service in Britain,* and Harold J. Laski, *The British Civil Service,* Civil Service Assembly . . . , Special Bull. No. 3, January 1937; Hiram Stout, *Public Service in Great Britain* (University of North Carolina Press, 1938).

tions, are not embraced in the Treasury grades, nor are they under any service-wide classification plan.

The British plan of classification for clerical, executive, and administrative positions developed out of the recruiting principles originally adopted as the foundation of the service. To the difference in British recruiting practices compared with our own may be ascribed many of the differences in classification structure and refinements.[44]

In the 1850's, coincident with the beginnings of the elimination of patronage, the British began civil service operations on a distinctive theory of recruitment, the principal features of which were "the admission of young people into the Service at prescribed ages" through open competitive examinations, and the design of these examinations to indicate general ability and intelligence rather than technical preparation or subject-matter specialization for the duties of a particular occupation or specific activity. Thus, basic to the adopted recruiting practice was the coordination of national education and entry into the service.[45]

This theory of recruitment necessitated a method of identifying the positions to be covered. That method came with an Order in Council of 1870 which divided the clerical classes into Class I and Class II, corresponding to "intellectual" and "routine" work, respectively. Class I was recruited by examination based on university curricula and was assigned duties of an administrative and policy-forming nature. Class II was recruited by a less exacting examination, roughly corresponding to secondary school curricula. The great bulk of the clerical work was to be done by this group.

Thus was established the principle of a broad division of work—not on the American basis of recruiting persons for individual positions—but on the basis of dividing the work of government into large blocks for which persons taken from particular stages of the national education system were judged to be best suited. Out of this

---

[44] "In contrast to the American policy, the British Government has insisted upon broad services defined in rather general terms in order to permit greater leeway for assignment. Furthermore, in paying attention to the career aspects the British have stressed a division of labor which is determined partially by a broad definition of the duties in the respective classes and partially by a scheme of selection designed to secure for each class a definite type of worker who normally will be content to remain in the single class for a long career. The classification makes promotion from one class to a higher class difficult but not impossible." Morris B. Lambie, *op. cit.*, p. 415.

[45] Herman Finer, *The British Civil Service* (London: George Allen and Unwin, Ltd., 1937), pp. 44–45.

beginning has grown a series of broad "Treasury classes," or "Treasury grades," covering clerical, executive, and administrative positions (but not all positions of these types), which receive somewhat distinctive treatment compared to the rest of the service.

These general or "Treasury" classes took their present form in 1920 when the recommendations of a Reorganization Committee of the National Whitley Council were largely accepted by the Treasury.[46]

The Administrative Class includes positions which involve duties "concerned with the formation of policy, with the coordination and improvement of Government machinery, and with the general administration and control of the departments of the public service."[47] Within this class there are several ranks: "assistant principal," the entrance rank; "principal," "assistant secretary," "principal assistant secretary," "deputy permanent secretary," and "permanent secretary."[48]

The Executive Class, having two ranks or grades, includes

the higher work of supply and accounting departments and of other executive and specialized branches of the civil service. This work covers a wide field,[49] and requires in different degrees qualities of judgment, initiative, and resource. In the junior ranks it comprises the critical examination of particular cases of lesser importance not clearly within the scope of approved regulations or general decisions, initial investigations into matters of higher importance, and the immediate direction of small blocks of business. In its upper ranges it is concerned with matters of internal organization and control, with the settlement of broad questions arising out of business in hand or in contemplation, and with the responsible conduct of important operations.

In this class there are two grades, (1) a Training Grade and (2) the Higher Grade.[50]

[46] National Whitley Council, *Report on the Organization, etc., of the Civil Service,* February 17, 1920, reprinted in Leonard D. White, ed., *The Civil Service in the Modern State* (Chicago: University of Chicago Press, 1930), p. 33, from which the work descriptions given below are quoted.

[47] A more detailed description of the responsibilities of the Administrative Class is given in Appendix VIII to *Minutes of Evidence, Royal Commission on the Civil Service (1929–30),* Statement submitted by the Association of First Division Civil Servants (London, 1930), pp. 4–8.

[48] All the higher positions are normally filled by progressive promotion from the assistant principal grade. See Harvey Walker, *Training Public Employees in Great Britain,* Monograph 6, Commission of Inquiry on Public Service Personnel (New York, 1935), p. 9.

[49] Including actuarial, legal, auditing, accounting, supply, and statistical.

[50] Finer, *op. cit.,* p. 76. The Executive Class is recruited normally by promotion. In the absence of suitable promotees, direct recruiting is on a full secondary education basis at ages from 18 to 19.

The Clerical Class includes

all the simpler clerical duties in the public departments, in so far as these are not assigned to Writing Assistants in accordance with the principles already stated [see below], and in addition the following duties: Dealing with particular cases in accordance with well-defined regulations, instructions or general practice; scrutinizing, checking and cross-checking straight-forward accounts, claims, returns, etc., under well-defined instructions; preparation of material for returns, accounts, and statistics in prescribed forms; simple drafting and precise work; collection of material on which judgments can be formed; supervision of the work of Writing Assistants.

In this class there are two ranks: a Higher Clerical Class and the Clerical Class. The higher rank is employed only in departments having no Executive Class officials.[51]

The Clerical Assistant Class is composed largely of a former Writing Assistant Class, which is to be

employed on work preliminary to machine operations (punching, tabulating, etc.); on hand-copying and transcribing work (writing out acknowledgments, filling up forms, warrants, and bills); on the addressing of letters; on the counting and routine examination of postal orders, insurance cards, etc.; on the casting and preparation of schedules and lists, and the writing up of simple cards; and the custody of card indexes.

This class is also engaged on the actual operation of card punching machines, calculating machines, and bookkeeping machines, and in the performance of other somewhat less routine tasks.[52]

Clerical Assistants are employed in only a few departments where there are large blocks of work of a simple routine or mechanical character. Where such work does not exist in large blocks, it is assigned to members of the Clerical Class during the initial stages of their employment.

The Shorthand Typist and Typist classes, forming the fifth general group recommended by the Reorganization Committee, stand in sharp contrast to the other groups in being much more homogeneous in duties content. In this group there are four grades, rising to the Superintendent of Typists.[53]

These Treasury classes, upon which so much emphasis has been placed by American writers, cover only a part of the British civil service. The professional, scientific, and related positions are not

[51] *Ibid.*, p. 77. Recruiting is at ages from 16 to 17 (among boys) and from 16½ to 17½ (among girls) on the basis of the intermediate stage of a secondary school course; or by promotion.
[52] Recruiting is among women only, at ages of from 16 to 17.
[53] Lambie, *loc. cit.*

included. In addition, there are a number of "departmental classes," each covering positions in one department, such as the outdoor staff of the Customs and Excise department, the tax inspectorate of Inland Revenue, the employment officers of the Department of Labour, the immigration staff of the Home Office, and prison governors and deputy governors. Other positions, mainly in the Post Office, are grouped in the "Minor and Manipulative Classes." There are also large groups of industrial workers in the trades and crafts and messengers, porters and charwomen.

The approximate number of officials and employees in each of these groups is shown in the accompanying tabulation:

TABLE SHOWING THE NUMBER OF EMPLOYEES IN VARIOUS CLASSES IN THE BRITISH CIVIL SERVICE (1937)[54]

Treasury or General Classes:

Administrative	1,300
Executive	4,453
Clerical	33,233
Clerical Assistants	7,944
Shorthand Typists and Typists	7,012
TOTAL	53,942

Other Classes:

"Other" executive[a]	12,320
Clerical	37,074
Typists	2,961
Assessors, Collectors, Distributors and Clerks to Commissioners of Taxes	1,780
Inspectorates	2,278
Professional, Scientific, and Technical[b]	6,504
Subordinate Supervising and Technical[c]	10,831
Minor and Manipulative Classes[d]	182,000
Industrial Classes	145,000
Messengers, porters and charwomen	18,000
TOTAL	418,748

[a] "Other executive" means departmental classes engaged on duties broadly similar in character to those assigned to the general executive class.

[b] Includes barristers, solicitors, doctors, architects, engineers, and scientific and technical research staff.

[c] Includes subordinate technical personnel, such as draftsmen, technical assistants, certain supervisory staffs in industrial establishments, clerks of works and foremen of works.

[d] Mostly Post Office employments.

[54] Not including those serving abroad. Figures taken from Herman Finer, *The British Civil Service* (London: George Allen and Unwin, Ltd. 1937), pp. 74, 79.

Outside of the Treasury classes the refinements in classification are parallel to those that would be drawn in this country.[55] To illustrate: classes of First Class Officer, Second Class Officer, Third Class Officer, Employment Officer, and Employment Clerk have been established in the Ministry of Labour, each with its distinctive pay scale. Similarly, in the Admiralty are found classes of First Grade Clerk, Second Grade Clerk, and Third Grade Clerk, with relatively narrow pay scales.

The messenger group is classified into one grade "for supervisory duties and for attendance on Ministers and high officials," and another grade for general messenger duties. Also, departmental classes of clerk-shorthand-typist and clerk-typist have been established to cover a merger of routine clerical duties with typing and shorthand work.

Positions which are not in the Treasury classes are recruited for under designations as specific as those under American systems. For example, reports of the Civil Service Commission record tests and appointments under a multiplicity of class titles, such as Junior Legal Assistant, Assistant Civil Engineer, Audit Assistant, District Forest Officer, Inspector of Factories, Inspector, Dangerous Drugs Branch, Immigration Officer, Assistant Director of Industrial Planning, Messenger, Assistant Inspector of Taxes, Supervisor Duplicator Operator, Nurse, Attendant, Deputy Head Porter, Postman, Telephonist, and so on.[56]

In particular, the professional and scientific services are as finely classified as they are under American classification systems. In 1929 the Royal Commission on the Civil Service was informed by the Institution of Professional Civil Servants that there were "more than 500 distinct grades, differing not merely in technical nomenclature but also in their standard of remuneration."[57] The Institution

---

[55] "Passing from the clerical classes, which are broadly conceived, we find much the same variety of specialized classes in the departments as would be found in corresponding American services. The Post Office has a great number of specialist classes peculiarly required for the handling of mails; the revenue services have specialist officers acquainted with the intricacies of income tax and customs legislation and regulations; the comptroller general has a variety of accounting and finance officers, and so on." Leonard D. White, "The British Civil Service," Monograph 2, Commission of Inquiry on Public Service Personnel, in *Civil Service Abroad* (McGraw-Hill, 1935), pp. 16–17.

[56] See, for example, *Report of His Majesty's Civil Service Commissioners on the Year 1937* (London, 1938); *Civil Service Examinations;* Subjects of Examination and Limits of Age (London, 1936).

[57] Royal Commission on the Civil Service, 1929–31, *Report*, p. 49. Cf. the following statement: ". . . Classification has developed along very different lines in

proposed a "graded technical service," to be arranged in 30 general and 17 special grades, closely related to the general or Treasury grades. This proposal, however, did not meet with the approval of the Commission.[58]

Other important exceptions to the "Treasury classes" are the "departmental classes," i.e. classes which are set up for particular departments, examples of which have previously been mentioned. From time to time there have been proposals by the Reorganization Committee[59] and others for assimilating some of these classes into the general or Treasury classes on a cross-departmental basis. These departmental classes, however, continue to exist, even to increase. Involving as they do separate pay scales and separate examinations for recruitment, they are certainly a limitation on the British principle of broad general classes and an illustration of the need of more specific position-classification than the general "Treasury" classes permit.

From this brief summary it may be said that, with the exception of the treatment of Treasury classes, position-classification in Great Britain was, at least before the war, not evolving so differently from that in the United States. The one major difference, i.e., the existence of the Treasury classes, is due to the carefully planned introduction of a limited number of generally trained young people

---

the United States from those in England. The British recruit generally qualified individuals, upon the basis of broad educational tests, and then train them to do any specialized or technical work. It is accordingly necessary to have only a few broad classes—typists and shorthand typists, writing assistants, clerical, executive, and administrative classes—geared into the several stages of the general educational system. With very few exceptions there are no job specifications in the British service; no sharp division into occupational or vocational groups." Mosher and Kingsley, *Public Personnel Administration* (1st ed.; New York: Harper and Bros. 1936), pp. 355-57.

[58] *Ibid.*, p. 53. "Here the chief point to note is the broad autonomy of the department in the classification of its own personnel [in the departmental classes], subject to review by the Establishments Division of the Treasury—a review which has not been effectively used in the interest of consolidation of classes. The prevailing view is that apart from the Treasury classes the departments should be left to handle their own classification problems. This attitude is especially emphasized with respect to the professional, technical, and scientific officers. Here a multiplicity of titles exist, with varying rates of pay, peculiar to each department or scientific institution. Continuous efforts on the part of the professional officers to secure simplification of classes and pay structure have failed to convince the responsible departmental authorities that simplification is desirable." White, *op. cit.*, p. 17.

[59] "We suggest that departmental classes engaged on duties analogous to those assigned to the general administrative, executive, and clerical branches of the Service should be brought within the scope of the revised classification; and we recommend that the possibility of assimilating these classes should be explored departmentally at an early date." *Op. cit.*, par. 65.

at two different levels—after college and after high school, and training of these employees for executive and administrative positions respectively.[60]

PRIVATE INDUSTRY

In private industry, the analysis, evaluation, and classification of positions as a systematic management process originated in job analysis for "scientific management" purposes and later, concurrently with the growth of personnel departments and industrial relations activities, developed along modified lines with emphasis upon the use of position-classification in personnel management.

The expansion of private industry during the latter part of the nineteenth century and the transition from small shops to large factories made manufacturing and production methods a fruitful field for study. Industrial engineers undertook detailed analyses of factory, machine, and laboring jobs for the purpose of increasing production, lowering costs, and establishing wage rates and incentives based on output.[61]

Concurrently with the functionalization of personnel management as a distinct phase of over-all management and the consequent rise of centralized employment departments in industry, job analysis took on additional significance. Employment managers, needing detailed, organized information about job-content and job-qualifications for hiring purposes, followed the example of the industrial engineer and obtained this information through studies of work being done and interviews with foremen and employees. Brief notes prepared in this way for the use of employment interviewers soon gave rise to narrative job descriptions and check lists of job data on standardized forms.[62]

The World War period gave still further emphasis to the value of job specifications as definitions of standardized job terminology and as tools in the proper placement of men. A Committee on Classification of Personnel in the Army was established by the Secretary of War on August 5, 1917, for the purpose of furnishing advisory, research, and planning service to the various military units in solving the problem of effective placement of civilians inducted into the

[60] For a critical treatment of the promotional problems involved in attempts to copy the British "Treasury classes," see E. O. Griffenhagen, *Report on a System of Personnel Administration for the Commonwealth of Virginia* (Richmond: 1937), pp. 20–26.

[61] Frederick W. Taylor, *Shop Management* (Harper & Bros., 1911).

[62] R. S. Uhrbrock, "History of Job Analysis," *Administration*, February 1922, pp. 164–68.

Army.[63] An Index of Occupations was prepared, covering the fundamental civil occupations and trades needed in the Army. Each trade or occupational name was defined in a Manual of Trade Specifications.[64] As an additional aid, the Committee developed a series of "Personnel Specifications," defining the duties of positions in the various military units, under their Army titles, and connecting each such specification with the nearest equivalent civilian occupational description as shown in the Index of Occupations and the Manual of Trade Specifications.

In 1918, at the request of the War Labor Policies Board and in response to an urgent need on the part of governmental wage adjustment agencies and representatives of workers and industry, a summary report was prepared on standardization and adjustment of wages for skilled and unskilled labor, on a national scale, based on position-classification methods.[65]

In 1921 there was completed a duties classification of railroad occupations for the U. S. Railroad Labor Board. This classification, with minor modifications, is still being used by the carriers in reporting wage and compensation information to the Interstate Commerce Commission.[66]

Such activities as these did much to stimulate the interest of industry in similar techniques.

From shortly after the World War to the present, paralleling a similar movement in the public service, there has been an active interest in private industry in job analysis and job classification as tools in the facilitation of personnel programs, pay plans, and the conduct of employer-employee relations.[67] Position-analysis for

[63] *The Personnel System of the U. S. Army*, Vol. 1, *History of the Personnel System* (Washington, 1919). See also C. B. Ross, "Industrial Job Classification from Viewpoint of Mobilization," *Commercial Standards Monthly*, June 1932, pp. 352–53.

[64] *War Department Document No. 774*, Office of the Adjutant General, March 21, 1918.

[65] *Preliminary Statement of the Objects, Principles, and Procedure for National Wage Standardization and Adjustment*, Prepared for the War Labor Policies Board by J. L. Jacobs, United States Shipping Board Emergency Fleet Corporation, August 27, 1918 (mimeographed).

[66] United States Railroad Labor Board, *Rules for Reporting Information on Railroad Employees together with a Classification and Index of Steam Railroad Occupations*, May, 1921 (Prepared under the supervision of J. L. Jacobs & Co., Chicago).

[67] While the position-classification movement did not spread rapidly until the period following 1918, some concerns had been giving serious consideration to methods of grouping positions on the basis of their duties and responsibilities before that time. As early as 1912 the Commonwealth Edison Company, a large public utility, had written position descriptions and classified its 5,000 employees upon this basis.

personnel management purposes has rapidly improved and spread from one industry to another, from factory and process jobs to office positions. As job specifications were perfected, their value in personnel processes increased. Employment managers have recognized their value not only in original selection but in making transfers, in developing promotion plans, in furnishing data necessary for administering position-classification plans, in coordinating rates of pay, and in supplying a useful tool in wage and salary administration. Effective use of job analysis information for purposes of personnel management has also been accelerated by increased emphasis upon effective industrial relations.[68]

The application of job analysis and classification techniques to office and professional positions has generally lagged behind their use in connection with factory positions. However, the larger industrial concerns have perceived the broad usefulness of position-classification and in these concerns the rational analysis of white-collar occupational groups is coming to be commonplace.[69]

During this developmental period the methods used have varied from establishment to establishment and have not followed the same basic principles and approximately uniform pattern which underlie

[68] "Undoubtedly, one of the most important developments to come out of management's current preoccupation with labor problems is the new emphasis placed today upon job classification and rating, and merit rating. The principle, of course, is not new; it is the organized, scientific application of it that is of present significance. It is discussed at practically every meeting of production or personnel executives, and impressive work in developing methods of applying it in wage administration in specific industries is being done by trade associations." Carl Heyel, *Human-Relations Manual for Executives* (McGraw-Hill, 1939), p. 183.

[69] In 1936 a study covering 2,452 companies and 4,502,608 employees showed that job analysis studies were being conducted by 434 companies for 2,111,645 employees, job descriptions were being maintained by 323 companies for 1,746,666 employees, and salary classification plans were being administered by 345 companies for 1,620,311 employees. National Industrial Conference Board, *What Employers are doing for Employees* (Board Studies No. 221, 1936), pp. 24–25. In the same year a study made of 64 companies employing 309,317 workers showed that 48.4 per cent of the companies were carrying on job analysis programs affecting 55 per cent of the total number of workers covered by the survey. Donald S. Parks, "1936 Personnel Trends," *Factory Management and Maintenance*, December 1936, p. 39. A study made in 1935 for the National Office Management Association, covering 254 companies and 649,681 employees (202,922 of whom were office workers) showed that 109 companies, or 43 per cent, had analyzed and evaluated their office jobs and established minimum and maximum salaries for each class. Thirty-eight per cent had adopted the same procedure for their non-office jobs. The survey covered 57 banks, 74 industrial concerns, 50 insurance companies, 31 merchandising stores, 14 public utility companies, and 28 others. Peirce School of Business Administration, *Current Personnel Practices* (Philadelphia, 1935). See also recent study of prevalence of salary and wage administration practices in National Industrial Conference Board, *Personnel Activities in American Business* (Studies in Personnel Policy No. 20, 1940), p. 9.

position-classification methods in the public service. Some concerns have adopted techniques parallel to those being used in the public service. Others have developed different methods.[70]

70 For general descriptions of the various methods, see Harold B. Bergen, "Principles of Scientific Salary Administration," *Report by the Committee on Salary Standardization of the Office Executives Division of the American Management Association,* (1925) pp. 12–21; *idem.,* "Salary Administration and Promotion," *Handbook of Business Administration,* W. J. Donald, Ed. (McGraw-Hill, 1931), pp. 857–65; E. H. Little, "Some Considerations in Installing a Salary Administration Plan," *op. cit.,* pp. 1148–51; Felix E. Baridon and Earl H. Loomis, *Personnel Problems* (McGraw-Hill, 1931), pp. 45–55; Samuel L. H. Burk, "Salary and Wage Administration," *The Personnel Journal,* September 1936, pp. 105–15; Metropolitan Life Insurance Company Policyholders Service Bureau, *Salary Standardization and Administration,* 1937, pp. 18–25; John W. Riegel, *Wage Determination* (University of Michigan Press, 1937), pp. 53–68, 79–99; Z. Clark Dickinson, *Compensating Industrial Effort* (Ronald Press, 1937), pp. 196–214; Life Office Management Association, Clerical Salary Study Committee, *Job Evaluation for the Establishment of Salary Standards,* Report No. 1 (1938), pp. 17–28; *ibid., Life Office Salary Administration,* Report No. 2 (1939), pp. 69–121; Eugene J. Benge, "Relative Salaries and Wages," and H. Barrett Rogers, "What is Your Job Worth?" in *Proceedings of the Wage Conference* (Third Industrial Conference), Industrial Management Society, April 7–8, 1939, pp. 24–34, 13–18; Kent F. Bradbury, "Job Evaluation Analyzed," *Advanced Management,* January-March 1940, pp. 16–20; C. Canby Balderston, *Wage Setting Based on Job Analysis and Evaluation* (Industrial Relations Counselors: 1940), p. 9 *et seq.,* and Appendix; National Industrial Conference Board, *Job Evaluation* (Studies in Personnel Policy No. 25), 1940. Footnote references to additional and more detailed sources are given on pp. 83–84 (footnote).

Chapter III

Fundamental Concepts

I<small>N THE</small> development of the human race, classification stands out as one of the earliest and simplest methods by which man discovered relationships among things. The human mind naturally seeks to find order in the world about it. An environment in which each object is given a separate and distinct name and is considered individually without reference to its possible similarity to other equally familiar objects would be much too complex for the reasonable conduct of everyday affairs. Accordingly, to simplify the things with which it has to deal, mankind from earliest history has sought to group together things that are related in some essential points, and to call by the same name things which have attributes in common.

The process of classification, considered abstractly, consists in grouping things in classes. We place in the same class the things that are alike in one or more characteristics and we place in different classes the things that are different in those characteristics. These characteristics constitute the *basis* of the classification.

In order to classify any aggregation of things we must decide beforehand what the basis of the classification will be. Naturally, this basis will be a quality or attribute in respect to which the things are alike or different. Since most things are alike or different in more than one respect, they generally lend themselves to classification on more than one basis. The selection of the particular basis to be employed in a given instance depends, therefore, on the purpose of the classification and the uses to which it is to be put. Different purposes usually require different bases of classification.[1]

[1] "It is obvious that in any aggregation of miscellaneous units countless bases of classification could be devised and applied, such as form, color, weight, size, density, structure, source, value, or any one of numerous other factors or combinations of factors. An arrangement on any such basis could be made a truly scientific product if carried through consistently in accordance with rule and principle. But its value after it had been made would be another question. Any classification becomes a mere game unless it is designed and adapted to meet clearly-visioned purposes." "The Classification Plan for the Massachusetts State Service" (Excerpts from report of Griffenhagen & Associates), *Public Personnel Studies,* January 1927, p. 11.

To illustrate: It is the purpose of many "natural" classification systems, such as those for birds, soils, or minerals, to catalog our knowledge of them for reference, study, and further investigations. Such a classification may be made on the basis of their natural characteristics, such as coloration, density, etc., rather than on the basis of any factor or group of factors deliberately selected by man. But other, or man-made classifications may be developed to meet particular needs or to assist in the solution of particular problems. For example, soils may be classified on the basis of their lime content; metals on the basis of their electrical conductivity; books and documents on the basis of their subject matter. In such cases the basis of the classification is purposely selected and defined in such a way as to make the resulting classification serve the purposes for which it is intended.

Systematic nomenclature and definition are necessarily associated with the process of classification. After deciding on the basis for classifying a given set of objects or qualities, the various classes must be segregated and designated by distinctive names or other means of identification to serve as common vehicles of expression. Then each such class must be described or defined so as to indicate its content and boundaries. The definitions, when formally recorded in writing, give each of the class names a standard, uniform meaning and serve as sources of future reference. Additional items may then be classified in conformity with the original plan.

The Basis for Classifying Positions

As with any other group of things, in order to classify positions, we must first select that basis, from among all those possible, which best serves the predetermined purposes of the classification and the uses to which it is to be put.

Postponing for a moment consideration of formal definition of a "position," it is possible to prepare a lengthy list of points in respect to which positions will be similar or different: e.g., (1) salary or pay; (2) method of fixing salary or pay; (3) duration or intermittency of employment; (4) method by which they are filled; (5) organizational location; (6) work involved.

Conceivably, therefore, positions may lend themselves to classification on any one of several different bases, depending on the purpose for which we may wish to use the completed classification. We may use one basis for one purpose and another basis for another purpose. If we choose bases that are at all significant, each such classification, after it is completed, will have some, although perhaps a limited, practical use.

If, for example, our purposes are purely statistical, many bases of classifying positions are available, each of which will produce the foundation for an interesting and useful statistical study.[2]

Also, if our purpose is to determine the degree of legal jurisdiction or authority of a civil service commission over the filling of positions, we would be interested in a "jurisdictional classification" of positions.[3]

However, the purpose of position-classification, as the term is used here, is different from either of the illustrations cited. To carry on effectively over a period of time the continuous operations of personnel administration such as fixing pay, establishing qualification standards, recruiting and testing personnel, and maintaining effective working forces, certain tools of administration are required. One of the most important of these administrative aids is that which facilitates the establishment and current maintenance of a logical and consistent relationship among: (1) the duties and responsibilities of positions, (2) the standards of qualifications to fill them and, (3) where employment conditions are substantially the same, the salaries paid. Position-classification is this tool. It is the purpose of position-classification to facilitate the attainment and maintenance of this relationship and to serve in this and other respects as a principal tool for personnel administration.[4]

Let us examine briefly this triangular relationship in order ٭to appreciate why it is so important in public personnel administration.

[2] To illustrate: Classifying all positions in a given state or city according to the department in which each is located will provide a means of tabulating their numerical distribution by departments; classifying them according to their existing salary rates will provide a means of constructing a salary distribution table and of computing average, median, and modal rates of pay. Classifying them on both these bases concurrently will permit the development of salary distribution tables by departments, the comparison of the frequencies in different salary groups in the various departments, and the comparison of minimum, maximum, average, median, and modal rates and salary costs, between one department and another. Statistical classifications of these broad types are frequently made for budget, estimating, and appropriating purposes.

[3] See p. 5, second paragraph.

[4] It is also the purpose of position-classification to facilitate the clear consideration of employment conditions (including economic factors) and to keep the determination of their effect on pay scales separate from the effect of duties and responsibilities. Such matters are problems of a pay plan, which will be discussed in a future publication of the Civil Service Assembly. Note the final phrase in the definition of a "class of positions," p. 45 (lines 23–25).

It is easy to see the practical logic of the idea that work done by an employee and the salary paid him by the government should be directly related. Expenditures taking the form of salary have as their purpose the receipt of benefits by the government in the form of personal services rendered. The government should pay salaries in accordance with the value of services rendered. The taxpayer has a right to expect that the government should not pay high salaries for simple work, which would be a waste of funds, or low salaries for the more difficult or more responsible work, which would attract only mediocre employees and thus tend toward incompetency. The employee is interested in obtaining an adequate salary for the work he does, in receiving the same scale of pay as others receive for the same work, and in receiving higher pay than those who perform simpler or less responsible work. Accordingly, from three points of view it can be said that equal work should call for equal salaries; the more exacting and responsible work, the higher salaries; and the less exacting and the simple work, the lower salaries. Thus, the salary of a position should be based upon the character, difficulty, and responsibility of the work involved.

It is equally easy to see that work done and the standards of qualifications necessary to do that work are logically related. In determining what qualifications are necessary in a given position, the work of that position must first be examined, and from analysis of the duties and responsibilities involved or other evidence certain inferences or conclusions may then be drawn as to what combinations of education, experience, knowledge, and ability are required to carry them out efficiently. Obviously, equal work requires equivalent qualifications; the more difficult or more responsible work requires more extensive or exacting qualifications; and the simpler work requires simpler or less exacting qualifications. Thus, the qualification standards of a position should be based upon the character, difficulty, and responsibility of the work involved in that position.

Finally, we see that the salary of a position and the standard of qualifications required to fill it should also be definitely related. The government offers a salary, not only as payment for the services rendered in that position, but also as an inducement to persons possessing the necessary qualifications to seek that position and apply those qualifications to the tasks or responsibilities it involves. Moreover, salary scales, individually and collectively, should serve as an incentive to employees to remain in the service, to continue to do increasingly effective work, and to prepare themselves in knowledge and ability for higher assignments requiring higher qualifications and carrying higher pay. There should, therefore, be a logical and consistent relation between qualification standards, which are in the nature of specifications for personnel, and the salaries offered to persons who meet those standards.

Clearly, then, from a practical standpoint, this desirable relationship of logic and consistency among the duties and responsibilities, the qualification standards, and the pay scale of *one* position can be secured by making both the qualification standards and the pay scale depend on the character, difficulty, and responsibility of the work involved in that position. However, when we wish to accomplish the same result for a number of positions—some of which are alike and some different—we need (1) to identify and group together in one "class" all positions which involve work sufficiently similar to call for the same pay scale and the same tests of knowledge and ability and other qualification standards; and (2) to determine the direction and magnitude of differences among these "classes," i.e., whether one is higher or lower than another and to what extent. These, however, are nothing but the essential processes of position-classification. We adopt the work of each position as the basis for its classification, place in the same class those positions involving work sufficiently similar to warrant like treatment, and arrange all the classes of positions according to kind of work and level of difficulty and responsibility so as to show how each class of positions is related to all the other classes in these respects. For identification purposes, each class is given a distinctive and appropriate class name or title, defined and described by a "class specification," in terms of the work and qualification standards of the class of positions to which it relates.

Positions that fall in the same class are designated by the class name, filled by using the same qualification standards, and paid (under the same or substantially the same employment conditions) according to the pay scale for the class. Moreover, since the various classes are arranged in order of their difficulty and responsibility, qualification standards and pay scales may be developed so as to ascend or descend in amount and quality reasonably proportioned to the ascending or descending order of the classes, and so that differences in the work of the positions are reflected by corresponding differences in pay scales and qualification standards. Equal work, equal pay scale, and equal qualification standards go together; the simpler work, the lower pay scales and the less exacting qualification standards go together; the more difficult and responsible work, the higher pay scales, and the more exacting qualification standards go together; all in coordinated, well-ordered procession.

"POSITION" DEFINED

A significant definition of the term "position" should emphasize those characteristics that serve as the basis for its classification. We may say, therefore, that *a "position" is a group of current duties and responsibilities, assigned or delegated by competent authority, requiring the full-time or part-time employment of one person.*[5]

Under this definition a position consists of assignments of duties and delegations of responsibilities. It may be part-time or full-time, temporary or permanent, occupied or vacant. It comes into existence through the action of management or other controlling authority proceeding through supervisory operating officials who formally or informally specify work for individuals to do and delegate responsibilities for them to exercise. In the public service the initial steps to create positions may be taken by a legislative body, a chief executive, or the head of the department or establishment in which the position is to be located. At any given time a position is characterized solely by all its duties and responsibilities, as they exist at that time, and so long as these attributes remain the same, the position itself remains the same regardless of any other considerations.

The duties and responsibilities of a position are, however, not always fixed and immutable. They may change from time to time, abruptly or gradually, and for a number of different reasons.[6] Hence, since a position is characterized by its current duties and responsibilities, it follows that when these change, the position itself changes. This is true even if it is still called by the same *organizational* name (such as Chief of the Mails and Files Division), and occupies the same place in the organizational structure of the department. Since

---

[5] For similar definitions, see D. A. Straight, "Establishing the Position Specifications and the Position-Classification Plan," *Salary Administration in Henry L. Doherty & Co.*, American Management Association (Office Executives' Series No. 34, 1928), p. 7; Harold B. Bergen, "Salary Administration and Promotion," *Handbook of Business Administration*, W. J. Donald, Ed. (McGraw-Hill, 1931), p. 861. *Cf.* the definitions in Arthur Young & Co., *Report of Transmission to Accompany the Classification of the Civil Service of Canada* (Ottawa, 1919), p. 3; and in the Federal Classification Act of 1923, Public No. 516, 67th Cong., 42 Stat. 1488, U. S. Code, Title 5, sec. 662.

[6] See pp. 285–88.

the classification of the old position may not be appropriate for the new one, a new application of the classification process is necessary. The basis for classification is always the duties and responsibilities of the position as they *currently* exist. In fact, an integral part of the administration of a position-classification plan consists in keeping the classification of individual positions currently attuned to changes in their duties and responsibilities as they occur.[7]

From a broad management standpoint, a group of duties and responsibilities to be performed by one individual, i.e., a position, may be regarded as essentially a final subdivision of the functions of the organization in which it is located. It is the ultimate functional unit of organization. For example, an organization is established to design and construct a building. To accomplish this objective requires the conduct of several types of functions: design, preparation of working drawings, purchase of supplies and equipment, construction operations, supervision, inspection, and incidental correspondence and record-keeping work. In order to carry out these functions each of them must be subdivided into unit functions each capable of being performed by one person. This involves the creation of a number of positions each with its own duties and responsibilities, including engineering, drafting, clerical, mechanical, and laboring groups. Within each group some will be identical in all respects and some different. In classifying these positions, their respective duties and responsibilities, considered as subdivisions of the functions of the organization as a whole, are the controlling factors. Those which are alike will fall in the same class; those which are different will fall in different classes.

"Position" Does Not Mean "Employee"

Position-classification, as the term implies, is a classification of positions and not a classification of the employees occupying them. To classify employees according to their qualifications and abilities is a useful function in some phases of personnel administration, particularly in placement and service-rating procedures. Such a classification, however, is different from position-classification in principle and purpose. Position-classification, for example, serves as the basis for salary equalization and standardization. If positions were placed in classes according to the actual qualifications of their incumbents and the pay scale for each class applied to each incum-

[7] See pp. 47–49.

bent in that class, all persons having the same or equal qualifications would receive the same scale of pay. Thus, one who performs easy and routine tasks would be paid the same as one who performs difficult and responsible tasks, simply because both have the same or equal qualifications.

In order to assure proper position-classification, it is necessary to stress the distinction between the characteristics of a position and the characteristics which the employee occupying it may happen to possess or lack.[8] This, of course, is not in conflict with the fact that position-classification is of benefit to employees and that the qualifications and characteristics of employees have weight in other phases of personnel administration.[9] Position-classification is but one function of personnel administration. To achieve equity, orderliness, and clarity in all kinds of personnel transactions, the considerations governing that function should be distinguished from those involved in recruiting, testing, rating, and rewarding efficiency, and placement (assignment, transfer, promotion, and reassignment). In such processes the applicant's or employee's qualifications have an important and controlling influence, and in carrying them out employees or applicants are frequently grouped or "classified" according to their actual qualifications and relative performance.[10] This is different, however, from classifying their *positions*.

[8] "We find it necessary constantly to keep before our supervisors the fact, that in interpreting and using the system they must bear in mind that it is the work that is the subject of the analysis, and not the personal performance, ability or characteristics of the employee who performs the work, that employee rating is a distinctly separate thing. If the two become confused in their application, we are just where we were before the principles of job analysis were discovered, and management has in its hand only the crude measuring stick of unrelated opinions rather than a precision instrument." E. B. Roberts, "Position Analysis and Classification," *The Management Review*, July 1935, p. 205.

[9] "A 'real' job classification [i.e., one made on the basis of fundamental relationships] in an enterprise does not restrict dealing with people as individuals. Instead, it facilitates dealing with individuals equitably. It enables us to *reach or find* the individual—to specify and evaluate his job so that we may assign to him the particular rate of compensation which his individual proficiency merits within the range related to the status of his job." J. O. Hopwood, *Salaries, Wages and Labor Relations* (Copyright 1937, The Ronald Press Co.), p. 85.

[10] One should not fall into the error of thinking that position-classification carries the entire burden of personnel administration and that classifying a position takes the place of other personnel transactions. "The matter of the fitness of an individual employee or applicant for a position of a class, his efficiency in such position, the specific rate that he should receive at any time within the limits of compensation set for his class, his status for promotion or transfer, are matters for separate consideration and treatment. They should be subject to rule and orderly procedure, and are much simplified by adequate classification and compensation plans." Joint Committee on Economy in the Public Service of Ohio, *Report on State Administrative Agencies*, Part I, General Administration, 1929 (Griffenhagen & Associates).

A position, as we have indicated, is composed of assignments of duties and delegations of responsibilities. It does not depend for its existence or identity upon whether or not it is occupied by an employee. It often exists as a vacancy before it is occupied by any one and it resumes its status as a vacancy when an incumbent is separated from it. A vacant position is characterized by its duties and responsibilities quite as much as an occupied position, and therefore is classified on the same basis.[11] Thus, the concept of a *position* is distinct from the concept of an *employee*. This might seem to be merely a statement of an elementary and obvious fact. Experience indicates, however, that the two are not infrequently confused.

The idea of a position should be held up as something distinct and apart from an employee. That is not at all to say that the incumbent does not often influence the nature of the position, but it means that the concept of a position should be of things to be done rather than of the doer.[12]

Confusion always arises and mistakes frequently are made when position-classification is uncritically regarded as classifying the employee himself. Attempts to correct this view are met with the loose argument that the employee "makes his own job." It is, of course, a common experience, with respect to work which is not routinized, to find that after an employee has been inducted, his qualifications, or lack of them, as tested in actual work, have resulted in an addition to, or subtraction from, or alteration of the assignments or responsibilities originally contemplated for him. We say in such cases, more or less loosely, that the man makes the job. Nevertheless, regardless of the reasons why a position has been created or changed in a particular manner, clear thinking demands that we distinguish between *what* the employee does and *what* he is actually responsible for, on the one hand, and *how well* he does it and *how effectively* he bears his responsibilities on the other. The former are attributes of positions, which control their classification. The latter are purely attributes of employees, which are not classification factors, but rather

[11] It is a usual provision of law or regulation in the public service that vacancies must be classified before they are filled. Where the salary scale and qualification standards for a position depend upon its classification, the classification of newly created vacancies is an obvious necessity, for otherwise the entrance rate of pay and the qualification standards would not be known for recruiting and employment purposes.

[12] E. O. Griffenhagen, "Classification and Compensation Plans as Tools in Personnel Administration," *Handbook of Business Administration* (McGraw-Hill, 1931).

factors that are pertinent in administering other phases of personnel management or certain phases of a pay plan.[13]

Some Common Misconceptions

Obscurity in thinking that the classification of positions depends on the employees occupying them results for the most part from one or all of the following errors:

1. Failure to discriminate between (a) the *causes* of change in the duties or responsibilities of a position and (b) the *effect* of such change on the position.

2. Failure to distinguish between (a) the *qualification requirements of a position* and (b) *the actual qualifications* of the particular employee who happens to occupy the position at the moment.

3. Failure to differentiate between (a) the *duties and responsibilities* performed or exercised by the employee, and (b) the *relative efficiency* with which he carries them out.

Normally, the same position, its duties and responsibilities unchanged, may be occupied successively by different employees whose individual qualifications, although perhaps varying greatly, have not affected the basic operations of the position as indicated by the assignments of work and the delegations of responsibility involved. In some lines of work, however, by reason of the employee's individual traits or ability the character of the position to which he is originally appointed may materially change, and its value to the organization be enhanced or decreased. This is especially true in organizations where a variety of work is available, where administrative officers are allowed considerable latitude in authorizing and assigning duties, where the employee is assigned to duties and responsibilities which are considerably below or above his capabilities, or where his position is not enclosed in a framework of administratively imposed procedures and routines. Under these circumstances, the current duties and responsibilities of an employee's position may have evolved in their present form because of his personal characteristics, may further change from time to time as his ability advances or diminishes, and no doubt would be different if someone else were the incumbent.

[13] "It appears almost too obvious to state that the job content and requirement be rated and not the attributes of the men in the job; however, all too frequently job surveys fail because the individual, and not the job has been considered." Samuel L. H. Burk, "Salary and Wage Administration," *Personnel Journal*, September 1936, p. 113.

In such cases, in order to avoid the error of classifying the employee instead of the position, we should recognize that changes in the duties or responsibilities of a position may take place from time to time for any of a number of different causes, and that among these causes are the capacities or deficiencies of its incumbent. His capacities may have led his supervisors to assign to him, or to permit him to undertake, tasks of greater scope, difficulty, or complexity, or to delegate to him responsibilities of greater weight or import. On the other hand, his deficiencies may have led his supervisors to assign to him, or to permit him to do, simpler or less exacting work, or to transfer his responsibilities to someone else, whose own position is also thereby changed. In such situations, what the employee's status will be depends on the civil service or other rules of the jurisdiction respecting promotions and demotions.[14] In either instance, however, it is to be recognized that the change in his position is a fact, and that for position-classification purposes the change is the important thing, his abilities or deficiencies being simply the reason that his position has developed or changed. They are *causes* and, like all the various causes of development or change in the characteristics of a position, are for position-classification purposes to be clearly distinguished. from their *effect*, namely the changed or developed duties and responsibilities themselves.

Position-classification, accordingly, adheres strictly to the view that the current duties and responsibilities of a position are the sole basis for its classification, and recognizes at the same time that these may be changed in character, difficulty, or scope by reason of the capabilities or deficiencies of the employee occupying the position, resulting in a consequent change in its classification and raising the question of a possible readjustment of his legal status.[15]

Again, confusion between "position" and "employee" is caused by failure to distinguish between the qualification standards of a position and the actual qualifications possessed by the particular employee who happens to occupy the position at the moment.

---

[14] See pp. 330–35.

[15] "In some instances . . . the individual *makes his job* what it really is. If he is not held down he may gradually take to himself additional and larger duties or he may enlarge his original duties and develop his job to a higher level of work. Its acknowledgment is a *promotion*. On the other hand he may do the opposite by permitting responsibilities to slip from him, or it may be that he cannot prevent changes which take from him responsibilities which he once had, and this brings about a *demotion*." J. O. Hopwood, *Salaries, Wages and Labor Relations* (Copyright 1937, The Ronald Press Co.), p. 72.

In the process of classifying positions, such qualification standards established through a process of objective reasoning and inference, and affording a measure of guidance in classifying positions, are to be sharply distinguished from the actual qualifications that the employee occupying the position at the time may happen to possess or lack.[16] The qualification standards of a position are the basic education, experience, knowledge, ability, skill, and personal traits that *any* incumbent of a position must possess upon original entrance. They are in the nature of inferences drawn from information about the character, difficulty, complexity, scope, and weight of the duties and responsibilities of the position. In a position-classification plan they are established *a priori* for each class of positions and are intended to apply to all future applicants seeking employment in any position in such class. They have a generic and impersonal significance, not a significance dependent solely upon the actual qualifications of one person.

When carefully and objectively prepared, they constitute an auxiliary or collateral consideration aiding in the classification of positions, for they reflect the characteristics of the positions to which they apply, and to state them is one method of indicating how difficult or complex the duties and responsibilities of these positions are.[17]

The classification of a position is based on the duties and responsibilities performed or exercised in that position, and not upon what its incumbent might do if he were reassigned to another position involving work more in keeping with the qualifications he possesses. "A Phi Beta Kappa may be working as a janitor. The job is still that of a janitor."[18] The actual qualifications of employees would constitute an erroneous and misleading basis for classifying the assignments and responsibilities given them in fact in their organizations. Sometimes the employee possesses less than the qualifications that would be required of future incumbents. That does not mean, however, that the classification of his particular position should be lowered, as long as it is a fact that the work he does would

[16] A frequently effective correction for a tendency to regard the ability or deficiency of the incumbent of a position as a direct and controlling classification factor is to imagine that the position is vacant and to fasten one's mind upon the qualifications that would be required of a new, but so far unidentified incumbent, at entrance.

[17] See pp. 128–31.

[18] National Association of Assessing Officers, *Personnel Administration in Local Assessment Offices* (Chicago, 1940), p. 15.

entitle the position to that classification if anyone else did it. Perhaps he possesses more than the required qualifications. That does not mean that the classification of the position should be raised, as long as it is a fact that the work he does would not entitle the position to a higher classification if anyone else did it.[19] Perhaps he possesses qualifications of a kind not needed at all in his assignments. That circumstance, being purely accidental, can have no bearing on the classification of the position he occupies.

To be sure, in the cases we have just mentioned there may be an administrative error in matching the employee to his job. Position-classification serves a very important function in bringing such administrative errors into focus. It displays the facts about the actual duties and responsibilities of the position to which the employee is assigned. If, in the interests of the employee or of the department, that assignment can be made more effective, it is a matter for correction, not through position-classification, but through placement procedures.[20]

Another common reason for falling into an unconscious attempt to classify the employee rather than the position is failure to distinguish between the duties and responsibilities an employee performs or exercises and the relative degree of efficiency or effectiveness with which he carries them out.

We have seen that positions are characterized by their duties and responsibilities and that these constitute the sole basis for position-classification. When different persons are assigned to identical duties and responsibilities they may carry them out with varying degrees of effectiveness. The jobs are no different, but the performances of the persons on the jobs are different. The particular degree of efficiency or satisfactoriness with which the duties and responsibilities of a position are discharged is thus not a characteristic of the *position;* it is

[19] "We must be mindful, also, of the fact that it is jobs which are being evaluated and *not the persons* who may occupy them. The individual's qualifications may be broader than his job requirements but this should not affect the evaluation of his job. College graduates may take jobs in the lower levels in shops and offices but this does not raise the jobs to higher levels." J. O. Hopwood, *Salaries, Wages and Labor Relations* (Copyright 1937, The Ronald Press Co.), p. 72.

[20] In general, maintaining the right relation or adjustment between an employee's ability and the work to which he is assigned is primarily a recruiting or placement function. However, position-classification points the way so that these functions may be intelligently and fairly exercised. "If individual employees are performing their duties inefficiently, or if others are doing exceptional work and should be given greater responsibility, these are problems of administration and management." Public Administration Service, Transmittal Letter Accompanying Report of Seattle Reclassification Survey, May 7, 1938.

a characteristic of the *employee* occupying the position at the time and hence does not serve as a factor in the classification of positions.

In particular, a position that belongs in a certain class because of the kind, importance, difficulty, or complexity of its duties and responsibilities is not entitled to be placed in a higher class simply because its incumbent performs those duties or bears those responsibilities with a high degree of success and efficiency, nor is it properly to be placed in a lower class simply because its incumbent carries on with a low efficiency.

Since variations in individual performance on identical jobs cannot be recognized by differences in classification, some other method of compensating for efficiency must be found. The recognized solution, of course, is to fix a salary range, instead of one flat rate, for each class. A salary range consists of a number of rates of pay. It includes (1) a minimum rate, which is the entrance rate of the class, below which no employee occupying a position in the class shall be paid, as long as his work is sufficiently satisfactory to warrant his retention on the same assignment; (2) one or more intermediate rates for the purpose of rewarding degrees of increased usefulness and efficiency; and (3) a maximum rate, beyond which no employee may be paid while occupying a position in that class, no matter how efficient he may be in such position.[21] The various degrees of efficiency which may be manifested by different employees in the positions falling in the class, without change of duties or responsibilities, or classification, may thus be recognized by this range of rates. The rewarding of the efficient whose duties or responsibilities do not materially change, the withholding of rewards from those who are barely satisfactory but are allowed to remain on the same assignment, and, in general, the recognition of various degrees of efficiency are properly provisions of a pay plan rather than ends of a position-classification plan.

The necessity of maintaining the distinction between "position" and "employee" in developing and administering position-classification plans is frequently emphasized[22] in reports dealing with per-

---

[21] See the report of the Committee on Pay Plans in the Public Service, a companion volume in this series.

[22] See, for example: Congressional Joint Commission on Reclassification of Salaries, *Report,* March 12, 1920, H. Doc. 686, 66th Cong., 2d sess., p. 153; Civil Service Commission of Canada, *Report of Transmission . . .* etc. pp. 7, 8.

sonnel administration in public jurisdictions. Many of those who have written on the subject in the field of job analysis or position-classification in private industry consistently have expressed cautions of the same nature.[23]

CLASS OF POSITIONS

It has previously been pointed out that the process of classification, abstractly considered, consists in grouping things in classes; that the nature of a class of items in any system of classification implies that each individual item which the class contains shall be like every other item in certain respects; that these respects depend upon the basis of the particular classification concerned; and that in position-classification we select as the basis of classification the duties and responsibilities of the positions being classified. Hence, a class of positions constitutes a group of positions which, irrespective of the particular operating units in which they are located, are, in respect to their duties and responsibilities, sufficiently alike for purposes of personnel administration. In a position-classification plan, the class is the fundamental unit.

One formal definition of the term "class" is the following:[24]

The term "class" means a group of positions established under these rules sufficiently similar in respect to the duties, responsibilities, and authority thereof that the same descriptive title may be used with clarity to designate each position allocated to the class, that the same requirements as to education, experience, capacity, knowledge, proficiency, ability, and other qualifications should be required of the incumbents, that the same tests of fitness may be used to choose qualified employees, and that the same schedule of compensation can be made to apply with equity under the same or substantially the same employment conditions.

The definition of the term "class" is the most significant of those involved in position-classification because it contains the basic principle for determining whether two or more given positions belong in the same class or in different classes. From the first part of the definition it will be observed that if two or more positions are "sufficiently similar in respect to their duties and responsibilities" they belong in the same class; otherwise they belong in different classes. It is the decision whether or not positions are in fact "sufficiently

---

[23] See, for example: E. S. McClelland, *Report of Committee on Job Analysis*, American Management Association, October 29, 1924; Roy R. Marquardt, "Scientific Classification of Trust Department Personnel," *Personnel*, November 1930, pp. 77–87; Roberts, *loc. cit.*

[24] Civil Service Assembly . . . , *First Draft of Report of Technical Committee on Rules for the Installation and Administration of Classification and Compensation Plans.* Presented at Eastern States Regional Conference, May 16, 1930.

similar" that constitutes the essence of classification.[25] The second part of the definition establishes four concurrent conditions to govern the making of this decision. If all four conditions are met, the positions concerned belong within the same class. If any one of the conditions is not met, they belong in different classes.

We should especially note that equality of value to the service is not alone sufficient to establish positions in the same *class*. Two positions that may properly be paid according to the same pay scale—one composed of stenographic work and the other statistical work—are not allocable to the same class of positions, because they do not conform to the other standards of sufficient similarity. For example, different qualification standards would be used in testing and selecting employees to fill them, and certainly they could not be aptly described by the same name.[26]

Particular attention should be paid to the requirement in the definition to the effect that the same pay scale may be made to apply with equity "under the same or substantially the same employment conditions." The purpose of this is to make it clear that variations in employment conditions—especially economic factors—are not usually determinative factors in *classifying* positions. They are reserved for appraisal and recognition in developing and administering a pay plan.[27]

From an administrative standpoint it is important to notice that a class of positions is a group of positions which are sufficiently alike in their duties and responsibilities to justify *group treatment* in nomenclature, selection, compensation, and other personnel processes. It is this fact that renders classification, or the grouping of positions into classes, a practical device of many administrative uses and advantages.

A "class of positions" is a group concept, as contrasted with "position," which refers to the duties and responsibilities performed (or to be performed) by an individual employee. In a given organization there are as many positions as there are employees and vacancies waiting to be filled, but there are only as many classes of positions as there are distinct kinds of positions, one compared with another. Two clerks keeping customers' ledgers, one taking A to K and the

---

[25] See p. 196.
[26] See Griffenhagen, "The Principles and Technique of Preparing an Occupational Classification of Positions in the Public Service," *Public Personnel Studies*, November 1924, p. 241.
[27] See pp. 52–54.

other L to Z, would be occupying two positions, but both these positions would fall in the same class. The duties and responsibilities making up a position may make it anything from messenger boy to head of department. The duties and responsibilities of a class of positions can, however, properly include only those having essential features of similarity.

While defined as a group of positions, a class may sometimes consist of but one position where no others of the same kind exist in the service. For example, in a municipal service, Director of Public Safety is a class containing but one position, and Junior Stenographer is a class which may contain hundreds of positions.

The records of classes of positions take two principal forms: (a) the classes are identified by their official class titles, and (b) these titles are defined and the boundary lines of the classes described in terms of their duties and responsibilities content in formal written statements called class specifications.[28]

THE PLAN ITSELF

As previously stated, a position-classification plan consists of (1) the system of classes and class specifications, and (2) a code of formal fundamental rules for the installation and maintenance of the classification plan and for the interpretation, amendment, and alteration of the classes and class specifications, to keep pace with changes in the service and in the positions therein.[29]

Keeps Pace with Changes in the Service

To comprehend its general nature, we should first observe that a position-classification plan is not something that is fixed at a particular time and unchangeable thereafter. On the contrary, it is active and growing in accordance with trends in the service itself.

In the course of time in any public jurisdiction, new positions are created, duties and responsibilities are materially altered, or positions are abolished.[30] Hence, some of the classes and class specifications, as of the time they are set up, will ultimately become obsolete by

[28] See Chapter IX.
[29] See p. 4. Frequently it is considered that the list or other form of record which identifies for each position the class to which it has been allocated is an integral part of the position-classification plan. Cf. Donald C. Stone, "What is a Classification of Positions?", *Public Management*, March 1938, p. 71. Such a list, however, may more logically be regarded as a record of the application of the plan, rather than as a part of the plan itself.
[30] See pp. 285–88.

reason of changes in the positions upon which they were originally based. Similarly, allocations of individual positions to classes may become inappropriate because of changes or development in the duties or responsibilities of such positions.

A position-classification plan faces these conditions and takes them into account. It anticipates the need for and lays down a method of action and procedure for the future as well as for the present, which is contained in the code of formal fundamental rules as an integral part of the plan itself. A position-classification plan, accordingly, contains within itself the procedure for its continued growth so that a *continuously current* arrangement and description of classes of positions, fitting the positions in the service as they themselves change, may be effectively and systematically maintained. Such a procedure will include, among other things, provisions for the interpretation, amendment, and alteration of the classes and the class specifications, for ascertaining currently the duties and responsibilities of positions as they may exist at any given time, for classifying additional positions, new kinds of positions, or materially altered positions, and for rendering decisions as to their classification or reclassification. The whole process of keeping a classification plan attuned to the positions it encompasses, and of maintaining the relationship of individual positions to the plan as a whole, is one of recognizing development and change in organizations, functions, duties, tasks, responsibilities, and qualification standards; of maintaining a perpetual inventory of things that change with time; of constantly fitting the classification plan to the pattern of an ever-changing service, so that at all times it will show and conform to current facts and conditions.

Thus, a position-classification plan is more than a logically arranged list of classes of positions, accompanied by a set of specifications appropriately defining and describing each class. The classes and the class specifications are vital, but they do not constitute the whole plan. A position-classification plan has one other important aspect. It is a *plan* in the true sense, in that it sets a program for the future. It recognizes that the classes and the class specifications themselves are designed to reflect *current* duties and responsibilities of existing positions.

In this respect, it has been said that a classification plan for positions is analogous to a perpetual inventory of supplies and equipment. Both are based upon the characteristics of items as they currently exist. Changes in the characteristics of existing items, the introduction of new items, or the elimination of old items induce corresponding changes in the classification or inventory structure.

Descriptive and Not Restrictive

Classes and class specifications are not intended to and do not create a rigid system of classes which cannot be changed, and to which positions and assignments of work to employees must at all times conform. Their function is not to limit or prescribe the kinds of positions that may be created from time to time, or to fix, control, or prescribe the duties that particular employees shall perform or the responsibilities they shall exercise.[31]

Their purpose simply is to portray, for each class of positions, the duties and responsibilities which *if present in an individual position* will cause the position to fall in that class. Nothing in a position-classification plan interferes with any lawful authority that an operating official may possess in creating new positions, abolishing existing ones, changing the character of the duties and responsibilities of any position, or changing an employee's work assignments or responsibilities. When such authority is exercised, the effect may be to require changes in the classification of individual positions or in the classes and the class specifications themselves. For example, the creation of new positions which do not fall in any of the existing classes may call for the establishment of new classes and the writing of new class specifications; the abolition of all the positions falling in a given class may necessitate striking out that class from the classification plan; and material changes in the duties or responsibilities of individual positions frequently may require that they be reclassified, or that existing classes or class specifications be revised in the particulars necessary to reflect such changes, as made by operating or administrative officials. In other words, so far as the principles and rules of a position-classification plan are concerned, administra-

[31] For erroneous concepts of the nature of a position-classification plan in this respect, see National Institute of Public Administration, *Report on a Survey of the Organization and Administration of the State Government of New Jersey*, 1930, where it is said that "specifications defining duties and responsibilities necessarily limit appointing officers in assigning work to appointees"; and *Report of the Connecticut Commission concerning the Reorganization of the State Departments* (Hartford, 1937), pp. 196–97, where it is said that "the prescribing of specifications of the duties and responsibilities of each class of positions in a classification plan is to assure that a person employed for such position shall . . . perform the duties of that position." See the discussion and footnote references in Chapter IV, pp. 70–72.

tive officers, by creating new positions materially different from those already in existence, or by making changes in work-assignments or responsibilities, may set in motion a train of events leading to changes in the classification plan itself or in the classification of one or more individual positions. It is an essential function of the agency responsible for maintaining a position-classification plan to take such changes into account when they are contemplated or immediately after they are made, to determine, and to take the necessary action to recognize, the effects of these changes upon the classes, the class specifications, and the classification of individual positions.[32]

The distinction between a position-classification plan and other phases of general management or personnel administration should be kept entirely clear. Although the creation of, or changes in, positions are not restricted or controlled by a position-classification plan, they may be, and frequently are, controlled by the limits of available appropriations, by statutory schedules of positions allowed, by other specific legislative action, or by the administrative authority of a budget or fiscal agency or an agency controlling matters of organization and procedure. Furthermore, the assignment of employees to positions, and changes in their work assignments from time to time, may be subject to administrative regulations and civil service laws and rules, which also are instruments of control distinct from a position-classification plan itself.

However, the existence of budget, fiscal, or civil service controls over changes in positions and the assignments of employees should not lead to confusion in respect to the status of a position-classification plan. Where these controls do exist, they would continue to exist even though no classification plan were in effect. The operations of a position-classification plan may, however, reinforce and give meaning to these controls and render them more effective by closing loopholes and making avoidances harder to conceal. At the same time, a position-classification plan makes it possible to conduct studies, discuss mutual problems, prepare recommendations, and take actions on the basis of job terminology that is understood by the operating departments as well as by the staff agencies.

An Administrative Instrumentality

In the field of personnel management, a position-classification plan has the status of an administrative tool. Broadly speaking, it is not an

[32] See Chapter X.

end in itself, but a means for facilitating the accomplishment of many ends of personnel administration. Since it is a mechanism of management, its reason for being is that it furnishes a logically arranged factual basis about positions and their duties and responsibilities, which is essential for large-scale operations in other personnel processes, such as the recruiting, testing, selection, transfer, and promotion of personnel and the fixing of pay. Like any other mechanism, its value depends upon its being kept fit for current use.[33]

By itself, the process of classifying positions might hold only an academic interest if it were not for the fact that a position-classification plan is a definite, practical tool for the handling of the important and intricate operations that go to make up personnel administration.[34]

Although it clears the way for the solution of many problems of personnel administration, a position-classification plan solves, by itself, only two problems. First, it overcomes the limitations of the human mind in not being able to surround at once a large, unorganized mass of information about positions and to decide which positions warrant like treatment and which justify different treatment. It accomplishes this result (1) by placing together and identifying all individual positions involving substantially the same work, thus creating a much smaller number of classes of positions, and (2) by differentiating the various classes among themselves according to the character, difficulty, and responsibility of the work involved. Second, it solves the problem of establishing a uniform, defined terminology for positions. It accomplishes this result by associating with each class a distinctive, descriptive name or title, applicable to the class and to each position within it. Thus, a position-classification plan is an instrument for over-all management and for personnel administration, valuable and indispensable because it names positions uniformly, defines these names, presents information about their duties and responsibilities in condensed form, and arranges them in a logical pattern of relationships.

[33] See pp. 47–50, 285–88.
[34] E. O. Griffenhagen, *Classification and Compensation Plans as Tools in Personnel Administration*. Office Executives' Series, No. 17, American Management Association (New York, 1926). In the subsequent discussion of this paper, H. B. Bergen remarked: "I think the word 'tool' is very aptly used. These devices are but tools of management. In the office, we think of personnel administration not so much as an operation of putting the right man in the right job, but rather as a process of making continuous adjustments between men and their work. . . . Job classification and salary standardization are tools which facilitate the making of these adjustments."

Distinct from Pay Plan

The fact that a position-classification plan is an administrative tool designed to facilitate other techniques is strikingly illustrated in its use in developing and administering a pay plan.[35] But however close the association between a position-classification plan and a pay plan, there are definite lines of demarcation between them that must be constantly borne in mind.

The classification of positions is sometimes popularly regarded as synonymous with salary equalization and standardization and the impression is thus created that the only purpose of preparing a classification plan and classifying positions in accordance with it is to afford a basis for fixing fair pay for work performed and equal pay for equal work. That this is an extremely important purpose of position-classification is, of course, true. It is not amiss, however, to point out the error of confusing a position-classification plan with a pay plan and of thinking that a classification of positions is the same thing as fixing salaries.

A position-classification plan and a pay plan are distinct in basis, purpose, and technique. A position-classification plan is a system under which positions, on the basis of their current duties and responsibilities, are grouped into properly arranged classes, each class designated by a descriptive title, which is defined by a statement of duties, responsibilities, typical tasks, and qualification standards. In addition, it contains a code of rules for its installation, amendment, and continuous administration. A pay plan, on the other hand, is a plan by which the scales of pay for positions, *as previously arranged under a classification plan,* are determined. A pay plan also includes a code of formal fundamental rules governing its installation, amendment, and administration.

In other words, a position-classification plan serves to separate positions into classes; a pay plan serves to establish the pay scale for each class of positions, the pay scale for each individual position, and the pay rate for each employee at any given time. A position-classification plan does not, therefore, constitute a pay plan, but is, in fact, an entirely separate thing. In fact, it may exist without a pay plan. For example, a position-classification plan might be made solely for the purpose of providing a basis for suitable entrance requirements and tests for employment.[36]

[35] See pp. 61–64.
[36] For a description of an interesting city-wide position-classification project not designed for pay purposes, see Oliver C. Short, "The Classification Survey

Authority to establish and administer a position-classification plan does not include the power to establish and administer a pay plan. Each must be distinctively conferred. In some jurisdictions one agency possesses both types of authority. In others, the central personnel agency having control over the administration of the position-classification plan does not fix pay policy or pay scales, this activity being retained as a function of the appropriate legislative bodies. In New Jersey the State Civil Service Commission establishes and administers a classification plan for counties and municipalities which have voted by referendum to come under the authority of the Commission, but it has no control over the salary policies of these local governments.[37]

There are, of course, various elements which enter into the construction of pay scales and a pay plan that do not fall under the head of duties and responsibilities, and are therefore not considered in classifying positions. Some of these factors are socio-economic, administrative, or fiscal in nature, the consideration of which determines the liberality or economy of the general wage policy adopted. Among these factors are: cost of living as represented in reasonable family budgets; changes in the cost of living; comparison between pay levels in private industry and the public service; relative benefits of public and private employment other than those expressed in wages; present rates of pay and their payroll cost; recency and effect of previous salary adjustments; immediate and ultimate cost of proposed pay levels and financial ability or willingness of the jurisdiction to meet this cost.

Obviously, such socio-economic, administrative, and fiscal factors have a broad and important bearing on pay scales. They should be

---

of Positions in Industry and Commerce in Baltimore and Cumberland, Md.," *Summary of Proceedings,* Fourth Eastern States Regional Conference of the Civil Service Assembly . . . , 1932, pp. 18–22.

"The primary objectives for making the survey and preparing the community wide classification plan are: to furnish the educational authorities with data upon which they may formulate or reformulate educational programs to meet more closely local requirements; to furnish the vocational guidance department with correct information as to employment statistics, job specifications, and employment possibilities; to point out promotional opportunities to those already employed; to furnish placement agencies with information from which they will be able to do qualitative placement and thereby aid employers in securing workers whose pre-employment qualifications have been measured against job specifications; to improve personnel practices in the various organizations covered by the survey." Short, "Maryland Cross Classification Plan," *The Personnel Journal,* October 1932, pp. 169–73.

[37] New Jersey State Civil Service Commission, *Civil Service Organization and Routine in New Jersey* (Trenton, 1931), p. 7.

considered, their weight and effect determined, and the results given practical expression in terms of pay policy and pay scales. They should not, however, be given consideration in the classification of individual positions. So far as pay levels and the pay for individual positions are concerned, the position-classification plan must operate within the limitations set by the pay plan, and no attempt should be made to avoid these limitations in classifying positions by taking into account socio-economic or fiscal factors of the types mentioned.

Distinctions like that between the process of classification and the process of fixing pay do not, of course, constitute new or strange ideas. They are frequently encountered in everyday affairs. Two merchants may have on their shelves articles of exactly the same kind, style, and quality, which would be classified in their respective inventories under exactly the same name and description. Yet for various reasons they may have cost the merchants different amounts, and the merchants may sell them at different prices. Again, for transportation purposes commodities may have the same freight classification; yet the rate for the service may differ, because it depends upon other factors in addition to the classification of the shipment.

A position-classification plan is concerned only with the duties and responsibilities of positions. It does not take into consideration or give effect to every element bearing on the question of appropriate salary. In determining the pay policy of the jurisdiction, the pay scales for classes, or the pay rates of individual employees, many factors in addition to the duties and responsibilities of positions are involved. These are for consideration, separately from the matter of classification, in the development and administration of a pay plan. The problem of fixing pay is not solved by a position-classification plan alone; it needs the application of both a position-classification plan and a pay plan, with the decisions as to policy and rates that the latter entails. Nothing but confusion results from an attempt to regard every factor influencing pay policy or pay rates as one which should be influential in determining the classification of positions.

Chapter IV

Principal Uses and Advantages

GENERAL CONSIDERATIONS

THROUGH experience in the use of a position-classification plan there have been developed many important advantages that appeal readily to the official confronted with problems of general administration, personnel administration, or budget control.

Among other things, the law in a civil service jurisdiction would give to the central personnel agency the task of examining applicants to determine their fitness, preparing lists of qualified persons for each kind of work, and certifying the names of such persons to appointing officers when vacancies occur; to the managerial and fiscal officers the task of preparing the annual estimates for personal services; and to the legislative body the task of appropriating money periodically for such personal services. None of these agencies can properly perform these tasks unless there is some common understanding as to what kinds and numbers of jobs really exist, what their duties and responsibilities are, what each kind is to be called, what qualifications those appointed must possess, and what their pay ought to be. A position-classification plan provides the basis for this common understanding.

A position-classification plan is one of the most important steps which can be taken toward efficient personnel and budgetary administration.[1] The work necessary in establishing and maintaining such a plan where none has previously existed has everywhere been well repaid in the substitution of definiteness and fact for uncer-

[1] "The classification plan is the all-important foundation upon which all other personnel transactions are based. Without the basic classification plan to provide for equality in rates of pay for comparable types of work; to provide the necessary statement of background and skills and abilities on which recruiting and testing activities are based; to define the interrelationship of classes in such manner as to make clear the lines of promotion and transfer; and to provide the terminology by which the personnel agency, the budget authorities, the department heads, the employees, the legislature, and the public may refer conveniently and accurately to recognizable classes of employment; most of the work of personnel administration would be difficult if not impossible to do." California State Personnel Board, *Thirteenth Biennial Report* (1936–38), p. 14.

tainty, confusion, and conjecture. A position-classification plan establishes a uniform occupational terminology; serves as a base for an equitable and logical pay plan; facilitates the preparation of informative budgets for personal services; serves as a foundation for the recruiting, testing, and certification activities of the central personnel agency; clarifies promotion and transfer transactions; aids in developing service-rating plans and training programs; aids in planning, clarifying, and improving organization; facilitates the development of good employee-management relations; makes it possible to compile meaningful personnel statistics; and in general tends to systematize and facilitate the determination and execution of many types of personnel policies and specific personnel or pay transactions.[2]

A discussion of some of the specific uses and advantages of a position-classification plan follows.[3]

UNIFORM OCCUPATIONAL TERMINOLOGY

One feature of a position-classification plan that makes its benefits felt in many directions is that it establishes a common language, a uniform, significant, and defined terminology for the naming of positions.

[2] A good many advantages of a position-classification plan in everyday administration arise simply out of the fact that certain orderly, significant records are currently maintained about positions and the duties and responsibilities of which they are composed. These records consist mainly of (1) individual descriptions of the duties and responsibilities of each position; (2) class specifications or summarized descriptions of all positions that are sufficiently alike for personnel, fiscal, and management purposes, showing qualification standards, class by class; (3) a list of uniform and coordinated class and position titles, defined by the specifications; (4) a list showing the class to which each position belongs and therefore its appropriate job title and the qualifications required to fill it; and (5) records showing (a) at any given time the classification of the position held by each employee and (b) the classifications and the duties, responsibilities, and qualification standards of the various positions held by him from time to time during his official service.

[3] For additional discussion of the uses and advantages of a position-classification plan, see especially: Lewis Meriam, "The Uses of a Personnel Classification in the Public Service," *Annals*, May 1924, pp. 215–20; "The Uses of an Occupational Classification of Positions," *Public Personnel Studies*, October 1924, pp. 220–25; Garret L. Bergen, "Uses of Job Study," *Personnel*, November 1929, pp. 85–100. Public Administration Service, *Personnel Programs for Smaller Cities as Exemplified by Installations in Various Cities in Michigan*, Publication No. 73, 1940, pp. 14–16. For summarized lists of advantages, see, for example, Congressional Joint Commission on Reclassification of Salaries, *Report*, March 12, 1920, H.Doc. 686, 66th Cong., 2d sess., pp. 26–27; Griffenhagen, "The Principles and Techniques of Preparing an Occupational Classification of Positions in the Public Service," *Public Personnel Studies*, November 1924, p. 240; Civil Service Assembly . . . , *Classification and Compensation Plans*, Technical Bull. No. 1, pp. 7–8 (Chicago, 1928); "The Development of Classification and Compensation Plans for the Library Profession," *Public Personnel Studies*, September 1926, pp. 251–52.

Short descriptive expressions are, of course, time-saving vehicles of communication in everyday affairs and in many scientific activities. This is also true in personnel administration, where positions are named in order to identify them in a wide variety of payroll, budget, and personnel transactions and documents. Names of positions, like any other names, are most useful when they have single and unambiguous meanings, are used uniformly by all persons in their intercommunications, and are supported by definitions or explanations of their meaning in a written form convenient for reference. They are least useful when they are fictitious, misleading, undefined, used in good faith with different meanings, or deliberately used in such a way as to conceal the true nature of positions; for in that event the names alone are not reliable substitutes for the more lengthy explanations or descriptions of positions that they are intended to supplant in documents, schedules, statistical tables, correspondence, codes of rules, and other papers, and in telephone or other oral transactions.

In the absence of a position-classification plan, comprehensively developed and currently maintained, names of positions are apt to be nondescriptive or misleading. The same name is used to refer to different kinds of positions. Different names are used to refer to the same kind of position. No attempts are made to define the position-titles used, and different persons have different understandings of what the same name means.

Survey after survey has vividly demonstrated the chaotic condition into which position terminology falls in the absence of system and control. In one early survey it was found that the title "laborer" was being used to refer to a position the work of which was "sorting and filing mail in the file room"; that a "highway inspector" was engaged in simple blueprinting; that an "inspector of masonry" was doing routine clerical work; and that approximately 943 fictitious, misleading, unnecessary, or nondescriptive titles of positions were used in fiscal and personnel transactions and records.[4]

In another survey it was found that 133 persons each carried on the payroll as "miscellaneous helper" were in fact engaged in some 35 different capacities, such as registered nurse, pastry cook, hostler, physician, chauffeur, power plant laborer, stenographer, motor truck driver, and others.[5]

[4] State of New York, *First Report of the Senate Committee on Civil Service,* March 27, 1916 (Albany, 1916), pp. xvi–xvii, 768–918.
[5] Pennsylvania Civil Service Association, *The Growing Municipal Payroll in Philadelphia* (1928), p. 16. In commenting on the confusion in job titles, the

In another survey it was found that a chauffeur, a motor boat pilot, a painter, a pharmacist, a salad maker, a telephone operator, a clerk-typist, a graduate nurse, and a superintendent of laundry were all officially called "attendants" on the payroll and employment records; and for the purpose of illustration it was shown that 33, 43, and 79 different titles, respectively, were in effect for three groups of positions which would be classified as junior stenographer, junior storekeeper, and assistant fiscal accounting clerk.[6]

In another study it was found that the title of "clerk" was being used to cover positions involving work of such distinctiveness as to kind and rank as to require 21 different titles, including not only more significant clerical titles, but also such titles as Junior Library Assistant, Junior Accountant, Associate Executive, Junior Statistician, and Dietitian. On the other hand, it was found in the same study that 34 payroll titles were in actual use to cover positions that would all be called Junior Clerk under the proposed classification plan.[7]

In developing a salary and wage administration program for certain manufacturing activities of the Atlantic Refining Company[8],

> The first problem to be met by the company was the fact that the job titles used and developed over many years were rapidly becoming obsolete, at last for rate-setting purposes. The job titles had little, if any, significance to men and management in general, because in a large number of cases they gave no indication of the work performed, afforded no reflection of the qualifications necessary to the performance of the work or of the varying degrees of responsibility, and were variously interpreted in different locations. . . . As a result of these inaccurate job titles, management found it almost impossible to compare jobs in various plants or even in different divisions of the same plant. There was no systematic, standardized basis for discussion of comparable work, rates, etc., with employees. Difficulty was experienced in hiring, promotion and transfer unless personnel department employees were quite familiar with the actual work of all the positions, but the chief difficulty was that top management was unable to give cogent consideration to wage problems.

Association said: "An ace of spades should be recognizable every time it turns up, and not camouflaged half the time as a trey of hearts or a deuce of diamonds."

[6] U. S. Personnel Classification Board, *Closing Report of Wage and Personnel Survey*, H.Doc. 771, 71st Cong., 3d sess., pp. 96–113.

[7] Griffenhagen & Associates, *Report on Classification and Compensation of Positions in the Commonwealth of Virginia* (Richmond, 1937), pp. 36, 41–43.

[8] Samuel L. H. Burk, *A Case History in Salary and Wage Administration* (American Management Association, 1939), p. 4.

Illustrations of this sort can be multiplied indefinitely.[9]

It is not surprising if under such conditions confusions and misunderstandings are prevalent in personnel and fiscal processes. As was said by the Public Service Commissioner of Australia in reporting on the classification of the Commonwealth Public Service required by an Act passed in 1902:[10]

To have classified the service on the assumption that an officer's existing designation could be accepted as an indication of the nature of his duties and responsibilities would have created serious anomalies and injustice, and have made confusion worse confounded.

Lack of definiteness and system in the establishment and use of the titles by which positions are known provides a fertile ground for attempts to justify high rates of pay by high-sounding titles applied to simple work. Under such conditions, salaries are fixed not on the basis of what the employee does but on the basis of what the department calls him. It is impossible for the public to find out or understand the exact kinds of services for which the taxpayer's money is being spent. The time of operating departments and personnel agencies is wasted in repeated explanations of the meaning of position-titles and in clearing up misunderstandings due to mere differences over words. Budget schedules are not susceptible to clear analysis. Appropriating bodies provide funds for the operating departments without adequate information or with information that misleads.

The authority of a central classifying agency to specify the proper class title for each position and to define these titles controls uniformity of use, and prevents the setting up of fictitious titles as a basis for attempts to mislead personnel or fiscal authorities. This control is a simple recognition of the importance of class titles as common language devices for records, correspondence, and other communications that may be necessary in personnel and fiscal administration.[11]

[9] See, for example, the following additional sources: Congressional Joint Commission on Reclassification of Salaries, *Report*, March 12, 1920, pp. 44–49; Philadelphia Civil Service Commission, *Classification and Compensation Plans* (Extracts from Report to City Council, October 10, 1930), pp. 19–22; Joint Legislative Committee on the Classification of Positions in the Civil Service of the State of New York, *Report*, January 21, 1932, pp. 24–31.

[10] Quoted in Arthur Young & Co., *Report of Transmission to Accompany the Classification of the Civil Service of Canada* (Ottawa, 1919), p. 21.

[11] "The usefulness of a standardized system of titles in personnel management and in the operating procedures of the various organizations should need little explanation. A uniform classification of expenditures is commonly recognized

A position-classification plan thus designates or earmarks positions by names corresponding to the work which each position involves. A uniform terminology is established by which all concerned—taxpayer, legislator, administrator, and employee—may speak or write or read about positions in mutually understandable terms.

After administrative and personnel officers become familiar with the classification plan in operation, the class titles are used and referred to more frequently than the class specifications themselves. The designation or title identifies the position concisely, and users quickly or gradually become familiar with its exact meaning in terms of duties and responsibilities. Until they become familiar with its significance, it is a simple matter to look up the meaning of the title in the set of class specifications. One would consult the detailed specifications just as one consults a dictionary for the meaning of a word.

As will be seen in the following pages, the coherent system of occupational terminology supplied by a position-classification plan assists good public administration by eliminating confusion and uncertainty in many directions. In particular, it enables civil service administrators, department officers, budget officials, the legislative body, interested citizens, and taxpayers to get an inventory view of the government service, to find out how it is organized as to kinds of personnel, what numbers and kinds of positions exist, how the various appropriations are distributed as to jobs, what kinds of positions are found in each department or smaller organization unit, the distribution of employees and positions by occupations or vocations, and similar items of information on a reliable fact basis.[12]

---

as a prerequisite to satisfactory accounting and auditing control. A uniform classification of supplies and equipment is also recognized as a necessary accompaniment of purchasing and stock control. In each case the particular class of expenditure or of supplies or equipment is always designated by a name and usually a symbol number. In the same way it is proposed to classify positions, each with a precise name and symbol number, with specifications serving as definitions of what is included under the title, much as a class of expenditure or a class of supplies or equipment may be defined by analogous specifications." U. S. Personnel Classification Board, *Closing Report of Wage and Personnel Survey*, pp. 165–66.

12 "As a sound matter of business a corporation would not think of publishing a false inventory; nor is there any reason why the City of Philadelphia should in making its annual list of employees designate many of its employees by misleading titles. For example, calling by the single title 'laborer' some 75 inspectors, 44 watchmen, 34 truck drivers, 23 clerks, and 10 asphalt rakers. Similarly it is indefensible for the City to hide the clerical nature of a position by calling one who should be designated as 'clerk' by such masquerade titles as patrolman, foreman, auto machinist, auto driver, guard, or supervising engineer." Pennsylvania Civil Service Association, *Philadelphia's Quota of Government Employees*, 1930, p. 6.

BASE FOR PAY PLAN

In establishing and administering pay rates for positions in the public service and apart from any other factor of salary policy, one of the most important objectives is plain equity. Under the same employment conditions, employees doing work of the same difficulty and responsibility should enjoy the same pay scale; those doing harder or more responsible work should receive more; and those doing easier or less exacting work should receive less. In a given jurisdiction the pay scale at any time for a stenographer doing a certain class of work should be the same whether the Department of Health, the Department of Highways, or the Department of Parks pays the salary. Positions involving duties and responsibilities of higher order should be compensated in due relation to those of less importance. In other words, scales of pay must be logically and consistently related to work performed.[13]

A position-classification plan, which groups and designates positions according to the likenesses and differences in the work which they involve, provides a sound basis for accomplishing this objective. In order to put into effect the principle of "equal pay for equal work," it is necessary first to find out what the work of each position really is, and next to find out what work is, in fact, "equal." This is determined during the course of preparing a position-classification plan. Classifications and designations are controlled by a central agency serving all departments of the jurisdiction alike, and are uniform across departmental lines. Under this procedure, the fact that two positions are in the same class and have the same class title shows that their work is substantially equal(Hence, under the same employment conditions, one pay scale can be established for a class of positions with the assurance that if it is right for the whole class of positions, it is right for each individual position within the class.) Similarly, the ranking sequence of the classes as set forth in a position-classification plan permits the association of higher pay scales with higher work, and lower pay scales with less exacting work. Differences in difficulty and responsibility of work can definitely be

[13] "Any plan of wage-rate determination must, in order to be satisfactory, satisfy the workers affected on two questions that they raise either explicitly or unconsciously, viz: (1) Are the earning rates sufficient? (2) Are the various rates fair, relatively, one to another? The question of sufficiency refers not merely to what is needed for living but to other rates for the same grade of work in the community. The question of fairness involves such ideas as 'equal pay for equal work,' 'more pay for harder work,' and the like." Frank J. Becvar, "A Method of Grading and Valuing Operations," *Annals*, March 1922, p. 17.

recognized by corresponding differences in pay scales. Thus, through the use of a position-classification plan as a base, the same pay scale is made to apply to all positions involving equal work under the same employment conditions; and different pay scales are applied in proper sequence to positions involving different work.

Experience has amply indicated that it is not possible to create or maintain anything like equitable pay conditions without developing and administering a position-classification plan to support them. They can never be brought about under a system by which the pay of each position is determined separately and on the supposed merits of the individual case. It is only by a comparison of the value of the work of any position with the work of every other position paid from the same treasury that there can be a complete application of principles of equity, fairness, and uniformity.[14]

Where several thousand positions are involved, however, the appraisal of each position by itself and the determination of the relationship between each position and every other position are tasks that are impossible if each position is to be considered as a separate item for study and comparison. To accomplish these tasks and reduce them to manageable proportions it is necessary to group positions, considering as a unit those that are substantially alike in duties and responsibilities. A position-classification plan provides such a grouping. To develop such a plan is to organize information about the different kinds of positions, their duties, responsibilities, and qualification standards, and the relative difficulty and importance of the duties and responsibilities of the different kinds of positions from the lowest to the highest. It compacts these pertinent facts to a form that can readily be held in the mind while making the necessary comparisons and examinations of the relationships among positions. The problem of comparing thousands of positions one with another is reduced to the process of comparing the relatively much smaller number of classes to which such positions have been allocated in advance.

In practice, where no position-classification plan has been prepared and such comparisons among positions are, therefore, not feasible, administrative and legislative officials responsible for setting pay rates are handicapped. There is nothing to tie to. The administrative officer rarely has a general view of all positions in the

14 Griffenhagen & Associates, *Report on Classification and Compensation* . . . *in* . . . *Virginia*, p. 36.

service; he has no convenient source of reference. He must, as well as he can, recommend the establishment of pay rates for new positions he desires authorized and the continuance or revision of rates of existing positions, without much regard to uniformity throughout the service or coordination with any general plan, for none exists.[15] Except in those relatively few instances where he is able to secure more comprehensive information, the legislator must be governed largely by the undefined titles of positions used by different departments or units in their individual recommendations. In the absence of the uniform, official terminology provided by a position-classification plan, nothing is more unreliable than to conclude that positions deserve the same pay scale because they are called by the same name, or that a position called by a title that sounds important is really an important position.[16] The whole pay-fixing process is further confused by pressure for special pay increases on the part of individuals or groups.[17]

[15] Griffenhagen & Associates, *ibid.*, p. 37. Note the following testimony: "It is well known that in any large organization the salary paid in individual sections is very often conditioned by the attitude of the superior. In one unit the person in charge feels that only the professional people are important and they, therefore, should be highly paid to the disadvantage of the necessary and important clerical workers. In another unit, the reverse may be true. In still another situation the supervisor may feel that public funds should be conserved and that Government employees should be paid as small a salary as possible. In another unit, the supervisor may feel that the more money one can pay his employees, the more likely he is to get the best of the crop. As a result, envious comparisons arise between the employees of the respective units. . . With the introduction of a sound classification plan personal considerations do not condition the classification. To the contrary, there is a uniformity of compensation developed. The result is that not only is there a better attitude on the part of the workers, but there is much less moving about of workers not only between units of the same agency but between agencies, since the only financial inducement that can then be offered is that which can appropriately be advanced with the increase of responsibility in the new position." F. C. Harrington, Administrator of Works Progress Administration, Hearings before the Senate Committee on Appropriations, 76th Cong., 1st sess., on H.J.Res. 326, pp. 119–20.

[16] "Dignified titles were used as a smoke screen to legislative inquiries. Thus a 'building superintendent' has become under job analysis a mere 'clerk, class B,' and one 'chief clerk' is now a 'clerk typist,' . . . and another who told the legislative world he was a 'statistician' is now a 'tabulating machine operator.' . . . None of the people with these high-sounding titles did the work those titles called for. The titles were devised to get the money. Thus many clerk typists were put on the statutory rolls under the high-sounding title of 'recording clerk' and no legislator successfully got back of the window dressing to look at the goods that were being delivered for the pay." Clyde L. King, "How Shall Salaries of State Employees Be Fixed?", *Annals*, May 1924, pp. 204–05. See also Z. Clark Dickinson, *Compensating Industrial Effort* (Ronald Press, 1937), pp. 188–89.

[17] "Furthermore, in the common practices of fixing rates, just recited, the value of the work of *the position*, and the personality and ideas of the personal worth of *the incumbent*, are hopelessly confused, so that no clearcut idea is held of

The result is that positions involving the same work are paid at widely varying rates; the pay structure of the jurisdiction lacks rhyme or reason; there is both overpayment and underpayment; public funds are wasted; injustices and discrimination exist and are continually created; and the effectiveness of the public service is diminished.

In contrast with such methods, the use of a position-classification plan as a base for a pay plan contemplates the development and formulation of a definite salary policy; the expression of this policy in terms of scales of pay and operating regulations; the definite association of the scales of pay with the classes of the position-classification plan; and the determination of the scale of pay for each individual position through the process, controlled by a central classifying agency, of determining the precise class in which the position falls, on the basis of its duties, responsibilities, and qualification standards.[18]

INFORMATIVE BUDGETS

The same characteristics of a position-classification plan that make it an indispensable foundation for a sound pay plan have a useful role in budget-making. With respect to this function, the heads of operating departments, the general management executives of the

---

just what is being valued, and this further precludes the application of consistent judgment from case to case. Often the salary of a position is advanced by successive increments based on the continued service and the claimed increase of ability of the incumbent. But when such incumbent steps out, the fact that such increments were granted on grounds personal to the incumbent is often forgotten, and the new appointee starts off at the point that his predecessor attained only by years of service. There is thus a tendency to 'pyramiding' of rates." Griffenhagen & Associates, *Report of the Joint Legislative Committee on Classification of Positions in the Civil Service of the State of New York* (Albany, 1932).

[18] "In this situation when a department head wishes a new position, he asks for it under the specific title of the class that covers the particular kind of employment. The legislator needs but to turn to the specifications of the class in the classification plan to gain a clear idea of exactly the kind of position that is involved. He needs but to turn to the salary scale for the class to find out the salary that should be paid in the position if it should be authorized. He knows, under the procedure set-up as part of the plan, that there are administrative agencies constantly at work checking up on the classifications and allocations of specific positions and making adjustments as conditions change, and similarly bringing to his attention and that of his colleagues any desirable adjustments in the compensation plan, so that he can depend on the information that is supplied. The only times when he needs to concern himself with the propriety of any specific rates is when proposals are presented, with the facts, and reasons, for adjustments in the compensation plan and for periodic checks and revisions possibly every few years, to meet changed conditions." Griffenhagen & Associates, *Report of Joint Committee on Economy in the Public Service of Ohio* (Columbus, 1929), Part I.

jurisdiction, the legislative body, and frequently the personnel agency, are periodically in contact.

A position-classification plan aids in the development of cooperative relations and practices among these agencies and makes for increased efficiency in the administration of budgetary activities. Means of control can be established to insure that the will of the appropriating body in authorizing positions of certain kinds will be carried out and that the salaries appropriated will be paid for the kinds of services contemplated and no others. In the absence of such a classification there is little basis for common understanding, for consistent action, or for carrying out any policy.[19]

Because of the uniform, defined terminology it affords, the classification plan can be used by administrative officials as a definite tool for presenting requests for funds for personal services in comprehensible form. Schedules of positions are built upon the official class titles, having the same meaning to the writer and the reader of the schedules, each title being supportable, if necessary, by an official explanation in the form of a class specification. Masses of detail can be diminished greatly by the listing of positions by classes, showing the number in each class. The time spent in dealing with individually named positions, in comparing one position with another, in endeavoring to find out what unreliable position titles mean, can be saved and devoted to broader questions.

Furthermore, the executive and legislative agencies concerned with recommending or passing upon the requests of administrative heads for appropriations are enabled to get a clear picture of the organization and position-content of the different operating units as a basis for action. In any event, they must be in a position to discuss effectively with administrative officers the need for the number and kinds of positions already existing and the need for the number and kinds of additional positions, authority, or funds which are requested. In a position-classification plan they have a systematic device to which they may require administrative officers to conform in scheduling the number and kinds of existing positions and of additional or new positions being requested. Such schedules will show by descriptive titles what duties and responsibilities are or will be assigned to each of the classes of positions listed.[20]

[19] Griffenhagen & Associates, "Classification in Relation to Budget Making," in *Report on Classification and Compensation . . . in . . . Virginia*, pp. 38–40.
[20] "In the department estimates for appropriations each position would be designated by its official title of the class to which it has been allocated. The title would carry with it the specific definition provided in the specifications,

The importance of a modern position-classification plan in this respect can be illustrated by reference to instructions issued a few years ago by a state budget agency for the guidance of department heads in preparing estimates for personal services. These instructions contained a "Classification of Personal Services." Departments were to classify positions in accordance with the outline given, showing the minimum and maximum salaries under each classification. Observe, for example, the mixed content of the following groupings:[21]

Engineers, which term shall include all positions where qualifications of an engineering or cognate character are required, including civil engineers, levelers, surveyors, rodmen, architects, architectural draftsmen, engineering draftsmen, chief engineers, electrical engineers, dynamo tenders, electricians, steam engineers, firemen, engine drivers, and others.

Clerks, which term shall include all positions, the duties of which are of a clerical character, and which are not otherwise specifically provided for herein, including secretaries, chief clerks, clerks, recorders, registers, copyists, clerks with special educational requirements, bookkeepers, accountants, stenographers, typists, pages, office boys and girls, switchboard operators, and others.

Special agents, which term shall include all positions requiring analytical ability, including examiners for the banking department, examiners for the insurance department, examiners for the Comptroller and other State officers, examiners for the State boards and commissions, deputy factory inspectors, special excise agents, inspectors of milk, butter, cheese, vinegar, etc., and others.

Although reviewers of budget requests would have no means except further investigation of understanding a request for fourteen "clerks," they would understand (referring to the recorded system of class specifications, if necessary) what is meant by five Junior Stenographers, three Junior Accountants, two Telephone Operators, and four Senior Clerk-Typists. Moreover, they have a means of comparing the organization and operating effectiveness of different units engaged in similar work. Establishing standardized titles and re-

---

so that the department authorities, the budget officials, and the Legislature could be sure of thinking of the same thing in the same terms in the consideration of each item. If detailed appropriations are made authorizing positions under specific standard titles, there can be no doubt of the actual kinds of positions authorized, as the titles must carry the meanings expressed in the specifications." Griffenhagen & Associates, *Report . . . on Classification of Positions in the Civil Service of the State of New York,* pp. 35–36.

[21] State of Rhode Island and Providence Plantations, Office of the State Budget Director and Comptroller, *Manual of Instructions for the Preparation of Estimates of Expenditure and Revenue for the fiscal year ending June 30, 1938.* The state has since adopted a modern position-classification plan and the budget procedure has been revised.

quiring their use in budget estimates and reports helps to prevent the creation or maintenance of fictitious positions, too many positions, or higher positions than the nature of the work warrants.

As a control over the expenditure of lump-sum appropriations, a position-classification plan is especially significant. In fact, in the federal service the administrative operations which a position-classification plan involves were regarded as a sufficient control over the discretion granted to administrative officers in lump-sum appropriations, and the passage of the Classification Act of 1923 led directly to the final elimination of the practice of appropriating funds for personal services by direct statutory lists.[22]

RECRUITING, TESTING, AND CERTIFICATION

Civil service commissions and similar central personnel agencies are charged by law with the maintenance and enforcement of the merit system of employment. In this respect they must provide the operating departments with qualified persons to do the varied work of the public service. This involves the recruiting and testing of applicants for positions in the public service, the preparation of eligible lists, and the certification of the names of successful applicants to the operating departments.

A position-classification plan has a pivotal place in the effective planning of such activities and the conduct of the numerous transactions involved. It serves the central personnel agency as an orderly arrangement of facts about the duties, responsibilities, and qualification standards of positions. These facts form the basis for planning and preparing tests, for informing prospective applicants or other interested persons about the duties of the positions to be filled and the basic qualifications to be tested and rated, for preparing eligible lists, and for controlling their use in the filling of requisitions for the certification of eligibles.

In its contacts with the public in recruiting employees, the central personnel agency can effectively utilize a position-classification plan.[23] In some jurisdictions, the class specification covering the positions for which the test is to be held is reproduced bodily in the public announcement of the test, this being considered the best way to show the name of the positions, the work they involve, and the qualifica-

[22] *Cong. Record*, daily edition, January 10, 1924, p. 788; U. S. Personnel Classification Board, *Closing Report of Wage and Personnel Survey*, pp. 171–72.
[23] William Brownrigg and Louis J. Kroeger, *Toward Effective Recruiting*, Civil Service Assembly . . . , Pamphlet No. 7 (Chicago, 1937).

tions required or desired. Not only does a position-classification plan thus lend itself to the advertising of single examinations but it also aids in publishing information of broader scope and viewpoint with respect to the opportunities and requirements of government employment. For example, an inventory picture of whole occupational groups can be presented, with their numbers, duties, salaries, departmental locations, and qualification standards for entrance and for advancement, in such a way as to develop interest in a specific line of public employment and to attract desirable applicants who might not be drawn by the announcement of an individual test.

In the testing process itself, a position-classification plan is a tool that saves time, money, and confusion. The personnel agency does not have to travel the same ground over and over again in order to determine duties to be performed and qualifications to be tested every time a vacancy occurs, a new employee is to be hired, or an examination is needed. The classification of the position to be filled furnishes the basic facts.[24] Since positions in the same class involve work requiring the same basic qualifications, the personnel agency can key its testing activities not to individual positions directly, but to classes of positions. Consequently, instead of holding a large variety of tests—with perhaps only slight differences among them— for positions of the same kind but presumed to be somewhat different, the personnel agency holds one test covering all positions in a single class. This decreases the number of different kinds of tests held, and likewise decreases the number of eligible lists maintained to meet the needs of the operating departments.

Moreover, in deciding upon the scope and content of tests, the work of the positions to be filled must be thoroughly understood. The analysis and evaluation of the qualifications of prospective employees mean little except in relation to the work they are to do.[25] The specifications of each class of positions contained in the position-classification plan show what this work is. Each specification records the duties, responsibilities, and qualification standards of the positions in the class. This information when adequately set forth greatly

---

[24] For some types of tests a more detailed analysis of duties is sometimes required. See pp. 248–50; and footnotes on pp. 69, 266.

[25] "Two sets of information are essential for the successful operation of the employment division of any business organization. First, there must be available a considerable amount of knowledge concerning the requirements of each job, and second, there must be information with regard to the qualifications of individual workers. . . . In the absence of the data which job analysis yields, proper selection and placement are inconceivable except by accident." Watkins and Dodd, *The Management of Labor Relations* (McGraw-Hill, 1938), p. 119.

facilitates test-preparation. Further, distinctions in tests should conform to the distinctions in work upon which the different classifications rest. Class specifications, accordingly, serve the personnel agency as a sound base for its testing programs, as a useful instrument for discussions about tests with operating heads, and as a guide to such further analysis of qualifications as may be necessary for some testing purposes.[26]

In its contacts with appointing officers and administrative officials the central personnel agency has in a position-classification plan a common and understandable language. For example, in filling departmental requisitions for employees, uncertainty on the part of the personnel agency as to the meaning of the titles used in the requisitions often necessitates additional inquiry, investigation, or correspondence. This results in misunderstandings, mistakes, or delays. Sometimes inquiry is not made, and eligibles on the lists who are entitled to consideration and who would prove satisfactory employees are not identified; operating departments are not furnished with the qualified employees who are actually available; existing eligible lists, entirely appropriate, may be ignored; and provisional or temporary appointments may be needlessly authorized: merely because the position-titles used in requisitions do not correspond with those of any existing eligible list.

On the other hand, the defined terminology of a position-classification plan renders it practicable for appointing officers, in submitting requisitions for the certification of eligibles, to indicate clearly and definitely by title alone the class of vacant positions to be filled. Class titles, examination titles, employment list titles, and requisition titles would normally correspond, and the list from which certification should be made would be specifically indicated. Attempts to avoid the use of the proper list would be met by the proper classification of the position and a check of the requisition title against the standard class title. Where the civil service rules, through

[26] "In order to improve the methods of testing applicants to determine their relative qualifications for a particular position, research procedure includes the following studies: 1. Duties of the occupation. 2. The proficiency necessary in each of the duties. 3. The human qualifications necessary to attain such proficiency. These include: (a) Skill and knowledge—training and experience; (b) General intelligence—ability to learn and adapt to new situations; (c) Special aptitudes, including such qualities as ingenuity and constructive ability; (d) Personality, including tact, perseverance, aggressiveness; (e) Physical qualifications, general and special. 4. The relative importance of these qualifications for fitness in the occupation. L. J. O'Rourke, *Report of Research Section*, Fortieth Annual Report of the U. S. Civil Service Commission (1923), p. L. See also Donald J. Sublette, "The Preparation of Pencil and Paper Tests," *Public Personnel Review*, January 1941, p. 4.

"selective certification,"[27] permit the use of appropriate lists of other titles, the system of class specifications with which all employment lists could be correlated would permit intelligent action. A position-classification plan thus puts the filling of requisitions for employees on the same businesslike basis as the filling of requisitions for supplies.[28]

PROMOTION AND TRANSFER

The formulation and administration of sound plans, equitable regulations, and definite requirements governing promotions and transfers of employees from position to position within the service are constant challenges to public personnel agencies.

Clearly, before general policies can be determined and procedures laid down for promotions and transfers, much must be known about the positions in the service and especially their relationship to one another in kind and level of work. In fact, the very feasibility of a promotion or transfer is based on the assumption that intelligent comparison is possible between the position from which the employee comes and that to which he goes. Study and analysis of positions and their relationships need to be made and the results recorded. Because promotion is the movement of an employee to a higher position,[29] the relative place of each position in a promotional sequence needs to be known. Areas of activity from which employees may be drawn for higher positions need to be identified. The qualification standards for each position have to be known. All this in-

[27] "Where the Commission finds that there is no register in existence appropriate as a whole to fill a particular existing vacancy, the Commission in its discretion may certify selectively from the most nearly appropriate register, in order of their ranking, the names of any individuals thereon found by it to be adequately qualified to fulfill the particular requirements of the vacant position." Section 2 of Rule VII, U. S. Civil Service Commission.

[28] The following is contained in the rules of one public personnel agency: "In certifying to requisitions, the duties of the position to be filled, rather than the name by which it is called, shall be considered, and it shall be the duty of the Commission to inquire into the requirements of the position for which requisition has been made and to certify from the register of eligibles which shall in its judgment nearest conform to the requirements of the position to be filled." Obviously, in the absence of a definitive classification of positions, frequent investigation would be essential in order to reap the full advantage of such a rule as this. However, in this case investigations are not made and the agency does not recognize an employment list as being appropriate if it was made up under a title other than that used in the requisition. It does, however, use its power to approve or disapprove payrolls to prevent the deliberate switching of titles for the purpose of evading the civil service law.

[29] A position-classification plan makes possible a clear distinction between (a) a promotion, which involves selection to perform new duties of greater difficulty or responsibility, and (b) a salary advancement due to length of service or efficiency or a combination of the two.

formation is furnished by or can easily be compiled from a position-classification plan.

In a position-classification plan, the arrangement of classes of positions, supported by class specifications, identifies positions in their proper relationships for promotion and transfer purposes. Thus such a plan is a prerequisite for the clarification of promotion and transfer programs and transactions.[30]

With respect to promotional opportunities, a position-classification plan shows where career avenues are present and where they are lacking. It provides the basis for an analysis of the reasons why this is so and for an approach to proper remedies. If the service is not organized to provide a sufficient number of career avenues for employees, a position-classification plan is a useful analytical and factual tool in reorganizing and redistributing work and responsibility, for the purpose of creating promotional opportunities where they are needed.[31]

Further, the use of class titles in employees' service records and in the documents, correspondence, orders, or regulatory position-schedules relating to promotions and transfers frees such transactions from needless but common impediments.[32] Particularly is this manifested in cases which are simple in themselves but which require

[30] "A general plan of promotion which is not constructed on a foundation of specific and explicit specifications of positions in their proper sequences is foredoomed to failure. Men cannot be advanced from position to position presenting a spiral of responsibilities unless the nature and requirements of higher positions are definitely known. A careful study of jobs not only assures a correct line of advancement but frequently makes possible an escape from 'blind alley' jobs by linking them up with positions in the same or different departments which offer greater opportunities." Watkins and Dodd, *op. cit.*, p. 127. See also U. S. Civil Service Commission, *Nineteenth Annual Report* (1902), pp. 22–24; Frank B. and Lillian M. Gilbreth, "The Three Position Plan of Promotion," *Annals*, May 1916, pp. 289–96; Robert C. Clothier, "Organization for an Occupational Survey," *The Journal of Personnel Research*, February 1923, pp. 444–46; Mosher and Kingsley, *Public Personnel Administration* (Harper & Bros., 1936), pp. 260–61.

[31] Wallace S. Sayre and Milton Mandell, *Education and the Civil Service in New York City*, Office of Education Bulletin, No. 20, 1937, pp. 42, 44. For general discussion of the criticism occasionally encountered, to the effect that a detailed, descriptive position-classification plan restricts promotional opportunities, see Griffenhagen, "Personnel in Government," *Proceedings*, Sixth Eastern Regional Conference of the Civil Service Assembly . . . , 1935, pp. 14–15; and Ismar Baruch, *Facts and Fallacies about Position-Classification*, Civil Service Assembly . . . , Pamphlet No. 10 (Chicago, 1937), pp. 20–23. "The exact description of jobs has sometimes been misunderstood as a handicap to the career service idea. This is an error; the difficulty lies not in close classification but in too narrow recruiting, inadequate in-service training and above all in severe limitations on transfer. These handicaps are not essentially related to a system of closely defined classes or grades." Leonard D. White, *Introduction to the Study of Public Administration* (Macmillan, 1939), p. 333. See also Chapter III, pp. 86–9.

[32] See the discussion of the use of position-classification in handling transfers, in *Public Personnel Studies*, October 1924, pp. 222–23.

definiteness of terminology to avoid misunderstanding or confusion. Comparisons among positions, to see whether a promotion or a transfer is involved, and the application of pertinent regulations and requirements should not be made laborious by mere failure to name jobs correctly.[33]

OTHER PERSONNEL PROCESSES

In general, it may be said that there is no important phase of a modern personnel program in which a position-classification plan is not a convenient aid.

For example, an important phase of personnel administration is the evaluation of the performance of employees, a necessary step in discovering, developing, retaining, and utilizing to the fullest extent the most able and efficient employees.[34] The building of a service-rating program for this purpose is aided by the existence of a position-classification plan. In developing such a program, it is necessary to decide upon the items that will be used in rating the performance of each employee. Clearly, this requires an analysis of the work involved in his position. Under a position-classification plan, basic analyses have already been made and recorded in class specifications. Furthermore, the result of the classification process is to

[33] For example, note the following extract from a memorandum prepared some years ago in a public personnel agency operating without the benefit of a position-classification plan: "In the Z case, and in all other cases like the Z case, there is, in reality, no transfer at all so far as duties are concerned, but a mere, nominal transfer for the convenience of the department. The department did not want Z to serve as an elevator conductor at all; therefore, it was not necessary that he qualify as an elevator conductor. The department desires a messenger; Z is qualified as a messenger (having been promoted from messenger boy to watchman, but continuing on messenger duties), and is eligible to be continued or transferred as a messenger. The department has a position with the designation of elevator conductor (but no elevator) to which it desires to promote Z, he to continue, however, on messenger duties. When Z is thus transferred he still continues to have the status of a messenger, not the status of an elevator conductor."

In another instance, a public personnel agency authorized an operating department to appoint Miss M. as a "Junior Stenographer." The department made the appointment, but reported the name of the position as "clerk." This did not correspond with the authority granted, and the agency wrote to the department. The department replied: "In order to avoid multiplicity of designations it has long been the practice of the department to avoid the use of such designations as 'stenographer,' 'typist,' etc., and to carry employees engaged on such duties under the generic title of 'clerk.' Miss M. is assigned to a stenographic position."

[34] For summaries of the objectives of service-rating plans, see, for example, National Industrial Conference Board, *Plans for Rating Employees* (Studies in Personnel Policy No. 8, 1938), pp. 5–6; Home Owners' Loan Corporation, Personnel Department, *Service Rating Manual*, January 1937, pp. 1–2; J. B. Probst, *Service Ratings*, Civil Service Assembly . . . , Technical Bull. No. 4 (Chicago, 1931), p. 10.

allocate to the same class all positions to which the same rating factors would apply. A position-classification plan thus supplies the factual and analytical foundation upon which the further refinement and final determination of rating factors may proceed, class by class, instead of individual position by individual position.[35]

In some service rating systems, in the effort to make the rating factors apply to the work rated as precisely as possible in concrete terms of action or behavior, several or many sets of rating factors are used. In the absence of a position-classification plan, the applicability of each set of factors to each individual position and employee would be difficult to determine and prescribe. However, where a position-classification plan exists, administration is simplified by keying each set to the precise classes to which it is applicable.[36] Thus, in the actual application of the program, the record of the class in which the employee's position has been allocated will indicate the combination of rating factors—and the particular rating form—that is to be used.[37] For example, the rating scale of the Westinghouse Electric and Manufacturing Company for salaried employees, which embraces seven sets of items applicable to unskilled, skilled, interpretative, creative, executive, administrative, and policy positions, respectively, is developed from its job classification plan which recognizes the same groupings.[38]

Similarly, the analyses and class specifications of a position-classi-

[35] "Classification according to duties, responsibilities and qualifications is also essential to the development of sound efficiency rating systems. . . . Efficiency rating systems that get away from an analysis of the duties get away from the facts and the further they get away from facts the less their value." Lewis Meriam, "The Uses of a Personnel Classification in the Public Service," *Annals*, May 1924, p. 216.

"Much of the negative experience in rating practice is attributed to a lack of distinction, on the part of foremen and management, between men and jobs. For this reason many firms regard job classification as a prerequisite to effective employee rating." National Industrial Conference Board, *loc. cit.*

[36] Jack H. Pockrass, "Common Fallacies in Employee Ratings," *The Personnel Journal*, January 1940, pp. 263–64.

[37] California State Personnel Board, *Reports of Performance, A System of Service Ratings*, 1940.

[38] "The Westinghouse plan seeks to relate performance rating to position classification on the principle that rating is a refinement of the position classification and that both are tools in the hand of management in its work of determining the right compensation for the individual." National Industrial Conference Board, *ibid.*, pp. 9–11. See also the tabular coordination of definitions of characteristics for use in both job evaluation and employee rating which appears in Life Office Management Association, Clerical Salary Study Committee, *Life Office Salary Administration*, Report No. 2 (1939), pp. 38–39. This table shows, for each job evaluation characteristic (allocation factor), the definition of that characteristic used in job evaluation, the parallel definition used in employee rating, and "levels of performance" for use on forms for rating employee performance.

fication plan are of aid as a starting point in the development of employee training programs.[39] Before employees can be trained, the work for which they are to be trained must be described and analyzed, the necessary knowledges and abilities deduced, and a selection from among them made, to serve as a basis for the training program.[40]

PLANNING, CLARIFYING, AND IMPROVING ORGANIZATION

Organizations are set up for the achievement of particular purposes; unless such purposes exist, there is no need for the machinery. Viewed as a whole, the purposes of government are extremely complex, but those of individual departments, commissions, boards, and their subdivisions are reasonably specific and comprehensible. These segments of government have many of their objectives set out for them in the form of specific legislative enactments, or through appropriation measures which in turn have to be supplemented by administrative or legal interpretations or otherwise translated into particular projects and programs. However objectives may be defined, their achievement ordinarily requires some kind of hierarchical structure. "Organization is the arrangement of personnel for facilitating the accomplishment of some agreed purpose through the allocation of functions and responsibility. It is the relating of efforts and capacities of individuals and groups . . . in such a way as to secure the desired objective."[41]

It will be noted, accordingly, that organization is an arrangement of personnel relating the capacities of individuals and groups. This arrangement may be termed *organization structure* or the framework into which the staff is fitted. By no means is it inflexible or unchanging, but rather it is determined by such elements as quality of personnel available, character of the purposes or aims being pursued, the stage of development of a particular technology, and simi-

---

[39] "It is difficult to conceive of a successful training program in the absence of detailed information relating to the various jobs in the establishment. Positions must be classified, indexed, defined, evaluated, and related if a systematic program of employee training is to be maintained. Men cannot be prepared intelligently unless the nature, duties, and responsibilities of the jobs for which they are being trained are definitely described. The content of the training curriculum, length of the training period, and selection of candidates for training are alike dependent upon an adequate study of jobs." Watkins and Dodd, *op. cit.*, pp. 127-28. See also W. W. Charters, "New Developments in Personnel Work," *The Management Review*, June 1926, p. 164.

[40] Job analysis for training purposes is generally much more detailed than that customarily engaged in for position-classification purposes. See footnote, p. 248.

[41] John M. Gaus, Leonard D. White, and Marshall E. Dimock, *The Frontiers of Public Administration* (University of Chicago Press, 1936), pp. 66-67.

lar factors.[42] Thus, *organization* is the combination of personnel and organization structure, and as such embraces all the interrelationships between the various components of the total group. Administration or management, however, is creating and using the organization, i.e., "the vital spark which directs and controls the plan and procedure of organization."[43]

In the light of these definitions and concepts, it is clear that a position-classification plan, the processes of fact-finding and analysis it involves, and the agency which develops and maintains it, have special contributions to make in solving the technical problems of organization structure.[44]

By the orderly inventory and analysis of the duties and responsibilities of positions, the discovery of their supervisory relationships, and the tracing of flow of work—tasks all of which are carried out in classification surveys—facts are disclosed which serve classification and organization purposes equally.[45] Although the classification process does not of its own force carry with it the authority to prescribe or change organization structure, lines of responsibility, work-sequences, or the number of positions of each kind,[46] it must go into these features and the results show what exists in all these respects. The picture thus revealed, perhaps for the first time, may be so illogical or wasteful that it calls for attention and correction.[47]

[42] "Human abilities change through inherent adaptability, development through experience, health changes, aging, or other causes. Conditions of market, customer demands, public thought, technical processes, producing equipment, and other variables change, and with them change the requirements for combinations of abilities. These changes take place faster than is commonly realized. Organization, therefore, is a continuous process. An executive who does not reconsider his organization structure every six months in the light of the human and other changes is not covering his job." Thomas Roy Jones, "Dog Fights and Organization Charts," *Dun's Review*, December 1938, p. 7.

[43] James D. Mooney and Alan C. Reiley. *Onward Industry! The Principles of Organization and Their Significance to Modern Industry* (Harper & Bros., 1931).

[44] L. Urwick in "The Function of Administration" suggests that in order to achieve a science of administration, the structural aspects of organization should be treated as a technical problem and isolated from the human aspects. He recognizes, of course, that the two must go hand in hand. Luther Gulick and L. Urwick, Eds., *Papers on the Science of Administration* (Rumford Press, 1937), p. 122.

[45] "The group recognized the importance of sound application of classification as a tool for accomplishment of . . . clarifying organization structure and eliminating confusion as to lines of authority, placement of responsibility, and assignment of duties." *Report of Conference of Regional Personnel Officers of the U. S. Forest Service*, May 9, 1938, p. 17.

[46] See pp. 49–50.

[47] "Confusion in the distribution of authority, overlapping duties, and other sources of poor administration are almost certain to appear in the process of getting at the facts on which an allocation rests. This is one of the subsidiary but important advantages of a classification plan." White, *Introduction to the Study of Public Administration* (Macmillan, 1939), p. 335.

Whoever may be the official having the power to make the correction, the classification facts are his basic tools and the classes and class titles of the position-classification plan his language for expressing such corrections and making them plain to others.

Position-classification analysts are thus concerned every day with assignments of work, locations of responsibility, definitions or boundaries of responsibility, delegations of authority, and relationships between positions. The excellent opportunities to observe elements of this character are doubtless the basis underlying the statement that[48]

The study and planning of organization structure can readily be approached through the techniques of personnel administration that are employed in the classification of positions. This approach should be used concurrently with the budgetary approach and with due regard to the limitations of each. . . .

The detailed analysis of positions and their various relationships to one another should be used in large part as the basis upon which to build, revise, and modify the organization structure in which those positions function. Overlapping functions discovered through the classification approach suggest various alternative revisions of the assignments of duties and responsibilities. Conflicts and gaps in authority, if they exist, are almost certain to be revealed by the classification approach.

When an administrative officer or executive is charged with the duty of informing the central classifying agency of the precise duties and responsibilities of each position under his control, he necessarily must decide definitely on such phases of his work-program as (a) form of organization, (b) flow of work, and (c) delegation of various kinds and degrees of authority. Thus through the procedure incident to position-classification he is required to plan in advance or to review from time to time his working organization and methods. In particular, he finds it necessary to fix the responsibility for each specific type of action, recommendation, or decision, which is in itself a requirement of good organization.

Essentials of good organization require, among other things, that delegations of authority and responsibility be clear-cut and well

[48] Floyd W. Reeves and Paul T. David, *Personnel Administration in the Federal Service: A Staff Report to the President's Committee on Administrative Management* (Washington, 1937), pp. 58–59. See also Griffenhagen, "The Origin of the Modern Occupational Classification in Personnel Administration," *Public Personnel Studies*, September 1924, p. 192; Public Administration Service, *Personnel Administration in the State of Michigan* (Prepared for the Michigan Civil Service Study Commission), June 1936, p. 71; Bernard L. Gladieux, *Administrative Planning in the Federal Government*, presented before the Governmental Research Association, September 8, 1939, pp. 21–22.

understood by all concerned, that overlapping and gaps in responsibilities be avoided and that duplications of work be eliminated.[49] Any deviations from these essentials come to light in the classification process and their clarification or remedy is a material contribution to the achievement of the aims of the enterprise.[50]

Departures from other recognized management principles are also revealed through classification studies. Take, for example, the number of supervisory levels. Orders and decisions go down the line while information and recommendations rise to appropriate levels in the hierarchy. It is obvious that the larger number of hands through which matters must pass not only extends the time required for transmission but increases the hazard of misinformation or misinterpretation. Moreover, there is always the danger that somewhere along the line what is supposed to be a *conductor* is, in practical effect, a partial or complete *insulator*. Therefore, a minimum number of supervisory levels is closely related to effective organization. Since the classification staff is concerned with discovering what are the actual delegations of authority, it can well answer management's question, whether the number of levels in the supervisory line is too great for the most effective accomplishment of a particular objective.

Also, an executive's actual span of control is shown by a position-classification analysis of the relationships among positions in the same organization. If an administrator has too many intermediate supervisors reporting directly to him, he may have too little time to devote to broad matters of policy or administration. In other words, the administrator is exceeding a reasonable span of control—a concept closely related to the span of attention in psychology.[51] The classification study will indicate whether this is due to a disregard for the principle of grouping activities on the basis of homogeneity, or whether, if the diversity of activities within the bureau or depart-

[49] U. S. Department of Agriculture, Office of Personnel, *Personnel Bulletin*, July 1940; Emery E. Olson, "Scientific Management is Basic to Confidence in Government," *Civic Affairs*, May 1939, pp. 3–6. The latter article also appears in *Western City*, March 1939.

[50] "In the first place, much more careful attention will have to be given to organization relationships and the assignment of responsibilities to executive and departmental personnel. . . . What is needed in most companies is a thorough analysis of executive work to be done in terms of the kind of decisions to be made and in terms of the kind of influence to be exercised." W. J. Donald, "Essentials of Large-Scale Organization," *Handbook of Business Administration*, p. 1498. See also Harry A. Hopf, *Improving Management Through Job Analysis*, American Management Association, Annual Convention Series No. 62, 1927.

[51] See V. Graicunas, "Relationship in Organization" included in *Papers on the Science of Administration*, pp. 183–87.

ment is neither illogical nor too great, the executive's span of control has been exceeded because of a lack of conception of line and staff functions.

Major executives, responsible for administrative organization and organization structure, can with great advantage study carefully the pertinent facts collected by the classification agency in its investigation and surveys. Practical aspects of the situation suggest that classification staffs are in strategic positions to render advice on organizational matters.

EMPLOYEE-MANAGEMENT RELATIONS

It is good business, in private industry and in the public service, to take positive steps to maintain and improve the effectiveness of working forces. A basic policy in this direction is that personnel matters shall be administered according to definite policies, sound principles, and clear procedures, formulated in advance. Morale is an uncertain factor when personnel matters are decided in a haphazard way as individual cases arise.

In this respect, a position-classification plan has a definite contribution to make, because of the foundation it provides for broad planning and for uniformity and equity of action in many phases of personnel administration that are as conducive to good service as they are potential sources of friction and controversy.

To illustrate: Inadequate salaries and, particularly, discordances in pay scales are constant sources of irritation to employees.[52] Under such conditions, capable and progressive employees may be influenced to seek more lucrative and satisfactory employment; others who cannot leave become disgruntled and fail to give their best service. A rational and understandable plan for the payment of personal services automatically removes a large part of the friction which exists when pay matters are handled entirely on an individual basis. When a pay plan based upon a position-classification plan is

---

[52] "Salary inequalities are more potent sources of dissatisfaction than the general level of pay. Such inequalities indicate to employees the lack of recognition by the management of their individual status and progress. It might be mentioned that dissatisfaction over salary inequalities is not confined to the lower brackets of office employees, but that department heads and vice-presidents are often disturbed about these matters in their own situations." Harold B. Bergen, "Employer-Employee Relations in the Office," in *Attitudes and Emotional Problems of Office Employees,* American Management Association, Office Management Series No. 87, 1939, p. 6. See also Carl Heyel, *Human-Relations Manual for Executives* (McGraw-Hill, 1939), p. 184; Herman Feldman and Milton V. Smith, *A Personnel Program for the New Hampshire State Service,* A Report to the Governor and Council of New Hampshire, December 20, 1934, p. 12.

in effect, the class of a position, and consequently its scale of pay, is determined objectively, without any reference to the qualifications that the person holding it at the time the classifying is done may possess or lack, or to any other attributes or work habits that are personal to the employee. These personal factors are intended to be taken into account in the determination of the rate of pay of the incumbent within the range of the scale of pay established for the class.[53] A position-classification plan and a pay plan built upon it thus tend not only to reduce the effects of indiscriminate salary administration but also to prevent excessive turnover and provide incentives for efficient work.

Another illustration: a position-classification plan leads to methods of preserving to employees within the service opportunities for advancement—whether in their own bureau or department or in other departments. Without such a plan, the general lack of order and system make it impracticable to lay down and administer any general promotion policy. However, the establishment of classes of positions involving the same kind of work and the arrangement of these classes in promotional areas or sequences make it possible to develop equitable methods through which capable employees may be advanced to higher positions. Position-classification furnishes the basis for determining present lines of promotion and developing new ones, for defining career avenues, for determining the content of training courses designed to equip employees for higher assignments, for identifying misplaced employees with positions for which they are better qualified, and for determining where in the service there exist actual or potential sources of supply for filling positions of a given type.

From the employee's standpoint, the set of class specifications may be regarded as a sort of map showing where he is now with relation to where he might wish to go, with the roads and necessary equipment indicated. The descriptions of the duties and qualification standards of all classes of positions acquaint him with promotional opportunities of which he otherwise might not be aware. It has been rightly said:[54]

The ambitious employee inquires as to promotional possibilities and as to how he may qualify himself for these higher-grade positions. Specifications provide the answers to his questions. General knowledge of the duties

[53] See p. 44.
[54] Garret L. Bergen, "Uses of Job Study," *Personnel*, November 1929, pp. 85–100.

of a position is not enough on which to build a substantial self-improvement program but recourse to detailed information must be had.

Moreover, in educational and morale building value, emphasis should be placed not only upon final results of the classification process, such as written class specifications, but also upon certain of its inherent steps, particularly those which are involved in securing information about individual positions. In classification surveys executives, supervisors, and employees have the opportunity to write descriptions of their own work, to think about and discuss the relations of what they do with what others do, to become appreciative of the part their positions play in the whole activity of their organization, and perhaps to realize fully for the first time why their work is constituted as it is. The more clearly workers are encouraged to identify themselves with their organization and to appreciate their part in it, the more efficient as workers and the more happy as individuals they are apt to be.[55]

The clarification of job content and job relationships has recently been set forth as the first two steps of a formula for raising employee morale:[56]

1. Clearly define in writing the job to be done. This eliminates questioning on the part of the employee as to whether or not he is doing what he is supposed to do. Definiteness in respect to duties affects morale.

2. Clarify and describe in writing the relationships between the specific job under consideration and other related positions or activities. If carried through to a conclusion, this eliminates misunderstanding, jealousy, etc. It reduces the possibility of conflicting authority. It outlines possibilities for progression and educates all as to what others in the organization are doing. It establishes the importance of each individual job regardless of its nature. Such a procedure has a definite effect upon "zeal, spirit, hope, and confidence."

[55] "In addition to practical values in administration, the writing of job specifications may have large educational value in industry. For the various jobs in any plant are defined and assigned by management. Often workers do not understand the full scope of their work and its relation to the whole enterprise. The experience of writing for himself a description of his own job in the form of a job specification is then very useful to the worker. To do this, he must study his job and clarify his objectives. He begins to think consecutively about the things he daily does, sees, and handles and this stimulates interest in work and personal growth." American Council on Education, "Job Specifications," *The Educational Record* (Supplement), October 1927, pp. 7–8.

[56] Lawrence A. Appley, Supervisor of Education and Training, Socony-Vacuum Oil Co., "An Educational Program for Employee Morale-Building," *Proceedings of the First Personnel Institute,* May 12, 1938. Ohio State University, College of Commerce Conference Series No. 2, pp. 21–29.

The growth of employee unions in the public service and the prominence given in recent years to collective bargaining in private industry has had an impact upon the relationships between the managers of governmental units and the employees. On a larger scale than previously, public agencies are faced with the necessity for dealing with organized employee groups. Without going into the question of the differences that exist between public and private bodies as employers, it is clear that there are large areas for mutual exploration by employees and their supervisors in either setting. Certainly employee participation in management, whatever its degree, and mutual discussions of personnel policies and problems should not be clouded by such handicaps as lack of reliable information about the duties and requirements of positions, lack of order and system in the position-structure of the service, or lack of administrative tools to accomplish effectively what everyone agrees is a desirable objective. Such handicaps, common in services where position-classification plans do not exist, are overcome through the processes and records involved in such plans.

In addition to the records developed, the files of every classification agency are replete with job facts and statements of conditions that can be made available to the end that collective discussions in many instances can proceed on the basis of a full knowledge of the problems at hand. With greater dependence on actual conditions as contrasted with hearsay evidence or unsubstantiated opinions, negotiations can be conducted on a more even keel with less possibility of exhaustive dissertations composed of generalities or emotional appeals. Many problems in the field of human relationships arise simply because all the elements of a given situation either are not known or are not fully understood. The result is that opinions are founded on an erroneous base; however, the problems caused thereby in many instances dissolve when there is a full knowledge of the circumstances.

The availability of facts leads not only to sounder conclusions but makes possible the discussion of the full agenda in a minimum amount of time. Conferences are time-consuming. If the contribution of the classification process served only to conserve the energy of the conferees, it would be rendering a valuable service. Furthermore, the willingness of the employer to discuss all of the pertinent elements engenders a feeling of confidence and good faith on the part of the employees.

Nor is the availability of facts limited in usefulness to formal conferences. An active employee union will raise various questions with immediate supervisors who may be well down the line in the administrative hierarchy. The real place to settle grievances is right where they occur—on the job. Accordingly, supervisors can be encouraged to secure and utilize information from the classification files which will be recognized by all concerned as representing an impartial factual basis for discussion. Moreover, the classification agency should be sensitive to the contribution which a survey, audit, or review of individual positions may make to the solution of certain types of problems and should volunteer such services when those problems arise. It seems clear that the further down the line grievances can be settled, the less chance there is for the real issues to become obscured.

Chapter V

Position Analysis for Classification Purposes

THE NEED FOR ANALYSIS

I<small>T HAS</small> been previously pointed out that the duties and responsibilities of positions are the factual basis upon which classes of positions are established and individual positions allocated to their appropriate classes.[1] In carrying out the actual processes of classification, during both the development and the continuous administration of a position-classification plan, it is, therefore, of primary importance that the facts about these duties and responsibilities be adequately ascertained, logically analyzed, and evaluated by the exercise of informed and experienced judgment.[2]

---

[1] Pp. 32–36.

[2] In the public service it is not the practice to analyze or evaluate positions by mathematically scoring selected work-factors of specified weights. Some private manufacturing and commercial concerns use this method. Others follow practices which are parallel to those in public jurisdictions. Both methods have their proponents and critics in the industrial field. See, for example, the following: H. B. Bergen, "Salary Administration and Promotion," *Handbook of Business Administration*, W. J. Donald, Ed. (New York, 1931), pp. 857–65; Marion A. Bills, "A Method for Classifying the Jobs and Rating the Efficiency of Clerical Workers," *Journal of Personnel Research*, December 1922, and January 1923, pp. 384–93; Walter V. Bingham, "Classifying and Testing for Clerical Jobs," *The Personnel Journal*, November 1935, pp. 163–72; Hugh L. Clary, "The Zoning of Jobs," *Industrial Management*, May 1921, pp. 324–29; Samuel L. H. Burk, "Salary and Wage Administration," *The Personnel Journal*, September 1936, pp. 105–15; *idem.*, *A Case History in Salary and Wage Administration*, American Management Association, 1939; Z. Clark Dickinson, *Compensating Industrial Effort* (Ronald Press, 1937), pp. 196–99, 208 *et seq.*; Griffenhagen, "Classification and Compensation Plans as Tools in Personnel Administration," *Handbook of Business Administration*, pp. 1135–44; Edward N. Hay and Samuel L. H. Burk, "Job Evaluation by the Point Method," *Personnel*, February 1938, pp. 130–32; J. O. Hopwood, "The Grades of Labor, a Key for Job Classification and Appraisal," *The Personnel Journal*, August 1929, pp. 114–24; *idem.*, *Salaries, Wages and Labor Relations* (Ronald Press, 1937), pp. 28–72; Industrial Relations Association of Philadelphia, Salary and Wage Committee, "Salary and Wage Administration," *Personnel*, May 1939, pp. 149–64; A. F. Kindall, "Job Description and Rating," *Personnel*, February 1938, pp. 122–130; L. J. King, "Job Evaluation," *The Society for the Advancement of Management Journal*, May 1938, pp. 93–98; Forrest A. Kingsbury, "Grading the Office Job," *Administration*, March-June 1923, pp. 267–74, 393–401, 537–58, 669–80; and *Management and Administration*, July 1923, pp. 73–78; *idem.*, "Classification of Office Positions in the University of Chicago," *Personnel*

The duties and responsibilities of a position are identified by (a) tangible tasks and assignments and (b) intangible conditions bearing on the difficulty or the responsibility of the position, such as lines of authority, supervision, or review, which bind it to other positions in the same or a different organization unit. Tangible tasks can be covered by direct observation of the employee's work, where possible, and by analysis of the mental or physical processes involved. However, responsibilities and levels of difficulty are frequently not directly or at once observable. They come to light through study of the functions, structure, and flow of work of the organization. They may be specifically revealed by investigation of the work of all employees in the same organization unit and the connection of the work of one with the work of all the rest. Positions are not isolated entities, but their duties and responsibilities are interlaced with those of other positions in the same organization unit through the recognized lines of authority and flow of work. To ascertain and appraise correctly the duties and responsibilities of a position, one must study not only the position itself, but also at least that part of the organization in which it is located. A study of the position itself will develop the *kind* of work, that is, the subject matter or occupation involved, but only a study of the organization and the duties and responsibilities of other positions therein will develop its *level*.[3] "Level" is a relative concept and depends upon such essential facts as the kind and degree of supervision exercised upon the position from above, the kind and degree of supervision exercised over subordinates, the responsibilities carried which are other than supervisory, and the importance and difficulty of the work.

Moreover, when positions in different departments of a jurisdic-

---

Journal, August 1933, pp. 91–97; E. H. Little, "Some Considerations in Installing a Salary Administration Plan," *Handbook of Business Administration*, pp. 1148–51; Merrill R. Lott, *Wage Scales and Job Evaluation* (Ronald Press, 1926), pp. 46–84; Roy R. Marquardt, "Scientific Classification of Trust Department Personnel," *Personnel*, November 1930, pp. 77–87; Metropolitan Life Insurance Company Policyholders Service Bureau, *Salary Standardization and Administration* (1937), pp. 18–25; John W. Riegel, *Wage Determination* (University of Michigan Press, 1937), pp. 79–99; *ibid.*, *Salary Determination* (Bureau of Industrial Relations, University of Michigan, 1940), pp. 103–35; E. B. Roberts, "Position Analysis and Classification," *The Management Review*, July 1935, pp. 195–210; J. W. Rupley, *A Rational Salary Plan*, presented at the Fifth Annual Institute of Government, University of Washington, July 26, 1940, pp. 4–5. D. A. Straight, "Establishing the Position Specifications and the Position Classification Plan," *Salary Administration in Henry L. Doherty & Co.*, American Management Association Office Executives' Series No. 34, 1928, pp. 6–10. See also the footnote references in Chapter II, p. 30.

[3] See p. 209, footnote.

tion are studied for purposes of uniform classification, it frequently is found that differences in organization and in the distribution of tasks and responsibilities render very difficult the determination of likenesses or differences among positions. Positions in corresponding places in the "organizational pyramid" of different departments or offices may be far from equivalent in importance, difficulty, and responsibility. Organization units—even those of about the same size and having substantially the same purpose, such as mail and file units —may vary in the manner in which positions are arranged in them; duties and functions may be differently combined; specific responsibilities may not be vested in corresponding places. The result of these circumstances is that the classification of positions across organizational lines, particularly in large jurisdictions, requires detailed fact-finding and careful weighing of facts as to each individual position, including especially its relations to others.

During the course of the development or the continuous administration of a position-classification plan, it may be found that a position to be classified is like one or more positions already classified, or falls within the purview of a given class specification, except as to one factor. It may be a question of variety or difficulty of work, a certain type of nonsupervisory responsibility, or partial or complete supervisory responsibility. This one factor then calls for a detailed analysis to determine whether it is of sufficient or insufficient weight to warrant a different classification from the other positions or class of positions with which the position to be classified has been compared.

Thus, after guide lines and evaluation standards have been established, the process of analysis may sometimes lead to the determination that one factor is the controlling one to the exclusion of others. However, it should be recognized that consideration of many factors is inherent in the problem of analyzing and classifying a position. Each task and responsibility of a position should be considered and its influence or weight determined. The variety of possible combinations of facts about the duties and responsibilities of positions makes it desirable to proceed with a thorough analysis of all factors whenever the points to be decided are not at once clearly discernible. The position is broken down into its component parts, each part being then studied to determine its bearing upon difficulty or responsibility, first separately and then in combination with the other elements of the position, up to the point where the question of classification is narrowed down to one or a few issues.

GENERALITIES VS. PRECISION

To determine the difficulty of duties and the weight of responsibilities of a position, the classifier must have precise information. In actual practice, he is frequently presented with incomplete or undeveloped information, of which, the following are some of the danger signals:

1. Generalized, ambiguous terms, such as "assist," "handle," "prepare," etc., or terms not having a uniform scope, such as "supervise" or "review," unsupported by further facts that answer the natural question "how?" or "in what respect?"

2. Descriptions of duties solely in terms of the names by which papers, processes, etc., are called in the particular office concerned, with little or nothing to indicate the basic nature of the work.

3. Information going no further than to show the place of the position in the organizational structure of a department, bureau, or office, with little or no data as to just what duties are performed in the position or exactly what responsibilities are lodged therein.

4. Information going no further than to show the functions or work of the organization unit or group in which the position is located, with little or no data as to just what duties and responsibilities are vested in the particular position concerned.

5. Information covering only part of the duties of the position, with no indication whether these are the preponderant, frequent, or regular duties or whether they are infrequent and rare.

6. Conclusions or inferences unsupported by facts; for example,
   a. A statement that one position is "similar" to, or "identical" or "comparable" with another position, without a comparative analysis supporting the statement.
   b. The characterization of duties as "unusually difficult," "complex," etc., without supporting facts or examples to justify such inferences.

It is true, of course, that general statements serve a useful purpose in providing a background for the consideration of details; but when taken alone they are not, as a rule, reliable guides for classifying a position. They must always be accompanied by supporting details. In fact, experience indicates that in the consideration of practically all classification factors, such as supervisory or other kinds of responsibility, or difficulty and complexity of work, the principal problem is to get facts which are sufficiently specific and comprehensive to serve as the basis for evaluation of the degree, extent, or weight of these factors.

Common Ambiguities in Job Descriptions

The use of such ambiguous terms as "assist," "prepare," "handle," "edit," "examine," "conduct research," "supervise," "review," etc., without any explanation of the processes, tasks, or operations constituting the assistance, handling, or preparation almost invariably is a sign of inadequacy of information. While such terms are perhaps satisfactory for purposes of *general* or *approximate* description, they always call for elucidation and require supporting details before they may serve reliably as the basis for classification.

The word "assist," when used alone, is capable of so wide a latitude of interpretation as to render it almost meaningless for classification purposes. An employee who assists in a given piece of work may perform such simple duties as searching files and assembling material for the use of a supervisor subject to the latter's close supervision, or he may perform other duties ranging from the most simple ones all the way up the scale to the point where he performs exactly the same duties as the one whom he assists, the only difference being the element of higher responsibility for the work inherent in the senior position. Accordingly, wherever the element of assistance is involved, a detailed knowledge of the duties and tasks constituting such assistance is required, so that it may be clearly understood at what point they fall along the scale ranging from tasks of a routine and repetitive nature to those which are the practical equivalent of the superior's duties minus the element of final responsibility.

Much, or very little, may be contained within the meaning of the word "prepare." For example, "to prepare statistical tables (of a certain sort)" might mean that the employee on his own initiative seeks out or develops sources of basic information, plans the schedules or outlines other means of collecting the information required, designs the tables, and writes interpretative text as well; or it might simply mean that he copies numbers from given places on a schedule, posts them to a given column and line on a tabulation sheet, adds columns, and computes averages and percentages on a calculating machine. It is not possible to appraise accurately the task of "preparing statistical tables" until we know of what operations the task consists. Similarly, the statement that an employee "handles" certain work has no precise meaning. The significance to be given to it in an individual case depends upon the essential features of the work, the difficulty and responsibility inherent in the duties, the flow of work, the form in which it reaches the employee, the action he takes in regard to it, how nearly final is his responsibility, where in the organizational structure the work goes after it leaves him, and what further is done with it.

"Editing" has a wide range of significance. It might mean editing a statistical schedule to see that all questions have been answered, all blanks filled in, and that various items of information are consistent with one another; or editing a proposed publication in order to correct spelling, faulty phrasing, imperfect punctuation, and the like; or editing publications as to all such matters of form and in addition marking the manuscript so that the printer will be able to understand the desires of the office; or editing publications with the authority to review the manuscript critically from a subject-matter standpoint, checking and verifying the product of the original writer, condensing overelaborated topics, making additions where a topic is inadequately treated, rearranging material when not effectively presented, and correcting information, inferences, or conclusions that are not technically accurate—the task including the responsibility of maintaining a high standard of technical excellence as well as proper literary and printing form.

The word "examine" is another one which frequently is expected to carry by itself a load of significance for which it was never intended. Different positions may involve "examining" the same thing—a document, for example—from different viewpoints, for dissimilar purposes, by means of unlike procedures, and the taking of different species of action as the result of the "examinations." Considerable analysis, as a rule, is required to determine just what "examine" consists of in a given case.

The word "research" is also frequently used for the word "search" because it sounds more impressive. For example, the item, "to do research work in connection with sources of material for reports, papers, pamphlets and memoranda prepared by the chief statistician," has been used to mean that the employee by reference to specific reports looked up the number of adults in a particular age group or similar information readily available in printed form. "To do research in the archives of the office" has been used to describe the task of attempting to find a document that has a regular place in the files but is (it is hoped temporarily) missing.

Probably for the same reason descriptions beginning "I am responsible for" are frequently broader than the facts justify. For example, "I am responsible for checking tax liability" has been used to cover the process of checking, by arithmetic, the figure representing the amount of the liability. Similarly, if a supervisor states that he has delegated the responsibility for assembling facts and then afterward goes to the source material and checks the assembled facts himself, he has assigned the physical *task* of assembling facts but he himself is holding on to the *responsibility* for the accuracy of the work. Frequently, when its scope is accurately determined, the expression "I am responsible for . . ." or "I am in charge of . . ." means nothing more than "I do . . ." or "I perform. . . ."

Other terms, intended to be descriptive of an operation or function, are frequently found to be ambiguous, requiring explanation as to extent, purpose, and the "how" of the job.[4]

The "How" of the Job

The answer to the question, What does the employee do? is obviously something the classifier should know. There is need, however, for emphasizing that the answer to the question, How does he do it? should also be understood. For example, to say that an employee "cleans motion picture films" means considerably more when we add: "The cleaning consists in swabbing the film with a soft sponge wet with a weak chemical solution." Similarly, an entirely different light may be thrown upon two correspondence clerk positions when inquiry develops that one employee simply composes correspondence from data or information already prepared for such use and the other collects data or information from various sources before composing the correspondence, requiring a knowledge of what to look for, where to find it, and how to assemble it.

The following example shows that inquiry into the "how" of the job can throw light on the precise nature of the tasks involved:

A position-description stated that the employee examined bids filed by private hospitals for emergency treatment of government beneficiaries, and that "in case of competition he considered all necessary factors in determining the lowest bid."

Taking such statement at its face value, one would be justified, perhaps, in supposing that the employee through a mental process requiring mature

---

[4] Various meanings of "review" and "supervise" are discussed later. See pp. 106–07, 115–17.

judgment made a decision of some responsibility. As a matter of fact, the making of the decision as to which of the bids was actually the lowest had, in this particular type of contract, been reduced to an arithmetic process. Each item of the bid was given a predetermined weight. These weights multiplied by the proposed rates on each item gave a figure which automatically determined the lowest bid. While a great deal of mathematical calculation was involved in this procedure, it consisted almost entirely of multiplication and addition.

This example illustrates the advantage of inquiring into (a) the nature of the raw material or sources of information from which the employee works, and (b) not only what the employee does but by what mental or physical process he does it.

Obscurities of Terminology

Frequently the "how" of the job is obscured by the use of departmental colloquialisms, broad functional terms, and failure to reduce operations to common denominators. This phase of getting the facts as to the duties of positions has been well stated as follows:[5]

In the established classifications, the duties connected with the various clerical employments are often stated in terms of the particular significance of the work of the department concerned. The following are illustrative:
"Docketing and indexing railroad rate proceedings."
"Recording architects' certificates."
"Making out notices for the collection of interest and rental on stocks, bonds and riparian leases."
The three operations suggested here are, in all probability, made up of the same elementary operations as are involved in the clerical work of many other departments. In these other departments, the duties are stated in terms of the special phraseology of these departments. These statements in terms of departmental procedure are what often throw the classifier off the right course.

In the same paper, the author refers to an analysis of this task: "I make out all the cumulative analytical compensation tabulation sheets from the employees' triplicate adjustment reports." He shows that in fact it referred to a series of postings of simple data from cards to a tabulation sheet, requiring only care and accuracy.

Much light can be thrown upon all kinds of generalities by following such lines of inquiry as: In what form does the employee's work come to him? What has been done with it previously? What

---

[5] Allen M. Ruggles, "Classifying and Grading Individual Employments," *Proceedings*, Fifteenth Meeting of the National Assembly of Civil Service Commissions. June 1922, pp. 76–87.

does he do with it? Exactly how does he do it? In what form is it when he finishes? What happens to it after that?

ULTIMATE CLASSIFICATION FACTORS

Depending on the point of view taken and the occupational area to be covered, several different lists of ultimate classification factors could be prepared. If, for example, attention is confined to one group of positions, somewhat similar in occupation, more specific lists of factors pertinent for inquiry can be developed than if it is attempted to cover a wide variety of different occupations. For example, a writer in the industrial field has suggested the following points to consider in evaluating foremen's jobs: (1) number of people supervised; (2) trade knowledge or skill required; (3) number and variety of operations; (4) number and size of order; (5) number of setups; and (6) quality factor.[6] Another example is given in a statement issued by the United States Civil Service Commission on August 7, 1938, relative to the establishment of personnel divisions in the operating departments, in which the Commission stated that the classification of the positions of directors of personnel

will depend upon (1) the difficulty and complexity of personnel administration in the particular department or agency as indicated by its size and the complexity of its operating activities, i.e., the variety, breadth, and magnitude of the personnel problems which are to be recognized and tackled; (2) the degree of comprehensiveness of the personnel program in terms of its various functions, . . . and (3) the place of the director of personnel in the administrative councils of the department or agency, i.e., the degree of direct responsibility of the director to the head of the department or agency.[7]

In this chapter, however, the purpose is to state and discuss fundamental classification factors covering all kinds of positions normally encountered in the public service, as an over-all frame of reference for the analysis of such positions for classification purposes.

[6] Howard Tilson, "J. Jones, Foreman—What's His Job Worth?", *Factory Management and Maintenance*, September 1933, pp. 354–55.

[7] For other examples, see Appendix F. See also Industrial Management Society, *An Occupational Rating Plan for Hourly and Salaried Occupations* (1937); J. O. Hopwood, *Salaries, Wages and Labor Relations* (Ronald Press, 1937), pp. 41–56; N. D. Hubbell, *Salary Administration Plan for Factory Supervision and Staff*, American Management Association, Office Management Series No. 88, 1939, pp. 28–40; *Life Office Salary Administration*, pp. 23–32; Riegel, *Salary Determination*, pp. 53–71, p. 265. Reference should also be made to the discussion of check lists and specialized questionnaires, Chapter X, pp. 317, 328–29.

Ultimate Classification Factors Defined

The duties and responsibilities of a position can be factually set forth, studied, and analyzed according to certain basic elements, which are here spoken of as ultimate classification factors, namely, (1) subject matter, function, profession, or occupation represented; (2) difficulty and complexity of duties; (3) nonsupervisory responsibilities; (4) supervisory and administrative responsibilities; and, to the extent that they may not be involved in the other factors, (5) qualification standards. Accordingly, it is convenient to regard these factors as collectively constituting the basis for position-classification. It will be found that all classification factors of a more detailed character, or their effect, may logically be considered under one or more of these heads.

Broadly speaking, the determination of the relative difficulty or responsibility of the work of a position (i.e., its *level*) requires more exacting analysis than finding out what subject matter, function, profession, or occupation it involves (i.e., its *kind*). Many occupations or professions are represented in the public service in various degrees of difficulty and responsibility. Stenographers of different classes "take in shorthand and transcribe dictation"; and plant pathologists of different classes "carry on research in the cause of plant diseases." These phrases clearly define kind of work, but they do not indicate any of the factors that distinguish one stenographic class from another, or one class of plant pathologists from another. Thus, after having determined the field of work covered by the position, the classifier is faced with discovering and evaluating other basic allocation factors, namely, those that distinguish that position from, or render it similar to, other positions in the *same* field of work. These factors relate to difficulty and responsibility of work and the qualifications necessary to perform it, and are the discriminatives among the different classes in a given series of classes.[8]

Determinations as to Difficulty and Responsibility

Determinations of the degree of difficulty or complexity of the duties and the weight of the responsibilities of a position are conclusions drawn from facts showing the nature of the duties performed, the methods of work involved, the authority exercised, and

[8] A general check list of these factors is given in Appendix E. For an explanation of what is meant by a "series of classes," see p. 194.

a variety of other circumstances under which the work is performed. The mere statement of such a conclusion in the description of an individual position is of little value unless it is supported by factual details. It is to be regarded as an unproved hypothesis, the accuracy of which it is the duty and the responsibility of the analyst to test.

The fruits of direct investigation of a position are facts which bear pertinently on the question of the degree of difficulty or responsibility that is present. Such facts are obtained through interviews with employees and supervisory officials, inspection of records, visual examination of work in process, exhibits of finished work, study of organization structure and flow of work, and similar processes.

Difficulty and Responsibility are Relative

The degree of difficulty and responsibility is determined and expressed in relation to something else which serves as a basis for comparison. This basis for comparison may frequently cover positions in various occupational groups, but for practical purposes it is usually sufficient to consider the range of duties, tasks, and responsibilities occurring in the same and closely associated series of classes or occupational groups. For example, in evaluating the difficulty and responsibility of civil engineering duties, the entire engineering group, as well as all civil engineering positions, could be taken as a background.

Interrelation of Factors

The same type of information will often serve as the basis for conclusions as to more than one classification factor. Facts relating to organizational structure or flow of work, for instance, frequently affect conclusions as to both difficulty and responsibility in close relation. Facts about supervision likewise point toward both difficulty and responsibility. For example, strong administrative and technical supervision over an employee's work indicates a correlative reduction of responsibility for independent decision and action on his part. It may also indicate a reduction of the difficulty of his tasks as compared to similar tasks performed under more casual guidance and direction. Supervision restricted to administrative control indicates both an increased degree of technical responsibility on the part of the employees supervised and an increased difficulty of duties. Also, the existence of a position in which rests the authority to decide unprecedented matters for the guidance of employees limits both the difficulty and the responsibility of the work of such employees.

The ultimate classification factors themselves are thus closely interrelated. The degree or extent of one factor almost always has a material bearing on the others. Increased responsibilities frequently entail increased difficulties. A lessening of difficulty frequently means a lessening of responsibilities. The qualification standards of positions reflect the various degrees of difficulty and responsibility involved in them.

Factors Indicating Difficulty and Complexity of Duties

Occasionally the element of responsibility is so clearly controlling as to obviate any necessity for analysis as to difficulty. Generally, however, the determination of the degree of difficulty inherent in the duties and tasks of a position is an integral component of position-analysis. The "difficulty" of a task does not refer to the ease or difficulty which *any* employee might find in performing it. Operating a typewriter might be extremely difficult for a person without training in this task but relatively simple for a trained typist. Similarly, one of a group of engineers, all doing identical engineering work, might feel that because he "keeps the files" his work is more difficult than that of his associates. He finds the maintenance of the files novel and difficult for him as contrasted with his familiar engineering routine. Differences in the "difficulty" of certain tasks do not depend upon the personal reactions of the employees who perform them, for these reactions may arise simply out of accidental differences in temperament, attitude, or background.

The principal kinds of facts entering into the determination of difficulties and complexities of individual positions may for convenience be grouped under the following general headings: (1) status of work or stage of development of problem when first presented to the employee; (2) segregation or selection of assignments for the employee; (3) procedure followed, processes performed, plans or action initiated or developed, or decisions made by the employee; (4) control of employee's work by others; and (5) variety and scope. These items will be discussed in order.[9]

---

[9] While the discussion at this point will be confined to the bearing of facts of these types upon the degree of difficulty and complexity of duties, it is apparent that facts of the same type in many instances have a material bearing upon responsibility as well. Elements of responsibility, however, are described later in this chapter.

Status of Work When Presented to Employee

To secure the desirable attributes of completeness and adequacy in analyzing a position, consideration is always given to two groups of facts which, together, display neatly the connection between the position in question and all other positions in the same organization unit. These facts concern the organizational structure and the flow of work. We are concerned here with flow of work.

If we think of an organization as a territory through which work travels, we can regard flow of work as the "geographic" course which a given piece of work takes from inception to completion. A proper description or charting of flow of work would show the sequence of operations or tasks, where and by whom each step in the sequence is carried out, precisely what operation is performed at each point, and the purpose of each such operation; in short, a sequential listing of activities, orientated to the organizational structure.[10]

To ascertain and study the flow of work to and from a given position is important because a complete picture of a position for purposes of classification cannot always be obtained if attention is confined to its particular tasks. Reference must be made to other positions that may involve work on the same matter, problem, or case, both before and after it reaches the position in question. The reason for this is twofold. First, certain elements of difficulty and, particularly, responsibility are intangible in the sense that they are not usually ascertainable at once by direct inquiry or by visual examination. Second, difficulty and responsibility are relative. Accordingly, these work-factors in a position are to be determined in comparison with the analogous elements of any other positions concerned at any point in the same matter, case, problem, or task. This requires inquiry into these other positions and the manner and form in which the work in question proceeds among them and is disposed of, step by step.

With reference to a given position, we may, for convenience think of flow of work as falling into three phases: (a) before it reaches the position, (b) at the position, and (c) after it has left the position. The second phase consists of the operations performed in the position itself. These are the basis for the classification of the position. But the true degree of difficulty and responsibility which they rep-

[10] See John M. Pfiffner, *Research Methods in Public Administration* (Ronald Press, 1940), pp. 304–05, 319–23.

resent is in many instances apparent only when the first and third phases of the flow of work are examined to see how the operations performed by others, both previously and subsequently, affect the difficulty and responsibility of the position.

In some clerical operations, what has previously been done by others may have the effect of reducing an employee's tasks to the following of a certain routine. The completed product, as it comes from the employee's desk might very well bear evidence of the application of special knowledge and experienced judgment, and the solution of certain difficulties; yet this evidence might reflect the prior work of others. For example, contrast the difficulty of the work of A and B in the following situations:

A and B both do work requiring reference to certain sources of information. A is referred to such sources by another employee who has made a previous analysis of the matter and has selected the sources of information to be used, stating where they may be found. B, while using the same sources of information, does so because of his own analysis of the problem and selects and discriminates on his own account. (This situation is characteristic of some statistical compilations. Both A and B work from the same data. A is instructed as to what data to use. B selects the appropriate data himself.)

A and B are card punch operators. A works from a schedule that has been numerically coded. B works from an uncoded schedule, reads items direct, translates them into a memorized code, and punches the cards accordingly.

A and B answer letters. On all correspondence assigned to A the action to be taken is indicated by short notations written by others. A's problem is largely one of composition and phrasing. B, however, is assigned the same kind of correspondence as A, but initially makes the decision himself as to the action to be taken, and from then on does the same as A.

The work of positions of a more complex nature is also affected by operations previously performed by others. The matter or problem may be initially presented to the employee; or it may have been outlined, planned, or analyzed in advance; or pertinent data may have previously been collected and selected for use; or certain of the decisions necessary for the disposition of the matter may have already been made. For example, in classifying engineering drafting positions it is important to know to what extent, if any, the employee is faced with problems of engineering design and engineering computations, and to what extent these problems with reference to the structure or fabrication concerned have been settled by other employees previously. In the mechanical trades a foreman may or may not have the duty of making layouts and determining the methods to be followed by journeymen on all jobs involving any particular difficulties. In claims adjudication, the necessary facts may or may not have been collected; questions of law may or may not have been settled; and the work of the employee may or may not be confined to the application of existing precedents.

Work previously performed by others in or outside the service has a significant bearing upon the originality which the employee is required to apply to his problems. This is particularly true in research activities, the difficulty of which is indicated in part by their novelty or originality as measured by the present state of knowledge on the subject. If, for example, in research in the social sciences, the use of certain source material is original and requires the employee to develop new techniques for gathering the data, the research problem would be more difficult than where accepted techniques are already available. Similarly, if a certain field of data has never been organized and classified, the innate difficulty of the study would be greater than that of a similar study where the classification of data has already been established. Also, where a certain type of study has been made before, a somewhat less difficult process is involved in making the same type of study again. Such varying conditions as these emphasize the importance of giving due consideration to previous precedents, guide lines, or flow of work in determining the difficulty of the duties of an individual position.[11]

Segregation or Selection of Assignments

In getting the facts as to the arrangement of work within an organization unit it frequently is necessary to determine specifically on what basis assignments of work are made to certain employees.

It may be found, for example, that the work to be done consists of an array of individual cases, matters, or problems. In some organizations, the individual cases may be assigned without discrimination as to their difficulty or complexity. Each employee would then deal with the "mine-run," and over a period of time each would receive a mixture of cases representing all the various degrees of difficulty comprised in that sort of work. In such a situation, the aggregate difficulty of the duties of each position would be the same.[12]

[11] The effect of subsequent flow of work is, of course, equally important. See pp. 100–02, 107–09, 118–24.

[12] For a discussion of "mixed" positions, see pp. 131–36.

On the other hand, in some organizations before any assignments are made a supervisor or other experienced employee examines the cases, determines their relative difficulty, and segregates them into two, or possibly more, groups. The cases are then assigned to different groups of employees on this basis. In such a situation the degree of difficulty of the duties of employees in different groups varies materially, the extent of such variation depending, of course, upon a comparison of typical cases in each group.

A parallel condition is sometimes encountered where a segregation of assignments to different groups is made, not necessarily on the basis of difficulty, but on the basis of type of case—a subdivision by subject-matter within a group of cases of the same broad character, the work upon which has the same general purpose. For example, the work of auditing federal income tax returns in Washington is assigned to different groups, depending upon whether the return is that of (a) an individual, a partnership, or a fiduciary, (b) a single corporation, or (c) a consolidated corporation. In such a situation as this it is necessary to work out, by comparison, the relative difficulty of the several types.

Procedure Followed by the Employee

Generally speaking, although there are other elements which affect difficulty, the work done by the employee himself can be thought of most specifically in terms of the procedure he follows, the processes he performs, the plans or action he initiates or develops, or the decisions he makes on his own account.

Positions in different fields of work, however, are so different in their characteristics that no common comprehensive scheme for analysis can be worked out. Recourse must be had to examples and general suggestions.

For example, in considering the processes performed by instrument makers, laboratory workers, and skilled tradesmen, difficulty of work cannot be gauged unless it is known to what degree of precision the employee must work or what fineness of execution is demanded of him. Precision and fineness of execution are factors that are not always pertinent in other types of positions or even in all positions of the groups named, but where they are pertinent they are the very essence of the job and weigh heavily in the evaluation of its difficulty.

The clerical operation of filing may be of various degrees of difficulty, depending on circumstances. The system may be a simple alphabetical or numerical one, or it may be a complicated subject file. In the latter event the subjects may be in a nontechnical or a highly technical field. The material to be filed may have to be classified under a few, many, or a great many headings. Cross-references and indexes may or may not be required. The files may be merely storage space, or they may be in constant active use, involving searches for material on a particular matter or subject. Unless the processes performed in filing are fully analyzed, the relative difficulty of the operation itself cannot be judged.

The extent to which plans or actions are initiated or developed may mean one thing for one type of position and another thing for another type. When applied to positions of architects or authors, it may relate to the opportunity and necessity for creative work. In positions of research workers in the sciences, it may relate to the opportunity and necessity for the employee to choose his own problems, to develop his own technique, or to change the method of attack or the object of the research as the findings are coordinated and appraised.[13] In administrative positions it may apply to the formulation of policies, the organizing of work programs, and the determination of the scope of the work. In clerical positions it may relate to the working out of assigned problems where the information desired is stated but the method for securing it must be developed by the employee.

In any event a breakdown of the work done by the employee into its component parts furnishes a better understanding of its difficulty because it usually indicates clearly the mental processes or the manual operations involved. One point of view that is sometimes helpful is to regard the work as requiring the employee to accomplish certain major objectives or tasks. In all but the simplest jobs it will then be found that the major objectives are accomplished through lesser or contributing tasks, which can then be explained in detail.[14]

This may be illustrated by a recent study of the approach to the classification of social science research positions, in which the steps

[13] Cf. discussion of "novelty of problems" in the case of other workers in Riegel, *Salary Determination*, pp. 59–60.
[14] American Council on Education, *Instructions for Writing Job Specifications*, 1927.

involved in a research project are tentatively laid out and the work of the employee on each step examined. These steps in chronological order were:[15]

(1) Determination of the general nature of the study; (2) determination of its scope; (3) determination of the source material to be used; (4) gathering data from this source material; (5) verifying the data gathered with the original and/or additional source material; (6) analysis, classification, and compilation of the data; (7) interpretation of the data; (8) organization and arrangement of the material; and (9) recommendations for action.

A consideration of the duties of a position in the light of what qualifications are necessary and are actually utilized in doing the work aids materially in evaluating the degree of difficulty.[16] For example, a definite measure of the difficulty of many kinds of positions may be found in the abilities and information necessary to its performance. What "tools" must a new employee possess when he enters the job? What others does the office give him to work with? There is a considerable difference between positions where the employee is required to exercise memory of decisions or regulations laid down by others or knowledge of where to find them, and a position where he does not have such guides but is required to exercise creative or original thought.

It is helpful in appraising the difficulty of a position to consider its broader aspects, namely, problems inherent in or peculiar to the type of work performed that have to be solved by the employee himself. Also, the function or subject-matter scope of these problems and the obstacles or complications encountered in solving them are important. These items are particularly germane in determining the relative difficulty of the matters dealt with by the employee as compared with the entire range of difficulty encountered by all engaged in that particular type of work.

Control of Employee's Work by Others

Few positions are isolated entities. Most of them have definite connections with other positions in the same organization, and sometimes with positions in other organizations. Usually a given function or objective is accomplished in a sequence that involves, directly

15 J. M. St. John, *Survey of Social Science Research Positions*, Social and Economic Research Division, Department of Regional Planning Studies, Tennessee Valley Authority, May 1938 (typewritten).
16 See pp. 128–31.

and indirectly, a number of positions of varying rank. This makes it necessary, in appraising the difficulty of work in an individual position, to consider the duties and responsibilities of other positions in the same office, division, bureau, or department, the work of which has a close bearing on the work of the position being directly investigated.[17]

An analysis of the kind and degree of supervision exercised over the work of an employee is in most cases essential to an understanding of its difficulty and responsibility. At this point will be discussed its relation to the factor of difficulty.[18]

Theoretically, the work of every official and employee is subject to some kind of supervision by someone. However, it is not this fact, but rather the extent to which supervision is actually applied and the ways in which it is actually manifested that may affect the difficulty of an employee's work.[19] Consequently, the general characteristics and the details of supervision from above need to be inquired into. It is important to know, for example, whether supervision from above is confined to "housekeeping" matters, i.e., the business of maintaining an organization as a going concern, or whether it extends to functional or technical matters, i.e., the operations and functions for the performance of which the unit was created and to which it owes its reason for existence. It is also important to distinguish between supervision exercised before and during the employee's active performance of his assignments and that which manifests itself purely as a review. Purely "housekeeping" supervision over an employee's work seldom affects its difficulty. The fact that it is reviewed after he has completed it also has little effect upon its difficulty, although it may materially affect the degree of responsibility with which the employee is charged in relation to the responsibility

[17] See Griffenhagen, "The Principles and Technique of Preparing an Occupational Classification of Positions in the Public Service," *Public Personnel Studies,* November 1924, p. 241.

[18] Its connection with the factor of responsibility—which is even more important—is dealt with later. See pp. 107–09, 121–24.

[19] One should not assume that low-grade work is always performed under immediate supervision or that high-grade work is always performed under general direction only. It will be found sometimes that simple work performed under general supervision is allocable to the same class as somewhat more difficult work performed under immediate supervision. In other words, the type of supervision is but one element in allocation. Various degrees of supervision may be found in combination with various degrees of many other factors entering into the appraisal of positions. It is the result of all factors together that finally determines the allocation of the position, and the lightness of one factor may be balanced by the weight of another.

borne by others. If it is supervised functionally or technically, however, particularly during the planning stage and while it is in process, its difficulty is frequently lessened from a classification standpoint. In such a case the total difficulty is not concentrated in the employee's position but is shared by that of his supervisor.

In a typical situation of this sort, it may be found that the employee's superior does not merely assign problems or tasks, leaving the employee to work out his own ways, means, and results. Instead, he outlines and defines the problems, makes a partial or a complete analysis of the work to be done, specifies the particular tasks to be performed, the order in which they are to be carried out and the methods or the procedures to be employed, keeps constantly in touch with the employee's assignment, and is always available to lead the way through any difficulties. In such a situation the degree of difficulty inherent in the employee's position is much less than if he were subject to active supervision on housekeeping matters only or if he were expected to make contact with his supervisor only when he was ready to produce completed results.

Another situation in which the work of one position may materially affect the work of another from the standpoint of difficulties encountered is one where there is another employee (or a group of employees) whose duty and authority it is to render decisions and advice on the more difficult or the unprecedented problems, or to whom, by virtue of their longer experience or higher qualifications, matters ranking relatively high in the scale of difficulty are referred for action, advice, or instruction.

Variety and Scope

A position may be made up of a variety of different tasks which may be all substantially equal in difficulty or which may differ from one another in this respect.

At this point we deal only with the first type of situation in which the question concerns the effect of variety as such upon difficulty.[20] What, if any, difference in appraisal should exist between a position made up of one or a few tasks and another position made up of many tasks—all of the same degree of difficulty? As compared with a position involving one duty or one closely connected series of tasks, what additional burden is placed upon the employee and what

[20] In the second type of situation, the question is which duties and tasks of the position govern its allocation. This question is discussed on pp. 131–36.

additional knowledge and abilities must he possess because he deals with more than this one duty and perhaps with several series of tasks? In what respect is his position thereby rendered more difficult by the element of variety alone?[21]

It is true in general that the incumbent of a position involving the performance of a variety of duties must possess knowledge and ability covering each task or problem involved. To this extent qualification standards are enlarged over those for an unvaried position. However, it does not necessarily follow that a variety of tasks calls for exactly the same variety of qualifications at the time the employee is recruited. One type of qualification plus the ability to acquire the others on the job may be sufficient, or a broad fundamental background may be the requirement common to both the varied and the unvaried position. It is true, too, that an employee occupying a varied position must possess certain general qualities of mind and temperament necessary for shifting from one type of work to another, but these may be too intangible and of too little weight to serve as a basis for classification differences. Thus, no general rule can be laid down that mere variety automatically gives rise to differences in work-difficulty.

Whether or not work-difficulty is increased by variety depends collectively upon such factors as:

1. The degree of difficulty represented in each task or problem, considered individually.

2. The frequency of occurrence of the several types of tasks or problems.

3. The distinctiveness of each task or problem, and the consequent total scope of the duties and the qualifications required to perform them.

Variety and scope are relatively unimportant allocation factors where each task or problem is itself of a limited degree of difficulty, as, for instance, in the duties of messengers, janitors, under and junior clerks, or typists. The performance of a number of simple tasks demands little more in respect to knowledge and ability than does one unvaried duty. As the level of difficulty of the tasks making up the combination advances, variety may become more significant. An appreciably broader scope of knowledge and ability is called for when varied difficult tasks are combined in one position.

[21] The discussion here is limited to nonsupervisory positions. Cf. the discussion on pp. 126–27.

Frequency of occurrence of the several types of tasks or problems is to be taken into account. Where each item recurs often enough to become repetitive, the position really involves a continuing series of similar tasks. Once the suitable technique has been learned, it does not greatly vary. In such a case, circumstances calling for freshness of attack, keenness of discrimination in recognizing new questions, and initiative in solving them are not present, and the work-difficulty of the position is but little different from a less varied one involving some of the same tasks. This should be distinguished from a situation where the duties present a nonrepetitive succession of new demands to be met, new situations to be faced, new subject matter to be dealt with, and new objectives to be achieved and new methods to be applied. In such circumstances, greater difficulty is generally involved.

Much also depends on the distinctiveness of each task or problem and the consequent scope or comprehensiveness of the duties and required qualifications. Many positions are encountered in which the tasks or problems involved are different one from another. But one should not fail to consider how distinctive they really are. Variety may exist when such tasks or problems

1. Are intimately related to, or part of, the same occupation or field of work, and are collectively broad in scope, not being confined to a single narrow phase or aspect of that occupation, or

2. Lead toward the accomplishment of a given objective, each forming a part of a continuous process within a limited field, or

3. Are mutually distinct, each being characteristic of a different occupation or field of work, or

4. Signify a succession of assignments, or of problems presented for interpretation and decision. Each such assignment involves a new objective, a freshness of attack; perhaps a different body of governing rules and regulations or customary procedure; perhaps a somewhat different technique. The field of operations is widened; a broader knowledge of the whole field is required, together with quickness of perception and some initiative and judgment.

As a general rule, variety of work having characteristics like (1) and (2) above, where the tasks belong to the same or a closely related occupation or field of work, or are all parts of a process having a common objective, is of less weight as a difficulty factor than variety having characteristics like (3) or (4), where the tasks are mutually distinct, and represent a succession of different assignments, problems, processes, and objectives.

Variety of work is entitled to particular consideration as a difficulty factor when it entails the possession and use of a variety of techniques or bodies of knowledge which are so distinct that they usually are not or cannot be assimilated "on the job," but are such as are acquired (and are usually expected to be acquired) through different channels.

In putting the foregoing ideas into practice, it is frequently helpful to treat variety of assignments and tasks as a question of breadth of duties, knowledges, and abilities. To illustrate: In the accounting office of a large establishment, a voucher auditor may deal with vouchers covering but one or a few classes of expenditures, such as payrolls, or purchase and contract vouchers, or travel and communication accounts. As compared with such a position it is reasonable to regard as more difficult a position in a small office involving the auditing of vouchers relating to pay, travel, transportation, purchase under contract or otherwise, repairs, rentals, communications, etc., because the latter position requires the ability to apply a greater body of appropriation laws, regulations, decisions, and office practices governing a much greater variety of fiscal transactions.

Similarly, the scope and variety of work of an information clerk or a correspondence clerk would have an important bearing upon the classification of his position. The more restricted the subject matter or functions or activities concerning which information is given, or replies to correspondence made, the more routine or repetitive the position tends to be and the less likelihood there is that an appreciable number of the questions presented would be novel. Conversely, the greater the activities of the department concerned the more initial knowledge is required in the information or correspondence work and the more difficult it is to keep constantly in touch with changes, developments, and new policies therein.

Nonsupervisory Responsibilities

The proper analysis of a position invariably demands consideration of the responsibilities vested in it. Every position entails responsibility of some kind to some degree, for unless the work which it involves is a definite contribution toward the final disposition of the matter concerned, there is little reason for its existence. Not all responsibilities are, however, controlling allocation factors. For example, every position involves a responsibility for careful, honest, and industrious performance. Responsibilities of this type seldom have discriminative value as allocation factors.

Nonsupervisory responsibilities vary widely in level. They range, for example, from a messenger boy's responsibility for following an instruction to deliver a paper to a given person at a certain time, to a consulting expert's responsibility for furnishing to the head of a department, as a basis for executive action, critical advice on questions of outstanding importance.[22]

Nonsupervisory responsibilities also vary widely in kind. While it is not feasible here to discuss each in detail, some of them present matters of special interest.

Reviewing Work of Others

At first thought it would seem a simple problem to define the word "review." In ordinary usage "to review" means to make a critical examination of something initiated by someone else. Nice discriminations, however, must be made in order to appraise this function properly. The statement that one employee "reviews" the work of another must be clarified in all cases by an analysis of the purpose and the extent of the review. The necessity for outlining sharply these elements of purpose and extent arises from the fact that, from a classification standpoint, some types of review are differentiating classification factors whereas others are not.[23]

There are several types of review, varying greatly in purpose and authority and, therefore, differing in degree of responsibility. The reviewer may merely repeat the work of another employee, the authority of the two being equal. He may go into all the work done by another employee or his review may be confined to one or a few phases. He may or may not have the authority to countermand, or to change results.

A limited reviewing function is encountered in some calculating machine operator positions which involve, interchangeably, both initial calculations and reviewing or checking the work of other operators to make sure it is free from errors—going over the same ground and repeating the same processes, and referring errors to a specially designated "adjuster." This type of review amounts to an exchange of work after it has been performed initially, for the pur-

---

[22] The same wide variation in level is found in supervisory responsibilities. It should also be noted that some kinds of responsibilities that exist together in a supervisory position may exist separately in nonsupervisory positions.

[23] This type of responsibility is here treated in its nonsupervisory phase, in which it is frequently encountered. It also occurs as a part of supervisory responsibility.

pose of insuring accuracy, and is a negligible differentiating factor in classification.

Review that involves a check of the pertinency, accuracy, and completeness of the facts assembled; of the correctness of all of the more important work processes; of the validity of conclusions drawn and the propriety of the action taken; and that carries with it the authority to change the details of the findings and the action taken, is review in the fullest sense of the word, constituting a definite differentiating factor in classifying the positions of the reviewer and those whose work he reviews.

Intermediate between these situations is the one set forth in the following illustrative position-description:

He reviews the reports prepared by the examiners attached to the section for the purposes of (1) ascertaining compliance with office policies; (2) analyzing the examiners' conclusions and reasons therefor; (3) considering with examiners any issue which he feels has not been properly disposed of, or any conclusion with which he does not agree, or which is indefinitely or improperly stated; (4) approving the report or preparing a dissenting opinion or explanatory memorandum for the information of the chief of the bureau and the head of establishment in case he does not approve the report.

Thus it will be seen the function of "review" may involve widely differing degrees of responsibility. The proper approach is to secure a full understanding of the coverage of the review. This can be gained only through a thorough analysis of the duties and responsibilities of the position, including a determination of the purpose, extent and authority of the review, and a study of relationships with the duties of subordinate and superior positions in the same organization unit.

Independence of Action or Decision

The authority to proceed with more or less independence is present as a nonsupervisory responsibility in many different types of jobs of varying levels. In most jobs this is an important allocation factor.

Independence of decision and action means a variable measure of freedom of the individual from close personal supervision, and of his work from minute review, but this is not its whole meaning. It connotes, as well, freedom from prescribed work plans and methods and from routine techniques, and involves an initiation and development of details or programs and some degree of authority for finality of action. A clerk filing cards alphabetically may be physically located at a place that makes it necessary for him to work alone and with only infrequent personal contact with his supervisor, but plans and work methods for filing are laid down for him, which is, of course, a manifestation of supervisory control,[24] and the field of operations is so circumscribed that there is no necessity or even opportunity for special decision or action on his part. This is true for all work that is routine in character and that involves the repetition of certain previously well-fixed operations or the performance of a series of standardized manual procedures.

However, as work increases in difficulty and scope the possibility for independent responsibility may be expected to increase. A worker in a scientific laboratory may have limited responsibility in making measurements, tests, or computations where he is given precise directions and instructions to follow. Another laboratory worker may have a good deal more responsibility because he participates in the determination of methods of attack on specific problems.

Nothing will illustrate more strikingly that responsibilities are relative and that various positions in the same organization are interdependent than the classifier's effort to determine the degree of independence of action or decision that exists in a given position, and to appraise the contribution made by each position toward the final action or decision on any given matter. Almost always, responsibilities of this character are shared.

Consequently, to determine the degree of authority vested in each position in the flow of work, it is necessary to consider to what extent authority over or responsibility for the same matter exists in other positions in the organization. It is profitable to trace from beginning to end the full course of responsibility for a certain thing. Frequently, for example, it is found that a decision made by a legal employee in one office of a department is not effective until reviewed and approved by an employee in the office of the general counsel of the department.

The relationship between difficulty of work and the kind and degree of supervision exercised over such work has been discussed. While supervision affects difficulty, its connection with responsibility is more immediate. Work that is guided in every detail by instruction and review or by complete plans may be, task for task, like other work which is performed without reference to any such detailed

24 See p. 116.

guidance. There is a difference in the difficulty of two such positions, but the greatest difference is in their responsibility. Accordingly, in appraising independence of action and decision, special effort should be made in tracing the lines of control from above. The *kind* of control from above is particularly important. Is the supervision from above close or general? Is it applied to the administrative features of the work, or the technical features, or both? What matters have been delegated away from the supervisory position, and what are the limitations on such delegations of authority?

Administrative supervision is the supervision of the employee's time and general procedures and conduct in relation to the rules, regulations, and broad plans of the organization. Such supervision implies large technical responsibility on the part of the one supervised. This situation often exists in professional and scientific positions, particularly those involving research activities. On the other hand, technical supervision presupposes direction of the employee's activities, and a more or less close check-up of his methods. It may include as well a verification of his findings and a testing of the validity of his conclusions within his field of work—a technical review with authority to change. This type of supervision affects both difficulty and responsibility.

Thus, in general, control or supervision from above reduces independence of action or decision on the part of those supervised when it plans, lays down precedents or methods for, and reviews, or otherwise covers the same subject matter, function, process, action, or decision as those with which the persons supervised deal.

Hence, to develop the primary information as to the kind and degree of supervision received by an employee and its effect upon his independence of action or decision, it is necessary to ascertain the precise elements of which supervision consists.[25]

Recommendations Affecting Plans or Policies

Occasionally one encounters positions having little or no responsibility for actual operations or supervision that, nevertheless, involve certain items of responsibility similar to those more frequently found in administrative or supervisory positions. The task of reviewing the work of others, discussed above, is, of course, an illustration of this fact; it may be found as a single nonsupervisory responsibility or in combination with other types of authority as a part of a broader

[25] See pp. 118–21.

supervisory or administrative responsibility. Sometimes broad phases of planning are part of the work of nonsupervisory officials, such as coordinators, administrative analysts, standardizers of procedure, technical experts, and the like. Personnel of these types may deal with policies, plans, programs, and methods of work, but without direct operating responsibility in respect to general management, production, and results. In such cases, these responsibilities may be evaluated by consideration of the magnitude, scope, importance, and difficulty of the problems dealt with. Particular attention is necessary to conditions at the start of the worker's activities, for there are occasions when planning a course of action is more difficult than carrying it out.

When a position involves responsibility for recommendations or decisions determining or affecting plans, programs, methods, or policies, it is helpful (apart from the question of difficulty, which should be separately analyzed) to regard the consequence of the recommendation or the decision as a guiding element in evaluation. Plans and programs for major projects are obviously of more consequence than those for minor ones. The organizational relation of the adviser to the official in the department who finally accepts or rejects his proposals is a weighty factor in determining the consequence of the employee's decisions or recommendations. Important, also, are the "size" of the problems dealt with and their complexities.

Responsibility for the Safety of Others

The responsibility for the safety or the lives of others, when unusually immediate and direct, is recognized as an element to be given weight in analyzing positions. This responsibility is found in such tasks as the following:

To test and examine gas masks for their capacity to remove poisonous industrial gases under various conditions of use.

In connection with the administration of safety appliance acts, to inspect and report the adequacy and condition of safety appliances on railroad cars and locomotives; to secure evidence to be used as the basis of prosecution of carriers for violation of safety appliance laws; to appear as witness for the government and to confer and advise with district attorneys.

To pack parachutes immediately prior to their use by airplane pilots.

Little recognition, however, can be given to this factor when it is present only to a limited degree or where it is only a very indirect responsibility. For example, it is not especially significant in the case of elevator operators because the burden of responsibility falls upon the mechanical safeguards of modern equipment and those who install and inspect them. Many of these safeguards practically eliminate this type of responsibility on the part of elevator operators even when passengers are entering and leaving the elevator.

The Custody of Money

Another nonsupervisory responsibility occasionally encountered is the responsibility for the custody of money, securities, or other things of special value.

Experience in classifying positions has demonstrated that there is a tendency on the part of employees and administrative officials to emphasize unduly any connection a given position may have with money, negotiable securities, or other things of special value. The importance which these things assume in one's personal affairs and views makes it hard to avoid giving them an exaggerated effect. However, nothing seems to be clearer than the futility of augmenting classifications, over what they otherwise would be, on the basis that increased allocations are necessary in order to obtain employees who are honest and trustworthy or in order to keep them honest and trustworthy. Such a basis implies that employees will be honest if given a somewhat higher classification (and salary) and that they are apt not to resist temptation to be dishonest if given a somewhat lower classification (and salary). It is based on the idea that pay, rather than fundamental character, controls personal traits. Even if this were true, the pay necessary to overcome the results of weak character would have to be greatly in excess of what is legislatively and administratively possible. Accordingly, the evaluation of responsibility for the custody of money, securities, or other things of special value, must depend upon something more than the necessity for honesty on the part of the employee who is occupying the position.[26]

Moreover, as in the case of other nonsupervisory responsibilities, the degree of financial responsibility present in an individual position depends upon the control which exists over the employee's official tasks, acts, or decisions. In positions involving responsibility of this type, such control is usually applied not only by the oversight of a superior but also by certain procedural or legal safeguards or remedies, such as bonding, penalties, recoveries, checks by other em-

[26] See discussion of "trust imposed" in Riegel, *Salary Determination*, p. 67.

ployees, requirements for daily balances, and periodic or unheralded inspections and accountings.[27]

Thus, in order that responsibility for the custody of things of special value may be real and direct, and so worthy of special study, it should involve (a) real responsibility for extreme care in the oversight of things of special value, for safeguarding such things against the carelessness or dishonesty of others, and for carrying on such clerical or other functions as may be required with accountability constantly in mind, and (b) a reasonable degree of freedom from procedural or supervisory checks for considerable periods of time. The greater the directness, completeness, and frequency with which checks, balances, inspections, or accountings are made, the more is the financial responsibility shared by others. In weighing these items the chances and consequences of errors or oversights (as something the employee must guard against) are for consideration as one approach to the analysis of responsibility.[28]

Responsibility for Accuracy

Another type of nonsupervisory responsibility is responsibility for accuracy or for freedom from errors. In most positions, accuracy is a factor for consideration in determining the incumbent's efficiency of performance rather than one which distinguishes the position itself from some other position. In its usual sense, accuracy is a result of carefulness, thoroughness, industrious application to the work at hand, or similar qualities that are expected of employees no matter what positions they hold. If in a given case the degree of accuracy called for in the position involves nothing more than this, it is not a critical factor in determining the allocation of the position; its significance is that of a standard for measuring the efficiency of the employee and thus for deciding upon his rate of pay within the range of salaries for the class in which his position falls.

That the question of accuracy required may, however, enter into the proper classification of a position is seen when positions of different kinds are compared in this respect. As among different classes of positions there may be different degrees of accuracy. Accuracy is measured always against some standard which may vary

[27] See C. Canby Balderston, *Wage Setting Based on Job Analysis and Evaluation* (Industrial Relations Counselors, New York, 1940), p. 46.

[28] A personal financial liability for erroneous or illegal payments is not, accurately speaking, a responsibility of the position. In reality, it is a penalty imposed on the incumbent for inefficiency or carelessness. Thus the effect of an error should be measured, as a classification factor, by something more than the imposition of such a penalty.

according to the class of positions concerned. The standard is most frequently, but not always, perfection.

For example, in statistical compilations or in accounting records nothing but perfection of arithmetical computations can be recognized as a satisfactory standard. Such work is either right or wrong. In mechanical or engineering work, however, where accuracy is a matter of precision, a task may be considered accurate when its results vary from some standard by less than a prescribed tolerance. In such work, accordingly, there may be degrees of accuracy depending on the size of the allowable error. Similarly, where results are not mathematically or mechanically measurable, and where accuracy is a matter of freedom from misapprehensions, misconstructions, or misapplications of judgment, different degrees of accuracy required may be encountered in positions at different levels.

Consideration of these examples will show, too, that in certain classes of positions something more than carefulness and industrious application to the work at hand may be needed to achieve the desired degree of accuracy. Particular methods may be employed; special skills or special knowledge may be required on the part of the employee; or perhaps the kind of work is such that the desired standard of accuracy may be attained only after long experience. It is, therefore, pertinent in some cases to inquire whether accuracy is a factor of difficulty and advanced or special qualifications, rather than mere carefulness, and whether accuracy is required to a degree unusually difficult for the worker of normal training in that field to achieve. For example, note the following task:

To analyze a wide variety of commercial products and naturally occurring products, where the work requires a high degree of exactness to withstand checking by highly trained technicians employed by the manufacturers of such products or by other outside agencies, and requires such frequent readjustment of analytical methods as is necessary to overcome obstacles and difficulties.

In such cases as these, accuracy may well be considered an appropriate allocation element.

Relative responsibility for accuracy may be determined by considering the opportunities for errors and omissions that must be guarded against by the employee, as well as the potential consequences of errors.[29] This involves inquiry into the purpose to which the result of his work is put.

[29] "Of fifteen companies visited, fourteen note the seriousness of possible errors on each job when they grade work for compensation purposes." Riegel, *Wage Determination*, p. 35. He gives an example of grading of jobs according to this factor on p. 36. See also the same author's *Salary Determination*, pp. 60–62.

In summary, then, in order clearly to appraise a nonsupervisory responsibility for accuracy, it should be analyzed through the process of the following inquiry:

1. How *difficult* is it to achieve the desired standard of accuracy? Is it a matter of carefulness, alertness, or other quality that any satisfactory employee should possess or can acquire on the job in a reasonable time? Or must the employee initially bring to the job special skill, or special knowledge of a particular method, or advanced training or experience in that field, when compared to the requirements for like or associated positions generally?

2. How *responsible* is the work in the light of the necessity of that degree of accuracy? What is the purpose of the work? To what use is the result of the work put? What happens when the desired standard of accuracy is not met? What is the effect of errors usually? What might be an unusual effect of an error? What provision is there for the discovery of errors and for review, inspection, or correction of the employee's work by others?[30]

Responsibility for Public Contacts

In some kinds of positions the responsibility for public or official contacts may be a nonsupervisory responsibility worthy of separate consideration and appraisal.[31] This type of responsibility, like many others, varies considerably in extent, difficulty, and importance from position to position. Its evaluation depends upon a number of factors. Various classes or segments of the public or various levels of public officials may be dealt with. The subject matter involved may be simple or complex, narrow or broad in scope, controversial or commonly accepted. It may deal with policies requiring justification or only with procedures and methodologies. The purpose of the contact may be the giving of information or it may be negotiation, involving a responsibility for obtaining support and cooperation or for influencing others to take a certain course of action. The accomplishment of the purpose may be indispensable to the operations of the agency or it may be only a desirable goal. The purpose of the contact may or may not be forwarded by the requirements of law.

---

[30] "The mere requirement of accuracy does not make a task difficult unless errors are difficult to avoid and/or detect and such errors cannot be easily corrected and may result in loss of life, limb, property, money or goodwill. The number and nature of supervisory and other checks which limit or make impossible undetected and/or uncorrected errors must be considered." Detroit Civil Service Commission, *The Classification Plan for the City of Detroit* (1935), p. xii.

[31] See Elton D. Woolpert, *Municipal Public Relations: A Suggested Program for Improving Relations with the Public*, International City Managers' Association, 1940.

The degree of authority which the official or employee has to commit or represent his agency during the course of his contacts or to take official action on his own motion, and the extent to which he is free from prior and current direction or supervision in this respect are also, of course, important factors.[32]

SUPERVISORY AND ADMINISTRATIVE RESPONSIBILITIES

The term "supervisory and administrative responsibilities" is here used to denote a general class of responsibilities for administering, directing, and overseeing the work of others.[33] Such terms as "supervise," "direct," "administer," etc., are each susceptible of different meanings, and a reader does not always interpret them to mean what the writer has intended. Hence for the purpose of analyzing positions, special effort should be made to get behind the words themselves and determine the precise constituents of supervision, direction, or administration in a given case and how the presence of such control functions is actually manifested.[34]

[32] See the discussion of "personal influence to be exercised" and the function of "negotiating" in executive positions, in Riegel, *Salary Determination*, pp. 64–66, 202–06.

[33] No attempt is here being made to discuss differences between administrative functions on the one hand and supervisory functions on the other. Those interested in this question may refer to such sources as the following: Royal Commission on the Civil Service (1929–30), *Statement Submitted by the Association of First Division Civil Servants*, Appendix VIII to Minutes of Evidence (London, 1930), pp. 4–6, 11–12; Glen V. Cleeton and Charles W. Mason, *Executive Ability, Its Discovery and Development* (Antioch Press, 1934); Commission of Inquiry on Public Service Personnel, *Better Government Personnel* (McGraw-Hill, 1935); Leonard D. White, *Government Career Service* (University of Chicago Press, 1935); Lewis Meriam, *Public Service and Special Training* (University of Chicago Press, 1936); Chester I. Barnard, *The Functions of the Executive* (Harvard University Press, 1938); W. V. Bingham, *Administrative Ability, Its Discovery and Development*, Society for Personnel Administration, Pamphlet No. 1, April 1939; Arthur W. Macmahon and John D. Millett, *Federal Administrators* (Columbia University Press, 1939), pp. 3–24; Albert Walton, *New Techniques for Supervisors and Foremen* (McGraw-Hill, 1940), pp. 189–98; "Business Administration in a Changing Economy," *Proceedings*, Third Annual Conference of the Academy of Management, University of Michigan School of Business Administration (Michigan Business Papers, No. 3, April, 1939), pp. 5–10.

[34] See extracts from report of Griffenhagen & Associates to Massachusetts Commission on Administration and Finance, November 22, 1936, in "The Policies and Procedure Involved in Developing a Compensation Plan for the Massachusetts State Service," *Public Personnel Studies*, December 1926, p. 332; Riegel, *Salary Determination*, pp. 193–236; Home Owners' Loan Corporation, Dallas Regional Office, *Executive Development in Human Relations* (1940), pp. 2–4; Marshall E. Dimock and Howard K. Hyde, *Bureaucracy and Trusteeship in Large Corporations*, Temporary National Economic Committee, Monograph No. 11, 1940, chapters VI and VIII. For a discussion and analysis of the constituents of supervision in the field of education, see A. S. Barr, William H. Burton, and Leo J. Brueckner, *Supervision: Principles and Practices in the Improvement of Instruction* (D. Appleton-Century Co., 1938), pp. 3–76.

There are many variations in the mechanics of supervision or administration, both as to the methods used and their timing. As between the supervisor and those supervised, supervision may be carried out by direct personal and oral contact; by the issuance of written statements covering policies, working instructions, and guiding precedents; by indirect contact through intermediate supervisors; or by a combination of these methods. It may be manifested before assignments are made to the employees supervised, as where general instructions are given and the employees informed in advance of plans, policies, and work methods. It may be manifested while the work is in process, the supervisor exercising control step by step, or making test checks, or answering questions as to matters not clearly understood, or deciding matters of a type previously scheduled for reference to him. It may be manifested after the employee has completed his assignment, the results of the employee's work being inspected, reviewed, and checked for accuracy, adequacy, and compliance with instructions, objectives, and work methods.

More important, however, than the mechanics of supervision is the supervisory pattern, functionally considered. What are the respects in which the supervisor controls the work-methods, the initiative and judgment, and the work-results of those supervised? To what extent, within what segments of supervisory control, and on what matters have responsibilities been delegated? By what facts is supervision over employees recognized and its effect appraised? To which of their processes, actions, or decisions does it apply? How and to what extent? The kind and degree of supervisory responsibility or administrative responsibility involved in a given position depend on the precise respects in which supervision over others is evidenced, including both its direct and obvious phases and those which are more latent and less apparent at first glance.

It should again be mentioned that single elements of supervisory or administrative responsibility sometimes exist in nonsupervisory positions. For example, a technical responsibility for plans, flow of work, and work-methods might be found in positions of procedure analysts or others assigned to make studies of methods with a view to their improvement. Responsibility for review of results is frequently encountered in positions having no other supervisory aspect. Such circumstances frequently give rise to a claim for recognition of these single elements as "supervisory responsibility." Of course, they should receive full measure of recognition, but as nonsupervisory, rather than supervisory responsibilities.

Because of the frequency with which a reviewing function alone is erroneously considered to be "supervision," it may be well to draw this distinction between them: Both supervisory review and non-supervisory review may involve power to reject, revise, and modify the product. Supervisory review, however, also includes the authority to plan, assign, and reassign work, and to instruct those whose work is reviewed; and it also involves an operating or management responsibility for the work of those supervised. For example, the passing of correspondence or reports over a desk for examination and review, or for analysis and record, or analysis and further correspondence, does not create for the reviewing desk a responsibility properly characterized as "supervisory."

Factors Indicating Degree or Weight

The principal factors entering into the analysis of supervisory or administrative responsibilities may for convenience be grouped under the following general headings:

1. Number and types of supervisory action present.

2. Extent to which the initiative and judgment of those supervised are limited and the results of their work passed upon.

3. Size of the organization supervised.

4. Importance and variety of functions and the complexity of the organization supervised.[35]

As is true in the analysis of any position, questions of difficulty and degree of supervision by others should, of course, be explored in connection with questions of responsibility, with which they are closely interlocked.[36]

[35] "Common earmarks of supervisory responsibility are: the delegation of work, instruction in methods of work, coordination of efforts of subordinates, and accountability to higher authority for the progress, quality, and cost of group effort. Supervision exercised by the occupant of a position can be measured by the number of subordinates and the wages of subordinates." Riegel, *Wage Determination*, p. 39.

[36] "It is just as true that no adequate conception of the responsibilities pertaining to a position can be secured except through an understanding of the place of the position in the whole scheme of organization and of its relationships to all other positions both higher and lower in the scale of authority. It is not sufficient to know that the incumbent of a certain position is responsible for the work of others; it must also be known whether he is solely responsible, whether he is under the close supervision of a still higher officer who relieves him of many important decisions, whether he supervises both the work to be done and the method, whether he merely reports delinquencies or takes disciplinary action upon his own initiative, and whether those whom he supervises are in turn charged with the direction of others or are assisted by others." Griffenhagen, "The Principles and Technique of Preparing an Occupational Classification of Positions in the Public Service," *Public Personnel Studies*, November 1924, p. 241.

The "Supervisory Pattern"

The "supervisory pattern" or the function of supervision, including those phases which collectively are more commonly spoken of as administrative responsibilities, may involve control over:

1. *Policies* (broad principles of law interpretation, management, or ethics governing the conduct of the work). May range from the actual determination of policies by a high administrative official to their interpretation by supervisors for the benefit of workers.

2. *Objectives* (purposes of the work; the characteristics of the completed product). May range from the fixing of broad limits and the setting of the goal for complete work programs by a high administrative official to the determination by intermediate supervisors of purposes and characteristics of tasks to be performed by individual workers.

3. *Plans* (ways and means for accomplishing the objectives). May range from the creation of organizational structures and the making of provisions for personnel and equipment, with which a high administrative official is generally directly concerned, to the determination of details or precise techniques, upon which an intermediate supervisor may be engaged.

4. *Flow of work* (organizational and functional course which a given piece of work takes from inception to completion). May range from the determination of the general sequence of operations as a special phase of planning to the fixing by intermediate supervisors of the routine to be followed in the performance of those tasks allotted to particular organization units.

5. *"Housekeeping" management* (matters of personnel, discipline, leave, expenditures, supplies, equipment, space, etc.). Control over matters of "housekeeping" management is as a rule widely distributed downward in the organizational pyramid in logical progression. It may range from that of the head of the department who lays down general rules and regulations and makes the ultimate decisions on the more important questions to that of the intermediate supervisor who makes the initial recommendations and minor decisions.

6. *Assignments* (what the employees supervised are to do and the order in which they are to do it; selection of employees for particular assignments; determination of the priority of activities). May range from the exercise by an administrator of full authority in determining the characteristics of individual positions, in selecting

employees to fill such positions and in determining the order in which projects shall be undertaken, to the exercise by intermediate supervisors of a limited authority for distributing work of one type to a group of employees where there is no problem in the selection of the employee to whom the work is to be given other than that of expediting the work and equalizing the load.

7. *Work-methods* (the technique of doing the work; the sequence of steps by which the employee, using the appropriate technique, accomplishes the prescribed objectives). May vary widely. In some fields, for example the mechanical trades, where the work methods are standard, the administrator's control of this particular factor is negligible. Here the principal control exercised is through an intermediate supervisor concerned mainly with the degree of excellence of technique rather than with the kind of methods employed. In other fields, the work methods may be definitely prescribed by a specialist in the subject matter concerned (who may or may not be a supervisor). In other fields control over work methods may vary from determination by the administrator to overseeing by the subordinate supervisor to see that approved methods are followed.

8. *Coordination* (development and operation of mechanisms for proper consistency and gearing of varied functions and tasks). May range from that exercised by a high administrative official or a specialist in planning and establishing such mechanisms to that exercised by an intermediate supervisor in overseeing their operation for the purpose of insuring that procedures are being followed in accordance with instructions.

9. *Production* (amount of work done; promptness with which it is accomplished). May range from that exercised by administrators on broad matters of expenditures, equipment, personnel, etc., to that exercised by an intermediate supervisor of a small group in face-to-face supervision of routine details.

10. *Results* (the accuracy, adequacy, propriety, etc., of the work in the light of established policies, objectives, and work methods). May range from broad planning, policy determination, and layout as to methods, to general or direct oversight while the work is being done by individual employees and to inspection, review, or check (which may be carried out by a supervisor or an individual worker) after completion, with authority to change actions taken or decisions made by those supervised.[37]

[37] Cf. Riegel, *Salary Determination*, pp. 195–212.

Supervisory positions vary considerably in their pattern. Some positions of a supervisory nature are characterized largely by responsibility for face-to-face oversight of the work of employees, confined, for example, to matters of assignments, work-methods, production, and results. Others might be confined to minor phases of business management, and to assignments and production, with little responsibility for work-methods and the technical accuracy of the results obtained by the individual employees. When positions of higher administrative responsibility are reached, the indirect phases of control become more in evidence, such as those with respect to policies, objectives, plans, and coordination, and the direct phases of control become less in evidence, such phases being delegated to intermediate or subordinate supervisors.

Accordingly, in appraising the supervisory responsibilities in individual positions, it is important to know the phases of supervisory action involved.[38] Frequently the phases of supervisory responsibility listed above are delegated among several positions at different levels. Each of these positions, although supervisory in general nature, would include only a certain part of the totality of supervisory responsibility for the work of a particular group of employees. Direct inquiry as to exactly what types of supervisory control are vested in a given position will prevent giving undue weight, in connection with that position, to certain types of supervisory responsibilities that are really vested in other positions. This is particularly important because of the tendency to use such terms as "supervise" rather loosely. We should ask: Of what elements does the supervisory pattern consist?[39]

[38] "Obviously, supervision which consists of a mere passing out of work or work-assignments is extremely elementary and should not be considered as true supervision. Similarly, 'guard' duties in seeing that subordinates are busy at work is not true supervision." Detroit Civil Service Commission, *The Classification Plan for the City of Detroit.*

[39] Notice the following item contained in the instructions for filling out the classification questionnaire used a few years ago in developing a position-classification plan for the Indiana Unemployment Compensation Division: "Do not say that you have direction or supervision of others unless you actually have authority to assign or direct their work, to give them orders, to tell them what tasks to do and in what order, and usually to discipline them in at least minor matters. Inspecting, checking, or proofreading the work of others or answering their questions or making suggestions which they may or may not follow, does not constitute supervision or direction." Observe also the following comment quoted from a classifier's report in another jurisdiction: "The word 'supervises' means in this instance 'to inspect with authority to change' and was not meant by the department to have the more usual meaning of definite planning, laying out, assigning, advising, instructing, following through and directing the work of other employees."

Finding out just what phases of supervisory action are included in the responsibilities of a given position becomes of vital importance when this question arises: In a given case, may the class for a supervisory position be properly based on the classes of positions supervised? By making detailed inquiry and testing the facts against the supervisory pattern, it can be determined whether the supervision exercised is of a type which warrants basing the class of the supervisory position upon those of the positions supervised.

For example, a superintendent of building, appealing for the reclassification of his position, offered as his major contention that he "supervised," in addition to the usual cleaning and maintenance staff, two instrument makers and a glass blower. The facts were, however, that these employees had been attached to his organization for administrative or business management purposes only. The instrument makers and the glass blower designed and constructed scientific apparatus on their own initiative in contact with scientists. The superintendent did not pass upon their work or give technical advice to them in any way. His "supervision" was confined to such matters as approving leaves of absence and determining which assignments should be given precedence in execution. The classes of the instrument makers and the glass blower, had, therefore, negligible significance in determining the superintendent's classification.

Extent to Which Initiative of Those Supervised is Limited

This factor is always to be considered in connection with (a) particular activities or processes and (b) the particular types of supervisory or administrative action present in the position. It is understandable only when it is related to definite phases of supervision or administration, such as planning, organizing, setting objectives, prescribing work-methods, reviewing details of work, and so on. Obviously, it has a wide range of meaning. In the position of a high executive who has delegated to others the authority to act initially, it may indicate a strong responsibility for leadership and influence on major matters of policy, a personal responsibility for coordinating the different parts of his organization, and ultimate responsibility for results. In the position of the supervisor of a small clerical section, it may mean personal review of nearly everything that is done in his unit. Depending on the area of activity and the phases of the supervisory pattern involved, thoroughness of control may indicate a broad, heavy responsibility for over-all management and direction, or a much lighter responsibility only slightly above that of the individual workers supervised, or something in between.

Thoroughness of control requires consideration from two standpoints: that of the supervisor and that of the supervised. Generally speaking, the greater the extent to which the initiative and judgment of those supervised are limited and controlled by action of the supervisor on matters of the same kind and scope, the greater the degree to which responsibilities for these matters have not actually been delegated to the supervised positions and remain vested in the supervisory position instead.

Clarity of analysis demands constant attention to the principle that within the same segment of the supervisory pattern the factor of responsibility in the supervisor's position is the direct opposite of the factor of independence of work in the positions supervised. As one increases in degree, the other decreases.[40] What the supervisor has not delegated, the employee is not responsible for. Each factor is to be considered in the light of the facts about the other. Inquiry as to one serves as a check upon inquiry as to the other.

Experience indicates that confused thought in this respect frequently is due partly to an assumption that supervision always means close, constant, personal oversight and partly to a failure to realize that supervision has different aspects of application. An employee, A, might say that he is not subject to B's supervision because he, A, reaches his own conclusions and decisions independently on the matters assigned to him. This is the usual situation in the case of a trained, experienced employee. Nevertheless, supervision might be constantly present as the result of B's planning, organizing, setting precedents, establishing work methods, controlling production, and carrying out other phases of supervisory responsibility of which A may not be cognizant.

The following are examples of various degrees of supervision, written from the standpoint of the position supervised. They illustrate (a) the different situations arising with respect to control by a supervisor over the initiative and judgment exercised by individual workers, and (b) the variation in the matters to which control relates, depending on the segment of the supervisory pattern involved.

[40] "Supervising responsibilities may be greater in a group where the proportion of beginners, learners, or apprentices is relatively high, as contrasted with a group where most of the subordinates are journeymen or experienced workers." *Ibid.*

"Under Immediate Supervision"

Excluding supervision over an apprentice or trainee, this phrase indicates the greatest amount of supervision and control from above, the least personal independence of action, and the least breadth of matters upon which the employee makes his own decisions. It is a particularized supervision that is recognized by its specificity and its application to details. The supervisor has not only the responsibility for assignments, flow of work, production, discipline, and other management functions but also the responsibility for proper instructions as to objectives, plans, policies, procedures, and office methods, including specific responsibility for matters which are out of the ordinary or unusual when compared to the mine-run of work. The employee's assignments, his objectives, and sequence of detailed steps in his work are prescribed for him. Little opportunity is given him for the exercise of personal initiative, discretion, or judgment; or for the assumption of any real responsibility for results alone. Generally, he is held personally responsible for the accurate and proper application of steps in a well-recognized technique. If he has followed this technique and his instructions, his responsibility ends, because the responsibility for results rests with his supervisor or his supervisor's superiors. He is given no assignments requiring the exercise of experienced judgment except that gained by experience in a well-recognized, standard, or conventional routine.

The phrase "under immediate supervision" does not, however, imply that the employee work directly under someone's eye; that each stage of his work is reviewed and checked; or even that all his results are checked. He is a trained employee in work of a given class. He has familiarized himself with routine and with the methods or procedures affecting his particular position. He is presumed to be able to recognize instances which are out of the ordinary and which do not fall within his existing instructions, and upon which, consequently, he should obtain advice or further instructions. Hence, he is not constantly or continuously instructed, and reviews and checks of his work are applied only to an extent sufficient to keep the supervisor aware that instructions and methods are being understood and followed and that the employee is referring to others unusual matters for advice or decision.

When conditions such as those described above are encountered, the employee is said to be "under immediate supervision."

"Under General Supervision"

This phrase indicates that the control from above is not a particularized supervision, but a general control, not intimately bearing upon the details of the employee's work.

The difference between "immediate supervision" and "general supervision" may be found in the degree of control on both administrative and "technical" phases, or it may be evidenced almost entirely in the amount of direct control on "technical" aspects alone, i.e., the "how" of the job—methods of work and sequence of steps.

There is, for example, the employee who is under fairly close supervision from a management standpoint but from a "technical" standpoint is given a considerable amount of independence and responsibility. His assignments and objectives are prescribed for him, but his method is seldom supervised, reviewed, or controlled while the work is in process. He is expected to plan the sequence of detailed steps by using experienced judgment and discretion. He is expected to solve on his own motion most problems of detail that come up in the course of his work, except those of an unusual nature. He has substantive and personal responsibility for results, circumscribed by the scope of his assignments.

The principal indicia of general supervision on the technical aspects of a position are personal acccountability for accomplishing prescribed results and objectives, infrequent reference of matters of detail, and considerable freedom from control or oversight by others while the work is in process.

In those cases where the generality of supervision is found in both management and technical phases, there are present in addition to the foregoing conditions, such indicia as the following: Considerable freedom from control over sequence of assignments, the employee bearing a fair degree of responsibility for determining what shall be done next; and a substantial degree of independence in planning and organizing his own work.

"Under General Direction"

This phrase indicates an extremely general and somewhat remote control that manifests itself expressly only on detached occasions. Such phases as planning and organizing the details of work and deciding the methods to produce a given result are completely in the hands of the employee, who is expected to carry out not only all the ordinary affairs of his position but to meet unusual situations without advice or instruction other than that afforded by the general plans, policies, and purposes, applicable to all work in his unit, which he is expected to interpret and apply properly. Active control is manifested only where matters of broad policy and coordination, long-time planning, expenditures of funds, etc., are involved. And even in such matters the employee generally participates by making recommendations or developing ideas in conference with his superiors. Actual contact between the employee and his superior, personally or through memoranda, is, however, rather limited in point of frequency and matters covered, when compared to the whole scope of the employee's tasks, including details.

"General direction" is characterized by a heavy personal responsibility on the part of the employee for planning and organizing his own work, and for developing methods and carrying out work in accordance with established policies, by relative infrequency of reference to others for advice and instructions, and by practically complete freedom from supervision or oversight on working methods even when unusual problems are involved.[41]

---

[41] There are a good many other phrases that can be used to describe the type of supervision from above. For example, "under executive direction" may apply to the work of a bureau head who reports to the head of a department or establishment. "Under immediate supervision and continual instruction" may

Size of the Organization Supervised

Another factor to be considered in determining the weight of supervisory or administrative responsibility of a given position is the size of the organization supervised or administered. Usually this is indicated by the number of employees. For example, "to have general supervision over the clerical functions of the office of the chief of the division" can be interpreted more accurately when it is known that the office force consists of two clerk-stenographers.

Generally speaking, the number, classes, and levels of positions supervised are significant measures of many, although not all types of supervisory and administrative problems. The larger the organization for which the individual is responsible, the greater his responsibility for such supervisory actions as planning coordinated programs, flow of work, and work-methods, for carrying out matters of general management, and for securing proper results. The effect of magnitude should in any case be affirmatively established by direct inquiry as to what special problems of supervision or administration arise by reason of the magnitude of the organization.

Number of employees supervised is emphasized as a classification factor by those in charge of large forces and depreciated by those in charge of small forces. The fact is, however, that magnitude should never serve as the *sole* factor in analyzing supervisory responsibility. It is important only in combination with other elements. The scope of the supervisory position is shown not only by the number but also by the classes of the positions supervised. The nonsupervisory positions, particularly, reflect the inherent difficulty of the work for which the supervisor is responsible. One may direct a large force engaged on simple routine work and yet may have no greater supervisory responsibility in the aggregate than one who directs a smaller staff engaged on more important or more difficult work of a varied character. Thus, while magnitude is to be given due weight, all other factors, such as scope of the supervisory pattern, diversity, complexity, and importance of the questions to be settled, and the knowledge of subject matter, laws, regulations, precedents,

---

apply to an apprentice or trainee position. Likewise, the three phrases mentioned may be modified to indicate more precisely the scope of matters covered by supervision. For example, "under general *administrative* direction" would emphasize the independence of the worker on technical matters. "Under general *technical* direction" would emphasize technical control.

policies, procedure, etc., which is required on the part of the supervisor, also have important significance.[42]

Importance and Variety of Functions; Organizational Complexity

These are weighty factors in allocating supervisory and administrative positions. To evaluate them requires a study of the purposes, functions, and structure of the organization concerned.

The importance of the functions of an organization unit, is, of course, purely relative. An organization may be important from one of a number of different viewpoints, such as its (a) importance to the department, considered as an operating unit; (b) importance to the government, considered in the aggregate as one operating organization; (c) importance in respect to finance, industry, commerce, agriculture, public health and safety, or to other general economic and sociological factors; and (d) importance from the standpoint of effect or significance to the jurisdiction.

Manifestly, the relative importance of an organization varies according to the viewpoint taken. For example, if the importance of all organizations were to be determined with one viewpoint paramount, say government finance, it might be said that only those organizations which collect or produce revenue would be considered of major importance and those which expend and do not produce moneys would be considered of less importance. Generally speaking, attempting to apply to all organizations a single "external" viewpoint such as this is illogical. However, a single viewpoint is frequently helpful in comparing positions in two organizations of similar or parallel function.

The variety of functions for which the supervisor is responsible and the complexity of the organization supervised are other items worthy of thoughtful consideration in analyzing supervisory positions, particularly those at the head of organizations of some size. This is true not only because of the wider scope of knowledge and ability required, but also because, as a rule, difficult problems of supervisory action, such as coordination, are encountered directly by the supervisor. The geographic and organizational distribution of the employees supervised, and the number, types, functions, and locations of the various divisions and subdivisions thus become facts of significance. Further, the number and classes of positions super-

---

[42] See the measurement scale of responsibility for supervision in Riegel, *Salary Determination*, p. 127.

vised are good indications of the character, complexity, and variety
of functions of the organization itself. From such facts can be developed the special difficulties and complexities of supervisory or administrative action that bear directly upon the supervisory or administrative position concerned.

In the field service of the federal government, or within a state,
offices of generally parallel function exist in different locations. The
problem of determining the character and the scope, relative magnitude, and importance of the supervisory and administrative responsibility of the heads of these offices (as well as the difficulty of their
problems and programs) frequently can be approached through a
process of (*a*) selecting a number of significant factual items bearing on these allocation factors and (*b*) ranking each office with respect to the combination of these items. This procedure may be simple or complex. For example, the responsibility of administrative
positions in hospitals may be made to depend upon the kind of hospital and its bed capacity. On the other hand, the responsibility of
directors of certain agricultural regional offices may be relatively
measured by amount of appropriations or allotments available for
expenditure; number of states in the region; agricultural character
of the region; number, area, value, and type of farms; the normal
cash income from the farm products of the region; and the size of the
farm population and the number of farm tenants.[43]

The Fallacy of "Mechanical Organizational Parallelism"

In discussing with operating officials the degree of supervisory or
administrative responsibility present in a position, one frequently
encounters a superficial conclusion drawn from the form of organizational structure, and based on this reasoning: A's position is that
of chief of division falling in a certain level in the classification plan.
B is another chief of division in the same bureau or agency. Therefore B's position should fall in the same classification level as A's.

This reasoning assumes that the classification level of a position
can be based solely on organizational rank. However, positions which
are at parallel steps in the pyramid of organizational authority are

[43] Another example of this approach is afforded in the recent A.L.A. classification of chief librarians of municipal public libraries. Eleven classes of libraries
were distinguished on the basis of (1) size, make-up, and compensation of staff;
(2) budget per capita; (3) size of book collection; (4) book circulation per
capita; (5) per cent of population registered as borrowers; and (6) hours open.
American Library Association, *Classification and Pay Plans for Municipal Public
Libraries* (Chicago, 1939).

not always comparable in duties and responsibilities. Organizations differ, of course, in their method of placing duties and responsibilities in corresponding organizational subdivisions. All divisions of an organization are not alike. They do not entail the same variety and difficulty of functions and their heads do not always have responsibilities of the same weight. Furthermore, under some circumstances there may be no limit to the number of "divisions" of an organization that may administratively be created. The number of division-head positions may be increased in such a way that they are all on a parity with respect to flow of work and line of authority, but there may be vast differences among them with respect to difficulty and variety of work and weight of responsibility.

In short, to classify positions simply according to their mechanical parallelism as shown on an organization chart is to ignore all the other phases of duties and responsibilities that have to be considered in order to make an equitable allocation.

QUALIFICATIONS STANDARDS OF THE POSITION

Qualifications needed for the effective performance of the duties and the discharge of the responsibilities of a given position are not a distinct classification factor, but are a gauge or measure of, or a clue to, other factors: subject-matter, function, profession or occupation, difficulty of work, nonsupervisory responsibilities, and supervisory or administrative responsibilities.[44]

Bearing on the Classification of a Position

Stating the qualification standards for a given class of positions is one method of indicating how difficult or complex these duties and responsibilities are.[45] Simple duties require little training and experience. Difficult duties require longer training and experience and the demonstration of definite attainments.[46]

---

[44] "An occupational evaluation is an effort to differentiate between jobs on the basis of duties and responsibilities involved. The minimum qualifications required before an employee is capable of assuming the responsibilities of a specific job can be used as an aid in the grading process. These qualifications are a measure of the differences in the type of individuals preferred, and, consequently, a measure of the jobs themselves." Baridon and Loomis, *Personnel Problems* (McGraw-Hill, 1931), p. 45.

[45] See Griffenhagen, "The Principles and Technique of Preparing an Occupational Classification of Positions in the Public Service," *Public Personnel Studies*, November 1924, p. 252.

[46] "Every company whose grading plan was examined includes 'length of learning period' as a factor in job comparisons." Riegel, *Wage Determination*, p. 32. See also the same author's *Salary Determination*, p. 58.

For example, if the difficulty of an individual task be regarded as reflected in the degree of skill necessary to perform it, then, in the practice of one classification agency, it may be more or less accurately measured by one or more of the following factors:

1. Length of experience necessary to attain reasonable efficiency.

2. Length of schooling, formal or other training necessary either to profit by experience or to directly acquire a particular skill.

3. Relative scarcity of basic traits and aptitudes necessary for acquiring a particular skill. That is, a task that calls for traits possessed in a sufficient degree by the majority of persons to acquire skill readily would be considered less difficult than a task which requires traits possessed by a relatively small percentage of the population.

4. Possibilities of errors and the seriousness of the consequences of errors.

Three of these factors, it will be observed, are directly associated with qualification standards.[47] After the difficulty of each task is thus determined, the difficulty of all the tasks of a position taken as a whole may be governed by (1) the intrinsic difficulty of the separate tasks and (2) the complexity of the duties, i.e., the wideness of the field covered by the separate tasks.[48]

Statements of qualifications to be required of *any* future incumbent of a given class of positions are particularly enlightening in considering newly created positions while they are vacancies in the process of being filled. Their value lies in the fact that they are *standards*. They are intended to apply to *all* incumbents seeking employment in the class in which the vacancy falls. They have a significance which is generic, not dependent solely upon the qualifications of one person.

Possibilities of Error

Erroneous conclusions by reason of undue emphasis upon qualification standards as a classification factor may come about through one or more of the following causes:

1. The assumption that the qualifications possessed by the employee who happens to be in the position at the time it is classified are a reliable measure of the difficulties and responsibilities of the

[47] We have considered the fourth in connection with nonsupervisory responsibility. See pp. 112–14.

[48] Detroit Civil Service Commission, *The Classification Plan for the City of Detroit.* Additional factors are used in the case of supervisory positions.

position, i.e., an important guide to its classification level; whereas, as a matter of fact, his qualifications are frequently higher than necessary and sometimes lower. One should distinguish sharply, accordingly, between the qualifications to be required of *any* future incumbent of a given class of positions and those which a particular incumbent may happen to possess or lack.

2. Incomplete analysis in cases where a department desires to employ a person of designated qualifications in a newly created position which is to be allocated, the statement being made that a certain classification level (and therefore pay scale) is necessary in order to attract persons having these qualifications and that the qualifications justify the classification requested. In such cases it must also be found that the duties and responsibilities of the position are such that they require, as a minimum standard, qualifications of the kind and extent designated. Unless such a finding can logically be made, granting the classification requested is equivalent to classifying a position purely on the basis of the qualifications of the person who is to occupy it and not on the basis of its duties and responsibilities.

3. Inadequate appreciation of the fact that only *minimum* qualification standards properly reflect classification levels and distinctions. To a certain extent, it is desirable that employees possess qualifications higher than a minimum standard, as recognized by the general order of selecting employees beginning with those having the highest ratings. But qualifications of a level which is desirable may reflect other employment conditions, such as the wish to secure employees who will afford a good recruiting field for future promotions to higher lines of work.

These three comments, it will be observed, are directed toward a clarification of the principle that the concept of the minimum qualification standards of a position should not be confused with the actual qualifications possessed or lacked by some particular employee or applicant.[49]

Subject to the foregoing limitations, the degree of difficulty of the duties and the weight of the responsibilities of an individual position can be approached indirectly by ascertaining and considering the qualifications necessary to perform the work. The result will serve as an additional guide and will assist in clarifying issues and checking conclusions arrived at through other phases of the analysis. However, it should be recognized that qualification standards are

[49] See pp. 42–43.

generally inferences or deductions or empirical opinion. They do not stand upon the same footing as other facts about duties and responsibilities. Consequently, they should never be employed as the sole guide in classifying positions.

Determining Qualifications Standards

The qualifications standards of an individual position may be determined either by direct interview, in the same manner as any facts are gathered (except that opinions are also covered); by inference from the duties and responsibilities of the positions concerned; by inquiry as to past, present and (possibly) future recruiting practices; and by inquiry as to the classes from and to which promotions are made to and from the class to which the position in question belongs.[50]

Qualifications required in tests from time to time should always be checked against the duties and responsibilities of the class of positions before being used as a guide to its classification level, in order to see whether or not, for reasons of policy, they have been placed higher than would be required to perform the work. Examination qualifications may, for a number of proper reasons, be higher than those required by the immediate difficulty and responsibility of the class of positions to be filled.

For example, they may be placed at various levels above a minimum level, depending upon the available supply of candidates. They may be set so as to take advantage of a surplus market of employees of the kind to be recruited and to secure the best qualified candidates available, without the necessity of considering all candidates who could do the work. Again, qualifications higher than minimum may be required because the positions in question are used as a source of supply for promotion to higher positions, and it is desired in advance to take into consideration in some measure the qualifications needed for these higher positions. Also, examination requirements may properly include desirable qualifications as well as those considered necessary for one to do the work at all.

MIXED POSITIONS

The process of classification includes and necessitates investigation, analysis, and evaluation of *all* the duties and responsibilities of a position, whatever their nature or extent. Evaluating the facts as to

[50] See also the discussion on pp. 32–33.

duties and responsibilities includes, however, distinguishing between the material and the immaterial, and between the controlling and the insignificant duties and responsibilities. Hence, this question may arise: *Which* duties and responsibilities of the position shall govern its classification?

Mixed Positions Defined

The answer to this question is relatively easy to arrive at in the cases of positions of which the characteristics remain substantially the same month after month, and which are sufficiently homogeneous that all the various duties, tasks and responsibilities are of about the same level. However, a difficult problem arises where the duties and responsibilities of a position fluctuate from time to time so rapidly that an attempt to keep pace with each fluctuation by new classifications would violate common sense.[51] In such cases, the position is regarded as possessing in the aggregate all the characteristics that it has over a reasonable period of time in the present and future, and, for convenience, we refer to it as a "mixed position."

For the purpose of this discussion, a "mixed position" may be defined as one which is constituted of duties that are of different levels of difficulty, varying with time, where it is impracticable or not sensible to classify the position upward and downward from time to time to conform to such variation. In particular, it should be observed that this definition covers positions made up of a daily mixture of tasks of different levels of difficulty and responsibility, as well as those where the variation of task levels is apparent only when a longer view is taken.

Temporary Work-Assignments

With respect to positions giving rise to these particular types of classification problems, as a general rule exceptional, emergency, or incidental assignments are eliminated from consideration. The following views should govern:

1. Only those items of which there is reasonable assurance of continuance are germane for purposes of classification.

[51] It will be observed that this problem is connected with the rules of the classification plan relating to reports of changes in duties and/or responsibilities. These rules would require analysis of such changes and a new classification, if warranted, whenever it would be feasible and sensible to treat the position as changing from time to time into one of different characteristics. See Chapter X, pp. 285–88 and 311, for discussion of this allied problem.

2. Work-assignments made accidentally, temporarily in unusual situations, or for the purpose of trying out the employee's capacities should not result in a classification different from that which the regular tasks of his position warrant.

3. The position in question should be looked at over a length of time sufficient to neutralize the effect of any accidental assignments, whether those assignments detract from or add to the position. Obviously, a position should not be frozen at any particular moment for the purpose of inspection, for it may then present an entirely different picture from the one obtained from inspection over a longer period.

If the classifying agency as a matter of policy gives a position a new classification upward because of an *accidental or temporary* assignment to a task higher than the employee customarily handles, then it logically should not fail to inquire into assignments, accidentally or temporarily given to employees, lower than those which they customarily have, and take appropriate action toward the reduction of classifications. However, this would be a ridiculous policy technically, and particularly administratively, for it would mean a continual series of classifications upward and downward at short intervals. If it is agreed that the policy should be uniform, regardless of whether the temporary tasks add to or detract from the regular duties of the position in question, then this policy must be that the infrequent, occasional, or accidental assignment shall have no weight, and that the position shall be appraised over a period long enough to give a true picture.

Cyclic and Noncyclic Mixed Positions

In attempting to define the outlook that should be adopted with respect to mixed positions, one must consider how far into the past and how far into the future the duties and responsibilities of the position should be examined to collect a body of facts as the basis for the allocation. A distinction must be made between positions of which the duties are definitely cyclic and those which are not.

A cyclic mixed position may be defined as one in which the variations in duties take place more or less periodically. The cycle may be relatively short, as in the case of a payroll clerk whose activities vary in a fairly definite way during a pay period. The cycle may be relatively long, as in the case of a budget officer whose duties are cyclic by fiscal years, or an operating engineer in a heating plant, whose duties vary as between the winter and summer seasons. In cyclic positions there is a very definite certainty of recurrence of duties, because of the requirements of law or customary practice, and the cycle is not easily destroyed or disturbed through purely administrative action. The general rule in such cases is to consider the position over its complete cycle and to classify it on the basis of all the duties and responsibilities performed or exercised during the cycle.

In the case of noncyclic mixed positions, however, there is ordinarily not the same degree of certainty respecting the future recurrence of duties and responsibilities that existed at one time. In such instances the general rule is to consider the position in its past characteristics only to an extent that will throw light on its present or immediately future duties and responsibilities, on which its classification necessarily will be based. Further, if inquiry directed to the specific point develops no information to the contrary, it may be concluded that its present characteristics will continue far enough into the future to give rise to no doubts concerning the propriety of basing the classification upon them.

General Rule for Mixed Positions

It will be found that if certain of the components of a mixed position were assumed to occupy full working time the position would be allocable to one class, and that if certain other components were full time it would be allocable to a different class. Which components govern? How best can effect be given to all the components?

It is not possible to lay down a rule applicable under all circumstances to all types of mixed positions. However, the principle governing the allocation of the great majority of such positions is the familiar one that the preponderant duties and responsibilities of the position, i.e., those which occupy the major part of the employee's working time, are the basis for its classification. Although there are proper exceptions to this principle, it is sound as a general and an initial guide.

Proper Exception to the General Rule

Occasionally, in the process of allocating a mixed position, it is deemed proper to apply another principle which may be stated briefly as follows: The highest type of duty performed governs the allocation.[52]

[52] In describing a survey of office positions in the University of Michigan conducted in 1929–30, Z. Clark Dickinson says: "Another point emphasized in this

The typical circumstances under which it is proper to apply this exception, and the typical conditions, all of which should be met, are outlined below:

1. One or a combination of several of the duties of the position (although not preponderant as to time) is an outstanding characteristic and markedly different from the other duties of the position as to difficulty and/or responsibility.

2. This particular duty or combination of duties upon which the classification is to be based, although not preponderant as to time, must occupy a substantial portion of the employee's working time. It must not be an infrequent, minor, exceptional, or temporary duty or responsibility. Exactly what proportion is substantial cannot be mathematically defined. Generally speaking, however, 10 per cent is regarded as minor and 25 per cent as substantial.

3. This duty or combination of duties, furthermore, should be so different from the other duties of the position as to require unquestionably higher qualifications.[53]

4. The duty or combination of duties which is to govern the classification must be the basis for recruiting and selecting an employee for the position. In other words, the duties which control the classification are to be consistent with the qualification standards which govern (or would govern) the selection of an employee to fill the position.[54]

---

survey may as well be mentioned here: the case of double-classified positions, in which the worker is not fully occupied with his higher-grade operations, and has to fill in time doing lower-value work. In general it seems that such a person's pay is much more largely determined by the higher-grade work than by the other; and one benefit of any occupational survey, from the management's standpoint, is to bring out the quantitative aspects of such mixtures and thereby call attention to the need of giving each such employee the practicable maximum of the highest grade of work he can do." *Compensating Industrial Effort* (Copyrighted 1937, The Ronald Press Co.), pp. 200–01. See also C. Canby Balderston, *Wage Setting Based on Job Analysis and Evaluation* (Industrial Relations Counselors, New York, 1940), p. 45.

[53] An important question is whether or not there are other positions in the same unit to which the tasks of the higher type have been, are, or may be conveniently assigned for performance or referred for advice, instructions, or guidance, and whose existing classifications are, at least to some extent, predicated upon such tasks.

[54] "The argument in favor of evaluating chiefly, or even entirely, on the basis of the most difficult element is that it is a logical recognition of the fact that men must be hired in the market who can handle the most difficult element, regardless of how little time it occupies or how much less difficult the other elements are. This is quite sound, and in many cases it would be inexcusable to overlook it, as in the case of jobs which are mixtures of quite different elements, or tasks, or occupations; but, in operation, problems are encountered, such as tendencies to spread difficult work, with resultant necessity for determining what is a sufficient amount of more difficult work to warrant consideration in

When the foregoing conditions are met, the principle that the highest type of duty or responsibility should govern the classification of the position has considerable merit from the standpoint of setting qualification standards and recruiting. It is easy to conclude that qualifications conforming to the highest type of work performed are necessary and should be paid for. Consequently, recruiting should be carried out on this basis. If the highest type of work is made the guide, then the easier or less difficult duties and responsibilities will naturally fall within the capabilities of the employee, whereas if a lower type of duty involved is made the criterion for pay and recruiting there is no assurance that the more difficult duties in the position can satisfactorily be performed.

Since this principle is an exception to the general rule, it should be strictly confined and cautiously applied. The necessity for strictly limiting its application arises out of the fact that it permits the employee to draw the pay of a higher class for part of his time when he is actually performing duties of a lower class. A second, and perhaps more serious, point is that it too readily permits improper organization of offices and ineffective distribution of work if the desire of the responsible operating official to obtain higher classifications overcomes his desire to organize in the most effective way for production and general efficiency. Over the matter of organization and the methods of assigning work to employees, the classifying agency generally has little, if any, control. It does have control, however, of the application of the exceptional principle here discussed, which should not be regarded as applicable to a situation in which the duties of positions have been deliberately mixed for the mere purpose of securing higher classifications without regard to logical or effective distribution of work. This situation does not, of course, arise with respect to isolated workers occupying positions of mixed duties, but may occur where the department has spread two or more levels of work among all the employees of a group instead of assigning the work of each level to two or more separate groups.[55]

---

evaluation." Kent F. Bradbury, "Job Evaluation Analyzed," *Advanced Management*, January-March 1940, p. 17.

[55] For example, an office engaged in the adjudication of claims had two senior claims examiners whose duty it was to dispose of the more difficult claims, and four junior claims examiners who passed upon the simpler claims. After different classifications had been granted on this basis, the office decided to assign the claims indiscriminately to the six employees and requested that the four junior claims examiner positions be changed to senior claims examiner, on the ground that each of the juniors was spending one-third of his time on work recognized as of senior difficulty. Under such circumstances, however, the request was denied.

POSITION-TO-POSITION COMPARISONS

Comparing a position to be classified with positions already classified, for the purpose of determining differences as well as similarities, is always a desirable and frequently a necessary part of position-classification analysis.

After a position-classification plan has been placed in effect, such analytical comparisons will be aided by reference to class specifications, which reflect general standards of classification and illustrate the application of such standards to typical individual cases. However, it is not always possible to prepare each specification with such comprehensiveness and at the same time with such fineness of detail that it covers in so many words every task, duty, responsibility, and all their various combinations that belong in the class described in the specification.[56] For this reason it is helpful to regard individual positions, already correctly classified, as illustrations of the applicability of class specifications and of their scope and effect, in the same manner as samples illustrate the meaning of specifications for material, supplies, or equipment.[57]

Difficulty and responsibility are relative. Their appraisal depends upon a comparison with something used as a base. Positions already allocated to their proper classes furnish such a base from which one can proceed to determine and measure differences and similarities between the duties and responsibilities of the position to be allocated and those which are standard or representative in the various classes.

Purposes of Comparative Analysis

Since comparative analysis involves both equating and differentiating, its purposes are such as the following:

1. To insure for the position the same classification as that of like positions, previously classified, whether in the same or in other departments or offices.

2. To determine the interpretation of general terms employed in class specifications, such as "relatively small" or "relatively large"; "moderately difficult" or "unusually difficult"; etc.

[56] See Chapter IX.

[57] The question whether or not a given position comes within the specifications of a certain class is one for the determination of the classifying agency, which is given this responsibility because the specifications are for the most part expressed in terms that are relative, not absolute, and hence are not always interpreted alike by different individuals. The interpretations of class specifications by the classifying agency are shown to a considerable degree by its allocations of positions to classes.

3. To get the benefit of appropriate illustrations, when class specifications do not include specific descriptions or illustrations of the line or level of work of the position to be classified.

4. To ascertain gradations in difficulty and responsibility among existing positions and thus check the boundaries between classes and establish lines of measurement for the position to be classified.

5. To ascertain relationships when positions of different duties and responsibilities are interrelated because of flow of work or organization structure.

6. To determine, in the position concerned, the supervision exercised over others and the supervision received from above.

7. To determine from a study of other positions within the organization unit, the independence of action with which the employee works, when such independence of action is presented as an important factor.

8. To evaluate the effect of any elements additional to the main duties of the position, or to evaluate the duties of a position when they are so varied as to require the evaluation of tasks in several different lines of work.

Principles Governing Comparisons

Comparisons can aid the classification process only if they are thorough and analytical. Each of the positions concerned in the comparison should be dissected to determine not only the respects in which difficulty of work, nonsupervisory responsibilities, and supervisory or administrative responsibilities are of equal weight, but also the respects in which they are of different weight.

Within a single class, there may be hundreds of positions located in various departments and establishments. It is to be expected that although all these positions are sufficiently similar to belong to the same class, some of them are slightly more, or less, difficult or responsible than others. In a class having a fairly large number of positions, those that are typical of the class will naturally be in the majority. The others are in the border-line zones; weak marginal positions not very much stronger than the strongest position in the next lower class; and strong marginal positions not very much weaker than the weakest position in the next higher class.[58]

[58] It is frequently helpful to visualize classes in the same series as segments of an inclined plane (rather than a stairway), portraying the progression of difficulty and responsibility in a field of work. Within each class, individual positions fall along the inclined segment.

This concept of the position-content of a class becomes of vital importance when comparisons are made with a single position or a few positions, or when the classifier is presented with statements of comparisons, without information as to whether the positions taken as a base are typical or border-line. When border-line positions are known and treated as such, they are useful for comparison purposes because they tend to illustrate definitely the lower or upper boundaries of a class. However, when they are unknowingly accepted as being typical of the class, incorrect classifications may result.

One should avoid the tendency to regard a class as an absolute level, with *all* the positions therein *exactly* equal in respect to all allocation factors. For positions to belong to the same class they need only be *sufficiently similar*.[59] In fact, an essential background for making position-to-position comparisons is a full appreciation of the fact that all positions in a given class are not *exactly* identical as to difficulty and responsibility of work, and that therefore *any* difference in difficulty or responsibility in two positions does not necessarily mean a consequent difference in class.

Another basic principle, the observance of which will tend to assure proper comparisons, is that a position already classified does not serve as a standard for the comparison of a position to be classified unless the precise duties and responsibilities which controlled the class of the first position are also present in the second. This means that the position used for comparison must be studied sufficiently to determine the reasons and the facts upon which it was placed in the particular class. The basis for the classification may have been all its duties and responsibilities, taken collectively; or only some of them, the others being regarded as immaterial or not controlling. If the basis were all its duties and responsibilities, taken collectively, the question for decision is whether the points of difference between it and the position to be classified are sufficiently immaterial to justify the same classification, or whether they are sufficiently material and controlling to require different classifications. If the class of the allocated position was controlled by only part of its duties and responsibilities, the kind of work represented in this part must also be present to the same extent and degree of difficulty and responsibility in the position to be classified. A position under consideration for allocation may be on all-fours with an allocated position except as to one point, but if this point represents the crux

[59] See pp. 45–47, and 196.

of the classification cited, no indication of comparative equality, but rather a showing of comparative inequality, is thus developed.

Experience in passing upon requests for review of existing classifications indicates that officers and employees seldom have as comprehensive a knowledge of someone else's job as they have of their own. Frequently they cite certain classifications, in an effort to prove that certain classifications are too low, because they lack complete understanding of the positions cited, to which, because of their limited knowledge of them, their own positions seem equal.

It should be an obvious rule that the first step in comparing two positions should be to make an analysis to determine the likenesses and differences between all the duties and responsibilities of one and all the duties and responsibilities of the other. Sometimes an officer or employee will be perfectly correct in his contention that he "does the same thing" as an employee occupying a position in a higher class, but this may refer to one type of work or one task only, and the comparison between the remainder of the components of the positions may show clearly a material difference between them. For example, a time and payroll clerk may compare his position with one involving not only this type of activity, but also control over the procedure of personnel changes, such as appointments, promotions, transfers, reinstatements, retirements, and the like.

Sometimes comparisons made by the officer or employee concern an item of duties and responsibilities so incidental that it was ignored in the process of allocating the position cited for comparative purposes. Where this is true, the comparison, of course, has no significance. For example, an employee requesting that his position be reclassified contended that he was performing duties identical to those of other employees in the higher classification, because he reviewed reports as they did. It developed, however, that these employees conducted formal hearings as presiding examiners; that this was their main duty and responsibility, upon which the classification of their positions had been based; and that only incidentally did they review reports of other examiners.

Furthermore, a position which has undergone changes in duties or responsibilities that have never been reported to or considered by the classifying agency cannot serve as an illustration of classification standards, for in fact its current characteristics have not been appraised. Comparisons with classified positions must be confined to duties and responsibilities which were of record at the time they were considered and acted upon.

The finding of an inconsistency in classification does not always mean that the position immediately before the classifier for action is the one that requires a change of classification to correct the situation. He should always be conscious of the possibility that the position used as a comparison may itself have been incorrectly classified. It goes without saying that positions used for comparison must be correctly classified.

Chapter VI

Basic Legal Authority

THE development and continuous administration of a uniform position-classification plan in a public jurisdiction, covering all operating departments, are based on express legal authority. As distinguished from the power which may be found in the management authority of an individual operating department, the basic legal authority for a service-wide classification plan applies alike to all agencies of the jurisdiction. From it the rules, regulations, and decisions of the central classification agency obtain their legal effect.

SOURCES OF LEGAL AUTHORITY

Depending on the jurisdiction concerned, basic legal authority may be found in constitutions, charters, statutes, or ordinances. State constitutions or statutes may, on occasion, be designed to cover positions and personnel in the state service only or they may also cover county and municipal jurisdictions.[1] Charter or constitutional provisions may be brief, stating merely a fundamental policy without implementation, as in the New York and Ohio constitutions.[2] On the other hand, they may be more detailed, establishing administrative machinery and procedures, as in the amendment to the Charter of the City of Bridgeport, Connecticut, June 5, 1935, establishing a merit system.[3]

Where a constitutional or charter provision states a general policy only, further legislation is usually necessary before it can be translated into administrative action. In some instances, however, such provisions have been interpreted as being self-executing in the sense that compliance with their terms will be enforced by the courts, not-

---

[1] It should be observed in passing that the authority granted directly to a municipal public personnel agency in a city charter or in a state law is not so susceptible to change by the local legislative body as similar authority granted by local ordinance.

[2] See also National Municipal League, *A Model State Constitution*, 1936, pp. 18, 31.

[3] See also National Municipal League, *A Model City Charter*, 1933, pp. 63–75; and the recent amendment to Art. VI of the Michigan constitution, effective January 1, 1941.

withstanding the absence of statutory legislation.[4] Such an interpretation, of course, does not obviate the necessity for implementing legislation and the vesting of responsibility in executive agencies. There is at least one instance where constitutional provisions contain a statement that their requirements shall be self-executing.[5]

The basic legal authority for a position-classification plan is most frequently found within statutes or ordinances creating a merit system. In fact, the problems involved in establishing such authority can scarcely be divorced from those incident to drafting legislation for a general personnel program. No attempt will be made here to formulate and recommend "model" classification legislation.[6] Certain important criteria of adequacy will, however, be set forth.

CRITERIA FOR ADEQUACY

Classification laws or ordinances, in common with other legislation, must be constitutional, and free from defects of drafting. The language used must be sufficiently definite to avoid ambiguity.

Definite Position-Coverage

The positions to be included within or excluded from the scope of the position-classification plan should be clearly identified. Frequently this is done, or attempted, by including "all positions in the classified [competitive] service." Sometimes, however, the boundaries

[4] H. Eliot Kaplan, "The Merit System and the Constitution," *National Municipal Review*, February 1938.

[5] Sec. 5 (a), Art. XXIV, Constitution of the State of California, pertaining to the state merit system, provides: "The provisions of this article shall be self-executing, but legislation not in conflict herewith may be enacted to facilitate its operation."

[6] This is involved in the broader project of merit system legislation, being studied by a committee of the Civil Service Assembly of the United States and Canada, in cooperation with committees of the National Civil Service Reform League and the National Municipal League. The work of these committees has already resulted in the publication of a draft of a state civil service law, in which will be found "model" or typical provisions for the development, adoption, installation, and administration of a position-classification plan. National Civil Service Reform League and National Municipal League, *Draft of a State Civil Service Law*, pp. 7, 16–18. Reference may also be made to "The Personnel Problem in the Public Service, Preliminary Report of the Conference Committee on the Merit System," *Public Personnel Studies*, January 1926, pp. 18–19; National Municipal League, *The Merit System in Government*, Report of the Conference Committee on The Merit System, 1926; "A Draft of a Short Act to Create a Public Personnel Agency," *Public Personnel Studies*, February 1927, pp. 26–35; League of California Municipalities, *Suggested Forms of Civil Service Ordinances*, Report No. 14, 1938; *ibid.*, *Suggested Form of Civil Service Ordinance for City Manager Cities*, Report No. 15, 1938.

of classified [competitive] service and the position-classification plan are not the same. Much administrative and legal difficulty may be avoided by establishing the boundaries of the plan in such terms that it will include all positions except those that are definitely excluded.

The satisfactory administration of a classification and compensation statute, like the administration of any other statute, depends in part upon how distinctly the statute defines the things which are to be included within and excluded from its operation. One of the essentials of a classification and compensation statute is that it shall enable one to make clean-cut decisions as to whether or not the act applies to particular positions or groups of positions. . . . The boundaries of the scope of a classification and compensation statute should never be so vague that the interpretation of the applicability of the statute may be made to depend upon expediency or the resultant advantages or disadvantages in each individual case. Nor should the authority for making decisions as to the boundaries of the statute be so decentralized as to permit inconsistent action regarding like positions in organizations within the scope of the act. It is necessary accordingly to define explicitly in the proposed statute the kinds or groups of positions which are to be subject to the act and those which are not, or to set up administrative machinery for the making of such definitions, with the final authority, necessary for consistency and coordination, centralized in one agency. . . . There are four ways of defining exclusions from the position-content of a classification and compensation statute. These are: (1) Naming entire organization units, all positions within which, of whatever character, are to be excluded; (2) Naming certain kinds, classes, or groups of positions which are to be excluded under all circumstances; (3) Naming certain circumstances or conditions under which all positions are to be excluded; and (4) Naming certain kinds, classes, or groups of positions which are to be excluded under certain designated circumstances or conditions.[7]

Basis of Position-Classification

It is essential to indicate in basic law the basis upon which classes are to be established and positions classified.

For example, this has been done by stating that "there shall be created a classification plan which shall group all positions . . . in classes, based on their duties, authority and responsibilities," and that "every position . . . shall be allocated to the appropriate class in the classification plan on the basis of the duties, authority, and responsibility."[8]

[7] U. S. Personnel Classification Board, *Closing Report of Wage and Personnel Survey*, H.Doc. 771, 71st Cong., 3d sess. (1931), pp. 304–05.
[8] Art. XXIV, Constitution of the State of California.

In some city charters, position-classification authority has been based on a provision that the civil service commission "shall classify all the offices and places of employment in the city with reference to the examination hereinafter provided for."[9] Because of the limited use of classification thus implied, such a provision tends to be insufficient when the authority of the commission to classify positions for pay purposes is brought into question. Conflict of authority with city councils or budget officers in this respect may preclude the possibility of employing one sound position-classification plan for both purposes.

In other instances, the objective has been met by incorporating in the law the definition of a "class of positions." This is the preferable procedure.

Creation, Adoption, Installation, and Administration

The terms of basic legal authority should affirmatively require that a position-classification plan be (a) created or developed, (b) adopted, (c) installed or placed in effect, and (d) continuously administered.[10] Where time limits for development, adoption, and installation are specified, these should, of course, be feasible.

Functions Involved

It is desirable that the basic legal authority be broad enough to cover the principal functions involved in developing, adopting, installing, and continuously administering a position-classification plan. These include: (1) currently ascertaining facts about positions in the service; (2) establishing classes and class titles; (3) writing and publishing class specifications; (4) after adoption, establishing additional classes and dividing, combining, altering, or abolishing existing classes, with corresponding changes in class titles and specifications; (5) allocating and reallocating positions to classes; and (6) promulgating and enforcing rules for the development, adoption, installation, continuous administration, and interpretation of the position-classification plan, and amending such rules from time to time.

[9] Sec. 3, Art. XVI, Charter of the City of Seattle; the Detroit charter, adopted April 7, 1913, contains the same clause.

[10] In some instances, the development of a position-classification plan may be administratively or legislatively authorized without the power to install and administer. Further action in such cases depends, of course, on the enactment of legislation after the developmental report is submitted.

Placing of Authority

With respect to each of the foregoing functions, authority should be definitely vested.[11] Depending on policy, different officials or agencies may have a part in carrying them out and this part may be different during the periods of development, adoption, installation, and administration. In some instances, the central personnel agency may be given final authority to develop and recommend a position-classification plan to a governor, a city council, or other official or body, in whom rests the final power of adoption, modification, or rejection. After adoption, the central personnel agency may be entirely responsible for installation and future administration. For example, the Model City Charter prepared by the National Municipal League provides for a central administering agency (the department of personnel) which shall "prepare and recommend a classification plan and amendments thereto" to the city council and shall "administer the classification plan approved."

From an administrative standpoint this is not the most desirable division of responsibility. In the exercise of a direct authority to revise the position-classification plan from time to time, or in connection with budget or salary measures, a legislative body may establish classes of positions that are essentially fictitious; or by line-item budgets it may in effect allocate individual positions to classes inconsistent with the work actually being performed or to be performed. The continuous, over-all viewpoint necessary for the maintenance of an integrated, workable classification plan can best be afforded by an executive agency of the jurisdiction.

In the larger and intermediate-sized jurisdictions, where a central personnel agency exists as a distinctive unit, it is preferable to place the control over the position-classification plan in the hands of such a unit, rather than in a state legislature, a city council, or a county board of supervisors. When this is done, a further desirable division of authority may be made within the central personnel agency itself,

[11] "The basic law should give the personnel agency the authority it needs to exercise the functions imposed upon it. Personnel administrators in their day by day operations will, as a matter of course, use persuasion and cooperative methods in dealing with appointing authorities and others but long experience has demonstrated the practical futility of the work of a public personnel agency which cannot enforce its rules, regulations, and mandates when operating officers and others are stubbornly recalcitrant." "The Personnel Problem in the Public Service . . . ," *Public Personnel Studies*, January 1926, p. 19. See also National Municipal League, *The Merit System in Government*, p. 81.

based on the separation of administrative and technical responsibilities from quasi-legislative and quasi-judicial responsibilities. Under such a policy, the director of personnel of the central personnel agency is authorized to develop and recommend the position-classification plan and any future amendments to the board or commission at the head of that agency, which in turn is authorized to adopt, modify, or reject the position-classification plan, including the rules, and any proposed amendments. The director of personnel is made initially responsible for final action on allocations or reallocations of positions to classes, the board or commission entering into this function only in case of appeal.

Whatever may be the division of responsibility in the control of the position-classification plan and in its application to individual positions, each type of authority should be definitely placed and its nature specifically set forth.[12]

Use of Class Titles

The basic classification law should require the use of the position-classification plan in personnel, budget, and fiscal operations. This objective is usually sought to be accomplished through a provision like the following:[13]

The class titles so established shall be used in all personnel, accounting, budget, appropriation and financial records of all state departments, commissions, and institutions.

DEGREE OF DETAIL

The degree of detail with which the authority for developing, adopting, installing, and administering a position-classification plan is set forth in basic legal instruments varies considerably. Some laws will provide merely that a given governmental agency shall

---

[12] This is particularly important as between the legislative and executive agencies involved (e.g., a city council and a municipal civil service commission), and as between policy determination and management execution (e.g., a governor, mayor, city council, or board of civil service commissioners on the one hand and a director of personnel on the other). See Maxwell A. DeVoe, "Administrative Relationships of Public Personnel Agencies," *Public Personnel Review*, January 1941, pp. 21–23.

[13] State of Rhode Island and Providence Plantations, Chapter 661, Laws of 1939, Civil Service Act of March 9, 1939, Sec. 9 (2). "The class titles shall be used in personnel, budget, and financial records, and, if individual positions are designated in the appropriation ordinances, in designating such positions." National Municipal League, *Model City Charter*. Provisions like this are not interpreted to prevent the use of "office" titles for intradepartmental or public contact purposes.

"classify all the positions in the classified [competitive] service." Others will include specific items, such as the basis for the classification of positions, types of actions which the classification agency is empowered to undertake, and so on. Some go further and describe the detailed procedures to be followed.

There can be, of course, extremes in legislation of this sort. Merely providing that positions in the service shall be classified without stating the basis or principles therefor is not generally regarded as sufficiently full legislation, there being no standard set for the position-classification process. In unskillful administrative hands such a provision may be unsoundly administered. On the other hand, the setting forth of details to too great an extent might have the result of restricting and hindering good classification practice.

In general, procedural details relating to the individual steps involved in performing a given function and similar details of administrative practice should be omitted from charter or statutory provisions and authorized to be covered by rules and regulations. It is desirable, however, to provide specifically in basic legal authority that in certain kinds of action employees, officials, and the public shall be given a reasonable opportunity to be heard. For example, employees and officials should be afforded opportunity to be heard when positions are reallocated. They should likewise be given opportunity to comment or advise on important revisions of formal rules. Similarly, in some instances, where there exist legal obstacles to good classification administration, the basic legal authority may include detailed provisions to modify or repeal them. It should also be observed that the rules of a classification plan may also include provisions defining the status of employees when a position-classification plan is first placed in effect, or when their positions are reallocated.[14]

Especially is it necessary that basic legal authority be drafted in such form as to make it applicable to the service for a considerable future period as well as the present. The service itself and the positions it contains, and perhaps the very processes of classification administration, may change from time to time. Ordinarily, changes made desirable by new conditions in the service should be covered by rule or regulation rather than by amendments of the basic legal authority. Flexibility and promptness of amendment are necessary. Rules, of course, are more susceptible to prompt amendment than

14 See pp. 239–44, and 330–35.

are constitutions, charters, statutes, or ordinances. Hence, to require that all changes be made by amending constitutions, charters, statutes, or ordinances would handicap administration.

Accordingly, legislation, at least for large services, should be basic rather than detailed in character. In large services organized to allow wide administrative latitude in creating, abolishing, merging, or altering positions, it is essential to avoid a rigid statutory system that will tend to delay or hinder the amendment of the position-classification plan to keep pace with actual changes in the service.[15]

In the smaller services or in services where the position content of organization units (not merely lump-sum appropriation allotments) is legislatively controlled, and where the time or difficulty involved in securing amendatory legislation is not too great, legislation of greater detail is feasible, although cumbersome upon occasion, if a policy of current legislative rather than administrative control is desired in the jurisdiction.[16]

[15] "In the main the basic law should set forth principles relating to personnel administration and should not prescribe detailed machinery. This is a sound general principle, which is particularly applicable to personnel legislation owing to the fact that personnel administration through a central agency is as yet in its infancy and there is every likelihood that in the course of a very few years better means of dealing with many personnel problems will be devised than are now in existence. Laws can be changed only with considerable difficulty and a measure which sets up procedure in detail may, though it is advanced today, be a bar to good personnel administration five or ten years hence." "The Personnel Problem in the Public Service, . . ." *Public Personnel Studies*, January 1926, pp. 18–19; National Municipal League, *The Merit System in Government*, pp. 80–81.

[16] *Classification and Compensation Plans: Their Development, Adoption, and Administration* (Civil Service Assembly . . . , 1928) Technical Bull. No. 1, pp. 18–19.

Chapter VII

Development and Adoption

A NUMBER of preliminary steps are necessary to get an original position-classification project definitely under way. The kind and the extent of such preliminary work will depend upon a number of factors, including the size and type of jurisdiction (as indicated by the number and variety of positions it includes and the geographic distribution of its services),[1] and the conditions surrounding the classification project itself, such as basic legal provisions, personnel rules, legal interpretations and court decisions, administrative traditions, and group and agency attitudes. In general, however, certain major things must first be done. These are: selecting the agency to do the work; arranging for finances and staff; determining the positional coverage of the survey; making appropriate contacts for general cooperation of all affected or interested persons, agencies, and groups; assembling existing informative material, such as budget documents, salary ordinances, payrolls, organization charts, and operating manuals; and designing and reproducing a position-description questionnaire and instructions for filling it out.

SELECTION OF DEVELOPMENTAL AGENCY

The selection of the agency to do the actual developmental work is, of course, a matter of considerable importance.[2] The basic legal authority for this task will place the responsibility in some agency or organization of the jurisdiction—most frequently, the central personnel agency. However, this does not prevent the responsible agency from utilizing the technical services of other organizations, particularly if it does not have readily available an experienced staff of its own.[3]

[1] For a description of the preparation of a position-classification plan in a small jurisdiction, see Public Administration Service, *Personnel Programs for Smaller Cities*, Publication No. 73 (1940), pp. 11–14.

[2] This discussion should be considered as supplemented by that in Chapter X, on the selection of the agency to administer the position-classification plan after it has been adopted.

[3] "The classifying agency seems logically to be the municipal personnel agency, which in New York State cities is the municipal civil service commission. If an

Usually the legally responsible agency will be faced with four possibilities: (1) it may do the work with its own staff, aided where necessary by occupational specialists in the operating departments; (2) it may secure, on a contractual basis, the services of a technical organization outside the public service; (3) in cities or counties, it may enter into an arrangement with the personnel agency of the state; or (4) where such a unit exists, it may enter into arrangements with the personnel service unit of a league of municipalities.[4]

In reaching a decision, the legally responsible agency must weigh several factors: the characteristics of the jurisdiction, finances and staff available, and current administrative conditions.

In some jurisdictions there may be already available a competent staff technically trained for classification work in the employ of the central personnel agency. If so, there would be natural advantages in giving this staff the immediate responsibility for developing the position-classification plan. It already has a knowledge of the service, gained through other personnel processes such as recruiting, testing, and the handling of in-service transactions. It has already made numerous and helpful contacts with administrative and technical personnel in the operating departments. The values in knowledge and experience gained during the process of development will not be lost when the period of continuous administration begins. It will be able

---

outside agency is employed, the work should be under the supervision of the municipal civil service commission. In the villages the state civil service commission might provide the supervision if it does not actually do the work. Under the present set-up the local commission is in a better position to qualify for the work than any other city agency because of its existing relationship to the personnel problem involved. Among other things it (1) occupies an important and independent relationship to the various departments in the services; (2) it is responsible for recruiting and selecting many of the municipal employees and consequently is most familiar with the duties and qualifications required by the many positions which it is called upon to fill; (3) it is the one agency which will most use the results of the classification. Whether or not the local municipal civil service commission can handle such an assignment without outside aid, is, of course, an individual matter. It may be advisable and necessary in some cases for the commission to secure the services of a classification expert to assist in developing certain more or less technical parts of the classification procedure." Theodore B. Forbes, *Municipal Job Classification and Salary Standardization*, New York State Conference of Mayors . . . , Bureau of Training and Research, Publication No. 32 (1934), p. 4.

[4] Private companies face a parallel problem. The pros and cons on the question whether it is preferable for an insider or an outsider to have charge of job analysis and job classification work have been summarized in E. H. Little, *Some Considerations in Installing a Salary Administration Plan* (American Management Association, 1927). This summary is reproduced in C. Canby Balderston, *Wage Setting Based on Job Analysis and Evaluation* (Industrial Relations Counselors, Inc., 1940), p. 26.

to perceive readily the significance of the problems arising during the course of development. It should be able to reach decisions in the light of the contribution that the position-classification plan should make to the whole personnel program.[5]

If the staff of the personnel agency includes no one with substantial experience in the development of a position-classification plan, it would be better to secure the services of consultants from outside the service both to plan and schedule the original survey and to direct and train the staff of the personnel agency in the performance of some of the detailed operations involved.[6] Also, in case the jurisdiction is too small to justify a full-time personnel staff, or the personnel agency is understaffed, or, as in the case of a new merit system installation, the personnel agency has not been fully organized, the use of outside technical staffs would ordinarily be desirable.

It is not always true that the best classification work can be done by persons already familiar with the organization of the jurisdiction and who have knowledge and understanding of the positions in the service before the survey is undertaken. An outside staff can usually bring to the classification problems of a single jurisdiction the broad knowledge, insight, and technical skill gained by experience in many jurisdictions. Well trained in classification techniques, it has something to contribute not only because it knows and can apply these techniques, but also because it has a detached view.[7]

[5] "Some companies have assigned regular members of their organization to this technical work; other companies have employed consultants on a temporary basis. The assignment of a regular member of an organization to this work is advantageous in that he is more familiar with individual positions in the company and with its personnel than a consultant would be. Furthermore, after the comprehensive study is completed, a competent insider is needed to analyze new or changed positions." John W. Riegel, *Salary Determination* (Bureau of Industrial Relations, University of Michigan, 1940), Report No. 2, pp. 74-75.

[6] "The next step was the selection of the personnel of the group to do the necessary detail work (of job analysis and evaluation). For group leader, the company had the choice of selecting some present employee, who was not familiar with job analysis and evaluation, or of employing the services of an experienced job analyst new to the company. It was recognized quite clearly that both choices have certain advantages and disadvantages, but management felt that work of this importance warranted the attention of a specialist. Past experience had shown that, in matters requiring an objective approach, the outside viewpoint is valuable. Moreover, those responsible for the work were of the opinion that, by securing a specialist, the company could eliminate the time and expense that would otherwise be required to determine methods of procedure and to develop necessary techniques." Samuel L. H. Burk, *A Case History in Salary and Wage Administration* (American Management Association, 1939), pp. 6, 7.

[7] "Some disadvantages of an insider are that . . . he might have preconceptions or prejudices with reference to the values of the particular positions in the organization." Riegel, *op. cit.*, p. 75.

Sometimes, even if the local personnel agency is equipped to do the work, circumstances may make it highly desirable to engage an outside staff. It may be advantageous for the personnel offices to remain free from details, commitments, or complicated relationships with interested groups, until the plan is developed and ready for adoption and installation. Local political or other conditions may be such that only an outside staff would receive cooperation and create confidence. A local staff may be subjected to pressures which would not affect an outside organization. Under conditions of this sort, where completely impartial recommendations are needed, an agency with no local ties or affiliations is in the best position to make them.

Where an outside staff is engaged to develop and aid in installing a position-classification plan, the necessity of staff arrangements for continuous administration should not be overlooked.[8] To some extent, a nucleus can be provided through the plan of assigning, as assistants to the outside organization, persons upon whom the responsibility for the details of classification administration will later fall.[9] It should be emphasized, in passing, that this advantage as well as others will be secured only if the outside agency makes it a point to work in close collaboration with the central personnel or other agency established as the administrative body for keeping the classification plan up to date after installation.

TECHNICAL STAFF AND BUDGET

During the preliminary stage of the classification project, and in order to ascertain staff and budget requirements and to control operations, working procedures should first be outlined, broken down into assignments, and tentatively scheduled.

Qualifications of Staff

The qualifications and composition of the technical staff will vary with the size and nature of the service. There are, however, certain qualifications which should always characterize such a staff.

---

[8] "When these experts have left town all the pressures for exceptions, for leaving classifications alone despite changes in duties, for preferential treatment for this or that class come to bear upon the often very weak defenses provided by the local personnel agency. Before many years the classification plan has not infrequently become only a pale reflection of the actual facts." Leonard D. White, *Introduction to the Study of Public Administration* (Macmillan: 1939), p. 328.

[9] "Outsiders employed for this work have a method of procedure and an extensive knowledge of position values. They can train regular members of an organization to aid them in the original review of salaries. These trainees themselves then can continue the technical work in connection with salary administration after the consultant has completed his contract." Riegel, *loc. cit.*, footnote.

The development of a position-classification plan is a project in an administrative setting. An ultimate objective of this project is to enhance the value of the whole personnel program as an aid to the operating departments. Consequently, the technical staff should be broadly grounded in public administration, and each member should have basic training and experience which will enable him quickly to understand the activities and appreciate the needs of the operating organizations. Further, since the values of position-classification are in proportion to the extent with which it is integrated with the whole personnel program, the staff should represent a reservoir of broad knowledge of public personnel policies and practices, acquired through work-training and experience.

In particular, the technical staff should possess a specific, detailed knowledge of the principles, objectives, and techniques of position-classification. The classification process employs procedures and analytical methods which must be learned and developed by application and practice. The classifier must be able to recognize and define the essential differentiating factors found in various positions. This analysis requires understanding of the entire developmental program; grasp of the structure and operations of the organizations involved; comprehension of the nature, difficulties, and responsibilities inherent in each position; interpretation of the exact work-relation of each position to other positions; and appreciation of the demands which administrative officials make upon these positions and their incumbents. It involves digging into the facts; casual observation of positions is not a foundation for good classification work. Adequate analytical ability is therefore a prerequisite. The classifier must be able to recognize pertinent and salient facts, to isolate them from the immaterial, and to relate them one to another. He must be able to interview effectively without friction. He must be able to express himself clearly in speech and in writing.[10]

Although these are the general over-all characteristics required of a staff for classification work, its composition may vary depending on the type of project. In a relatively small service one person may do all of the work of classification, in which case he will need fairly extensive training and experience in similar classification work, preferably in the same type of jurisdiction, and a wide knowledge of occupations. The demands made on such a worker are likely to be broad, but not as intensive and specialized as might be required of workers employed on a large program.

10 White, *op. cit.*, pp. 337-38.

On a very large classification project there is a division of labor and specialized knowledges are utilized to a greater degree. Such a project may be divided into direction of work, planning and control, the general technical classification process, specialized analysis and interpretation, and clerical work. The general technical classification process in turn may sometimes be divided into the less difficult preliminary grouping or fact-finding work and the more exacting final analysis and determination phase. Certain specialized occupational knowledges are not required in smaller jurisdictions but are needed in large jurisdictions wherever professional or highly skilled operations are encountered.

The composite qualifications of the staff required for classification of a large service will provide a variety of individual capacities. The director of such staff should be a person with broad knowledge of the types of operations involved in the service being classified and an appreciation of the needs of the administrators of such a service; familiarity with the functions and processes of public personnel agencies; ability to listen, disagree when necessary, and still maintain pleasant relations; and ability to plan the program, schedule operations, and to direct and coordinate the work of subordinate staff members. The bulk of the professional classification work will be performed by persons trained and experienced in similar classification work. Adequate understanding of the duties and responsibilities and of the relative degree of difficulty involved in the numerous accounting, engineering, law, medical, and highly skilled mechanical trades positions found in a large public service frequently can be provided only by persons who have had intensive experience in analyzing and classifying such groups or who are trained and skilled in the respective professions and trades.[11] The inclusion of such specialists in the staff also serves to establish confidence and good relations with officials and employees, for they are more easily assured of adequate understanding of the difficulties and responsibilities of their positions. Unless there is an unusually large number of positions within a single profession, it is usually sufficient to use such specialists only as consultants and auxiliary workers. In some cases such specialized services can be obtained from within the service be-

[11] The position-classification staff of the U. S. Civil Service Commission includes several such specialists, who operate partly as classification consultants, reviewing and advising on positions in their fields of specialization, and partly as direct investigators carrying through the complete classification process. Further development in this direction is contemplated.

ing classified[12] or from other units or jurisdictions in the area. Where specialized occupational classifiers are necessary only as part-time consultants or analysts, the bulk of the classification work is done by the general classifiers. Their time may be conserved to some degree by the employment of junior or student classification workers—persons who have had desirable academic training or general operating experience but who are relatively inexperienced in the application of classification techniques.

Factors Bearing on Size of Staff

In discussing size of staff required, it is convenient to think in terms of staff time, because the size of the staff will be more or less inversely proportional to the time available for completing the project. The number of positions to be classified is the primary factor affecting staff time. Its effect, however, will be modified by other factors such as the predominant position characteristics of the service; relative occupational complexity of the service; administrative characteristics of the jurisdiction and its constituent organizations, including their operating methods; geographic distribution of positions; attitudes of employees, officials, and the public; and the problems involved in the internal control of the project itself. These factors are discussed below.

Predominant position-characteristics of the service. This is probably the most important modifying factor. Classes of positions whose salient features are clearly shown by the nature of their duties or by the supervisory level they represent are capable of rapid classification, whereas positions whose classification is determined only by a careful analysis of relative level of responsibility and difficulty take more time. In the first grouping will be found such positions as those in the uniformed forces, skilled trades, and labor supervisory positions. In the second group are found the engineering, accounting, and clerical series of positions. In the first group, the classes are readily recognizable; in the second, careful analysis is required, frequently supplemented by direct observation and personal study of individual positions by persons intimately acquainted with the techniques involved.

---

[12] See "Recruiting the Detailed Classification Staff," in *Report of the Congressional Joint Commission on Reclassification of Salaries*, H.Doc. 686, 66th Cong., 2d sess. (1920), pp. 163–66. Where such services are properly controlled and utilized, little question will arise as to the objectivity of results.

Relative complexity or diversity of occupations or activities. A service composed of a great number and variety of activities with relatively few individual positions in some classes, where bureaus and offices vary widely in organization structure, and where work units have a wide range of size and geographic distribution, will require more time and effort to classify than will a more homogeneous service having the same number of positions. Multifunctional organizations obviously encompass a greater variety of professions and occupations than do unifunctional; the increased number of classes thus necessary will multiply the classification work.

Administrative characteristics of the jurisdiction. A large number of poorly-defined positions, the incumbents of which perform a variety of duties on random assignments, will increase difficulty and staff time. On the other hand, a logical assignment of related duties will facilitate classification. A poorly planned, inadequately controlled organization requires additional work of analysis for classification purposes, while standardized procedures and uniform operating methods planned and controlled through competent supervision simplify the classification problem. A haphazard method of direction without adequate plan will ordinarily result in a confused concept by individual employees of their duties and responsibilities. The variety and complexity of supervisory levels and the problems of evaluating relative responsibilities and authorities are greater in federated or loosely integrated organizations than in unified services. Also, the relative stability of the service and of the duties and responsibilities of individual positions during the period covered by the survey is an associated factor affecting the staff time required.

Geographic distribution of positions. Where the positions to be classified are geographically separated, time is consumed in travel, and less complete execution of position description questionnaires may result from inadequate opportunities for personal explanations by the classification staff.

Attitudes of officials and employees. The cooperation of officials and of union and other employee organizations will tend to lessen time and effort, especially in the clearance of the establishment of classes and allocation of positions. On the other hand, demands for detailed legalistic hearings or an active opposition movement will extend the time required. Also, an initial classification plan is likely to be developed in less time than a revised classification plan in a jurisdiction where time and custom have entrenched individuals in faulty classifications which they may feel called upon to preserve.

Requirements for controlling the classification project itself. Coordination, supervision, and clearance necessary to maintain uniformity of action and interpretation among all members of a large staff engaged in a large jurisdiction involve additional staff time. On the other hand, small services will entail a disproportionately large amount of time per position for preparation and organization, while unusually large services pyramid the requirements for supervision and coordination.

Bearing in mind all these modifying conditions, the technical staff time (excluding clerical work) required completely to develop and install a satisfactory position-classification plan in an ordinary, comprehensive governmental jurisdiction will usually be between three and one-half and six man-months per 1,000 employees. A jurisdiction so small that it can be completely classified by a single competent technician, aided by an apprentice, will require the minimum total staff time of three and one-half months per 1,000 positions, unless the service comprises fewer than 200 or 300 positions. Favorable circumstances and the assistance of occupational specialists will decrease this estimate and unfavorable conditions will increase it.

In fixing the exact number of staff to be assigned to any project, the time available will be one of the determining factors. In general the work should not extend over much more than a year. A shorter period is desirable in the smaller services. Long developmental programs lead to complications. Continuous changes in duties during the survey make difficult an attempt to maintain current allocations before regular machinery is established for the purpose. Delays between field visits and recommendations may lead to uncertainty and perhaps lack of confidence or opposition on the part of officials and employees.

The figures cited for staff time include all technical and supervisory staff but do not include clerical staff time. Such time may be estimated at approximately three to four man-months per 1,000 positions. The need for clerical service is lightest during the earlier part of the work and heaviest during the writing of class specifications.

Budget

The budget required for the development of a position-classification plan can be computed from the estimate of staff time, rate of payment for such services, subsistence allowances, transportation if any, and equipment and supplies. In preparing such an estimate it is necessary to anticipate the amount of time required for each class of staff member (e.g., junior technicians, general classifiers, occupational specialists) and to determine the over-all cost rate of each class. The costs involved in assembling and returning temporary or consulting staff and the transportation charges incidental to the classification work are important items. Equipment, including files, typewriters, dictating equipment, duplicating equipment, and similar facilities, may or may not involve rental costs. Supplies consist principally of printed questionnaire blanks and instructions, pencils, paper, and other staples. If specifications need to be reproduced, printing or mimeographing expense will be involved.

It is frequently not possible, however, to make such detailed estimates of staff time requirements and costs at the time budget estimates for the proposed classification work are required. Consequently, the cost of developing a position-classification plan is often estimated by multiplying the number of positions by a unit cost figure. For a balanced public service of more than 100 or 200 positions, such as city, county, or state, the unit cost for a full development and installation program, including the time involved in allocations of positions to classes, will ordinarily vary from $2.25 to $4.00 per position, exclusive of clerical staff and supplies. The total cost including clerical services and supplies may be expected to vary between $2.75 and $5.00 per position. The same factors will need to be considered in making an estimate of cost as in estimating staff time. Under unusually favorable conditions unit costs may be lower, while a combination of unfavorable conditions will result in higher costs. Under no circumstances should these general estimates be applied to a service consisting largely of a single occupational group.

DETERMINATION OF POSITION COVERAGE

The determination of the positional coverage of the proposed position-classification plan involves the decision whether (a) all positions in the jurisdiction are to be covered or (b) some are to be excluded, and if so, which ones and upon what basis. This decision rests upon a variety of considerations, depending on the legal and administrative conditions in the jurisdiction.

It may be, for example, that the coverage of the position-classification plan has already been defined by statute or ordinance, the terms of which are so definitive as to leave little room for judgment or interpretation. In this event, such problems of coverage as may arise are legal rather than administrative. On the other hand, even though there is a statute or ordinance in existence, its terms may be sufficiently general to require a more specific application through administrative interpretation, discretion, or formalized rules. In such case, arrangements may be made with the appropriate legal official of the jurisdiction for the assignment of a qualified legal adviser to participate informally in preliminary conferences. To the extent that the matter of coverage is not settled by the law itself as interpreted by the legal offices of the jurisdiction, the following points require consideration.

In the first place, a sound approach to securing maximum usefulness is to recognize that the coverage of the position-classification plan may be broader than the coverage of an existing or proposed merit system of recruitment, or the coverage of any particular type of pay plan.[13] In some instances, it may be difficult to persuade executive and legislative officials to adopt this view, because of lack of appreciation of the essential nature and broad values of a position-classification plan.

Although it is frequently the case that the position-classification plan and the pay plan are coterminous with the merit system, this is not always true.[14] Furthermore, classification plans or surveys, which are not coupled with the adoption or extension of civil service laws, are by no means unusual.[15]

---

[13] For example, see *Classification Plan for the City of Atlanta, Georgia,* June 1940, prepared by Public Administration Service. Note also: "The Commonwealth is to be commended for having made substantial progress in assuring the proper classification and compensation of its employees. It is especially significant that the plans are applicable not only to the civil service employees but to the unclassified employees as well." Commonwealth of Massachusetts, *Report of the Special Commission on Taxation and Public Expenditures,* Part XV, Sec. II, April 13, 1938, p. 62. (Prepared by Public Administration Service.)

[14] It is this fact that sometimes has led to confusion as to the meaning of the terms "classification" and "classified service." See the discussion of this point in Chapter I, pp. 4–5.

[15] This, of course, is the situation in industry; see Chapter II, pp. 27–30. For examples in the public service, the following documents may be cited: State of North Carolina, *First Report of the Salary and Wage Commission,* October 1, 1925; State of Virginia, *Report on the State Personnel Situation in Virginia,* Senate Doc. 1, January 1926; City of Boston, *Report of Standardization Committee to Mayor,* April 1, 1927, Doc. 58; Commonwealth of Pennsylvania, *Report of the Salary Survey Commission,* 1929; ibid., *Classification and Compensation System of Personnel Service,* September 1, 1933; State of Minnesota, Commission of Administration and Finance, Division of Personnel, *Classes, Grades and Titles of State Employees, with Class Specifications,* January 1935; Farm Credit Admin-

As a broad guiding viewpoint, it should constantly be remembered that the use of a position-classification plan as an administrative tool in personnel administration is governed by laws and rules outside of those controlling the classification plan itself. However, certain positions or groups of positions have frequently been excluded from a position-classification plan because it was anticipated that those positions could not be subjected to a merit system of employment or to a particular type of pay plan or salary control. This reasoning is not essentially sound. Regardless of the method by which a given position is to be filled or compensated, the fact is that the selection of the employee is made by someone on some basis and that the pay of the position is also fixed by someone on some basis. In any event, a full statement of the duties and responsibilities of the positions to be filled and a statement of qualification requirements, at least in terms of knowledge and ability, are prerequisites for intelligent action. In particular, class specifications for exempt appointive positions would be especially informative for newly elected officials responsible for key appointments. Recently, following an election in the State of California, position descriptions and statements of desirable qualification requirements were prepared for all the principal appointive positions in the state service, on the basis of the composite knowledge and observations of a group of persons familiar with the service and the responsibilities and requirements of the positions. From this standpoint, the maximum interests of good administration would be secured if every position in the jurisdiction, elective, appointive, or otherwise, were to be included within the position-classification plan.[16]

The scope of a position-classification plan as such, accordingly,

---

istration, *Class Specifications for Positions in District Units,* 1936; Home Owners Loan Corporation, *Manual of Class Specifications for Positions in State and Other Field Offices,* August 1, 1938.

[16] "To be genuinely effective and to engender universal confidence that each receives his just due, a salaried position analysis must embrace all positions from the highest to the lowest, and every worker must come within the scope of its provision, the work of each being the subject of the same analysis and classification that is applied to every other." E. B. Roberts, "Position Analysis and Classification," *The Management Review,* July 1935, p. 196.

Only rarely are positions which are filled by the electorate covered or proposed to be covered in a position-classification plan. However, see Commonwealth of Massachusetts, *Report of the Special Commission on County Salaries, under Chapter 33 of the Resolves of 1929,* Senate Doc. 270 (Boston, January 1930); *Compensation and Classification Plans for the Officers and Employees of Suffolk County, Approved under the Provisions of Ch. 400, Acts of 1930,* Doc. 55 (Boston, 1931); Public Administration Service, *Classification Plan for the City of Atlanta, Georgia,* June 1940.

should be distinguished from the scope of other personnel processes which it aids. Especially should the legal provisions which are to control the coverage of the plan be considered distinct from those governing the coverage of other personnel functions.

It is clear, in the first place, that the scope of a position-classification plan should never be narrower than the scope of the merit system as such because of the sound base it provides for the processes of recruiting, testing, selection, and promotion. It is equally clear that it is a necessary tool in the conduct of noncompetitive recruiting practices because a knowledge of the duties and responsibilities of the position to be filled noncompetitively is necessary for both the nominating officer and the central personnel agency and because qualification standards are prerequisite to effective operation. So far as the department head is concerned, the same benefits would accrue through the inclusion of exempt positions within a position-classification plan.

There is another important benefit that would accrue to the central personnel agency and the departments alike through the inclusion of all noncompetitive and exempt positions within a position-classification plan. Necessarily, exclusions from the scope of a competitive merit system must be set forth with precision if the abuses and confusion incident to excepting positions as "deputies" or "assistants" are to be avoided.[17] There is no better way of indicating exceptions or exemptions in civil service rules than by the use of class titles having direct reference to and defined in terms of the very duties and responsibilities upon the basis of which it was deemed advisable or expedient to authorize the exemption.[18]

Furthermore, in many instances, it may be anticipated that the proposed position-classification plan will be used as a base for a

[17] For example, "deputy assessor" has been used to designate all kinds and levels of positions in assessors' offices, down to positions involving only simple routine clerical work. See National Association of Assessing Officers, *Personnel Administration in Local Assessment Offices* (Chicago, 1940), p. 15.

[18] "Another group as to which there has been a loose interpretation of exemptions is that of secretaries, clerks, and administrative employees. Paragraph 8 of Section 48608 (a) exempts 'three secretaries, assistants, or clerks, and one personal stenographer for each of the elective state officers, boards, or commissions.' . . . Few of the exemptions actually allowed under this clause are of secretaries, assistants or personal stenographers of the elective or appointive executive officers, boards, or commissions themselves, but most of the positions treated as exempt under this provision form integral parts of the operating organizations under the charge of such officers, boards, or commissions." State of Ohio, *Report of Joint Committee on Economy in the Public Service, Part I, General Administration,* 1929. (Griffenhagen & Associates.)

systematic and coordinated pay plan. Under these circumstances, no reason is apparent why excepting a position from the competitive scope of the merit system should likewise except it from the scope of the pay plan. It does not follow that because a legislative or executive authority deems it desirable or expedient to permit an operating head to select his own employees without competition, he should for the same reason be permitted to pay them out of the public treasury any amount that he desires. In order, however, for such positions to be compensated in accordance with the work which they involve, it is necessary first to place them within the purview of the position-classification plan.[19]

Occasionally, in anticipation of the adoption of a particular type of pay plan or policy, it has been proposed that certain groups of positions be excluded from the position-classification plan. However, the fact is that a classification plan serves as a sound base for any pay plan or for a number of pay plans differing in policy and detail. To include all positions within a common position-classification plan, even though they are to be compensated according to different pay plans, would permit uniform treatment of such positions across departmental lines and obviate nonuniformity in the application of each of the different pay plans that might later be adopted.[20]

In short, a comprehensive position-classification plan covering both the positions included within the merit system and those excluded from it is essential to clear-cut administration.

PUBLIC RELATIONS

Negotiations and conferences for the establishment of smooth public relations and for cooperation with the classification staff are important preliminary steps in the development of a position-classification plan. The major purposes of preliminary negotiations and contacts are: (1) to spread correct information about the objectives and methods of the classification project and its prospective benefits to various groups; (2) to explain the limitations of the scope of the survey; (3) to clear away misunderstanding, suspicion,

[19] Congress has frequently taken this view. For example, the basic law (Act of September 1, 1937, 50 Stat. 888) of the U. S. Housing Authority places all positions paying in excess of $1,980 per annum outside the scope of the merit system, but requires the salaries of all positions (except the head of the agency) to be fixed in accordance with the Classification Act of 1923.

[20] U. S. Personnel Classification Board, *Closing Report of Wage and Personnel Survey* (1931), p. 306.

and apprehension in advance; (4) to secure the support and cooperation of everyone who will later have anything to do with the progress
of the survey and the adoption, installation, and administration of
the classification plan; and (5) to pave the way for further contacts.
Before beginning the fact-finding procedures of the survey and during its entire course, the staff must develop and maintain satisfactory
relations with all who are concerned with or affected by the projected
classification.[21] This broad category includes legislative or council
members or committees, budget authorities, the central personnel
agency, administrators and supervisors in the operating departments,
organized and unorganized employees, professional and technical
associations, civic and taxpayers' groups, and the public press.[22]
Special effort to secure the confidence, cooperation, and definite support of these groups is well spent.

The form which these preliminary public relations activities
should take and the manner in which initial contacts may best be
made depend upon conditions in the jurisdiction. Accordingly, as
a basis for planning, the developmental staff should explore the history of over-all and personnel administration in the jurisdiction. To
aid in formulating explanations of the project which will be germane to local problems, the conditions and events which gave rise to
the urge for a systematic position-classification plan should be
known. To aid in programming contacts and conferences, the authorities, officials, or employee groups displaying active interest in the
matter should be identified. To aid in making physical arrangements,
the cooperation of personnel and administrative agencies should be
solicited.

Generally speaking, certain kinds of public relations activities may
be anticipated in any jurisdiction.

Always in order are measures designed to furnish all concerned
with an understanding of what is to be done, and why, and how it
is to be done. Interviews, open group meetings, and written materials should all be used. Legislative, budget, and administrative
authorities, interested civic groups, and the public press should be
given an adequate explanation of the broad objectives and methods

[21] *Report of the Congressional Joint Commission on Reclassification of Salaries,*
pp. 151–52. For a summary of some of the difficulties that may be encountered,
due to attitudes of various groups, see discussion by Charles P. Messick, in *Proceedings, 14th Annual Meeting of Assembly of Civil Service Commissions,* June
1921, p. 35.

[22] See State of Rhode Island . . . , Department of Civil Service, *First Annual
Report* (1939), p. 6.

of the classification survey and the reasons for the project, and any misunderstanding on these points should be eliminated. Supervisory officials and employees should be made thoroughly familiar with the same information. They should be given an understanding of the practices and methods involved so that they may understand the kinds of data required by the classification staff and why, and so that uneasiness or skepticism may not arise. Especially should they be completely informed on the distribution, execution, and use of the position-description questionnaires.[23]

Another step toward beginning classification work, especially in a jurisdiction which has never had a position-classification plan in effect, is an adequate explanation to interested groups of the principles, purposes, and limitations of position-classification in general. Emphasis should be placed on eliminating any misunderstandings of what position-classification is. For example, it is usually necessary to explain that classification deals with the duties and responsibilities attached to the position rather than with the qualifications which the person occupying the position happens to possess or lack; that the classification staff has no authority to change duties and responsibilities or alter lines of authority; that the classification survey is in no wise an efficiency measure or evaluation of individual performance; and that classifying positions and fixing their pay are two distinct processes.[24] In addition, there should be specific applications of these explanations and distinctions to the personnel or other administrative problems of that jurisdiction.[25] In each instance, the discussions of the contemplated survey should be keyed to the special interests, questions, and problems of the group concerned.

The preliminary conference period also should be regarded as an opportunity for negotiations to establish working relations with various groups for specific cooperation during the whole developmental process or at certain stages. In every jurisdiction there are officials or groups who are in a position to make contributions by furnishing information or advice, by passing judgment on technical problems, or by making intermediate decisions which may be needed to clear the way for later stages of development.

As early as practicable, calls by the director of the classification

---

[23] See pp. 169–81, 184–86.
[24] Pp. 37–45, 49–54.
[25] For example, in a new civil service installation it will always be necessary to explain the relationship between the classification survey and the qualifying testing program of the civil service agency.

staff, accompanied by a key personnel official of the jurisdiction, should be made to acquaint the chief executive and his principal supervisory officials with the objectives and general procedures of the classification survey and to arrange to have a person in each major administrative unit designated to serve as liaison man between the unit and the classification staff. Enough time should be spent to insure complete understanding between the executive office and the personnel department. If appropriate, similar visits should be made to legislative officials. The first meetings with operating officials will be largely for the purpose of establishing relationships, for further meetings will be required during the progress of the survey. In general, personal contact should be made with all individuals and agencies who will be in key positions during the progress and clearance of the results of the classification project.

Obviously, the necessary work-relationship of the classification staff to the legislative body, budget authorities, the central personnel agency, and the operating departments, and the connections between their programs or schedules, should be made clear at the beginning. For example, the developmental period may include the time when a budget is being prepared and passed upon. The legislative body and budget authorities may plan to use the position-classification plan at that time for pay purposes. If the classification work is being done for a central personnel agency, but not by its regular staff, the relations between the developmental staff and the central personnel agency are especially important.[26] A civil service commission may have been in existence for some time, or the law authorizing the classification plan may have also established a merit system initially. It may be that the position-classification plan is needed in installing a merit system. In any event, it will be the foundation for later recruiting and testing operations. Both the budget and the personnel agency, accordingly, will be interested in seeing that the position-classification plan is being developed in a way to meet their needs and schedules.

In addition, negotiations may be conducted looking toward the participation of employees and officials and the cooperation of professional and technical associations. This has the dual benefit of providing the classification staff with technical or special assistance

---

[26] In such cases, it is frequently well as a general policy to arrange for all press contacts to be made with the central personnel agency; and to make conferences with officials and employees a joint project, with both the developmental staff and the regular staff represented.

and maintaining favorable relations. In several large classification studies, definite arrangements were made to set up advisory committees of employees representing occupational groups and to utilize representatives of employee organizations. Through these group committees or representatives, all employees or employee groups were afforded channels through which they could present factual data and make known their opinions on matters involved in the classification work.[27]

Conditions in the jurisdiction are sometimes such that it is necessary almost at the outset to inform officials and employees on certain policies or procedures that will be used in the actual installation of the classification plan. This is especially true if a position-classification plan and a pay plan are to be concurrently installed, or when a position-classification plan is being initially installed in a jurisdiction where a merit system has been in effect for some time. What will be an employee's civil service status when the title or classification of his position is changed? What will happen if the survey finds him in a position for which he has not qualified under existing civil service rules? Will an employee receiving pay above the maximum rate of the finally approved pay scale be reduced? Questions like these are raised by employees very early. If it is possible to have the policies on such points set and published at the beginning much will have been done to create confidence.

At the beginning and throughout the project, the interest of administrators and employees should be recognized and encouraged. Objectives and techniques should be thoroughly explained to them in order that they may see that their ends are served by impartial and scientific approaches to classification problems. In the effort to reach officials and employees who, by reason of geographic distribution or large size of the jurisdiction, would not be able personally to confer or to attend meetings, all organized channels of communication to them should be used, including departmental distribution channels, employee magazines, house organs, union publications, and the public press.

[27] See State of New York, *Report of the Joint Legislative Committee on Classification of Positions in the Civil Service* (Albany, 1932), p. 40; Frank L. Tolman, "The State Employment Study," *Bulletin of Association of State Civil Service Employees of the State of New York*, January 1931. For discussions of employee participation in industry, see, for example, Ordway Tead and Henry C. Metcalf, *Personnel Administration* (New York, 1926), pp. 262–65; Z. Clark Dickinson, *Compensating Industrial Effort* (New York, 1937), p. 216; A. M. Hammond, "A Salary Administration Plan for Your Business," *American Business*, December 1939, p. 42.

The availability of the classification staff to individual employees, groups of employees, or their representatives for explanation or consideration of all matters pertaining to the survey should be thoroughly impressed upon all those concerned. The survey staff must welcome suggestions and demonstrate its open-mindedness and reasonableness; open dealings and adequate explanations will do much to dissipate suspicion and uninformed opposition. Advantages secured during initial contacts can be conserved through the employment of professional workmanlike methods in conducting the survey.

SURVEY TOOLS

A position-classification plan must be based upon facts about the positions themselves and facts about the setting in which the positions exist—the service and the structure and functions of its operating departments. In a large service these facts are many and varied, and there is no royal road to their collection, analysis, and evaluation. Where no position-classification plan or scientific pay plan is in existence, titles of positions will not reliably indicate their duties, and salaries are not a good index of job responsibilities. It is necessary to break through such outward coverings and get down to the administrative setting and the duties and responsibilities of positions as they exist.

Ascertaining the necessary facts involves the acquisition and study of different types of documents. Chief among these are budget documents or salary ordinances which list the numbers and kinds of positions under each department, employee rosters or payrolls, position-description questionnaires and accompanying instructions for filling them out, functional and personnel charts of organization structure, departmental manuals of practice or reports of activities, and legal material such as charter provisions, civil service or personnel laws, rules and decisions.

Budget Documents or Salary Ordinances

In order to do preliminary planning, it is desirable as early as possible to know the general position-characteristics of the service. As previously pointed out, the number and types of positions involved will have an important bearing in determining the number, kinds, and time of the staff members required for classification work. The same information aids also in designing the position-description questionnaire and accompanying instructions to fit the particular jurisdiction, and in arranging meetings with employee groups. Budget documents or salary ordinances or acts listing the number and kinds of positions falling under the various departments will give sufficient general information for these purposes, supplemented, where necessary, by departmental reports or organization charts. Some budgets, like that of the State of California, serve admirably by providing, in addition to information about positions, brief summaries of the activities of each department. With the aid of such documents and brief descriptions of the activities of operating departments, the preliminary stages of the survey can be intelligently planned.

Employee Rosters or Payrolls

As a basis for establishing an inventory control over the coverage and progress of the survey, it is necessary to have a complete, up-to-date list of all employees by organizational units. In most cases the current payroll will serve excellently. It can be used to determine the number of questionnaires needed for each organizational unit, to check them in as they are returned, and to note changes in personnel.[28] During the course of the survey the payroll can be used as a source of reference to assist in the control of progress on the analysis and classification of the questionnaires.

Position-Description Questionnaires and Instructions

The possible methods of reaching qualified sources of information about the duties and responsibilities of positions include: (1) interviews with employees and supervisors and observation of the work by a trained analyst; (2) questionnaires; and (3) a combination of these two methods. The decision as to which of these methods will be adopted on an original survey depends on considerations of cost, time, and general practicability. Usually a combination of interview and questionnaire methods is used.[29]

[28] For a discussion of position-lists and their use on a specific project, see *Report of Congressional Joint Commission on Reclassification of Salaries* (1920), pp. 154–55, 159–62.

[29] "The questionnaire method, when used alone, is inadequate because employees are inclined to overstate the importance of their jobs, or fail to record pertinent data. However, there is an advantage in having selected workers fill out the questionnaires, because this procedure (a) insures a feeling of participation in the study, (b) gives the analyst useful background information, and (c) yields details which otherwise might be overlooked. In any event, whether the interview is used alone or in combination with a questionnaire, it is essential that the foremen and other immediate supervisors be consulted at the outset,

From a technical standpoint, very satisfactory results are secured through interview, observation, and recording by trained analysts, without the use of employee-supervisor questionnaires. However, this method is also the most expensive in time and money. On the basis of conditions surrounding the initial development of a position-classification plan in most, if not all, jurisdictions, it is not feasible of adoption in large original surveys.[30] Only infrequently has this method been followed in the original development of a position-classification plan in the public service.[31] Generally speaking, considerations of time and economy lead to a compromise; the employee-supervisor questionnaire method is initially employed and where necessary or desirable is supplemented by interview or observation techniques—"work-audits"—applied to sample positions, key types of positions, and cases or problems demanding special inquiry. This procedure, it is commonly agreed, is the least expensive and most satisfactory in an original survey. As a general rule, written instructions for filling out questionnaires should be considered a necessary supplement to the questionnaire itself.

In connection with both oral and written instructions for filling out the questionnaire, an adequate explanation of the objectives and processes of the classification survey should be made. As an introduction to a written set of instructions, it is desirable to summarize what has been or may be said in group meetings; namely, to explain why the survey is being made, the nature of the classification plan, and its advantages to the employee; to point out to the employee that a firsthand description of each job is desired; and to make it plain that the classification survey is in no wise an investigation of the relative merits or capabilities of present incumbents or an investigation for rating employees for decreasing the force.

---

so that their knowledge and experience will be utilized and their active participation secured." Industrial Relations Association of Philadelphia, Salary and Wage Committee, "Salary and Wage Administration," *Personnel,* May 1939, pp. 153–54.

As to methods of obtaining position-descriptions in private industry, see the analysis of the advantages and disadvantages of (a) the employee questionnaire method, (b) the analyst interview method, (c) the analyst-supervisor conference method, and (d) the incumbent-supervisor-analyst method, in Life Office Management Association, Clerical Salary Study Committee, *Job Evaluation for the Establishment of Salary Standards,* Report No. 1 (1938), pp. 9–13.

[30] Compare the procedures for obtaining accurate job descriptions in the course of making a classification audit or an organization for the purpose of maintaining a position-classification plan after it is installed, pp. 321–27.

[31] See Robert C. Clothier, "Organization for an Occupational Survey," *Journal of Personnel Research,* February 1923, pp. 427–50.

The principal purpose of written instructions is to give to each employee and supervisor a clear, adequate explanation, accompanied by illustrations, of the specific types of information solicited by each item of the questionnaire. In addition, the instructions suggest the mechanics of filling out the questionnaires; indicate what, if any, supplementary exhibits should be filed with them or otherwise submitted to the classification staff; direct how the original and each duplicate questionnaire, if any, is to be routed and used; establish the time limit for return of questionnaires; and lay out the procedure for distributing, listing, and routing the questionnaires back to the classification staff.[32]

As questionnaires and instructions are basic instruments in the classification procedure, their form warrants considerable study.[33] The major problems have to do with (a) who will fill out the questionnaire or otherwise initially record the basic information as to the duties and responsibilities of each individual position; (b) the use of a single, general type of questionnaire as against several types of specialized questionnaires, each designed to cover a particular occupational group; (c) the extent to which the questionnaire will call for data about the employee as distinguished from his work; (d) the coverage of information about the employee's position, the detail with which it will be requested, and how the employee and his supervisor will participate in furnishing it; (e) the mechanical setup of the questionnaire and instructions in terms of size, paper stock, color, and ink used for printing; and (f) the number of questionnaire copies (original and one or more duplicates) that will be required.

Who will fill out the questionnaire? To ascertain the facts about the work of each position, the best sources of information are the employee doing the work and one or more of his supervisors. Both from a technical and a public relations standpoint, their participation and cooperation are essential. Accordingly, the questionnaire form gives to each employee an opportunity to describe the duties he performs and the responsibilities he bears; and gives the supervisor an opportunity to check his employees' statements, amplify or comment upon them, and, to some extent, to analyze or evaluate each position under

---

[32] Instructions to employees and to supervisors should preferably appear on the same sheet or folder. If they are printed or reproduced separately, both sets of instructions should be made available to each group.

[33] On questionnaires in public administration generally, see John M. Pfiffner, *Research Methods in Public Administration* (Ronald Press, 1940), Chapter XI.

his jurisdiction.[34] It also makes available to the classification staff a tangible document representing each position to be classified—a considerable help in administrative control of the project. Further, through the initial analysis of the executed questionnaires, points to be developed or clarified by later investigations or work-audits can be noted, and the burden is avoided of securing all information, including routine data, through this more expensive method.[35]

General and specialized questionnaires. In most original classification surveys one type of questionnaire is used for all kinds of positions in the jurisdiction. The question occasionally arises, however, whether better results would be secured through the use of a number of specialized questionnaires, each designed to fit a single or a homogeneous occupational group. In executing a questionnaire of specialized type, the employee is asked to answer or check a series of definite questions or items, rather than (or in addition to) describing his tasks and responsibilities in his own words. Specialized questionnaires have some decided advantages.

For practical reasons, however, they can be used during an original classification survey only in rare instances when the positions to be covered comprise a single occupational group or several closely related groups.[36] Obviously, in order to prepare specialized questionnaires, the designer must know intimately the details of the tasks and responsibilities of the positions to be covered. This means that he must have made some analysis of them beforehand on the basis of information previously collected. Such information or the time to acquire it is seldom available during an original survey. Further, if more than one homogeneous group is involved, there must have been a previous study made of the positions, sufficient to identify which of the employees are to fill out each type of form. Ordinarily

---

[34] "The immediate reason for having employees participate in position description is to obtain complete and accurate statements of position content. A second reason . . . is that thus management can consider the employees' conceptions of their duties. An employee's summary of his duties which shows misconception affords his supervisor an opportunity to clarify for him the objectives of the position and the relative importance of the duties and responsibilities delegated to it. The improvements in the organization and performance of work which result from such conferences may be worth more than the cost of analyzing the positions." Riegel, *Salary Determination*, pp. 76–77, 86.

[35] Only occasionally is adverse criticism of the employee-supervisor questionnaire method encountered. See William E. Mosher and J. Donald Kingsley, *Public Personnel Administration* (New York, 1936), pp. 366, 367.

[36] To some extent, however, the same advantages can be secured during an original classification survey by directing specific sections of the written instructions to particular occupational groups. See Appendix A.

no factual basis would exist to permit the prompt preparation and effective distribution of specialized questionnaires in an original classification of a multifunctional organization or jurisdiction of some size. In general, therefore, specialized questionnaires find their usefulness mainly in surveying unifunctional organizations or homogeneous occupational groups and in making resurveys or audits during the continued maintenance of a position-classification plan.[37]

Coverage of personal and other data. A study of questionnaire forms used in original classification surveys in the public service indicates a wide variation in the types of information collected.[38] Occasionally rather simple questionnaires are used, covering a small number of generally worded items. Sometimes the items are numerous but confined to information which would be directly useful for classification purposes. More frequently, however, the questionnaire forms go further and ask for information that is to be used for civil service record purposes, for the development of a pay plan, for the improvement of working conditions, or for statistical compilations.[39]

Circumstances at the time a classification survey is initiated may make it necessary to couple the survey with a general personnel audit of the jurisdiction. For example, a classification survey is frequently one phase of installing a merit system in a jurisdiction where no centralized or reliable records of employees, their service, educational or employment record, age, marital status, number of dependents, or other personal data are available. The civil service commission, of course, will need data about the employees as a basis for establishing its employee rosters or service records, to be used in the administration of the personnel transactions involved in the merit system. Sometimes it is decided to ask for this information from each employee at the same time that he is requested to give information about his position. Sometimes, too, the personnel, budget, fiscal, or legislative agency desires personal information about employees

---

[37] Chapter X, pp. 328–29.

[38] For specimens of analogous questionnaires in industry, see Riegel, *Salary Determination*, pp. 80–85, 92–93; A. F. Kindall, "Job Description and Rating," *Personnel*, February 1938, p. 124; Metropolitan Life Insurance Co., *Salary Standardization and Administration*, 1934, pp. 11–16; J. O. Hopwood, *Salaries, Wages and Labor Relations* (New York, 1937), p. 37; L. C. Lovejoy, *Salary Standardization* (American Management Association, 1939), pp. 21–22; Life Office Management Association, Clerical Salary Study Committee, *Job Evaluation for the Establishment of Salary Standards*, Appendix, pp. 9–10; *ibid., Life Office Salary Administration*, Report No. 2 (1939), pp. 58–61, 67–68.

[39] For a comprehensive list of items in job analysis in industry, see Gordon S. Watkins and Paul A. Dodd, *The Management of Labor Relations* (New York, 1938), pp. 130–32.

for purely statistical purposes, and suggests that this be secured in connection with the classification survey.

It should be recognized that the inclusion in a position-description questionnaire of requests for purely personal information will seem inconsistent with the principle that the classification survey is concerned with the work of the employee's position and not with his personal characteristics or qualifications. In the mind of the employee the mere presence of such items on the questionnaire has a tendency to diminish the effect of explanations of the meaning, purposes, and basis of position-classification. Consequently, every effort should be made to separate the job information needed for classification purposes from the personal information needed for service record or statistical purposes.

This can be accomplished through the use of two separable questionnaires on one form. In a recent merit system installation, a four-page (two-sheet) folder was designed, perforated at the top. One sheet covered personal items and the other included classification items. The form contained a suitable explanation of the use of each questionnaire.

This method involves only a slight duplication of items, and the effect upon the employees and officials of the service and upon their understanding of position-classification as something distinct from employee appraisal is well worth securing.[40]

Coverage of classification data. This discussion will cover the items designed to produce an initial factual basis for classifying positions. Those needed for the development of a pay plan will be discussed in a later publication.[41] Questionnaires and accompanying instructions covering personal, statistical, and pay, as well as classification, items may be referred to in Appendix A and elsewhere.[42]

---

[40] The method here described was used in Minnesota, Arkansas, and Rhode Island by Public Administration Service. An inexpensive device that has been employed in using one questionnaire is to insert as a heading before a series of personal questions a statement such as the following: "This information will not be used for classification, but is for the records of the Commission."

[41] See the report of the Committee on Pay Plans in the Public Service, a forthcoming companion volume in this series.

[42] Griffenhagen, "The Principles and Technique of Preparing an Occupational Classification of Positions in the Public Service," *Public Personnel Studies*, November 1924, pp. 246–47, reproduces questionnaire used in Philadelphia, 1920, survey; U. S. Personnel Classification Board, *Report of Wage and Personnel Survey*, H.Doc. 602, 70th Cong., 2d sess., pp. 476–87, reproduces questionnaire and instructions to employees and supervisors used in 1928 survey of the federal field service; City of Philadelphia Civil Service Commission (J. L. Jacobs & Co., consultants), *Classification and Compensation Plans of the Personal Service in the Executive Departments* (1930), pp. 603–06, reproduces the Philadelphia 1930

A questionnaire confined to classification items would identify the position covered, indicate its status as to permanency or continuity, show adequately what the duties, tasks, responsibilities, and organizational relationships of the position are, and contain a certification as to completeness and accuracy by a responsible official of the organization.

For identification purposes, the questionnaire would call for the name of the employee,[43] the geographic and/or street location of place of work, the organizational location of the position (name of department, bureau, division, section, and unit), its payroll title, and its usual or working title (which may or may not be the same as the payroll title). This identifying information may be filled in by the employee himself or by a payroll or other administrative office before the questionnaires are distributed to supervisors and employees.

Permanency or continuity or the part or full-time character of the position is shown by information as to the number of working hours a day or week, number of days a week or month, or by a general characterization of the position as permanent, temporary, intermittent, or seasonal.[44]

The questions dealing with duties, tasks, responsibilities, and organizational relationships of the position are the crucial items of the position-description questionnaire. Their prime purpose is to elicit data permitting the development of the essential and differentiating characteristics of each position. They call for a detailed description written by the employee in his own words, and usually additional answers by the employee to controlled items relating to supervision received and supervision exercised over others, if any. This is supplemented by information furnished on the question-

---

questionnaire and instructions for department, bureau, and division heads; Mosher and Kingsley, *Public Personnel Administration*, pp. 364–65, reproduces the New York State 1935 questionnaire (Griffenhagen & Associates); Lewis Meriam, *Public Personnel Problems* (The Brookings Institution, 1938), Appendix C, pp. 410–31, reproduces questionnaire and accompanying instructions prepared by the U. S. Civil Service Commission in 1925 for the Territory of Hawaii; Public Administration Service, *Personnel Programs for Smaller Cities*, p. 12, reproduces the work-description questionnaire of the Michigan Municipal League; State of Rhode Island . . ., Department of Civil Service, *First Annual Report* (1939), Appendix, reproduces questionnaire prepared by Public Administration Service.

43 Cf. C. V. Putman, *Systems for Identifying Positions without Reference to the Names of the Incumbents,* Paper presented at the 23rd Annual Meeting of the Civil Service Assembly . . . , 1930.

44 Experience indicates that such terms should be defined in the instructions in the light of local terminology and employment tenures.

naire by the employee's supervisor, including check of accuracy and adequacy, additional comment, some evaluation of the essential characteristics of the position, and an opinion as to the qualifications needed to perform the work described.

The main core of such data is the employee's narrative description, for which, of course, a great deal more space is furnished on the questionnaire than for any other item. Because of its importance, the instructions for writing it should be not only plain and specific but also comprehensive. Usually, in order to give the employee all the space possible on the questionnaire form itself, it is preferable that such instructions be set forth in a form separate from the position-description questionnaire. If this is done, the questionnaire itself need contain only a brief introductory direction to indicate the purpose of the space allotted.[45]

The separate written instructions, covering all the items on the position-description questionnaire, provide specific, detailed directions and suggestions to the employee in respect to the form and content of his work description, give examples of what are and what are not adequate responses, request him to make an estimate of the proportion of his time spent on different activities, and emphasize the point that the description is to be his own individual statement.

Employees should be encouraged to execute questionnaires with as little assistance as practicable from their supervisors or other employees. In no case except when positions are vacant or when an employee is on extended leave of absence should the supervisor dictate the answers to be provided by employees. Sometimes, in the effort to be helpful, employee groups or organizations will provide their members with a standardized description of the duties involved in a group of positions to be copied by them on their individual questionnaires. This procedure, however, is not helpful or satisfactory even when it seems that the work of the positions is standardized. It is essential that the classification staff know exactly what duties are being performed in each individual position. While most of such positions may be practically identical, some may be essentially dissimilar. Moreover, several original descriptions taken together give the classification staff a better picture than a common description written in collaboration and possibly after some compromises as to what shall or shall not be included.

[45] Examples of these and other instructions mentioned here are given in Appendix A and in references previously cited.

The most extensive part of the instructions has to do with the effort to secure precision in the employee's description of the duties, tasks, responsibilities, and organizational relationships of his position. In a questionnaire of general type, the necessary breadth of some of the questions or items sometimes leads to inadequate or undiscriminating replies. To avoid this result, care is taken to make the instructions detailed and specific and to show the employee both unsatisfactory and satisfactory responses.

In a large service it may be found desirable to provide a number of examples of types of answers which would be suitable for each of the major occupational groups. For example, there might be a number of descriptions of work in each of a number of major occupational groups. Such examples should be carefully designed to conform to the terminology and nature of work involved in the type of position used as an example and should illustrate the need for detailed descriptions of each separate operation involved in each position. For example, a set of instructions used in a recent classification project in a large municipality gives examples of suitable responses in seven occupational fields—labor, mechanical, engineering, clerical and related fields, accounting, police and fire, and medical. These examples cover two pages of a letter-size folder.[46]

Information regarding the specific nature of duties and tasks needs to be supplemented by information indicating weight and extent of responsibilities. This is in anticipation of the existence of positions in the same line of work which are separated by lines of supervisory responsibility or by demarcations of difficulty or nonsupervisory responsibility. In such instances, a simple description of operations involved in the position is not likely to be sufficiently definitive. It is necessary to know how work assignments are made, what instructions are given, what supervision is provided during the course of the work, what check or review is provided, how working procedures and programs are formulated, what initiative is required, what supervisory or nonsupervisory responsibilities are involved, and in general what are the working relationships of each position to other positions within the same organizational unit.[47]

[46] City of Los Angeles, Board of Civil Service Commissioners, *Instructions and Suggestions for Filling out the Classification Questionnaire,* 1939, developed by Public Administration Service. The instructions are reproduced in Appendix A. For a parallel discussion and analogous examples with respect to position analysis in industry, see Riegel, *Salary Determination,* pp. 86–89.
[47] Chapter V.

To secure such information from the employee, specific supplementary questions or instructions are employed. One of these asks the employee for the name and title of his immediate supervisor. There are usually many supervisors in the line of authority above him, and consequently it is necessary to explain what the term "immediate supervisor" means. For example, this expression has been defined as "that person who, normally, in the regular course of your work is the one from whom you receive your work assignments, as well as to whom you are responsible for the work you perform." [48]

Another item asks the employee for the names and working titles of any employees who work under his supervision; or the names and number of employees in organization units he supervises; or the names of divisions or sections supervised and the names of their respective heads. The use of such questions as these, identifying the employee's immediate supervisor and any employees or units that he himself supervises, will make it possible to construct rough organization charts from the questionnaires themselves. [49] The instructions should also provide specific suggestions for describing the details of supervisory and administrative responsibility. [50]

Answers to questions of these types, together with the work-descriptions on the questionnaires for both the supervisor and the employees supervised, will ordinarily indicate the supervisory responsibilities within a given organizational unit. However, where it is necessary to ascertain the exact pattern of supervisory responsibility, further inquiry during the work-audit must generally be made. [51]

After the employee has filled in his part of the questionnaire, provision is made for participation of each supervisory official in completing questionnaires covering positions subject to his supervision. First, after conference with the employee, if necessary, the supervisor should comment on the accuracy and completeness of the employee's statement. The supervisor allows the employee's statement to stand as written. In a separate statement he makes appropriate comment, indicates wherein the employee's statement may be incorrect or in-

[48] Los Angeles County Civil Service Commission, *Questionnaire Instructions*, 1937. The instructions should also provide that more than one such supervisor may be listed, as in the case of a mechanic under both a "straw boss" or "leadman" and a foreman, or a scientific worker who has both a technical and an administrative supervisor.

[49] Pp. 190–91.

[50] See, for example, U. S. Personnel Classification Board, *Report of Wage and Personnel Survey* (1929), H.Doc. 602, 70th Cong., 2d sess., pp. 479, 483. These instructions are reproduced in Appendix A.

[51] Chapter V, pp. 118–21.

adequate, and furnishes any additional description or statement that seems to him pertinent. In this way, both the employee and his supervisor are given a collective opportunity to present a fair and adequate description of the position in question.[52]

The considered opinion of competent supervisors should be of value regarding the knowledges, abilities, experience, and training desirable for the positions under their control. They have had occasion to observe the performance of various incumbents in such positions and consciously or unconsciously should have observed the qualities shown. They may have given definite thought to the qualifications desirable or necessary for proficiency. During the questionnaire survey, such observations and opinions should be obtained for consideration in the development of specifications, as well as for their secondary value, when reliable, as indicating levels of difficulty and responsibility among the several positions or groups under each supervisor's immediate supervision. It is rare, however, that such opinions have been sufficiently well thought out to be objective and consistent over large groups of positions of different kinds and levels. They must be carefully analyzed and evaluated in use.

When opinions as to qualification standards are sought from supervisors, the instructions to them should make it clear that such standards need not bear any necessary relation to the actual qualifications of present employees.

In devising classification questionnaires, some agencies have adopted a fairly long series of short-answer items, to be filled in by the immediate supervisor of the position, including both qualification items and so-called "evaluation" items. Evaluation items, in effect, ask the supervisor to analyze the positions as to relative degrees of difficulty or responsibility in certain respects.[53] Answers to

[52] Rarely does the employee's knowledge that a check of his statement will be made, either by his supervisor or by a classifier on a work-audit, handicap him in giving a fair and adequate description of the duties he performs. In some instances, of course, it may tend to encourage him to avoid a superficial statement or obscure or loose expressions. Differences, if any, between the facts given by the employee and those given by the supervisor have the advantage of leading the classifier directly to points on which work-audit is necessary. Under the employee's narrative statement of duties and responsibilities, a space should be provided for the work auditor to insert notes in a form which will be intelligible to others who work on the same questionnaires.

[53] See Appendix A; also New York State Civil Service Department questionnaire, 1933; Bridgeport Civil Service Commission "classification sheet"; questionnaire reproduced in *Manual of Procedure for Municipal Civil Service Commissions*, published by the New York State Department of Civil Service in 1939, pp. 4–5; Portland, Oregon, Civil Service Board, *Work Description Questionnaire for Employees*.

such questions, like supervisors' opinions as to qualification standards, are helpful only to the extent that they represent considered judgment. Too often they place such a burden on the supervisor of a large group that good results cannot be expected within the time allotted for the execution and return of the questionnaires.

After the questionnaires have been completed by the employees and their immediate supervisors, the head of each major organization (or some one designated by him) is accorded an opportunity to review the questionnaires of his organization (personally or by delegation) before they are transmitted to the classification staff. Space is provided on the questionnaire to permit the appropriate official to note any comment and to affix his signature as an indication of completeness and accuracy.

Mechanical setup of the questionnaire and instructions. The preferable mechanical setup of position-description questionnaires is one sheet, letter size, $8\frac{1}{2}''$x$11''$, printed on both sides. Most classification questionnaires have been of this type, although a few have been printed on legal cap. Questionnaire folders which are not to be torn apart in use are not desirable for handling and filing purposes. Separate instructions in folder form are not, of course, objectionable, nor is it essential that their size correspond to that of the questionnaire. Frequently, they have been approximately $6''$x$9''$.

The position-description questionnaire should be printed head to foot, as turning the questionnaires vertically is more convenient for those who read them than turning them horizontally. The employee's narrative description of his duties and responsibilities should appear completely on one side.

If more than one copy of each questionnaire is to be required, the stock should be light enough in weight to permit the making of three or four clear carbon copies. The spacing between the lines should, of course, conform to that of typewriters.

Although in printed questionnaire forms black ink is commonly employed, if the items are printed in brown ink the black typewritten answers stand out better. In reading the questionnaires, the classification staff is interested in the answers; the questions themselves are not consciously read.

The method to be employed for producing questionnaires will depend upon the size of the service. For large jurisdictions the printed form will be most economical and satisfactory, while for small jurisdictions mimeographed or dittoed forms will suffice.

Number of copies required for each position. The number of copies of the questionnaire form which should constitute a set for one position will depend upon the needs of the classification staff and the desires of employees and administrative officers to retain copies in their files for record or general administrative purposes.[54] There has been considerable variance in this respect. Many large surveys have required but one copy of each questionnaire. In others, four copies in each set have been required. One copy is a work sheet to be filled out by the employee and to be held by him (or returned to him by the department after it is typed); one copy is retained by the departmental official; and two copies are forwarded to the classification staff.[55] When more than a single copy of the questionnaire is prepared for each position, the various copies should be of different colors to facilitate handling, e.g., white (original), green, yellow, and pink. In smaller jurisdictions a single copy will serve the purposes of the classification staff. Printing requisitions should allow about 20 per cent above the number of positions to be classified in order to take care of spoilage, change of position occupant, lost questionnaires, and similar contingencies. An excess allowance of 5 to 10 per cent is sufficient for instruction sheets.

Organization charts

Important relationships among positions in an organization unit are conveniently portrayed by the use of organization structural charts, and such charts are, accordingly, useful instruments of classification.[56]

For the purpose of the classifier, organization charts should indicate the nature of the activity encompassed in each organizational unit and the names and payroll titles of the personnel, or in some

[54] Operating officials should be encouraged to keep copies of these position-descriptions and informed of their use in administrative and personnel matters.
[55] See p. 190.
[56] "Properly constructed, an organization chart is a distinct aid to management because it permits an easy spread of knowledge of a company's structure. In order to present this picture completely, however, it is usually found necessary to prepare two charts. One of these, the 'functional organization chart,' shows the relationship of functions and the lines of control in the concern, and from it one may get a picture of the authority and responsibility of each individual. The other, the 'personnel organization chart,' substitutes for functions the persons who are responsible for the performance of the functions. This type of chart further emphasizes the exact scope of individual control." T. M. Heggland, "Organization Charts," *Civic Affairs*, September 1938, p. 1. The drafting of organization charts is discussed in this and a following article appearing in the October 1938 number. See also Pfiffner, *Research Methods in Public Administration*, Chapter XIV.

cases the number and payroll titles of positions in the unit, arranged in such a way as to indicate the supervisory relationships of the positions. In the larger or more complex organizations, more general organization charts are required to define the relationships among a number of organization units. A general or "master" chart coordinates the more detailed charts and needs to include only the names of key supervisory personnel and descriptions of the major activities of each unit. For large organizations, functional organization charts are drafted separately from personnel charts by reason of the space that is required. In small organizations, however, functional and personnel information can be combined on the same organization chart. In personnel charts used in the original development of a classification plan, names of persons are generally more useful for identification purposes than the existing titles of positions. In work-audits and other conferences, executives talk in terms of persons rather than in terms of positions. Names of employees, however, would not generally be required where they work in large groups of identical positions.

At the beginning of a classification survey all agencies should be asked for copies of such organization charts as they may have.[57] Occasionally, suitable charts prepared by operating agencies for administrative or budget purposes may already be available and can be used by the classification staff with minor adaptations or changes made as a result of a check against the information about supervisory relationships given on the charts. However, in most instances it will be found that sufficiently detailed up-to-date charts are not maintained and it then becomes the task of the classification staff to draft them from all the initial information secured. It is not necessary, of course, that such organization charts be drafted with mechanical excellence, since they are to be used only in the work process, and undoubtedly will be revised and annotated from time to time.

A study of organization charts by the classification staff brings forth gaps or conflicts in the data furnished on questionnaires, indicates where further information is required, clarifies other points, and assists materially in getting an over-all view of organization units and of the interrelation of positions. The charts also provide a basis

[57] For an example of such a request, suggesting briefly the manner in which charts may be designed, see Circular No. 26, August 9, 1928, reproduced in U. S. Personnel Classification Board, *Report of Wage and Personnel Survey* (1929), pp. 487–88; also see "Classification and Compensation Work in the Wisconsin State Service," *Public Personnel Studies*, July 1927, pp. 140–41.

for clearer understanding of the operations of the organization unit, assist in delineating the various levels of supervisory responsibility, and provide a ready reference to the organization location of positions. In addition, the charts will be found of material advantage during the course of interviewing employees and supervisory officials in the work-audit process, for by referring to the charts the classifier is able to carry in mind the location and nature of positions mentioned by the employee or supervisor in his explanation of operations or responsibilities.

Ordinarily the best time for the preparation of such organization charts is immediately following the receipt and sorting of the position-description questionnaires to organizational order.[58]

Other Written Material

A number of other types of written material need to be assembled for use, particularly departmental manuals of practice or reports of activities and legal material such as charter provisions, civil service or personnel laws, rules, and decisions.

At the beginning of a classification survey, the classification staff must orient itself with respect to any legal provisions or decisions which might affect the development of the position-classification plan or its administration. Accordingly, an examination and compilation should be made of charter provisions, ordinances, or statutes, constitutional provisions, legal opinions, and court adjudications bearing directly or indirectly on position-classification. Where civil service or personnel rules exist, they too should be reviewed and their connection with the classification problem determined. If many legal aspects are involved, it is helpful to index all legal provisions in accordance with the specific phase of position-classification to which they relate. From an analysis of such provisions the staff can prepare statements of controlling principles or exceptions.

Available manuals of practice in the operating departments should be obtained and read. Practice manuals are not always kept up to date and sometimes they reflect how the department desires work to be performed rather than how it actually is performed. However, such manuals may provide a basic understanding of the work of organization units, together with the work processes employed. While they are of general assistance in providing a preliminary

[58] Pp. 190–91. See "Charting the Organizations," in *Report of the Congressional Joint Commission on Reclassification of Salaries* (1920), pp. 167–68.

understanding, any work descriptions contained in the manuals should be verified before they are accepted.

Periodic and departmental reports containing summary descriptions of activities also will aid the classification staff to understand the work and problems of the operating units. Special or individual reports constitute specific examples of work performed by the department and sometimes establish in vivid fashion the difficulties, characteristics, and responsibilities of positions.

Flow-of-work charts or statements are sometimes available and may prove of some assistance. Material of this type, however, is not frequently encountered and it is always necessary to verify it against actual operations.

In some services it may be found desirable to request each department head to furnish through his subordinate officials a narrative statement covering the functions, responsibilities, and procedures of the various organization units in his department. Where an undue burden is not placed on departments, such statements will provide valuable material in a form convenient for use.

Samples of executed forms, records, exhibits, or other specimens of work are useful in illustrating to the classifier the actual operations involved in work procedures. Ordinarily, such material can best be collected during the course of the survey, usually at the time of the work audit.[59]

SURVEY PROCEDURE

Through the preliminary steps previously discussed, the positional coverage of the classification survey is determined; classification staff, finances, space, and equipment are provided; proper public relations contacts for general cooperation are made; various written documents are assembled; and the position-description questionnaire and instructions are made ready for distribution.[60]

Meetings with Employees and Supervisors

The oral introduction of the questionnaire and accompanying written instructions to employees and supervisors is a desirable step,

[59] This avoids the excessive duplication that might occur if such material were required to be submitted with each questionnaire.

[60] For a description of the procedure involved in distributing questionnaires, holding employee committee meetings, and getting the questionnaires promptly returned to the classification staff, in a survey covering 104,000 positions, see "Distributing and Collecting the Questionnaires," *ibid.*, pp. 158–59.

although the time available or the size or geographic spread of some jurisdictions may limit the extent to which this can be done. In some instances, perhaps the best that can be done is to use all available channels of communication to employees—departmental distribution systems, employee-organization letters and magazines, and the public press. The time and effort spent at the beginning in trying to have the questionnaires well executed saves much more time and effort in subsequent processes.[61]

In large jurisdictions it is also generally desirable to meet with groups of departmental officials, designated liaison men, and supervisory officials, to discuss classification procedures, enlist the assistance of supervisors for distributing questionnaires, having employee answers typed from work sheets, and returning the questionnaires properly and promptly to the classification staff. In some cases separate meetings with groups of foremen or other direct supervisors may be necessary to equip them to advise their employees in the execution of the questionnaires and the understanding of the written instructions. Such meetings should precede employee meetings.

At all meetings, special effort should be made to establish the true purpose of the survey in the minds of the supervisors and the employees. The position-description questionnaire and instructions are reviewed, item by item, with explanations and illustrations of what each item calls for. Emphasis is laid on the necessity for a detailed description of the work and responsibilities of each position, and for full cooperation from employees and supervisors who, being more familiar with the positions, can therefore provide the most complete and exact descriptions.

Distribution and Return of Questionnaires

At the appropriate time the survey staff will arrange with each department head to designate a liaison man to be definitely responsible for the distribution and return of the questionnaires for his department,[62] and enough forms for his department or administrative subdivision are turned over to him.[63] With each group of question-

---

[61] In connection with this discussion, see also pp. 163–68.

[62] The questionnaires and accompanying instructions may be distributed either before or after the meetings with employee and supervisory groups, depending on circumstances. It is sometimes better to distribute them before such meetings, thus enabling employees and supervisors to discover the points not clear to them and to raise questions at the time of the meeting.

[63] Where large numbers of employees, wide geographic area, distance from headquarters, or similar factors are involved, priority in distribution is indicated.

naires in the larger services, there should be included a letter addressed to the head of the administrative unit summarizing the objectives of the survey; requesting assistance; outlining a procedure for distributing the questionnaires within the department, and having them typed, collected, and returned to the classification staff; and suggesting that he prepare a request for cooperation in the survey, to be distributed over his own signature throughout his organization.[64]

After the questionnaires are filled in, those from each administrative unit should be returned to the classification staff at once rather than a few at a time. Naturally there may be a few positions which are temporarily vacant or for which, because of the absence of employees, questionnaires cannot be executed immediately, but these should not be allowed to hold up the rest of the group. They may be covered for the time being by "temporary" questionnaires.

The time consumed in executing and returning questionnaires in a large service is likely to be a great deal more than the estimate. While careful planning of each step and constant follow-up will be repaid in more prompt returns, with even the best planning, the classification staff will need to allow for the fact that some units may take ten times as long as others to supply the completed questionnaires.

Checking-In the Questionnaires

Before the questionnaires are distributed, the survey staff should prepare a control schedule showing the number of employees in each department or administrative division and providing columns for noting the date of distribution, number of copies furnished, promised date of return, and date of return. As the groups of questionnaires are returned, the date of receipt is entered on the control schedule and each individual questionnaire is checked against the payroll or other position list. A list of all questionnaires missing without explanation should be transmitted to the appropriate liaison

64 For examples of such a letter, see: Appendix B; "Classification and Compensation Work in the Wisconsin State Service," *Public Personnel Studies*, July 1927, pp. 140–41; and Los Angeles City School District Personnel Commission, *Instructions to Employees Concerning Classification Inquiry*, 1939. For examples of similar announcements of programs of position-analysis in private enterprises, see: Life Office Management Association, Clerical Salary Study Committee, *Job Evaluation for the Establishment of Salary Standards*, Appendix, p. 8; *ibid.*, *Life Office Salary Administration*, pp. 53–54; Riegel, *Salary Determination*, pp. 77–78.

man, with a request for advice regarding them. A follow-up should be continued until all questionnaires have been returned.

It is inevitable that some of the questionnaires received will be filled out inadequately or incorrectly. Ordinarily, however, it is not worth while to delay subsequent steps while all the questionnaires are inspected for deficiencies, the forms returned with instructions for correction, and the questionnaires checked in again as second receipts. In addition to the time this would consume, it is not a desirable procedure from the standpoint of cooperative relations. It is better not to examine the questionnaires for deficiencies until they are being studied for the purpose of sorting them organizationally and occupationally. Then those seriously defective can be noted for specific coverage in the later work-audit program.

In two types of situations, however, an immediate return of defective questionnaires might be warranted: (1) where the questionnaire does not contain the employee's own description of his work, there being no reason (such as the employee's absence) for this defect; and (2) where a group of employees have agreed upon a stereotyped, uniform statement to describe their positions, instead of submitting individual statements.

Keeping Information Current

The questionnaire survey is in effect an inventory of the positions in the service as of the date the forms are filled in. It is obvious, however, that the service, its positions, and its employees will not remain static while the position-classification plan is being developed. Additional positions will be created, some of which will be different in kind from any previously reported, and additional employees will be hired to fill them. Some employees who filled out questionnaires will be promoted or transferred to other kinds of positions, and some will resign from the service. Under ordinary circumstances, it is agreed that changes occurring during the developmental period should be covered before the position-classification plan is put into effect. The question is: Should they be covered (a) continuously during this period by a formal procedure in the nature of a perpetual inventory, or (b) only through the work audit, followed by a definite check-up during the installation process?

The principal types of changes to be recognized occur:

1. When a new employee is hired who is not taking the place of a former employee. In such cases, a new position is added to the pay-

roll, for which a position-description questionnaire should be required.

2. When a new employee is hired to take the place of a former employee but not to perform substantially the same kind of work. In this case, the questionnaire for the former employee and position should be eliminated and a questionnaire for the new employee and position substituted.[65]

3. When the duties and responsibilities of a position are materially changed while the same employee continues to occupy it. This calls for elimination of the employee's former questionnaire and the substitution of a new one showing his current work.

To keep information current as to these changes requires that distinctive forms and instructions be devised for use by departments, employees, and supervisors in making periodic reports to the classification staff. Whether such a procedure should be employed depends on local conditions. Factors for consideration are: (1) the size and complexity of the jurisdiction and the number and kinds of changes that may be anticipated; and (2) the length of time it is estimated will ensue before the installation procedures actually get under way.

In a small jurisdiction, or in one where changes are not numerous or frequent, reports can be required and currently taken into consideration by the classification staff without anyone's assuming a heavy burden of additional work. Where changes are both numerous and frequent, they have their greatest effect upon the classification plan being developed and at the same time require the greatest amount of work in reporting and recording them. Accordingly, it must be considered whether this procedure is worth while in the light of time and staff available and the other objectives of the survey.

In some instances, where the legislative channels have not been cleared for the installation of the position-classification plan immediately after development, it may be apparent that a substantial delay will occur. In this event, it probably would be better to plan for a complete check-up as the initial installation step, rather than attempt to maintain a perpetual inventory of the duties and responsibilities of all positions in the meantime.

In other instances, where development and installation constitute

---

[65] If the new employee simply replaces the former employee on the same kind of work, or if an employee is separated without immediate replacement, a change or an elimination of name on the records is all that is necessary.

an unbroken program, already authorized, and the period of development will be longer than one year, a formal procedure, begun after basic classification work is well under way, should be instituted, if staff available will permit.[66] During a long period in a large service changes are very likely to occur that will vitally affect the structure of the classification plan and the number and kinds of classes to be established; and to delay securing information until the beginning of the installation process may mean an unusual delay because of a sudden peak-load of important amendments and changes to be studied and determined by the classification staff. Where the developmental period is short, however, the danger of a peak-load is not acute and the acquiring of information as to changes—at least through formal procedures—may be postponed for a check-up as a part of the installation process.[67]

DEVELOPMENTAL PROCEDURE

From the time the questionnaires are checked in to the time the processes of installation are encountered, the development of a position-classification plan in a fairly large service normally involves the following procedures: (1) Arranging questionnaires in organization order and, after studying them, preparing rough pencil charts of organization structure; (2) arranging questionnaires occupationally; (3) analyzing positions; (4) determining classes tentatively; (5) determining relationships among classes; (6) selecting class titles; (7) preparing working definitions of classes; (8) allocating positions to classes tentatively; (9) conducting work audits; (10) revising classes, class titles, allocations of positions to classes, and working definitions of classes; (11) writing class specifications; (12) drafting code of rules for the installation and administration of the plan; (13) obtaining

[66] For a description of such a procedure, see "Keeping Current Records of All Changes in Personnel and Positions," *Report of the Congressional Joint Commission on Reclassification of Salaries*, pp. 159–62. "The earlier deliberations of the Commission had made it clear that several previous classification projects had been rendered less valuable than they otherwise would have been because no means were adopted to maintain, while the classification work was under way, records of changes in incumbency and changes in organization which so altered positions as to affect their classification. . . . The experience of the past eight months or more has shown that the information required to maintain these current records can be supplied by the departments without a prohibitive effort and that the central records covering every position in this present classification can be maintained with accuracy by a force whose size is not out of proportion to the results obtained." *Ibid.*, pp. 160, 162.

[67] See Griffenhagen, "The Principles and Technique of Preparing an Occupational Classification of Positions in the Public Service," *Public Personnel Studies*, November 1924, p. 245.

final criticisms and adjusting disagreements; and (14) adopting the position-classification plan.[68]

In some original classification projects, the classifiers have worked with two copies of each questionnaire—the original and a duplicate. The purpose of this procedure was to make available for the concurrent use of the staff engaged on work audit and those engaged on coordination, class-specification writing, and checking processes, sets of questionnaires continuously arranged in the two ways which experience has shown to be desirable. One set is sorted and maintained in organization order, while the other set is kept in class order, as classes are developed. The organization-order set is used in the work audit and is a source of information more comprehensive and more detailed than organization charts, showing the organizational relationships of each position. The class-order set is used for coordination and class-specification writing. Whenever comparisons need to be made among positions in the same field of work across organizational lines, this set furnishes the basic information for such an analysis.

So far, experience has not indicated that the technical advantages of this procedure outweigh the clerical expense of maintaining an additional questionnaire file, locating corresponding questionnaires, and constantly transferring field audit or other notations from one set to the other. Many of the advantages of the organization-order set can be secured through a first sorting of the questionnaires in organization order, as indicated below, if the questionnaires are given code or serial numbers, keyed to the charts. This will facilitate re-sorting them into the original organization order whenever it is found that the organization charts will not supply the necessary information.

The following discussion assumes that the classification staff will work with one copy of each questionnaire.

Arranging and Studying Questionnaires Organizationally

Arranging questionnaires in organization order is a process of sorting according to organization units and lines of supervisory responsibility. The questionnaires as received from the operating de-

---

[68] The sequence of procedures indicated is for the purpose of convenient discussion. Several of the steps are carried out simultaneously, and it is not intended to imply that each step must be completed before the next one is begun. In small jurisdictions or under certain conditions the first or second step may be omitted, or their sequence reversed. This will be indicated in the subsequent discussion.

partments should be grouped by organization units, but these units may be large or small and within each unit the questionnaires may be only approximately in organization order. The items on the questionnaire which will aid most in the organization-order arrangement are those which identify the positions, employees, or units under each supervisor and those which identify the immediate supervisor of each employee.

As the physical result of this sorting process, the questionnaires of all employees under the same supervisory official fall together, the questionnaire for the immediate superior coming at the top of each lot. Thus the questionnaires are in blocks corresponding to the blocks on the conventional organization chart. When this is done, the questionnaires are given a significant code or serial number to facilitate sorting them back to organization order, in whole or in part, whenever that might be desirable. These code or serial numbers should be indicated on the corresponding organization chart.

The major purposes of this process are (1) to facilitate the drafting of working charts of organization structure, so that the place of each position in relation to lines of authority and supervision may be known; and (2) to permit the raising and noting of points respecting organization structure or supervisory responsibility on which the questionnaires apparently are in conflict.

At the same time that the questionnaires are being arranged in organization order, the classifier should be alert for discrepancies and apparent inconsistencies as to lines of authority and responsibility and other matters which will affect later decisions. He also should watch for indications of missing information or similar errors which necessitate obtaining additional data. In this way, points to be covered either immediately or later during the process of the work audit are recorded for future coverage.

In small classification projects, or in any case where reliable and current organization charts are available or can be constructed without reference to the questionnaires, the preliminary step of arranging the questionnaires in organization order may be omitted. The first physical sorting is then on an occupational basis, discussed below. Under these circumstances, questions of missing or erroneous information are raised during the occupational sorting; but questions about supervisory relationships and responsibilities usually must be deferred until classes are being tentatively established or work audits are being made.

Arranging Questionnaires Occupationally

After rough organization charts have been prepared, a sorting of another type is made. In jurisdictions having as many as a thousand positions it will usually be found that the analysis of positions and the recognition of the classes that exist can be carried out most conveniently only after questionnaires representing similar, analogous, or associated occupations have been identified and grouped together for concentrated study. This calls for a preliminary occupational sorting.

First, the occupational groups into which the questionnaires are to be sorted are determined. These groups are selected more or less arbitrarily on the basis of a general knowledge of the service, in order to bring together for working purposes questionnaires covering positions that involve the same or associated professions, trades, vocations, lines of work, or fields of endeavor. For example, positions filled by engineers, draftsmen, and inspectors of engineering or fabrication, are sufficiently related functionally so that they should be studied together later, with a view to ascertaining what classes exist and how such classes should be described. Similarly, for working purposes, most positions involving the operation of office appliances, such as calculating machines, graphotypes, addressographs, etc., should be studied together because analogous classification problems arise in those cases.

The groups used as a basis for preliminary sorting form a working basis to facilitate the proper assignment of the personnel of the classification staff, to show where the services of subject-matter consultants might be used to advantage,[69] and to provide a means for effectively concentrating the study of classes during the next processes of analyzing the positions and tentatively deciding upon the classes which actually exist. Those experienced in the classification of engineering positions are confined to the group of questionnaires sorted to the engineering group; consultants in a given field, for example, accounting, are assigned to accounting questionnaires, and so on.

These groups may be few or numerous, depending somewhat on the size of the survey. In very large surveys many groups should be established, so as to avoid so far as possible the necessity later on of going through an additional sorting process. Sometimes, where a

[69] This is particularly important where the services of specialists or consultants are available for only a short time.

large or partly inexperienced classification staff is engaged, it is necessary to define these groups in writing, and to illustrate the kinds of positions falling in the various groups and the lines of distinction among the groups.

The preliminary sorting can be done by rapidly reading the information on the questionnaire describing the duties of the position. In the course of this process, no attention is paid to any of the following points:

1. Difficulty or responsibility ranking. Such important differences are taken up later on.

2. Organizational location. The sorting is cross-departmental.

3. Any finer segregation than that indicated in the predetermined occupational groups. Such finer segregation according to branches or specialities will be involved in subsequent steps.

Accordingly, the result of the preliminary sorting process will be an arrangement of the questionnaires into broad occupational groups, regardless of demarcations as to difficulty, responsibility, or occupational specialization.

This preliminary step is not so necessary in smaller jurisdictions where experienced classifiers can sort the questionnaires for the most part directly to classes or series of classes.[70] However, if the staff includes a number of inexperienced workers, the preliminary occupational sorting is desirable in the interests of training such workers, making the best use of their services, and conserving the time of the experienced members of the staff.

Analyzing Positions

After the questionnaires have been arranged occupationally, detailed analysis is begun. The considerations entering into this proc-

[70] Where the number and complexity of positions is not too great, experienced classifiers can sort questionnaires and tentatively decide upon the classes of positions which exist, more or less concurrently. This does not mean, however, that time will be saved or accuracy secured by adopting in advance a ready-made classification plan. It is essential, of course, that the classification plan being developed will fit the particular jurisdiction and the positions it contains. "The idea has been expressed at times that a set of services and series and even classes can be established once and for all, for all classification purposes everywhere. This idea can be disposed of rather summarily in view of the principle that the classification of a service should be a classification of *that* service—adjusted to provide for the employments as they exist under conditions which are peculiar to that jurisdiction. Furthermore, there are any number of questions of pure policy which make every difference in the detailed form of a classification and which are always decided somewhat differently in different projects." Griffenhagen, *ibid.*, p. 248.

ess and the kinds of facts and factors requiring evaluation have been discussed in a previous chapter.[71]

The preliminary occupational groups into which the questionnaires have been sorted are studied to determine (1) the kind or character of work, irrespective of level, and (2) the relative degree or level of difficulty and responsibility represented in each position.

First, as to kind of work, a segregation of the positions is made according to any distinct branches or specializations within the preliminary occupational group with which the analyst starts. For example, within a clerical group may be found stenographers, law clerks, statistical clerks, telephone operators, and other distinct lines of work. Each one of these breakdowns of the preliminary occupational group usually will be the over-all occupational area of what is known as a "series of classes."

A "series of classes" consists of several classes of positions closely similar as to line of work but differing in responsibility and difficulty, arranged in a ladder of steps in a normal line of promotion.[72]

Having defined, according to character of work, the occupational limits of each series of classes derived from the group of positions being studied, the next step is to consider the relative level of each position within each series. Following the technique of analysis discussed previously, there is determined, tentatively, the comparability, relative ranking, or gradation of the positions in each series, based on the difficulty and weight of their duties and responsibilities. Within each series this is at first an over-all, "vertical" arrangement without definitive ranks. Care is taken to recognize as accurately as possible the lowest and the highest positions in each series, and to make detailed notes of work-factors or difficulty or responsibility items having a controlling or contributory bearing on the relative

[71] Chapter V.

[72] "Where a number of 'classes' of positions are substantially similar as to the type of work involved and differ only in rank as determined by the importance of the duties, the degree of responsibility involved, and the amount of training and experience required, such 'classes' constitute a 'series,' and each is given a title containing a common term descriptive of the type of work, with a modifying term indicative of the relative rank." *Report of Congressional Joint Commission on Reclassification of Salaries*, p. 73.

For example, an aeronautical engineering series of classes may consist of the following classes, ranked in ascending order of difficulty and/or responsibility: Junior Aeronautical Engineer; Assistant Aeronautical Engineer; Associate Aeronautical Engineer; Aeronautical Engineer; Senior Aeronautical Engineer; Principal Aeronautical Engineer. A stenographic series of classes may include: Junior Stenographer; Intermediate Stenographer; Senior Stenographer. Sometimes there may be but one class in a series, where there are no other classes in that line of work in the jurisdiction.

order in which the positions appear to fall. This process establishes, in a preliminary way, the lower and upper limits of each series of classes and places the positions therein in a continuous rank-order.

The next objectives of the analysis are (1) to break up this continuous rank-order into discrete blocks, zones, or levels within the series of classes, i.e., to cut the series "horizontally" into individual classes of positions, and (2) to determine the relationships among classes in different series as to kind and level of work. These objectives involve, as a part of the problem of determining classes, the comprehension and definition of such lines of demarcation as may exist between the lower and upper limits of the series, as previously decided upon. They also embrace the problem of "pegging" classes, according to kind and level of work, not only within a given series of classes, but in the whole classification structure. These problems will next be discussed.

Determining Classes

With respect to their effect upon the operating processes of personnel administration, the most important decisions in the development of a position-classification plan are determinations of the classes to be recognized and established. In tackling this problem, attention is confined to the positions as they currently exist in the service. Although during the course of the continued administration of the position-classification plan (after it is adopted and installed) new and changed classes may be established,[73] the initial plan is regarded as a current inventory of the service, and usually, therefore, no classes are established during the process of development unless one or more positions belonging in these classes actually exist.

The classes into which the existing positions in the service fall are perceived and identified through analysis of their duties and responsibilities and the determination of the extent to which these duties and responsibilities are alike or different. The technique of analysis has already been discussed.[74] As a result of analysis, the similarities and divergences of the positions in the service—both as to kind of work and level of difficulty and responsibility—will have been explored and determined. To proceed from that phase of the classifier's work to the actual recognition and establishment of classes requires the application of sound judgment in personnel matters,

[73] Chapter X, pp. 306–08.
[74] Chapter V.

based (a) on the basic concept of a *class* of positions and (b) on the purposes of a position-classification plan as a facilitating instrument for personnel administration.

The definition of a class, as a fundamental concept of position-classification, requires that positions regarded as falling in one class shall be *"sufficiently similar" in respect to their duties and responsibilities,* and leaves to sound judgment the question of precisely what constitutes a sufficient degree of similarity, in the light of the four concurrent criteria stated in the definition, namely, the propriety of using the same title, the same qualification requirements, the same tests of fitness, and the same pay scale (under the same employment conditions) for all positions in the class.[75]

If, for example, in studying a group of positions, the classifier finds that some of the positions require treatment different from others in one or more of these respects, he knows that he cannot consider the group as a single class. He must break it up into two or more smaller groups, until the position-content of each group is so nearly uniform in character that each position in the group may be treated in the same way for personnel and pay purposes. At this point, then, he has recognized the groups or "classes" represented in the positions under his study. After making a memorandum record of his analysis, the classes recognized, and the lines of differentiation among them, he proceeds to carry out the same process for other groups, always referring back to classes already recognized to maintain consistency of viewpoint and judgment.

In some instances, the establishment of classes is not difficult. In very large organizations, where the division of labor is fine, some positions will be almost exactly alike in their duties, tasks, and responsibilities and significantly different from all other positions— so much so that it would be obvious to any one that they should be treated alike in personnel administration. For example, it may be found that the service includes a mechanical statistical tabulating unit in which there are 40 employees whose sole duty is to punch tabulating cards, using the same type of machine, the same type of statistical schedule, coded by a uniform system, and the same "fields" of the card. The classifier knows immediately that each of these 40 positions falls in the same class. Similarly, some positions will be easily recognized as falling in such classes as patrolman, building inspector, the journeyman classes in the trades and crafts, or other well-known groups, and the necessity for the establishment of these

[75] Pp. 45–47.

classes clearly perceived. Other kinds of positions require more study. For example, should separate classes be established for index clerks, payroll clerks, copyists, comparers, and other positions involving routine clerical work or should all such work, notwithstanding some differences in its type, be included within a single class? If such differences are not deemed sufficient to require separate classes, are the differences between clerks recording routine accounting data and those recording routine statistical data of greater significance? Does a working supervisor position in a group of three clerks require a separate class? Such questions as these are typical of those arising when classes are being recognized and established.

The grouping of positions into classes generally necessitates a definitive consideration of how material or immaterial their similarities and divergences are in the light of the uses to which the classification plan will be put.[76] Where positions are alike in some respects and different in others, do the similarities or the differences have the greater effect for personnel, administrative, and pay purposes? If the similarities of two positions are sufficiently strong and their differences sufficiently minor to make it logical and feasible to treat the positions alike from the standpoint of nomenclature, qualification standards, and pay (under the same employment conditions), they belong to the same class.[77] If not, they belong to different classes.

The question is sometimes asked, How many classes shall be established? There is no formula that will give the answer in the light of the conditions in the particular jurisdiction and the variety of positions it contains.[78] The question gets its importance from the

[76] Chapter IV. See also Griffenhagen, *op. cit.*, p. 249.

[77] "Whereas at first glimpse two positions may seem to be so dissimilar that it is felt they could not possibly be put in the same class, it may be that it is merely the media with which employees in the two positions are working that confuses the classifier. For example, routine posting of financial information to a ledger of accounts is really not different insofar as basic manipulations involved are concerned from posting information from statistical reports relating to a number of traffic accidents to summary form. Yet differences in the media involved in two such positions might lead to a hasty assumption that two classes would have to be established to comprehend them." Public Administration Service, *Personnel Administration Survey, Sioux City, Iowa* (1939) p. 5. See also Chapter V, pp. 86–91.

[78] "The number of classes in a given jurisdiction or industrial concern of course depends upon the size and complexity of the service classified, particularly the number of different functions exercised and activities pursued. An industrial concern if large and complex may have several hundred classes of positions. In a small city or county service, there may be as few as a hundred classes, while in a large city, state, or federal service, there may be 2,000 or more classes." "The Uses of an Occupational Classification of Positions," *Public Personnel Studies*, October 1924, p. 221.

effect the number of classes has upon the apparent clarity and simplicity or the apparent obscurity and complexity of the position-classification plan and the personnel transactions based upon it. The argument is that if too many classes are established, the recruiting, testing, promotion, and other civil service processes become voluminous in detail and expensive; there is too much "red tape" involved in reassigning employees to slightly different work; budget schedules become unwieldy and not easily understood; the lines of demarcation among the classes are apt to be so thin and the differentiating factors so obscure that it is difficult to allocate positions to classes convincingly; and much opportunity is afforded for controversy as to the class in which a given position properly belongs for pay purposes, promotion examinations, lay-offs, and other administrative processes. On the other hand, if too few classes are established, it is said, the classes themselves will be so broad in content that the recruiting needs of the service are not met by the production of specifically qualified eligibles through general tests based on these broad classes; there is so much flexibility as to encourage favoritism and injustice; there is often an ignoring of those differences in duties that should give rise to corresponding differences in the pay and other treatment of employees; and the data used in developing a pay plan—particularly outside wage data for comparable employments in private industry and in other jurisdictions—become to a large extent inapplicable or meaningless.

Of course, the question of *how many* classes are to be contained in the position-classification plan is not so important as the question of *what* classes are to be included. If the latter question is wisely settled, the former should be considered disposed of. Position-classification exists for administration. The classes established must therefore serve administrative purposes. If they do this well, then whatever the number of classes, whether large or small, that number is justified and necessary. Consequently, the problem is not one of holding the number of classes to a minimum or of establishing as many classes as possible, but is one of deciding in specific instances upon the degree of refinement to which the classification of positions must be carried in order that the plan may effectively serve its purposes.

It is simple enough to lay down a general rule that, in studying a group of positions, the classifier should establish such classes as are necessary to make the position-content of each one sufficiently homogeneous for these purposes. The application of this rule, however, is not simple. A series of problems always arises during the development of a plan requiring decisions on the breadth or narrowness of the classes being established. In this respect, certain position-classification plans have been criticized because they classified too finely [79] and others because they classified too broadly.[80]

Of course, immaterial distinctions among positions—those that are of too little weight to require that the positions receive different treatment in personnel or pay actions—are ignored. The classification of positions is not carried out to a philosophical extreme, in which human ingenuity is allowed full sway.[81] Considerations of clarity and usefulness are important. From the standpoint of pure logic, taking stenographic dictation of a medical diagnosis and taking stenographic dictation of an engineering specification are tasks that could be regarded as falling in two different classes. But from a practical standpoint, the recognition of small differences in kind of work would bog down with minutiae the position-classification plan and the personnel transactions based upon it.

[79] "The Congressional Classification of the Federal Service was published March 12, 1920. It contains 884 pages. . . . To my mind it is clumsy, unnecessarily verbose, difficult to understand and extremely difficult for the civil service commission to use. I do not think it is well suited to the examination requirements of the United States Civil Service Commission. For example, the following separately classified positions had the same or similar qualification requirements: Junior file and record clerk, under clerk, under securities clerk, junior recorder, under counter clerk, dead letter clerk, miscellaneous appliance operator, junior publication distributor, junior mail routing clerk, junior mechanical file clerk, under purchasing clerk. Instead of simplifying the terminology and expediting the work of the Civil Service Commission the classifiers have added to the complexities and difficulties of administration. Nearly all of the above named positions could be filled from two or three eligible lists. . . . The test of a good classification is its usableness. Its value lies in the fact that it gets itself used, the fact that it is practicable, sensible, and acceptable to reasonable men." F. E. Doty (Secretary and Chief Examiner, Los Angeles County Civil Service Commission), *Proceedings,* 14th Annual Meeting of the Assembly of Civil Service Commissions, June 1921, pp. 29–30.

[80] "Many of the classes are too general. Thus there is a class of 'associate technician,' but neither the title nor the definition of duties throws much light on the kind of position to be included. Elsewhere it appears, however, that this class is to include botanists, seed analysts, entomologists, actuaries, market specialists, and foresters." New York Bureau of Municipal Research, *Organization and Management of the State Government of Virginia* (Richmond, 1927), p. 33.

[81] "In preparing a classification plan for any objects, items, or things, the refinements that may be indulged in are limited only by human ingenuity. The same thing is true, of course, of the classification of positions. From a practical standpoint, however, the degree of refinement to which a classification plan should be properly carried is limited by consideration of the usefulness of the plan so prepared in the normal processes of personnel management." *U. S. Personnel Classification Board, Report of Wage and Personnel Survey* (1929), H. Doc. No. 602, 70th Cong., 2d sess. p. 26.

Similarly, too fine distinctions between positions in respect to degree of difficulty or level of responsibility are ignored. In a group of positions in the same field of work, the increase in difficulty or responsibility of work, from least to most difficult or responsible, is more on the order of an inclined plane than by a succession of definite steps. For classification, recruiting, and pay purposes, it would be impracticable to recognize each slight increment in difficulty or responsibility in a position, as compared with another one in the same line of work, even if classification methods could be developed to a point where such increments could be measured with scientific exactness.

In actual practice, accordingly, the degree of refinement is determined by working advantages to be gained and by considerations of principle, practicality, and common sense, in the light of local factors or conditions that vary in their effect from jurisdiction to jurisdiction. Among these are:

1. The local situation in respect to the merit system.

2. The precise ways in which the classes will later be used in personnel, fiscal, budget, and administrative operations.

3. The legal requirements of such formal rules or the character of such established practices as may exist, governing (a) recruiting, testing, and appointment processes, and (b) in-service transactions, such as promotion, transfer, lay-off, and reemployment.

4. The degree of variation in the kinds of work-assignments given in the course of operating administration to employees in the group under consideration.

5. Environmental conditions peculiar to certain kinds of positions.

The local situation in respect to the merit system is one of the first things to consider, by way of general background, because of its bearing on the use of the classes. There may be no civil service system and no formal rules of procedure in effect or in contemplation. In this event actual recruiting policies and practices need to be explored and understood. A merit system may be in process of development and installation concurrently with the position-classification program. In this case the civil service rules, being in process of preparation, may be so developed as to coordinate nicely with the character of the classification plan and to cover situations that could be met only awkwardly in the process of establishing classes. There may be in current effect a merit system, the formalities of which may be so firmly established that there is no possibility of revision within a reasonable time. When this is true, the classes to be established must serve the purposes of administration as effectively as possible in the light of the existing rules.

The fundamental guide to action on the problem of how fine the classification should be, is, as we have indicated, the purpose and use of position-classification as an administrative tool. Hence, in order to determine intelligently what classes shall be recognized, it is necessary to understand thoroughly the precise ways in which the classes will later be used in personnel, fiscal, budget, and administrative operations; for example, their use in recruitment, transfer, promotion, lay-offs, and reemployment, and in developing and expressing rules for the conduct of these and other transactions; in the establishment and administration of pay scales and a pay plan; in the preparation and control of payrolls; in the preparation of budget estimates and the legislative authorization of appropriations for personal services; and in facilitating the work of operating agencies.

Generally, it will be found that the selection of classes is governed by the degree of refinement made necessary by recruiting practices. Any classification of positions that is sufficiently fine for recruiting, testing, and promotion purposes is usually fine enough for all other purposes.[82]

Recruiting principles and practices, however, may vary according to the type of position. In some instances no outside competition may be available, and persons with broad, fundamental background are recruited and trained in the specialized work of the position. In other instances, recruiting is largely from outside the service of persons who already possess the required specialized qualifications. Classes sufficiently refined to serve adequately the first kind of recruiting process may be too broad to serve the second kind.

A good illustration of how the selection of classes is controlled by local recruiting practices is afforded by the testing and selection of laborers. In some jurisdictions recruiting practices may recognize only a difference between unskilled (or common) labor and the type of semi-skilled labor falling below mechanic's helper. In other juris-

[82] Differences in positions which are not such as to affect seriously their treatment as a unit in personnel work have been disregarded. In nearly every class there will be found, therefore, positions that differ from one another in minor particulars. . . . In setting limits to classification refinements the more frequently occurring needs of selection processes have governed." U. S. Personnel Classification Board, *Preliminary Class Specifications of Positions in the Field Service*, H.Doc. 772, 71st Cong., 3d sess., 1930, p. 5. See also Griffenhagen, *op. cit.*, p. 250.

dictions, the breakdown for test and selection purposes is much finer and such classes as farm laborer, power plant laborer, highway laborer, and building construction laborer, among others, may call for recognition in the classification plan.[83]

In some instances the character of the local "labor market" may require the creation of particular classes. The weight of this factor depends on whether the functions of the jurisdiction are purely governmental or whether they include proprietary functions in which the jurisdiction competes in the locality for particular types of employees. In the latter case, particular classes may be set up to permit recognition of the classes of specialized personnel available in the locality. For this reason, one classification plan recognizes a separate class of "cotton mill machinist" in addition to a general class of "machinist."

Especially important are the legal requirements. For example, in a new civil-service installation, present incumbents may be covered into the civil service without examination, or through noncompetitive or qualifying tests, or through open competitive tests. In the last situation, it may be required that the classes first established should recognize finer distinctions among positions than would be necessary after the regular recruiting program begins. Again, the rules for certification of eligibles have a bearing. In a few jurisdictions the first eligible on the list must be certified and selected; in others, the appointing officer may select from three eligibles to fill each vacancy; in still others, he may choose from a larger number. Certification rules may be very rigid or somewhat flexible. Where the appointing officer's field of choice is very much restricted, finer classes as a basis for recruiting will tend to provide him with eligibles having the specific qualifications the vacancies demand, and classes which are too broad or dissimilar in position-content will not serve adequately for recruiting for all the positions in the class.

The effort to fit the classes to the legal requirements of formal rules or the character of established practices in respect to in-service transactions, such as promotion, transfer, lay-off, and reemployment, may prove somewhat difficult, particularly where such rules or prac-

[83] See Fred Telford, "The Classification of Labor Positions and the Testing of Labor Applicants in the Public Service," *Public Personnel Studies*, January-February 1924, pp. 5–11; "The Method of Testing Laborers used by the City Service Commission of Milwaukee," *Public Personnel Studies*, November 1928, pp. 229–30. The Civil Service Board of Portland, Oregon, has recruited from different lists street-cleaning laborers, painting laborers, park laborers, sewer laborers, and regular laborers.

tices are inflexible in type. The use of the classes in personnel transactions may lead to changes of practice or revisions of laws or rules,
but for the time being, a realistic view sometimes gives rise to disturbing questions.

If, for example, the civil service rules provide that no employee
may be promoted from one class of positions to a higher class except
through competitive promotional tests, there might be a temptation
to establish classes as broadly as possible in order to provide administrative flexibility in the assignment of employees, and to avoid
bogging down the personnel agency's testing activities with a multiplicity of promotional tests. However, the establishment of classes
which are sufficiently broad for these purposes creates another difficulty in the preparation and holding of open competitive tests, in
that eligibles may not possess the specific qualifications necessary.
Thus, an attempt to aid operating officials by facilitating placement,
promotional, and transfer transactions may handicap them in the
selection of new employees whose qualifications do not fit the positions they have to fill as precisely as they deem necessary.

A few attempts have been made to avoid this apparent conflict
by adopting one classification arrangement for original recruiting
purposes and another arrangement for promotion, transfer, or lay-
off purposes. Clearly, such a procedure is undesirable. The better
practice is to recognize the classes that actually exist, having one
official classification for all purposes, and by the use of the appropriate class titles, to indicate in the civil service rules (a) the kinds
of positions between which promotions or transfers may be made
without formal test and (b) those between which promotions or
transfers require formal tests.

It has been suggested that the central personnel agency should not
favor, for original recruiting purposes, the recognition of a multiplicity of classes on the basis of special skills and knowledges which
are acquired only in the performance of the work and cannot be
tested for in the initial recruiting process. For initial recruiting
purposes, therefore, only such classes should be recognized as are
based on essentially different skills and knowledges which can be
tested. For other purposes, however, it is suggested that finer classifications, called "sub-classes," be adopted.[84] These sub-classes, it is
stated, are not used for recruiting purposes but are devices "to con-

[84] "Sub-Class. Whenever the Commission shall find that any class consists of
two or more positions which may be recruited with propriety from the same em-

serve the City's investment in training by facilitating lay-offs and reemployment in accordance with specialized experience secured with the City." The sub-classes are, accordingly, suitable for such processes as lay-offs and reemployment, payroll, and other official purposes; promotion and transfer tests and transactions; and service ratings. This plan, however, is in actual use only to a limited extent.

Another factor that has a bearing on the breadth or narrowness of classes is in the degree of variation in the kinds of work-assignments given to employees in the group under consideration. This is conditioned by how well work is organized and by the size of work-units. Generally speaking, the larger the work-unit, the more finely the operations of the unit are subdivided, and the more homogeneous the work of each individual position within the unit is apt to be. The smaller the work unit, the more likely it is that positions of widely varied duties-content will be found. For example, some positions may fall entirely within the class of carpenter; others within the class of electrician; but others, especially in institutions, may involve work in different trades, requiring the establishment of a class of handyman or general mechanic.

Again, consider a position which involves a more or less constant interchange of clerical and drafting tasks. Shall it be placed in a clerical class, because as a whole it does not warrant the same pay scale as a draftsman? Should it be placed in a drafting class, because drafting qualifications are needed to do the work and clerical qualifications alone would be insufficient? Or, should a separate class of clerk-draftsman be established? The answers to such questions as these can be made to depend on their effect on the recruiting process. If the additional labor of conducting specialized tests for clerk-draftsman would not be justified by the results, compared with the

---

ployment list but which by reason of work specialization or other reasons develop qualifications of skill, knowledge, and other requisites peculiar to one or more such positions and which specialized qualifications make difficult or undesirable, complete interchangeability of the experienced incumbents of such positions, the Commission in its discretion may create sub-classes of such class for the following purposes only: (a) Lay-offs and reemployment; (b) payroll and other official purposes; (c) promotions and transfers including promotional and noncompetitive tests; (d) service ratings; (e) such other purposes as the Commission shall designate, except recruiting. The Commission may restrict the use of a sub-class and the title thereof to one or more of the above purposes. Before the expiration of the probationary period, each new employee shall be allocated by the employing Department, subject to the approval of the Commission, to the appropriate sub-class. Transfers between sub-classes will be treated in the same manner as transfers between classes." Detroit Civil Service Commission, *The Classification Plan for the City of Detroit,* 1935, p. iii.

use of a draftsman list, the position in question could with propriety be classed with other drafting positions and a separate class of clerk-draftsman not recognized.[85]

In some instances, the conditions under which the work is done have such an important bearing on recruiting practices or standards as to require the establishment of specific classes. There is the steam-fitter working constantly in a steam tunnel; the marine fireman in the engine room of a vessel as contrasted with the fireman in the stationary power plant of an institution; the technician in a danger-ous-disease laboratory; or the worker whose position is unusually hazardous because of his environment or unusually undesirable be-cause of the geographic isolation of the employment.[86] Experience indicates that special recruiting devices usually have to be employed to secure qualified eligibles who are willing to accept positions of these kinds.

Determining Relationships among Classes

Each class that has been tentatively established represents both a kind of work and a "level" or zone of work in terms of relative de-gree of difficulty and/or responsibility. Among themselves, the classes have relationships in these respects. Two classes may cover work in the same general field, e.g., engineering, but one may be broader in scope than the other, as in the case of civil engineering contrasted with hydraulic engineering. This is a relationship of *kind*. Also, the same two classes have another type of relationship in that one may involve work of a high degree of difficulty or re-sponsibility and the other may include simpler or less exacting pro-fessional activities. This is a relationship of *rank, level,* or *degree.*[87]

[85] Example taken from Griffenhagen, *op. cit.,* pp. 249–50.

[86] The Federal Classification Act of 1923 has recently been amended to auth-orize the President to add a salary differential of not to exceed 25 per cent of the minimum rate of each pay scale for unusual isolation, excessive physical hardship or hazard, or extra-continental location. In lieu of establishing such differential, the statute also permits consideration of these factors in establishing classes and allocating them to classification and salary grades. Act of November 26, 1940, Title II, Sec. 3 (c), Public 880, 76th Cong.

[87] "The most logical and significant, and otherwise best available, bases that have been found for distinguishing among positions of different kinds are two: *kind* and *degree.* Here 'kind' would be represented by the character of the work done, which may be regarded for purposes of graphic representation as a hori-zontal coordinate, and degree being represented by the rank or level of difficulty and responsibility or other measure of relative value of work done, which may be regarded as the corresponding vertical coordinate. By these two coordinates any position may be located on the field of possible employments, with definiteness and certainty, in theory at least, and in due relation to each and every other

Until the classes are studied, each in relation to the others, and both types of relationships among them determined and recorded, the classification plan as a whole is not completed. In fact, the processes of analyzing positions and establishing classes, and the later processes of selecting class titles and writing class specifications, depend for their completion upon decisions as to how each class is related to all the others as to (1) kind and (2) degree of difficulty and responsibility of work. It is necessary, accordingly, to consider at this point the methods and principles by which the tentative list of classes, among which the interrelations have been only partly determined, may be finally transformed into an integrated and articulated classification plan of maximum usefulness.

The initial steps of analysis have grouped positions tentatively into classes and classes into series of classes. The connections among some classes as to kind or character of work are thus indicated by their assignment to the same series of classes. Also, the connections among some classes as to relative level within a given series of classes (such as stenography, mining engineering, or the machinist's trade), consisting of two or more classes, will already have been established. Thus some relationships have been determined, at least in a preliminary way.

To complete the classification plan it is necessary to go further with the analysis in order to determine and show the relationships of classes within the whole classification structure. This problem presents little difficulty so far as relationships as to kind or character of work are concerned. The determination of relative levels, however, is a difficult task.

Kind-relationships among classes are most commonly indicated by grouping the various series of classes into "services" or "occupational groups." A "service" or an "occupational group" is a general aggregation of classes of positions grouped regardless not only of departmental and organization lines, but also regardless of rank, on the basis of outstanding common characteristics or general factors of similarity, selected more or less arbitrarily to aid in the

---

position. No other possible coordinates have been suggested or have been found in use that seem to afford any logical ground for any claim to produce such a result. It is by such a result only that any justification for calling any set of titles and descriptions of positions a 'classification plan,' can be found." Griffenhagen & Associates, *Distinctive Features of the Classification Plan of 1938,* Memorandum No. 31, submitted to Michigan State Personnel Director, July 15, 1938, p. 2.

process of classification.[88] As a rule it embraces several series of classes of positions in associated or related occupations, professions, or activities.[89] These occupational groups or services are used to help make a complex classification plan comprehensible as a whole.[90]

Customarily, in the smaller jurisdictions, it is necessary only to gather the classes into either "services" or "occupational groups," no larger groupings being required for proper understanding of the position-classification plan.[91] Occasionally, however, in the largest jurisdictions, both such groupings are desirable. In this event, the series of classes are grouped into "occupational groups" and these groups are then brought together in a limited number of services. In such instances, services are broader in content than are occupational groups.

To illustrate: Under the Federal Classification Act of 1923, as amended, all classes of positions are grouped into five services: the professional and scientific service; the sub-professional service; the clerical, administrative, and fiscal service; the custodial service; and the clerical-mechanical service. The scope of each service is described in the statute. Administratively, occupational groups are recognized in each service. For example, the professional and scientific service includes such occupational groups as the economics and political science, agricultural, biological, and physical science, medical, veterinary, engineering, and legal groups. The custodial service includes various occupational groups such as the messenger, labor,

[88] *Report of Congressional Joint Commission on Reclassification of Salaries,* p. 73.

[89] For example, an engineering service or occupational group would normally include all engineering series of classes, although each series represents a distinct engineering branch, such as aeronautical, automotive, civil, electrical, or mechanical. A stenography, typing, and correspondence service or occupational group would include several series of classes, comprising the typist, clerk-typist, stenographer, clerk-stenographer, correspondence clerk, dictating machine transcriber, and stenographic reporter series.

[90] "What does the term 'service' really mean? The writer suggests that a service should be used to describe as a unit all those positions which normally appeal to the same general type of mind of potential public employees." Albert Smith Faught, "Highlights in Twenty Classification Studies," *Proceedings,* 13th Annual Meeting of Assembly of Civil Service Commissions, June 1920, p. 49. It should be observed that the expression "service" as used in classification matters has therefore no connection with the word "service" as used in such organizational names as Meat Inspection Service, Forest Service, or Indian Service.

[91] In such cases common practice omits the use of the term "occupational group" in favor of the term "service." A typical list of classification services in a municipality is: Clerical and Administrative; Engineering; Public Health; Welfare; Police and Fire; Domestic and Janitorial; Skilled Trades and Labor. In the smallest jurisdictions, even such services are not necessary, and series designations will suffice.

mechanical trades and crafts, guard and fire-protection, and domestic activities groups. These, it will be observed, are very broad services, making it necessary, for convenience in use, to segregate series of classes into occupational groups within services.[92]

The arrangement of classes into occupational groups or services is not a process essential to position-classification, but one of usefulness and convenience. Although perhaps unnecessary where the classes are few, such an arrangement is frequently adopted administratively in large jurisdictions, even though not required by statute, ordinance, or regulation, because it has certain advantages. When grouped together on the basis of similarity and equivalence of duties and responsibilities, positions form classes; classes, when ranked in a natural ladder of promotion, form series; series, when grouped together by closely associated occupations, fields of work, or functional activities, comprise occupational groups; and occupational groups, when brought together according to more general or broader associations, constitute services. This arrangement permits a logical association of classes, facilitates the analysis of the classes thus associated, and assists in the appraisal of their relative difficulty, value, or rank.

In the study and use of a position-classification plan in connection with personnel activities and problems, it is often desirable to concentrate attention on one class or one related group of classes at a time. Sometimes the problem is such that we wish to concentrate on a class of positions such as Junior Aeronautical Engineer; sometimes on all aeronautical engineering positions, in which event we would study the aeronautical engineering series of classes; sometimes on all engineering positions, in which case it would be helpful to have an engineering occupational group; and sometimes on all professional and scientific positions, such as engineers, lawyers, medical officers, economists, and so on, in which event it is helpful to be able to identify a professional and scientific service. The arrangement of classes into these groups furnishes segments conveniently available for study, and makes it possible to comprehend the plan in detail.

The existence of recognized services, occupational groups, and series of classes also provides a short way of describing comprehensively all classes having certain common characteristics. This may be convenient in drafting regulations governing personnel transactions.

[92] See the schematic chart of the federal classification system, in Pfiffner, *Research Methods in Public Administration*, pp. 340–41.

Moreover, in presenting a position-classification plan to administrative officials, legislative bodies, employee groups, and the general public, it is practically always necessary to group the classes so as to make them stand out in some orderly fashion. When problems arise as a result of this presentation, or when changes in the position-classification plan are required before its adoption, the arrangement permits easy segregation of the classes to which the problems refer, and the identification of other classes affected by the changes.

The development of a pay plan is also facilitated when the relationships among all classes have been worked out in terms of series, occupational groups, and services. This arrangement assists in setting certain broad matters of policy, entrance rates for the lowest classes in any service or occupational group, or maximum rates for the highest classes in any service or occupational group—decisions which have the effect of setting the general level of the pay plan. The arrangement also obviously affords a means for the legislature or the personnel or fiscal agency to see in advance the kinds of positions directly and indirectly affected by its decisions and to express its decisions cogently by associating pay scales with an orderly arrangement of classes.

The arrangement of classes which we have been discussing creates within each occupational group and each service a number of series of classes. Within each such series, the classes will be ranked in a ladder according to their relative difficulty and responsibility. Like real ladders, the various series may not all be of equal length, they may not all have the same number of rungs, and the rungs themselves may not always be the same distance apart. Furthermore, the series of classes have not as yet been ranked with relation to one another; that is, the arrangement does not tell us at once whether the feet of the various ladders are level, or whether their tops reach to the same level, and, if not, what and how much the differences are in these respects. Until series of classes are evaluated in relation to one another as to levels of work within the same service or occupational group, or within the whole classification structure, it may be said that positions are not fully classified, because the relative levels of the classes to which they are allocated have not been completely determined.[93]

[93] "In order to know fully what a person's job is we must know not only the *kind* of work in which he is engaged but also the *grade or level* reached by his activity in the operations of the enterprise. Each of these considerations necessitates a *separate* classification. The one is a *functional classification* and the other is a *graded classification*." J. O. Hopwood, *Salaries, Wages and Labor*

This problem of evaluating and relating the various series of classes, one to another, as to levels of work is most frequently tackled by developing from a study of the classes and series of classes a "vertical" frame of reference—a sort of master ladder to which the various series ladders would be referred. This frame of reference may be regarded as composed of "classification-grades" or zones, ranks, or levels of difficulty and responsibility of work.

"Classification-grades" are groupings of classes from a relative difficulty and responsibility standpoint. Each classification-grade includes all classes of positions which are substantially equal in difficulty and responsibility, even though these classes may vary widely in character, subject-matter, function, or occupation. The term "classification-grade" in lieu of "grade" is used to emphasize that basically it is a duties-rank concept (one phase of classification) rather than a pay or salary range concept. It is a zone of difficulty and/or responsibility to which the pay plan may attach a single scale of pay, uniform for all classes in the classification-grade, or pay scales of different lengths or of somewhat different levels, depending on the structure and policy of the pay plan and the extent to which variations in employment, geographic, or economic factors may warrant specific recognition in pay scales. Accordingly, "classification-grade," as here defined, should be distinguished from "pay-scale." A classification-grade recognizes only a certain level of difficulty and responsibility of work; a "pay-scale" recognizes this factor and many others that it should reflect, if properly determined.[94]

The fact that two classes fall in the same "classification-grade," or zone of difficulty and responsibility, does not, without further thought, lead to the conclusion that, when a pay plan is developed, they should be compensated by exactly the same pay scale. This

---

Relations (Copyright 1937, The Ronald Press Company), p. 84. See also J. W. Rupley, "A Rational Salary Plan," *Proceedings,* Fifth Annual Institute of Government, University of Washington, July 26, 1940, pp. 3–9.

[94] Confusion in this respect will arise wherever classification-grading is thought of as synonymous with pay-fixing. Note the following descriptive statement: "The final step in the over-all methods is fitting the jobs, as ranked, into grades which cut across all departments. The grading plan is the framework by means of which like jobs in different divisions and jobs of different kinds, but nevertheless of equivalent value, are given the same rate of pay. Theoretically the number of grades depends only upon the number of distinct levels of difficulty, responsibility, etc.; but, actually, the number is often based on opinions as to appreciable differences in rates of pay. Sometimes the unscientific practice is followed of developing the grade framework first and then merely sorting jobs into grades without previous ranking." Kent F. Bradbury, "Job Evaluation Analyzed," *Advanced Management,* January-February-March, 1940, p. 17.

should be the result, of course, where all other factors are the same. But where factors bearing on pay scales, other than difficulty and responsibility of work, are not the same, they may require a differentiation in pay scales as between two classes in the same classification-grade. For example, prevailing rates in nongovernment enterprises, economic conditions affecting recruiting, or degree of opportunity for promotion out of the class, are pay factors which would not always have a uniform effect upon each class in a classification-grade.[95] Classification-grades are based solely on variations in the relative levels of the duties and responsibilities of positions and do not reflect variations in these other pay factors. Hence, some difficulties may be anticipated in preparing and administering a sound pay plan if it is sought to integrate the pay plan formally or legislatively with classification-grades in such a way that one and only one pay scale is associated with each classification-grade.[96]

In establishing classification-grades, the underlying assumption is that we can so develop them that (a) all classes in the same grade will be substantially equal in respect to difficulty and responsibility of work and (b) classes in different grades will be in correct relation to one another in this respect. When this is done, the classification plan will have a "horizontal" framework consisting of series of classes within occupational groups and services, across which there will be a "vertical" framework of classification-grades. Thus each class and each position will be "pegged" horizontally and vertically in the whole classification plan and its place therein definitely determined.[97]

In order to develop classification-grades, classes of positions, after they are established, are analyzed and evaluated comparatively, using principles and factors the same as those upon which the analysis and comparative evaluation of individual positions are based.[98]

[95] See Chapter III, pp. 52–54.
[96] The use of classification-grades in developing a pay plan will be more fully discussed in the report of the Committee on Pay Plans in the Public Service, a companion volume in this series.
[97] With respect to the analogous problem in industrial personnel management, see Hugh L. Clary, "The Zoning of Jobs" *Industrial Management*, May 1921, pp. 324–29; Marion A. Bills, "A Method for Classifying the Jobs and Rating the Efficiency of Clerical Workers," *Journal of Personnel Research*, December 1922 and January 1923, pp. 384–93; J. O. Hopwood, "The Grades of Labor," *The Personnel Journal*, August 1929, pp. 114–24; Walter V. Bingham, "Classifying and Testing for Clerical Jobs," *The Personnel Journal*, November 1935, pp. 163–72; J. O. Hopwood, *Salaries, Wages and Labor Relations*, pp. 28–72; Riegel, *Salary Determination*, pp. 262–64; C. Canby Balderston, *Wage Setting Based on Job Analysis and Evaluation* (Industrial Relations Counselors, 1940), pp. 9–12.
[98] Chapter V.

In this evaluation, classes of positions having substantially the same rank as to difficulty and responsibility of work are grouped together and identified as belonging to the same "classification-grade." These grades are revised as necessary during the subsequent processes of developing the position-classification plan. Current records of the results of this study are maintained by preparing charts showing graphically, by class title, the various zones in which the classes are "pegged." Such a procedure provides a constant source of reference and aids materially in coordinating the classification plan.[99]

As thus established, classification-grades have the status of a working tool for the classification staff. Usually they are not defined otherwise than in the language of the specifications of the classes they contain; by reference to such classes and specifications, their characteristics are deemed to be adequately illustrated.[100]

The principal advantages of developing classification-grades during an original classification project are as follows:[101]

1. As an integral part of the development of the classification plan and at the time all differentiating factors among positions and among classes are being studied, it is necessary to explore and evaluate the facts as to relative ranking as well as to differences in character. This leads to more careful judgment and the current disclosure and definition of ranking factors, as contrasted with the frequent practice of leaving over-all ranking relations to be determined during the process of developing the pay plan.

2. Ranking factors can be described in class specifications and elsewhere in systematic and consistent terms with logical treatment from one part of the classification plan to another. The nomenclature of class titles can be better standardized across occupational lines, particularly in respect to ranking adjectives or symbols. Qualification requirements or standards in different series can be better coordinated.

---

[99] See J. W. Rupley, *op. cit.,* p. 8.

[100] In some instances, where definite integration of pay scales and classification-grades has been the objective, formal definitions varying in detail have been worked out. See Griffenhagen & Associates, *Distinctive Features of the Classification Plan of 1938,* p. 6; Section 13 of the Federal Classification Act of 1923, as amended, U. S. Code, Title 5, Secs. 661–74, 678. Cf. the "classification scheme for grading positions," in J. O. Hopwood, "The Grades of Labor"; and the frame of reference for the classification of positions in a large industrial company given in Riegel, *Salary Determination* (University of Michigan, Bureau of Industrial Relations, 1940), pp. 262–64.

[101] Griffenhagen & Associates, *op. cit.,* pp. 6–9; Detroit Civil Service Commission, "Purposes and Uses of a Grading Plan," *The Classification Plan for the City of Detroit,* pp. xxxvi, xxxvii.

3. The arrangement of classification-grades is an over-all guide to future changes in the classification plan such as those made necessary by expansion of activities, reorganizations, or the creation of new activities; such changes can be made on an orderly basis correlated with the whole plan.

4. Like the grouping of classes into series, occupational groups, and services, a grouping into classification-grades aids in explaining the position-classification plan and the allocations of positions to legislators, executives, fiscal agencies, employees, and the public. A common base is afforded for intelligent discussion of relative levels of difficulty and responsibility.

5. Where a pay plan is to be developed and a salary scale for each class established, a system of classification-grades facilitates initial action and later control and revision. It simplifies the problem of understanding the relationships among a large number of individual classes, and makes it easier to secure proper coordination among the pay scales for classes differing in kind and level of work.

In some jurisdictions, the principle of zoning classes of positions into classification-grades within services has been recognized by statute, although this fact is frequently obscured by their close integration with the pay plan. For example, the Federal Classification Act of 1923 divides each of the five classification services, previously mentioned, into zones of difficulty and responsibility called grades.[102] Each classification-grade is broadly defined in terms of general characteristics of work. These definitions show the degrees of difficulty, importance, responsibility, and complexity that are characteristic of each classification-grade.[103]

[102] The Act defines the term "grade" as follows: The term "grade" means a subdivision of a service, including one or more positions for which approximately the same basic qualifications and compensation are prescribed, the distinction between grades being based upon differences in the importance, difficulty, responsibility, and value of the work. Until the amendatory act of November 26, 1940, one and only one pay scale applied to each grade. The Act of November 26, 1940, permits variations due to unusual hazard, exceptional isolation, or extra-continental location. See the schematic chart of the structure of the federal classification system reproduced in Pfiffner, *Research Methods in Public Administration*, pp. 340–41.

[103] For example, Grade 1 of the professional and scientific service (the lowest grade) includes all classes of positions the incumbents of which are required to be technically trained scientists or professional workers whose duties are to perform elementary professional work within their respective fields. Grade 8 includes all classes of positions the duties of which are to act as the administrative head of one of the largest and most important professional or scientific bureaus, or to perform professional or scientific work of equal importance, difficulty, and responsibility. For a description of the Michigan plan, see Griffenhagen & Associates, *op. cit.*, p. 6.

Some limitations in using classification-grades are recognized from a technical classification standpoint. Illustrations can be cited to indicate that no one system of grades will exactly fit all the classes that may exist or permit the differentiations among the classes that the facts warrant. The various series or ladders of classes must all have their rungs at the levels of the classification-grades; and in order to fit into a limited number of classification-grades, it is said that classes must be "forced" slightly up or down, away from their correct relationship to adjacent classes in the same series; or, a given series having in fact four distinct classes may have to be compressed to three or extended to five classes.[104]

Such limitations have their greatest force where classification-grades are fixed by statute or ordinance as a basis for continuously administering a position-classification plan. However, when they are developed by a classification staff on an original project and can be controlled and revised through administrative action, their number can be fixed at a point where they can be (a) consistently and systematically grasped in concept, (b) recognized and identified in their application to positions having varied patterns as to organization relationships, subject matter, and procedures, (c) defined in available terms that can be standardized, (d) clearly distinguished in statements of qualification requirements or standards, and (e) maintained as valid and reliable in the process of administering and maintaining the position-classification plan. In short, classification-grades can be made sufficient in number to meet every valid distinction in level among the various classes.[105]

Selecting Class Titles

The class title is a definite, descriptive title or name applied to a class and to each position in the class. Its meaning is set forth in the corresponding class specification, and it is always to be used and understood in that sense, even though it may in other connections have a broader, narrower, or different significance. It is the official designation of the class and of each position in it, and is intended for use in all personnel, accounting, budgetary, and other communicating reports, and records.[106] Because of the frequency of their use,

---

[104] See Phillip M. Mayer, "Facing the Federal Classification Problem," *Personnel Administration*, May 1939, pp. 1–4.

[105] Griffenhagen & Associates, *op. cit.*

[106] See Chapter IV, pp. 56–60. "Following the adoption of the classification plan and the allocation to classes therein of positions in the classified service,

class titles should be as descriptive as possible of the relative rank and both the general and specialized nature of the work and yet be reasonably short.

The following major qualities are thus sought in selecting suitable titles of classes:

1. Descriptiveness. The title should indicate both the kind of work and the rank of the class with relation to other classes. This is the most important requisite of a good title.[107]

2. Consistency with the titles of other classes in the position-classification plan. For example, titles of classes of equivalent rank in different fields of work that are closely associated in the position-classification plan should customarily have the same prefix, such as Junior Chemist, Junior Radio Engineer, Junior Entomologist, etc.

3. Brevity. Supervising Telephone Operator is better than Telephone Operator in Charge of Multiple Switchboard.

Illustrations of good class titles are Senior Statistical Clerk and Junior Civil Engineer. "Senior" and "Junior" indicate rank or responsibility; "Statistical" and "Civil" indicate the kind of specialization; and "Clerk" and "Engineer" indicate the general kind of work of the class.[108]

Class titles should be selected according to some definite plan, in order that the system of nomenclature may be internally consistent. The utility of the titles is increased if they are made to follow a systematic title scheme, under which the differences and relations between classes are indicated as clearly as possible, with due attention to the need for brevity and conciseness.[109] This is especially true in the selection of terms indicating the relative rank of the class. Among

---

the class titles set forth therein shall be used to designate such positions in all official records, vouchers, and communications. No persons shall be appointed to or employed in a position in the classified service under a class title which has not been approved by the Director as appropriate to the duties to be performed." National Civil Service Reform League and National Municipal League, *Draft of a State Civil Service Law*, 1939, Sec. 14.

[107] "We classify when we use *titles* to designate like positions by the same name, and the title generally indicates, although very roughly and often by implication only, both kind and grade of work. . . . The title is a composite statement, however it may be abbreviated, of the two ideas and we must not lose sight of their requiring independent consideration." Hopwood, *Salaries, Wages and Labor Relations* (Copyright 1937. The Ronald Press Company), pp. 84–85.

[108] Fred Telford, "The Titles in an Occupational Classification Plan," *Public Personnel Studies*, May 1925, pp. 142–46; "The Development of Classification and Compensation Plans for the Library Profession," *Public Personnel Studies*, September 1926, pp. 257–58.

[109] Griffenhagen & Associates, *Report on Classification and Compensation of Positions in the Service of the Commonwealth of Virginia* (Richmond, 1937), p. 6.

different jurisdictions, there is no standard method in this respect.[110]
Some typical examples of ranking terms follow:

Junior	Junior	Junior
Senior	Intermediate	Assistant
Principal	Senior	Associate
Supervising	Principal	Senior
Assistant Supervisor	Chief	Principal
Supervisor	Head	Chief
Consultant		
Director		

In some services ranking prefixes are used for all classes except one
in a series, for example, Junior Accountant, Accountant, Senior Accountant; or Junior Civil Engineer, Assistant Civil Engineer, Associate Civil Engineer, Civil Engineer, Senior Civil Engineer, etc. This
has the disadvantage of being confusing in that the same name such
as "accountant" or "engineer" will inevitably be used to mean two
different things, (1) specifically, the name of the class in a series, and
(2) generically, the name of the occupation or the name of the series
as a whole.

Although there should be orderliness and system in deciding upon
the form of class titles, it is not feasible in practice to adhere to a
single adjective formula for all kinds of occupations. Different series
of classes may be composed of from one to six or seven, or more,
classes, and different series may begin and end at different levels with
relation to one another. Consequently the same set of ranking adjectives may not be applicable uniformly.

Class titles, being also the titles of the individual positions in the
class, should appeal to employees as being reasonable, not misleading, and not too depreciative of dignity. For example, "there should
not be a 'chief probation officer' unless there are others over whom
he is 'chief,' and human nature may object to serving as 'second class
clerk' while entirely willing to be known as 'assistant clerk.' "[111] Simi-

---

[110] In some jurisdictions "Assistant" ranks below "Junior," in others higher.
Similarly, "Head" may rank either below or above "Chief," depending on the
jurisdiction concerned. In the federal service, the Classification Act of 1923
establishes grades which are named as well as numbered, with such titles as
under, junior, assistant, main, senior, etc., in the Clerical, Administrative and
Fiscal Service, and such titles as junior, assistant, associate, full, senior, principal,
etc., in the Professional and Scientific Service. These terms furnish a convenient
series of rank-prefixes for class titles that can be generally, although not always,
followed with clarity.

[111] Albert Smith Faught, "Classification of Jobs in Public and Private Employment," *Proceedings*, 14th Annual Meeting of the Assembly of Civil Service Commissions, June 1921, p. 63. Obviously, blunders like "Mentally Handicapped
Arts Teacher" are avoidable.

larly, objections may be anticipated when "engineman" is used instead of "operating engineer";[112] when "medical inspector" is used instead of "district physician"; when "senior bookkeeper" is used instead of "treasurer"; and when "principal clerk" is used instead of "secretary to the Board of Public Utilities."[113]

The diminutive effect of such prefixes as "junior" or "assistant" is frequently objectionable to employees, particularly in their contacts with the public,[114] and in such instances the use of other organizational or functional titles for such contact purposes has been a reasonable solution. Another possibility is the use of an unmodified title to indicate the lowest rank in a series of classes. In other cases, the solution has been to maintain the ranking prefixes for official purposes but to drop them in correspondence and public contacts.

Occasionally the approach to remedying this and other difficulties has been the omission of ranking adjectives, using instead suffixed capital letters or Roman numerals.[115]

This scheme has been recently used in the position-classification plan for the State of Michigan in which class titles such as Accountant I, Accountant II, etc., and Account Clerk A, Account Clerk B, etc., were developed. The ranking symbols used corresponded to ten normal ranking levels into which the whole classification plan was divided.[116] These symbols were adopted as a substitute for the more

[112] See, for example, "Statement of William J. Reynolds, representing the National Association of Stationary Engineers," *Joint Hearings before the Committees on Civil Service, Congress of the United States, relative to the Reclassification of Salaries,* May-June, 1921 (Washington, 1921), pp. 752–58.

[113] See Charles P. Messick and Fred Telford, "The Development and Administration of Classification and Compensation Plans in the State Service of New Jersey," *Public Personnel Studies,* April 1925, p. 126.

[114] For example, consider the community reaction to "Junior Public Health Nurse" where the incumbent is the only public health nurse assigned to the community.

[115] "Where various grades of importance of duties or responsibilities were involved, the following modifying designations were to be used: Principal, Head, Chief, Assistant, or A, B, C, D, etc., the A referring to the lowest grade in the series. Examples: Assistant Chief Clerk, Head Janitor, Lineman C. The words 'Junior' and 'Senior' were to be used very sparingly, or not at all, because of the suggestion of inferiority which sometimes attaches to the word 'Junior' when it is applied to a job assigned to a worker advanced in years. The alphabetical sequence, with A as the lowest, was selected so that higher grades could be added in later years without disturbing existing titles, and also so that the title would not, itself, indicate the number of higher grades of the same title." John A. Williams (Niagara Hudson Power Corporation), "Job Evaluation and Salary Standardization," *Office Personnel Administration* (American Management Association, 1938), Office Management Series No. 84, p. 16.

[116] In other jurisdictions, however, the symbols have ranking significance only within a series of classes, and such titles as the following are used: Mining Engineer II, Graduate Nurse II, or Janitor II.

usual ranking terms of junior, senior, principal, etc., largely as an experiment and for three principal reasons: (1) because of the lack of standardization of ranking adjectives; (2) because of the objections commonly encountered on the part of those who regard terms like junior, assistant, and associate in their popular ordinary senses, rather than their technically defined meanings; and (3) because words appropriate for ranking prefixes have not been sufficient in number.[117]

Although the practice of using letters or numbers in lieu of adjectives to indicate rank is increasing somewhat, it is not common at the present time. Proponents testify that it is accepted and understood readily by officials and employees and avoids time-consuming and needless discussions of the propriety of the customary adjective prefixes.

Where parallel kinds of work in commerce or industry or in the professions are known by reasonably descriptive occupational names, class titles for work of the same kind should be selected, if possible, so as to adopt, or at least to be consistent with, industrial, commercial or professional terminology. For example, it is customary to use the already well-recognized titles of the mechanical trades—such as Carpenter's Helper, Carpenter, and Foreman Carpenter. Similarly, Junior Accountant in the public service should not designate a class that is parallel with semi-senior accountant or senior accountant in the public accounting field. A too wide variation from industrial, commercial, or professional practice where the positions concerned are more or less parallel may result in confusion and misunderstanding in the conduct of open competitive tests, especially in their public advertisement under the heading of the official class title.

On occasion, the exercise of an authority conferred by statute upon officials or employees identified in the statute as "special agents," "deputies," etc., may be questioned unless the employees are appointed under these designations and are so known to the public. For example, in one jurisdiction the class title of "Sanitary Inspector" had to be changed to "Sanitary Policeman" because of the provisions of a statute.[118] In some instances of this type, the use of the class title and the legal title (the latter in parentheses) may be a necessary and desirable compromise, to be authorized generally in the rules for the administration of the position-classification plan.

[117] Griffenhagen & Associates, *Distinctive Features of the Classification Plan of 1938.*
[118] "Building up a Municipal Personnel System—Cincinnati," *Public Personnel Studies,* April 1928, p. 84.

Where all the positions embraced in a given class or series of classes are located in the same organization unit, some classification plans have used titles showing the name of such organization unit, such as "Senior Clerk, Bureau of Education," or "Senior Inspector, License Division." Generally speaking, selecting titles on this basis is not the best practice, as it seems to depart from the principle of classifying positions on a work basis, irrespective of their organizational location.[119] Even in the case of one-position classes, where the tendency to use organizational titles is strong, such titles as Unemployment Compensation Administrator or Transportation Regulation Administrator have been suggested as preferable to Director of the Division of Unemployment Compensation or Head of the Bureau of Traffic. Others, however, have taken the view that in the case of higher administrative one-position classes, organizational identification may be used advantageously as a part of the class title.

While the class titles as used in a position-classification plan are intended to be used in all official procedure relating to personnel, appropriation, and payroll processes, there is nothing in the plan to preclude the use of "operating titles" or the ordinary department variations in carrying on the internal affairs of the department and in correspondence or other outside contacts.[120] Nevertheless, it is well to bear in mind the possibility that sometimes a slight variation in the class title may make it usable for all personnel, budget, and administrative purposes without change. The important thing is that whatever the class title is, all concerned in its use should agree on its meaning and agree to use it with that meaning in all personnel and fiscal processes.

In preparing specifications of "groups of classes,"[121] in order to

---

[119] "Every effort was made in selecting titles to choose those that would be adequate for the purpose of identifying the class but that would not be unduly restrictive. Departmental titles, such as 'Water Department bookkeeper,' were carefully avoided because they tend to obscure the essential similarity of positions, especially when new positions are being established in the service. An unnecessary multiplication of classes will almost certainly result from an indiscriminate use of departmental titles." Public Administration Service, *Personnel Programs for Smaller Cities*, 1940, p. 13.

[120] "The titles assigned to positions by their allocation to the classes established by the classification plan shall be used in all personnel, accounting, budget, appropriation, and financing records and communications of all state departments, institutions, and agencies. . . . Titles used in the course of departmental routine to indicate authority, status in the organization, or administrative rank may continue to be used for these purposes." Sec. 4, Rule V, Arkansas Civil Service Commission, adopted April 28, 1938. Similar provisions appear in other civil service rules, e.g., those for the State of Rhode Island, approved by the Governor, December 20, 1939 (Sec. 4, Rule IV); and in some statutes, e.g., Ch. 400, Acts of 1930, Massachusetts.

[121] See pp. 279–81.

show both the common characteristics and the distinctiveness of each class, a common title is selected for the group, and the class titles are formed by adding a parenthetical expression to the title of the group of classes, such as, Junior Chemist (Inorganic); Assistant Translator (Romance Languages); or Associate Physicist (Aerodynamics).

Preparing Working Definitions of Classes

During the process of determining the classes to be established and selecting class titles, the lines of demarcation among the classes are necessarily major subjects for discussion and formulation. Some classes, or distinctions among classes, may be definitely regarded as only tentative in character, to be analyzed again in the light of the results of investigations or work-audits, the allocations of individual positions to the classes, or criticisms and suggestions by supervisors and employees. Other classes will go through the developmental stage without material modification. In either event it is important that decisions, even though tentative, as to classes and the differentiations among classes shall be reduced to writing as soon as made, accompanied by questions and notes for later attention. They should then be kept available to each member of the classification staff for reference and use during the following phases of the program.

This written record provides a good working tool for work-audits, conferences with supervisors and employees, the preparation of class specifications, and the allocation of positions to classes. It will call attention to the specific points to be covered or the questions to be asked in work-audits or conferences. It will bring up definite points for consideration by supervisors and employees. It will make sure that the various problems involved in establishing classes are continually kept in mind, and the decisions thereon later reflected in the class specifications. It will bring the different members of the classification staff into a common understanding of the position-content of the classes. This is an important item where work-audits, investigations, or conferences with supervisors and employees may later be assigned on a departmental basis, in which event the same staff member will have all the positions in specified organization units, falling in various classes, within his assignments. The purpose is simply to record decisions for the time being, so as to make them definite enough for the raising of specific issues requiring further analysis.

Such a record may conveniently consist mainly of a series of preliminary or working definitions of classes, prepared concurrently with the establishment of classes and class titles, as tentative decisions are made. Each working definition includes the class title and a short statement of what the class consists of in terms of work-factors, and is confined largely to setting forth, as clearly as possible at that time, the factors that differentiate that class from all others. The following will serve as illustrations of such working definitions:

Telephone Operator—Operates standard branch exchange telephone switchboard and performs simple clerical tasks associated with this work, such as keeping records of long distance calls; on duty one shift as assigned by supervising telephone operator; responsible for own work only.

Supervising Telephone Operator—Supervises the work of a small squad of telephone operators, not more than five as a rule; responsible for quality of performance of these operators and for seeing that the work runs smoothly; assigns shifts and gives instructions to the operators, especially to new operators; operates one shift personally in most instances; in full charge of the board and reports to a building superintendent or other supervisor having many other types of responsibility.

Guard I—This is the first level of prison guard positions. It includes wall guards, shop guards, kitchen and dining room guards, dormitory guards, turnkeys, and searchers. It also includes two watchmen at St. Peter who are armed with shotguns and patrol egresses from the institution. Guards maintain order, supervise conduct of inmates, and attempt to prevent escapes.

Guard II—Performs responsible guard duty, not necessarily involving supervision of other officers, but involving work at key positions or work having general management responsibilities. Employees may have charge of a detail of other guards three days a week. Includes chief turnkey (keys and armory) and chief cellhouse keeper at St. Cloud Reformatory, and, at Stillwater Prison, cell hall captains and a half-time deputy warden who performs guard duties at other times.

Such working definitions as these are, of course, constantly subject to revision in the light of the results of later steps in developing the classification plan. They should therefore be kept up to date, as changes are made or new ones written, so as to provide a constant guide and control as to classes and differentiating factors, up to the time when the information is incorporated in a class specification.[122]

[122] If a pay plan is being concurrently developed, these working descriptions will serve very well as definitions of "key" jobs on which outside wage data may be collected and compiled.

Tentatively Allocating Positions to Classes

For purposes of clarity and convenience, the problems and procedures involved in analyzing positions, initially determining classes,
selecting class titles, and preparing working definitions of classes
have been discussed separately. This does not mean, however, that
these steps are carried out in a definite sequence, one procedure being completed before the next one is begun. As a matter of fact they
are, in most instances, conducted as different aspects of a single
operation.

The same thing is true of tentatively allocating positions to classes.
Since the classes and their characteristics are derived directly from
the individual positions and their characteristics, it follows that the
determination of the content of classes in terms of duties and responsibilities and the lines of demarcation between classes involves
an identification of all the positions falling within each class. Further, the task of recognizing the classes of positions existing in the
service is, of course, not completed until the classes collectively cover
the whole service and every position fits within one class. Thus the
recognition of classes and the identification of the position-content
of each class are virtually simultaneous operations.

As the questionnaires are studied, differentiating factors decided
upon, classes tentatively determined and named, and working descriptions written, all questionnaires falling in a single class are
placed and kept together. When these steps are completed, at least
for the time being, for a particular occupational group, each questionnaire is labeled with the title or symbol of the class in which
it falls.

Conducting Work-Audits

The primary purpose of a work-audit is to clarify, verify, or supplement the facts about positions, as given on the position-description questionnaires, and thereby to increase the classifier's understanding of such positions. Its method is that of personal interview,
observation, and conference.

The extent to which work-audits may be carried out during the
developmental process is governed not only by the necessities of securing or checking information but also by the time and personnel
available. In an original survey project the whole jurisdiction has
to be covered in a limited time, and hence it is usually necessary to
confine the work-audits to the time and staff available, and to the

kinds of questions or problems on which it is essential to make further inquiry.

In any service, personal interviews with employees, supervisors, and administrators conducted by the classification staff pay dividends in good will, cooperation, and common understanding of the duties and responsibilities of the positions being classified. To the extent that they are carried out during the developmental stage, the work of installation is facilitated. In a large and complex service, the personal interviews and conferences constituting the work-audit procedure are substantial parts of the developmental program. Even after the utmost care in the design of the questionnaire and in instructing supervisors and employees as to what information is required and how it should be presented, some questionnaires will be too inadequate to be analyzed properly and others will contain apparent inconsistencies or errors that should be looked into. In addition, it is always well to cover thoroughly (1) positions which are typical samples of large groups, (2) positions which represent key or important classes in the classification plan, (3) positions which are of uncommon types, and (4) positions the classification of which will raise unusual or controversial issues, when such classifications are later used in pay-fixing, recruiting, or other personnel processes.

In general outline, the procedure used in work-audits during the development of a position-classification plan is parallel to the investigation and audit procedure used in keeping such a plan up to date after it is adopted.[123]

Members of the classification staff are assigned to specified organization units and are given the questionnaires for such units arranged in organization order. Arrangements are made with the liaison man or other official of the operating department for a preliminary conference with the department head on the work-audit process. At this conference the investigator advises the department head of the present status of the classification survey, outlines the procedure and purpose of the work-audit, and inquires whether there are particular points that he wants covered in the field audit. The over-all organization and functions of the department are discussed, using as a basis the rough organization chart prepared from the questionnaires. The department head should suggest key personnel to be inter-

---

[123] For further details, refer to Chapter X, where investigation and audit procedures are more fully discussed.

viewed and any preferences as to scheduling so as to interfere as little as possible with current operations.

Somewhat the same program is followed in interviews with administrators or executives at the level next below the department head. The topics that would be discussed are the organization and functions of the unit for which the administrator is responsible, his working relationships with the department head and with his own intermediate supervisors, and the purposes and objectives of the work of his unit in relation to the work of the department. Frequently it is desirable in some kinds of activities to make a visual inspection of the physical layout, in the course of which the work-auditor is introduced to supervisors and other employees. The intermediate supervisors are next interviewed in the same manner and arrangements are made for interviews with employees.

As it is seldom possible for the developmental staff to interview every employee in the jurisdiction, a selection has to be made. Generally speaking, it is a good plan to contact some employees in every organization unit and, where the jurisdiction is geographically widespread, in every district office and institution. More specifically, an effort should be made to interview a representative number of employees in each class of the tentative classification plan, particularly any uncommon or unusual class of positions; and all employees whose position-description questionnaires have been noted for coverage in the work-audit, especially where the question raised during the preliminary classification is a major one. In addition, suggestions will have been made to the staff member by supervisors who will indicate employees having the best knowledge of a particular kind of work, together with the ability to give information clearly. Employees may have been suggested for interview by employee organizations or informal groups of employees having a common occupational interest. Other suggestions will have been received by the developmental staff in the form of letters and telephone calls indicating that particular employees should be interviewed or specific positions looked into by personal inquiry.[124]

It is frequently advantageous, particularly where there is any conflict in the facts collected by the staff member, to go back through the supervisory setup, both for the purpose of checking facts and for an opportunity to express appreciation for the cooperation received.

[124] Points to be covered in interviewing employees are discussed in Chapters V and X.

The results of the work-audit are reduced to writing although not necessarily worked into a formal report. Where the result is simply that the information given on the position-description questionnaire is verified and the staff member raises no question about the tentative class to which the position has been allocated, a notation to this effect may be placed on the questionnaire and no separate field notes need be written. Separate work-audit notes, however, are written in order to fill in any inadequacies or blank spots in the position-description questionnaires and bring out considerations bearing on the kind of work or the degree of difficulty or responsibility in the position. It is usually helpful to have the audit notes conclude with an evaluation showing the investigator's judgment as to whether the tentative allocation of the position is correct and if not what the proper allocation should be.

Both in collecting information during the work-audit and in reducing it to writing, the staff member should bear in mind that his notes will be used in conferences leading to revisions of tentative classes, allocations of positions to classes, and working descriptions of classes, and that they are intended to aid also in the writing of class specifications, in the conduct of hearings during the adoption and installation period, and to some extent in the continued administration of the classification plan.

Revising Classes, Titles, Allocations, and Working Definitions

Concurrently with the progress of work-audits, the project supervisor and other staff members conduct a coordinating review preparatory to the writing of class specifications. Work-audit notes are studied to determine their effect upon the tentative conclusions reached up to that point. As a result of additional information or changes in facts developed during work-audits, and with the aid and counsel of occupational specialists and field-audit men, revisions are made in the classes, class titles, allocations of positions to classes, and working definitions of classes. Appropriate changes in questionnaires and other records are made by the clerical staff. This process continues until all questions as to the facts or their evaluation, raised during preliminary analyses or work-audits, are cleared.

Writing Class Specifications

An important activity in the original development of a position-classification plan is the writing of definitive statements describing the characteristics of each class in terms of duties, responsibilities, and tasks, and the qualifications which the work of that class makes necessary or desirable. The form and content of such statements, commonly called "class specifications," require careful attention.[125]

After classes have been tentatively established, class titles selected, and working definitions of classes prepared, progress can be made on the writing of class specifications. However, this activity should be subordinated to necessary or desirable investigations, work-audits, and conferences. Such processes will add to the significant factual data available, will raise questions not perceived at the outset, and will tend to change the position-content of some of the tentative classes and the lines of demarcation among them. Hence, concentrated effort on the completion of class specifications should await that stage of progress where all, or nearly all, the facts have been secured and, so far as possible, checked, for the group of positions covered in each class specification writing assignment.

As is shown later, the form of class specification adopted herein is composed of the following parts: (1) class title, (2) general statement, (3) distinguishing features of work, (4) illustrative examples of work, and (5) qualifications statements.[126]

The working definitions of classes, already available at this stage of the developmental process, will furnish class titles, serve as preliminary drafts of general statements, and provide some material also for the distinguishing features statement. In drafting class specifications the writer works directly from the position-description questionnaires in class order, on which have been noted all additional information secured and comments made during the work-audit.

The preparation of statements of qualifications, in terms of knowledges, abilities, aptitudes, personal qualities, and required or desired experience, training, or education, generally brings up problems of policy and technique. The principal problem of general policy is whether qualifications shall be stated as prerequisites or as desirable preparation.[127] In jurisdictions where a central testing

[125] This section presents some of the procedural aspects of writing class specifications during the original development of a position-classification plan. Chapter IX is more extensively devoted to a treatment of the limitations, objectives, form, and content of class specifications. The problem of keeping class specifications up to date after the position-classification plan is installed is discussed in Chapter X.

[126] The form and content of each of the elements following the class title are explained in Chapter IX.

[127] See the discussion in Chapter IX.

agency, e.g., a civil service commission, exists, the commission's policy as to the relationship between qualifications statements in class specifications and qualifications requirements in tests will be a fundamental basis on which the form and content of such qualifications statements will be determined. As a matter of fact, because of the closeness of this relationship, the classification staff and the central personnel agency's testing staff should actively collaborate in the writing of the qualifications statements in class specifications. In some instances test technicians may be given responsibility in this respect and assigned to work with the classification staff.

After basic policies have been adopted, the class specification writer has before him a task requiring much judgment and understanding of personnel processes. He is usually presented with a variety of conflicting information and opinion about qualifications, given on position-description questionnaires or otherwise, which he must analyze and weigh carefully. In some instances, the opinions of supervisors or administrators may favor standards for positions under their jurisdiction which are much higher than necessary for the effective performance of the work. These opinions are understandable inasmuch as they largely stem from a desire on the part of the supervisors to secure highly competent personnel. In other instances, supervisors or administrators may indicate qualification standards in terms of an unconscious bias against or in favor of a particular kind of education or experience.

In the preparation of qualifications statements at this stage, emphasis should be placed upon thoroughly ascertaining the qualifications of knowledge, ability, aptitudes, and personal qualities needed and desirable in the various classes of positions. These are basic, and when correctly and adequately stated, remain the same so long as the fundamental position-content of the class is constant. On the other hand, statements of educational and experiential qualifications, being evidentiary and to some extent procedural, may be changed from time to time by reason of recruiting policies and practices, even though the class remains constant in its characteristics. Such statements when expressed as prerequisites often tend to be controversial, with the result in some instances that much time is spent during the development of the class specifications on issues which could be decided better later on. In any event, controversies over minimum or mandatory educational or experience requirements obscure the real issues involved and for this reason, among others, the use of statements of desirable qualifications as to education or experience is sometimes favored.

It should especially be observed that where a merit system and a position-classification plan are being simultaneously developed and installed, full and complete specifications, including statements of qualification standards, may be immediately necessary as a basis for qualifying or other types of examinations which the employees in the service may be required to take in order to continue in their positions. In such a case, it is desirable to complete the class specifications before the qualifying program begins.

When first drafts of class specifications have been prepared, they are subjected to critical review and revision by other members of the staff, occupational consultants, and, in civil-service jurisdictions, by members of the central personnel agency's examining staff. This review is both technical and editorial. Its major purpose is to assure that the specifications are technically sound, that they meet their objectives as written tools of personnel administration, and that they are consistent both as to content and phraseology. In the course of this reviewing process a good opportunity is afforded for reexamining the classes themselves, with the object of merging classes where separate classes are unnecessary, or dividing those classes which are too broad in content.

Drafting Code of Rules

During the course of developing a position-classification plan, and more or less concurrently with the establishment of classes and the writing of class specifications, a code of rules is prepared to govern the installation and the continued administration of the plan. It should be ready for adoption when the installation period begins.

A code of rules, of course, must be drafted in the light of local conditions. Attention must be paid to local processes of financial and personnel management, to the distribution of authority for fiscal and personnel decisions, to local statutes, ordinances, executive orders, and the opinions of law officers. All these have a positive bearing. Furthermore, in order to achieve a harmonious whole, rules governing the installation and administration of a position-classification plan should correlate with other rules governing personnel administration, such as civil service rules or rules governing hours of work and leave privileges.

The content of a code of basic rules, included as an integral part of a position-classification plan, is illustrated by Appendix D.[128] Broadly, the rules should cover (1) definitions of terms, (2) interpretation of class specifications, (3) availability to the public of official copy of the position-classification plan, (4) installation of the classification plan, (5) allocation of positions to classes during the continuous administration of the plan, and (6) amendment of classes, class specifications, and the rules.

Generally speaking, where the rules and their amendment cannot be easily and promptly revised, they should be confined as far as possible to fundamentals. Procedures can then be covered by regulations promulgated by the classification agency or its principal administrative official.[129]

The question may be raised whether the classes and the class specifications should or should not be made integral parts of the formal rules. The significance of this question lies in the fact that if they are so included, their revision or amendment would have to be accomplished as formally as a revision or amendment of the rules themselves. Generally speaking, it is not desirable to give the classes and the class specifications the same formal status as the rules themselves. Revisions of the class specifications, particularly minor changes of language, should not require the formal procedure of amendments of rules. In some instances, where the central personnel agency may itself amend its rules, it may deem it desirable to list the classes in the rules, the maintenance of the specifications of the classes being a responsibility of its principal technical officer.

[128] See also, for example, "Proposed Rules for a Public Personnel Agency, with Explanatory Comments," *Public Personnel Studies*, June 1928, pp. 117–55; Civil Service Assembly . . . , *First Draft of Report of Technical Committee on the Development, Adoption, and Administration of Classification and Compensation Plans*, presented at Eastern Regional Conference, May 16, 1930; City of Philadelphia, *Drafts of Proposed Ordinance and Rules Providing for and Governing the Adoption, Interpretation, and Administration of the Classification and Compensation Plans for the Offices and Positions in the Classified Service* (J. L. Jacobs & Co., 1930); City of Chicago Civil Service Commission, *Proposed Civil Service Rules Providing for the Administration and Interpretation of the City Civil Service Act* (J. L. Jacobs & Co., 1932); League of California Municipalities, *Civil Service Rules and Regulations Supplementing the Suggested Forms of Civil Service Ordinances*, Report No. 16, May 1938; New York State Department of Civil Service, *Model Municipal Civil Service Rules*, 1938.

[129] "The rules under which the personnel agency operates must cover in the main exactly the same ground as the law itself. The difference is that, whereas the law confines itself largely to statements of principles and objectives, the rules, which can be easily amended and which should be changed whenever the need arises, set forth a normal procedure for handling every employment transaction, together with means of setting aside this normal procedure when the circumstances are exceptional." "The Personnel Problem in the Public Service, . . ." *Public Personnel Studies*, January 1926, p. 19.

Obtaining Final Criticisms and Adjusting Disagreements

Before the classification plan, including the class specifications and the code of rules, is officially made the subject of a favorable recommendation to the personnel agency or to a higher authority, it should be reviewed and criticized by the classification staff in conference, and also by selected officials, employees, or other interested groups, particularly those whose cooperation during the progress of the survey has been especially helpful. This "clearance" concerns the merits and validity of the classes, the class titles, the class specifications, and the tentatively drafted rules. Questions touching the allocation of individual positions are reserved for consideration during the procedure of adoption and installation.[130]

The process of obtaining criticisms and adjusting disagreements relative to the classification plan itself involves (1) informal or preliminary conferences or contacts, (2) publication and distribution of the classification plan for comment and criticism, followed by conferences with the classification staff, and (3) hearings before the personnel agency responsible for adoption or for recommending adoption.

First, the classification staff in conference will critically review such aspects as the descriptiveness and consistency of class titles, the validity of each class, and the administrative features of each proposed rule. As the conference proceeds, any necessary revisions will be made.

Members of the classification staff will then discuss the classification plan with supervisory and personnel officials, employee representatives, and interested groups, in order to acquaint them with the results of the work, to familiarize them with the classification plan as a whole, and to discover any points giving rise to misunderstanding or misinterpretation.[131]

In large jurisdictions, the classification plan is necessarily lengthy and may not be readily understood by all those who read it. It is desirable, where possible, to enlist the aid of employee representatives in interpreting the plan to employees and employee groups. It may be possible, immediately prior to the general publication of

---

[130] See pp. 234–40.

[131] Depending upon the supervisory officials or group representatives, the types of classes, and the cooperative relationships existing, such clearances may have already been made in many respects during the course of the development of the position-classification plan, especially the work-audit.

information, for the classification staff to hold meetings with such representatives and explain the basis for the classes, the scheme of class titles, the application and use of class specifications, the implications of the rules, and the major points on which the proposed classification plan differs from any previous plan. The purpose of such meetings is to discuss the plan as a whole and not to go into matters involving specific allocations of positions to classes. Two points will need to be stressed: that each specification must be considered as a whole and not interpreted on the basis of one or two examples of duties or a phrase here and there; and that one of the principal purposes of discussing the plan in advance is to secure additional information to improve and perfect it.

After preliminary clearances and as a basis for general review and criticism, there should be duplicated four documents: (1) a list of classes by class titles, arranged in schematic order according to classification services, occupational groups within services, and series of classes within occupational groups;[132] (2) a full set of class specifications; (3) the proposed code of rules; and (4) an explanation of this material, with suggestions as to the topics or questions to which attention should especially be directed. There should be enough of these documents to permit officials, employee representatives, cooperative agencies and other interested groups to read and become familiar with them.[133]

This material should be distributed through proper channels, providing each department, agency, and interested organization with a number sufficient to meet its needs. It may not be necessary in every case to distribute a complete set of class specifications to each operating unit in the service as many units will contain only a relatively small number of classes in comparison with the total number of classes. However, enough copies of the entire classification plan, including the rules, should be made available so that all interested persons may review it with convenience. The problem is one of adequate coverage at minimum cost.

[132] In some projects this may be supplemented by a list of classes arranged in classification-grades, or zones of difficulty and responsibility.

[133] The method of reproduction will vary with the size of the service. In very small services typewritten copies may suffice. In large services they will need to be reproduced in large numbers. Where stencils are used, the date of reproduction should be indicated, or a distinctive color of paper should be employed in order that preliminary drafts may be recognized and later differentiated from final drafts. Such stencils can be retained, the date blocked out or changed, and used to produce additional copies for the final set when no subsequent changes are made.

Following the distribution of this material, opportunity should be afforded for officials, employees, their representatives, and other interested persons and groups to confer with the classification staff in order to suggest changes. Where errors or inadequacies exist, or where improvements are suggested, appropriate revisions are made. Where recommendations for changes are contrary to the best judgment of the classification staff, the persons making the recommendations should be advised fully of the staff's reaction and basis of judgment. If such persons still feel that their recommendations should be adopted, they will then be in a position to present their ideas intelligently at a later hearing to be held by the officials responsible for the immediate steps leading to the adoption of the classification plan. All discussions need to be maintained on an objective basis, and a full and open explanation of the reasons for decisions should be made, in order that everyone concerned may be aware of the controlling factors.

Following a reasonable period for these conferences with the classification staff, dates for hearings by the officials responsible for adopting the plan (or recommending it to higher authority) should be set. Adequate time should be provided. In a large service a single sitting will not usually provide opportunity for administrative and legislative officials, employees, and their representatives to express their views. Hearings should be conducted by responsible personnel officials. Representatives of the classification staff should attend in order to take note of suggestions advanced and to make such explanations as are required, without, however, engaging in argument with those making counter-suggestions or objections. During the course of such hearings, there will be instances in which the need will be indicated for further conferences between the classification staff and supervisors, employees, or their representatives. In such cases, suitable arrangements should be made promptly. Following the hearings and such further conferences with the classification staff as may be required, the classification staff should meet with responsible officials of the central classifying agency (or other body authorized to adopt the plan) in order that such officials may make final determinations with regard to classes, titles, class specifications, and rules.[134]

---

[134] For a description of a similar procedure for securing and acting upon criticisms of class specifications, see *Report of the Congressional Joint Commission on Reclassification of Salaries*, pp. 172–73.

Adopting the Position-Classification Plan

The officials authorized to adopt the position-classification plan should now be ready to consider it in detail and to make their determinations. They may take up one by one the points raised by those attending the hearings, give consideration to their suggestions, hear further discussion of each point by the classification staff, and receive a final recommendation on the basis of conferences held following the hearings or agreements reached. In many cases the officials will make their determinations on the basis of this discussion. In other cases they may wish to call in employees or their representatives or others for direct questioning regarding their views. In any event, the officials should proceed point by point to dispose of all issues and make final determinations.

The procedure for adoption will vary with the local situation. Some formal action is of course required before the procedure of actual installation can be undertaken. This action may be legislative, executive, or both. For example, the classification staff may, in some instances, be engaged as a technical group to assist a legislative committee. In other instances, it may be a part of or be employed by a central personnel agency which may be authorized to adopt the plan on its own authority. In still other instances, the central personnel agency may be authorized only to recommend the adoption of the plan to an executive official or legislative body of the jurisdiction such as a governor, mayor, city council, board of county supervisors, or state legislature.

As soon as the plan has been adopted, the specifications will be revised to conform with the determination of the officials and made ready to serve as the basis for the final allocations of positions to classes.

Although extensive clearance of class specifications and the classification plan in general is desirable, employees, their representatives, or supervisory officials of the operating departments should not be expected or requested to designate in writing their acceptance of the plan. The initial responsibility for the plan rests with the classification staff, and the responsibility for finally formulating and adopting it rests with the responsible officials of the jurisdiction.

Chapter VIII

Installation

THE legal provisions for the adoption of the position-classification plan may involve a lapse of time between the developmental stage and actual adoption. Depending on the length of this period, the details of the installation procedure may vary somewhat.

The installation procedure in general consists of finally applying the position-classification plan to the individual positions in the jurisdiction, that is, allocating each of these positions to one of the established classes. This involves preparing allocation lists, conferring with operating officials, notifying employees of the allocations of their positions, adjusting disagreements, approving the allocation of positions to classes, and recording the approved allocations in the personnel and fiscal records of the jurisdiction.

PREPARING ALLOCATION LISTS

The first step in the procedure is the preparation of lists showing the class to which each position in the service is proposed to be allocated. It is useful, if time and funds permit, to prepare these allocation lists in two forms: (1) *for each class of positions,* showing under major subheads by departments, broken down, if necessary, by organization subdivisions, the position-questionnaire number, name of employee, and present payroll title, of each position in the class; (2) *for each department, agency, or institution,* broken down, if necessary, by organization subdivisions, and identifying each position in the department by position-questionnaire number, name of employee, present payroll title, and title of the class to which the position is allocated.[1]

As already indicated, the process of allocating positions to classes starts with the first provisional assignment of a class title to the posi-

[1] One jurisdiction prepared allocation lists by typing on each class specification the names of the employees in a particular department whose positions fell in that class. Each department head thus had before him in one document the description of the work of the class and a list of his positions falling therein. Allocation lists serve as practical illustrations of the meaning of the various class specifications and show the distinctions among them in a fashion understandable to operating officials.

tion-questionnaire form and continues through a series of changes or verifications as further information is secured, classes established, and class specifications written. The extent to which these allocations are up to date depends, among other things, upon the completeness with which the facts have been ascertained, the attention paid to later changes, and the care with which information collected through the questionnaire method was tested and supplemented by work audits. In any event, before allocation lists are prepared, any remaining allocation questions should be reviewed and settled.

In addition it may be necessary to take account of changes in individual positions which have occurred since the original questionnaire survey. Even at the time the plan of classes and rules is ready for submission to officials and employees, there will usually remain a number of positions regarding which information is insufficient, conflicting, or doubtful, after all ordinary investigation processes have been completed. During the consideration of the plan of classes and rules, the classification staff should secure such additional information regarding those positions and determine the classification to be assigned. As positions are cleared, allocations are made definite and arranged for preparation of the lists.

CONFERRING WITH OPERATING OFFICIALS AND OTHERS

When, in the preparation of allocation lists, the greater portion of the positions in an administrative unit have been allocated and tentative assignments have been made to the others, conferences can be held with the supervisors concerned. Allocation lists are desirable for reference during the discussion, but conferences may be based directly upon allocations noted on the questionnaires, supplemented by a chart of the organization. As each series of classes comes into the conversation, a brief review is made for the officials of the essential characteristics and differentials of each class. Such a review will assist the supervisors to check the allocations. Then the tentative classification of each position, identified through the names of individuals, is read to the supervisors with requests for their comments. Positions whose allocations are uncertain in the minds of the classifiers are made the subject of critical analysis and discussion with the supervisors. Whenever an allocation is questioned, the reason for the questioning is developed and if any doubt exists in the classifier's mind at the end of the discussion the questionnaire is set aside for further study or investigation.

Clearance of allocations simultaneously with a number of supervisory officials in the same administrative unit provides the advantage of more than one viewpoint, and sometimes provides clues to factors not previously uncovered. For example, the simultaneous clearing of allocations with several foremen is particularly helpful in checking on the allocation of laboring positions involving varied assignments among two or three unskilled and semi-skilled classes. It is not practical to observe each worker for an extended period of time, and so other methods of securing information are required. Conference with a group of foremen ordinarily will disclose this information.

In many instances, similar clearance conferences at this stage with employee groups will prove advantageous. It may be impossible to secure agreement on all points, but respect for the fairness and competence of the classification process can be secured in most instances if the factors governing the classifiers' recommendations are fully presented.

But even after clearance and conference with departmental officials and others, and final weighing of all factors, the allocation of some positions will remain uncertain. There will be some positions that will be close to the border line separating the zones of two classes. The final decision should be made with due consideration of the effect on allocations of other positions having similar but slightly different characteristics. Experience indicates that an allocation of one position to a class more favorable than seems justified by comparison with other similar positions will cause dissatisfaction and agitation tending to break down proper zones of differentiation among classes.

Following or concurrently with contacts with operating officials and employees, and as a part of the procedure for revising or checking allocation lists, a conference should be held with the personnel director and other personnel officials of the jurisdiction in order to acquaint them generally with the lists and give them an opportunity to review the allocations of positions with which they may be familiar. Such personnel officials may ask for demonstrations of the basis for particular allocations and may critically appraise the thoroughness and soundness of the procedure which has been employed. If not satisfied with this review they may determine that a further audit of the allocations is required before the lists are released.

NOTIFYING EMPLOYEES OF ALLOCATIONS

Copies of applicable sections of the allocation lists are furnished to administrative units and an individual notice is given to each employee showing the allocation of the position he occupies. The notice to the employee may be mailed to him or distributed through official channels. A statement should accompany the lists and each individual notice, advising employees that the allocations represent the recommendations of the classification staff, that they relate to positions and not to persons, and that if any employee believes the allocation of his position is inaccurate he should file a written statement to that effect before a stated date, giving his reasons.

ADJUSTING DISAGREEMENTS

Before arrangements are made for hearings on appeals from the allocations of which employees have been notified, the classification staff should review all statements filed by employees. All new information should especially be considered and employees and their representatives should be given opportunity for discussing their cases with members of the classification staff. After these conferences and such reinvestigations as may be necessary, the staff will make such changes in the list of recommended allocations as seem indicated, and will give notices of the finally recommended allocation to all employees who filed statements.

At this point the allocation lists constitute the recommendations of the classification staff, whether a unit of a personnel or other agency or a consulting service organization. While the position-classification plan will have been developed under the general control of a responsible official or agency of the jurisdiction, such official or agency will not as yet have assumed responsibility for allocations of positions to classes. Accordingly, when the classifiers have made their finally recommended allocations, hearings should be arranged by the personnel or other official or officials responsible for advising as to allocations and for deciding upon them.

The purpose of these hearings is to permit the responsible officials to make sure of the correctness of allocations before official adoption; to provide them with opportunity to test the soundness of the recommendations of the classifiers; and to afford operating officials and employees opportunity to present in writing and orally further pertinent data bearing on the allocations of certain positions with which they are not satisfied.

Hearings should be scheduled according to the administrative units of the service and, in so far as practicable, they should be restricted to affected employees, officials of the administrative unit, employee representatives, and administrative and legislative officials. A special effort should be made to secure the attendance of the last-named in order that they may be acquainted with the manner in which the plan is put into effect. The chairman of the hearing, who may be the personnel director, chairman of the commission, executive officer, or other appropriate official, should explain the purposes of the hearing and the function and attitude of the agency officials. He may also request a representative of the classification staff, who will be present, to participate in the hearing.

The personnel officials will have at hand written appeals of employees, the corresponding position-description questionnaires, and other notes. These will be arranged by class and organization order. The employee's name, the previous classification of his position and its proposed classification, will be called as his statement is reached. Each such employee can be asked to address his remarks to the agency officials on points which will amplify or clarify the information given through the questionnaire and his appeal statement. The employee's representative and any of his supervisors may also be heard. At the conclusion or during the course of each individual's remarks, the personnel officials may request explanations or additional information. During the course of the hearing the classifiers should abstain from argument or general discussion, or from taking any action which can be interpreted as biased. They may give information when called upon, take notes, and may ask for submission of material or arrange for subsequent investigation.

Hearings should be scheduled and completed within as short a period as conditions permit. At the conclusion of each hearing, or of a group of hearings, the official or officials reponsible for allocations will need to review each appeal with members of the classification staff.[2] As each case is presented to the officials for review, the classifiers identify it, explain the work and responsibilities involved in the position, review the steps taken in the process of classifying it, bring out pertinent information, set forth clearly the factors

[2] Previous to such meetings the classifiers will have secured any additional information indicated as available and needed, and have all the material ready for consideration. If it is a large service, this will require that the supervisor of the classification work clear thoroughly with the individual classifiers who handled the particular positions and that the classification staff have in mind all facts bearing on each case.

upon which the allocation was made, and tie these to the class specifications. The effect of possible decisions on other positions and employees should be made clear. After conferences of this type and after such further investigation as may be necessary in a few cases, allocation decisions are made.

The responsible officials may, of course, raise questions regarding proposed allocations from which appeals have not been made. These are considered and disposed of in the same manner, except that if reallocations are contemplated, those affected should be afforded an opportunity for hearing.

Among the cases considered during the hearings will be some which in the opinion of the classifiers lie very close to the border line separating adjacent class zones about which it is sometimes best to secure the advice of the personnel officials in making the final determination. As classification is not a mechanical process, there are cases which do not permit a clear-cut allocation, and when such cases are considered by the personnel officials, the fact that doubt existed should be made known to them and their counsel solicited.

Hearings afford employees an opportunity to present every pertinent factor bearing on their positions and to have the recommendation of the classification staff reviewed. This process uncovers and corrects inaccuracies and thereby improves the position-classification plan and removes warranted discontent. But in addition to this it ties the responsible personnel or other officials into the classification process and affords them an opportunity to appraise it. If the process has been thorough, the classification staff will have full information and background on all but a few of the appealed cases, and will be able to display to the officials the procedure upon which recommended allocations were based.

APPROVING ALLOCATIONS OF POSITIONS TO CLASSES

Upon completion of the allocation hearings, the allocation lists will be revised to accord with decisions reached by the responsible officials, and the revised list adopted officially. All employees who have appealed will be notified of the final determination with respect to their positions, and heads of administrative units will be supplied with allocation lists covering their units.

It may be expeditious in some cases to hold in abeyance the final allocation of a small number of positions because of exceptional conditions, such as impending reassignment of duties, anticipated changes in the scope and nature of duties in an administrative unit, or other complicating situations. In such event the general list can be adopted and exceptions made of such positions pending clearing of the conditions creating the uncertainty.

With these minor exceptions the general allocation list should be adopted officially as soon as practicable following final decision on appeals. Material delays may bring changes complicating and partially invalidating certain of the allocations. Such changes can be handled after the classification is initially completed, but may endanger the whole plan if action is unduly delayed.

In a large service, some minor revisions of the classes or class specifications are likely to be required by developments arising out of the installation processes here described. Such changes should be considered and adopted simultaneously with the clearance and determination of allocations.

RECORDING APPROVED ALLOCATIONS

As previously pointed out, the new class titles, indicating the approved allocations, are to be used in all personnel, accounting, budget, appropriation, and financial records and communications of the jurisdiction.[3] This requires the entry of such class titles on current records of the personnel, fiscal, and operating agencies, the conversion of eligible lists to the new basis, the introduction of the new titles into the next appropriation or salary ordinance or statute or the schedules supporting such enactments, and the instructing of operating departments by the personnel and fiscal agencies.[4]

It is sometimes convenient to provide that during the period of transition in changing from old to new appropriation, payroll or service-record titles, payrolls, budget documents, and other communications shall carry both the old and the new titles, until the former are definitely supplanted.[5]

CIVIL-SERVICE PROBLEMS OF INSTALLATION

When a position-classification plan is adopted in a jurisdiction in which the merit system has been operating for some time, questions will arise as to whether employees in fact and in law are quali-

[3] See pp. 147, 215.
[4] See "Building up a Municipal Personnel System—Cincinnati," *Public Personnel Studies*, April 1928, pp. 83–84.
[5] For example, Sec. 4 of the rules of the Arkansas position-classification plan, adopted April 28, 1938, provided that "during the period until July 1, 1939, the

fied to continue in the positions in which the classification survey found them.[6] They are generally of two types:

1. Questions arising out of comparison of the employee's qualifications with the qualifications stated in class specifications.

2. Questions arising out of comparison of the employee's legalistic civil service status with that required, under the civil service laws and rules of the jurisdiction, for the class to which his position is allocated. These questions may be of two kinds: (a) where the employee is found in a position requiring competition when in fact he has never competed for any position but was originally appointed to a position exempt or excepted from the civil service rules; (b) where the employee is found in a position so much higher than or different from the one for which he originally competed and to which he was appointed as to require transfer or promotion.[7]

The first type of question arises when the employee is occupying substantially the same kind of position as that to which he was properly appointed, and when his qualifications as to education, experience, knowledge, and ability are compared with the qualification requirements or standards set forth in the specifications of the class to which his position is allocated. Lack of conformity may be revealed by this comparison, frequently due to the character of the qualification requirements or standards theretofore used in the recruiting, selection, and promotion of employees. What effect should this lack of conformity have? Obviously the classification of the position should not be lowered merely because the employee

---

present appropriation titles of positions shall be shown on payroll and budget documents, as well as the class titles established by the classification plan." A similar procedure has been used in New York State.

[6] These questions are not matters of position-classification, but are so closely connected with the problems involved in installing a position-classification plan as to warrant treatment here. The parallel problems arising during the course of maintaining a position-classification plan after it is originally installed will be discussed in Chapter X. The question of how existing pay is to be adjusted in the event of the installation of a classification plan and a pay plan simultaneously is not discussed here, but will be dealt with in the report of the Committee on Pay Plans in the Public Service, a companion volume in this series. The matters being discussed at this point should not be confused with that (not dealt with herein) of giving employees a civil service status when a merit system is introduced for the first time.

[7] Occasionally, where definite seniority or promotional rights have been fixed for some time by classes or groups of positions, another type of question appears; namely, how to define such rights in those cases where the former classes lose their specific identity. One jurisdiction solved this problem by translating such rights into terms of the new classes, by where they corresponded as to duties with the former classes.

who happens to be in the position at the time does not possess the qualifications set forth in the class specification.[8] Nor should the employee be demoted to a class for which he does meet the newly established qualifications standards. Having been selected for the position legally and having entered upon it in conformity with the recruiting and testing methods and standards then in force, a later revision or improvement of those methods and standards should not in equity have the effect of curtailing or terminating his services in that position.

To clarify this question, a general policy should be specified in the rules of installation and administration to the effect that minimum or other qualifications stated in class specifications are for future application and are not to be applied to present incumbents, whose employment is otherwise legal, in determining either the classification of their positions or their retention in the positions in which they are found when the plan is installed.[9]

Questions of the second type arise when, upon the installation of the position-classification plan, it is found that an employee is occupying, illegally or irregularly, a position for which he has never qualified under the civil service laws and rules then in force.

The status of employees in civil service jurisdictions depends on whether they were properly appointed to competitive positions (a competitive status), or whether they were appointed to positions exempt from the civil service laws and rules (an excepted or exempt status). The question, accordingly, may be raised as to what action shall be taken if, upon the installation of a classification plan, it is found that an employee who was appointed to an excepted or exempt position has been in fact assigned to the duties of a competitive position, and the violation or subterfuge is first disclosed when his position is classified. In such cases the employee should be separated, or, if possible, assigned to the excepted position in which he may legally be employed.

The status of civil service employees in civil service jurisdictions is also customarily tied in to the kind and level of the tests in which they have previously qualified for original appointment or promo-

---

[8] See pp. 42–43.

[9] A different policy, of course, applies to temporary or provisional appointments. If an employee is temporarily employed, there is nothing in the position-classification plan that gives him a permanent status. He must be separated in the regular manner upon the termination of his temporary appointment and if he desires to qualify for permanent employment he must pass the tests in force at the time, which should be based upon the new qualifications requirements or standards.

tion or transfer, and compliance with the rules governing such transactions. These examinations and, in some instances, the rules are in
turn correlated with particular kinds and levels of positions. Due to
lack of central control over work assignments, civil service employees
over a period of years may be shifted from duties, tasks, and responsibilities of their original positions to other duties, tasks and responsibilities which are disclosed for the first time during the classification survey and on which the final allocations of their positions are
determined. It is natural therefore that in some instances the final
allocations, being based on the work currently done, will reflect
changes of assignments within the competitive service which have
previously not been legalized. The central personnel agency is then
faced with instances in which the civil service status of the employee
does not conform to the status required for the position he is currently occupying.[10] For example, the work actually performed by
an employee having the civil service status of a Junior Clerk has
required his position to be allocated to the higher class of Senior
Stenographer.

The possible methods of dealing with these situations would include demotion or reassignment of the employee to a position in a
class for which he has appropriate civil service status; competitive
promotion test; noncompetitive qualifying test; or automatic con-
cordance of status without further test.[11]

Taking the employee out of his present position and reassigning
him to a lower one covered by his civil service status is clearly not
equitable if he has served in such position in good faith for a substantial time; further, there is the practical difficulty of finding an

[10] This refers to something more than a mere change in the title of the position. If that is all that is involved, there being no substantial difference between
the work-assignments and responsibilities of the position to which the employee
should properly be appointed and that currently occupied, the change of title
should be regarded simply as a revision of existing records. It may also be observed that if the employee's civil service status is higher than required by the
allocation of his position, and approximately in the same line of work, no question usually arises as to its legal appropriateness, although this situation may
naturally motivate the employee to seek a higher allocation or a promotion or
transfer to the higher class of positions covered by his status.

[11] In jurisdictions subject to a civil service law, it is necessary to keep the question of the civil service status which the employee happens to possess or lack
separated from the question of the class in which his position falls on the basis
of its duties and responsibilities. Where an employee has been assigned to the
work of positions for which he has not officially qualified, compromising on the
classification of his position in order to avoid raising the question of his civil
service status must be avoided. The question should be raised, faced, and
answered. The position should be properly classified and the matter of his future
status under civil service rules and his continuance in the position should be
covered by statutory or regulatory provisions such as are here being discussed.

appropriate vacancy and getting him appointed to it. Somewhat better than this procedure is to permit the employee to remain in his position, without acquiring a civil service status different from that which he already possesses.

A still better procedure as a general rule, is to improve the civil service status of the employee to conform to that required for the class in which his position is allocated. This would call for the application of existing rules governing transfer or promotion. Civil service rules differ in their rigidity or flexibility in these respects and therefore the simplicity or complexity of the problem of adjustment will be affected by the character of existing rules, the possibilities of amendment, or the adoption of special rules for the installation process. Little difficulty is encountered in those cases where the civil service rules of the jurisdiction permit an employee to be transferred or promoted noncompetitively, that is, without the necessity of engaging in competition with others for the position he occupies. However, if under existing law the promotion concerned can be made only after competitive examination, a real difficulty is encountered. In such and other instances, where existing law and rules do not permit equitable methods of adjustment to be worked out, special provisions should be adopted, to be applicable only upon the installation of the classification plan. Such provisions may vest discretion in the central personnel agency to require or waive formal tests of qualifications, or may establish a general right or privilege when certain conditions are met.[12]

---

[12] Note the following example (New York State): "Rule X—Temporary Provision Governing Status of Present Incumbents of Reallocated Positions.

"Section 1. The incumbent of any position reallocated by the Classification Board from one class to a higher or different class on or before September thirtieth, nineteen hundred and thirty-nine shall, with the approval of the Civil Service Commission, if holding the position on a permanent competitive or non-competitive basis, secure the same status under the reassigned title as though he had been originally appointed under such title; provided, however, that in each such case it is determined by the Classification Board that he has satisfactorily performed the work of the class represented by the reassigned title for the twelve months immediately preceding April sixth, nineteen hundred and thirty eight.

"Section 2. In each such case as described in Section 1 of this Rule, the Classification Board may require the certification of the immediate superior of the employee and that of the head of the department or agency in which the position exists as to the length of time during which the employee has fulfilled the same duties and responsibilities. The Classification Board shall also make such investigation and require such additional information and certification as to establish to its satisfaction the employee's right to secure status under the reassigned title without further examination as provided by law."

Chapter IX

Class Specifications [1]

A "CLASS SPECIFICATION" is a word picture or description of a class.[2] It normally contains the class title, a description of the scope of duties and responsibilities of the class, examples of work or typical tasks, and a statement of the qualifications required in order to perform the work of the class. The statement of qualification standards usually includes such elements as education, experience, knowledges, abilities, skills, and personal and physical attributes.[3]

The drafting of useful specifications is a difficult and exacting task which calls for analytical powers, creative ability, and the ability to express distinctions clearly and concisely. It also requires a thorough understanding of the subject matter, function, or activity involved in the class and the relationships which the class bears to other classes.

OBJECTIVES OF CLASS SPECIFICATIONS

Class specifications constitute a most important record of the position-classification plan. They show what the classes are, what

[1] In Chapter VII, pp. 225–28, were discussed the procedural phases of writing class specifications during the original development of a position-classification plan. In Chapter X, pp. 308–09, the revision of class specifications as a function in the continuous administration of a position-classification plan will be explained. This chapter, applicable to both the developmental and the administrative periods, will deal with the limitations, objectives, form, and content of class specifications.

[2] Sometimes such a statement is known as a "class definition" or "class description." The term "class specification" is the one in common use. It seems appropriate for a statement which indicates, for recruiting purposes, the kind and level of work for which employees are to be hired and the qualifications they should possess in order to do that work. In this respect a class specification is analogous to a specification used in purchasing material or equipment or in constructing physical structures.

[3] For comparative purposes, reference may be made to occupational or job specifications in industry. For example, see Samuel L. H. Burk, "Salary and Wage Administration," *Personnel Journal*, September 1936, p. 112; J. O. Hopwood, *Salaries, Wages and Labor Relations* (New York, 1937), p. 41 ff.; John W. Riegel, *Salary Determination* (Bureau of Industrial Relations, University of Michigan, 1940), pp. 100–01; Z. Clark Dickinson, *Compensating Industrial Effort* (New York, 1937), pp. 202–04; Watkins and Dodd, *The Management of Labor Relations* (New York, 1938), pp. 136–39; Ralph D. Williams, "How to Prepare a Job Manual," *Personnel Journal*, December 1939, pp. 219–26. See also American Council on Education, "Job Specifications," *The Educational Record* (Supplement), October 1927.

kinds of positions fall in the various classes, and what the lines of demarcation among them are in terms of work-factors and qualifications. Accordingly there are certain objectives which class specifications must meet as vehicles for communicating information in writing about the position-classification plan. Moreover, every objective of a position-classification plan as an instrument of personnel administration is equally an objective of class specifications; together with the rules for administration, they are the major written tools of the position-classification plan.

The principal objectives which class specifications must meet may be summarized as follows:

1. To define the boundaries of the respective classes; to differentiate them so as to distinguish each class from every other class, not only in terms of general character or kind of work but also in terms of difficulty and responsibility of work and qualifications.

2. To serve, consequently, as a guide for all concerned in the allocation of individual positions to classes.

3. To define and standardize the various class titles, which are to have the meaning, and only that meaning, given to them by the class specifications; to serve collectively as a dictionary of class titles.

4. To serve as a convenient, currently maintained, written record identifying the basic characteristics of any class for any purpose.

Thus the class specifications permit the understanding use of the position-classification plan, its classes and class titles and its arrangement of classes, by all concerned in recruiting and testing personnel, administering service-rating (or report of performance) systems, carrying out promotion, transfer, and lay-off programs, deciding upon pay scales, considering budget estimates and making appropriations for personal services, maintaining or administering the position-classification plan, and conducting other personnel, fiscal, accounting, and statistical transactions or operations.

First of all, a class specification must distinguish between the class named and all others and therefore as a whole should show differentiating factors clearly: first, by indicating them in the general statement of duties and responsibilities; second, by describing them in the statement of distinguishing features of the work; third, by illustrating them concretely in the enumeration and description of examples of work performed; and fourth, by reflecting them in the qualifications statements. When this objective is met, class specifications will serve as a guide to the allocation of positions to classes, both during the installation of the position-classification plan and its future administration. This is the most difficult phase of class-specification writing, and at the same time is the phase on which depends its primary value.

Involved in this objective is the purpose of defining the name by which, in all processes of personnel administration (not only position-classification), each class and each position embraced within it is to be known, that is, the class title. In personnel administration as in other fields, the value of names or titles is in direct proportion to the uniformity with which they are used and understood. In the development of a position-classification plan, class titles are selected and established as the common title of a group of positions substantially alike in duties and responsibilities. But if each user or reader of class titles is left to his own interpretation of what the titles signify, they may mean little or be actually misleading. If class titles are to serve their purpose as a common job language, they must be uniformly used and understood.[4] This is accomplished through the preparation of class specifications, the whole set of specifications thus serving as a dictionary of positions.

Finally, class specifications should serve as common sources of reference for those who have any kind of interest in public personnel management. They are written tools for personnel technicians, administrators, budget officers, and legislators in planning or conducting any phase of personnel or budgetary administration requiring a knowledge of the duties-content of positions and their arrangement in the classification plan. They afford a common understanding on such questions as the meaning of titles in terms of duties and responsibilities, or the relative value of various classes of positions, or the qualifications to be required or desired—questions that are time-consuming in the extreme if they have to be analyzed and discussed every time a problem or "case" arises. In particular, they serve as a broad base from which to start in the more refined and detailed types of job analysis sometimes required in test construction, the development of specific training programs, and the improvement of service-rating systems. They help employees to think in terms of the duties-content of positions; they display the basis for the differences and similarities in the classification of individual positions; and they indicate the qualifications for higher positions. In connection with a pay plan, they inform civic and tax-

[4] Pp. 56–60.

payers' groups of the kinds of services to which specified scales of pay apply.

A class specification should be clear and understandable. The results of the analysis of positions should be so preserved and the differentiating factors among the classes should be so emphasized that the reader does not have to engage in a new analytical process to discover them or dig them out of a mass of purely descriptive phrases.

LIMITATIONS OF CLASS SPECIFICATIONS

Class specifications, adequately prepared, are useful instruments in carrying out personnel activities. However, where very detailed job analyses are required, class specifications may provide only a broad base from which to start. The demands of the different branches of personnel work vary. Specifications developed to a sufficient degree of refinement for some purposes will not serve other purposes.

In the writing of class specifications there has been, generally speaking, a necessary emphasis on their prospective use as over-all descriptions of the positions in a class. This emphasis, however, has frequently made them too broad a tool for processes requiring a more detailed analysis of duties operations, e.g., for the purposes of the technician constructing some kinds of tests or developing in-service training curricula.[5]

Taking into consideration the limitations of time, funds, and staff, should the class-specification writer prepare the whole set of specifications to the highest degree of refinement demanded by any personnel activity or problem, or should the latter stages of this refinement be in part the responsibility of his colleagues in their respective fields? It may be doubted whether the super-refinement of class specifications is consistent with the administrative objectives of position-classification. One of the purposes of position-classification is to

[5] For examples of detailed job analyses for training purposes, see: Edward K. Strong and Richard S. Uhrbrock, *Job Analysis and the Curriculum* (Baltimore, 1923); U. S. Office of Education, *Training for the Police Service*, Bulletin No. 197 (1938); M. C. Wilson, *Training Extension Workers for the Job*, U. S. Department of Agriculture Extension Circular 315, November 1939; R. E. Bowman, "The Chemical Technician—A Trade Analysis," *Journal of Chemical Education*, January 1940, pp. 36–49; L. G. Stier, *Training for the Painting and Decorating Trade*, U. S. Office of Education Bulletin No. 193 (1938), ch. 14. See also Milton Hall, *Training Your Employees*, Society for Personnel Administration, Pamphlet No. 3 (Washington, 1940), p. 9; and *Employee Training in the Public Service*, Policies and Practices in Public Personnel Administration series. Civil Service Assembly (Chicago, 1941), pp. 18–20, 51. See also pp. 68–69, 265–66, and footnotes.

present salient information about positions in organized, yet compact and succinct, form. Specifications conforming to this purpose and sufficiently analytical and comprehensive for classification, allocation, and ordinary administrative processes may not be detailed enough for certain types of test construction problems or specific training programs. If they are expanded for these purposes, however, they are apt to be so long or so "technical" as to discourage their use in everyday operations by administrators and others who are not personnel technicians.

Progress for the future seems to lie in the direction of recognizing that any *one* type of class specification does not in fact serve *all* personnel purposes to the same extent; that it serves some better than others; that the degree of generality or specificity of class specifications and their form and content should be determined by considering the precise uses to which they are going to be put; and consequently, that there may be different degrees of refinement of specifications for different purposes. This view has been well stated as follows:[6]

Job specifications, in giving a clear picture of the duties and other requirements of each position or job, are necessary not only in making job evaluations for salary and wage ratings but also in interviewing applicants for employment and in developing tests and training programs. For salary and wage rating, our chief concern is the place of the *job as a whole* in relation to the other jobs in the system of the whole. The emphasis for this purpose is not on the details of the job but upon the pattern of the entire activity which the job represents in relation to the other job activities with which it is integrated in the organization as a whole. . . . For testing and training purposes, however, we *are* chiefly concerned with particular skills and other details of the job, regardless of its relations with other jobs in the organization. In the former instance, we are concerned with the jobs as *combined with other jobs,* but in the latter we are concerned with the *isolated job.*

Job specifications, therefore, are composed differently for these different purposes. In our present study, which is concerned chiefly with the problem of evaluations for salary and wage ratings, we are interested in the *general descriptive* form of job specification in order to obtain an over-all picture of the job for identification and comparison with other jobs in the system of the whole. Other forms of job specifications emphasize details of isolated jobs for the consideration of particular details in developing tests, examining individuals, and developing training programs. These are not adapted to our purposes here. In the descriptive form of job specification we must, of course, consider details of the job, but from the point of

[6] J. O. Hopwood, *Salaries, Wages and Labor Relations* (Copyright 1937, The Ronald Press Co.), pp. 38–39. See also Dale Yoder, *Personnel and Labor Relations* (New York, 1938), pp. 86, 87.

view of the *general scope* or comprehensiveness of the job rather than from the point of view of evaluating particular details of the isolated job.

Class specifications prepared as a part of a position-classification plan should be developed to conform to the objectives previously stated. Naturally, the specifications should serve to the greatest possible degree each of the many uses to which they will be put. However, in going beyond these objectives, in expanding the specifications or any of their parts, or in modifying them with different emphases for specific purposes, we encounter problems for the future which classification workers and their colleagues in other technical phases of personnel or public administration should explore in collaboration.

Trends in Class Specifications

Class specifications in different jurisdictions have taken various forms.[7]

The usual outline for a class specification has been as follows:[8]

(a) *The class title:* a definite title or name applied to the class and to all positions of the class, which shall be as descriptive as possible of the duties and responsibilities involved in the class.

(b) *The statement of duties and responsibilities:* a general, over-all description of the work—i.e., the preponderant duties and responsibilities— encompassed in the sum total of all the positions that fall in the class described.

(c) *The statement of examples of work performed:* specific illustrations of the duties performed and responsibilities exercised in typical individual positions embraced in the class.

(d) *The statement of minimum qualifications:* a presentation of the basic education, experience, knowledge, ability or skill, and personal attributes required for functioning in the positions in the class.

Refinements in the form of class specifications have been developed recently, of which the following outlines are examples:

State of Arkansas[9]
    Class Title
    Class Definition:
        General Statement of Duties
        Supervision Received
        Supervision Exercised
        Evaluation of Duties

[7] Some examples are given in Appendix C.
[8] "The Classification Plan for the Massachusetts State Service," *Public Personnel Studies,* January 1927, p. 14; "Classification and Compensation Work in the Wisconsin State Service," *ibid.,* July 1927, p. 142.
[9] Arkansas Civil Service Commission, *The Classification Plan for the State of Arkansas,* prepared by Public Administration Service, and adopted April 28, 1938.

    Examples of Duties
    Minimum Qualifications
        Experience and Training
        Specialized Knowledges, Skills, Abilities and Aptitudes

City of Seattle[10]
    Class Title
    Evaluation of Duties
    Supervision Received
    Supervision Exercised
    Examples of Duties
    Desirable Preparation

State of Alabama[11]
    Class Title
    Class Description
        General Statement of Duties
        Evaluation of Duties
    Interpretative Data
        Examples of Duties
        Supervision Received
    Entrance Qualifications Specification
        Required Knowledges, Skills, and Abilities
        Acceptable Experience and Training

State of Minnesota[12]
    Class Title
    Kind of Work
    Difficulty and Responsibility of Work
    Essential Requirements of Work[13]
    Examples of Work (Illustrative only; indicates kinds of work performed in the class outlined above.)

City of Los Angeles[14]
    Class Title
    General Statement of Duties
    Distinguishing Features of the Work
    Examples of Duties
    Desirable Qualifications

[10] Seattle Civil Service Commission, *Class Specifications of the City of Seattle, 1938,* prepared by Public Administration Service. The specifications were reproduced with the order of the last two sections reversed.

[11] *State of Alabama Personnel Department, Classification Plan,* approved November 29, 1939, prepared by Public Administration Service.

[12] *Minnesota State Civil Service Department,* 1940, prepared by Public Administration Service.

[13] In terms of knowledges and abilities.

[14] *Los Angeles City Civil Service Commission,* 1940, prepared by Public Administration Service. To the statement of Desirable Qualifications is added occasionally a statement of minimum qualifications, where they are clearly minima or are required by law. For certain classes, the kind of license or certificate required is also set forth. See exhibit in Appendix C.

A comparison of the form and content of class specifications, old and new, indicates several trends:

1. There is a decided tendency to make class specifications more understandable to those not trained in personnel administration. This has involved the adoption of a simple, report style of description, rather than the conventional infinitive-clause form. There is a collateral advantage in the use of declarative sentences phrased in the present tense, because this style conforms more with the idea that the specification describes duties as they are, rather than as they should be. The infinitive form frequently has a prescriptive connotation to those not grounded in classification techniques, and explanation is required to remove this impression. For example, if a class specification states that the duties of the class are "to do" a particular task or "to carry out" a certain operation, this can be interpreted to mean that the supervisor must assign the employee to that task or operation and under no circumstances to any other. It may be that this type of language has contributed to the idea that detailed specifications and the classes which they describe are in many instances too restrictive for sound administration.[15]

2. With the same purpose of making the class specification clearer it has been suggested that the nontechnical reader is accustomed to think in terms of whole positions and finds difficulty in grasping, or will misunderstand, the significance of tasks set out alone, when in fact they are each a part of an individual position. For this reason, it is thought that tasks which occur frequently should be mentioned, even though they are not typical in the classification sense, particularly when they can conveniently be set forth in combination with other tasks as they occur in positions themselves.[16]

3. There is a strong trend toward making class specifications more analytical or evaluative in character. Effort is made to set forth expressly the facts and factors which distinguish from all other classes the class being described. Thus the points on which the allocation of a position to that class hinges are made plain on the face of the specification instead of being left to the analytical skill of the reader. This trend is indicated by the inclusion of so-called "evaluation" statements or "distinguishing features" statements in class specifications and by attaching limiting or qualifying factors to typical tasks in order to give them a real differentiating effect.[17]

[15] See pp. 49–50, and the reference there given.
[16] Pp. 260–61.
[17] Pp. 262–64.

4. Statements of knowledges, abilities, and aptitudes are regarded as more fundamental than statements of education, experience, and training, and the two kinds of statements are therefore being set forth more distinctively. Qualification standards of education, experience, and training are being designated as evidentiary in character, that is, as evidence of the possession of certain kinds and extents of knowledge and ability.

5. There is also a tendency to omit statements as to lines of promotion and other data that are more pertinently included in records or rules relating to other phases of personnel administration.

FORM AND ESSENTIAL CONTENT

The class specification consists of five major parts.[18] First, as a general heading for the specification, the class title is given.[19] This is followed by General Statement, Distinguishing Features of Work, Illustrative Examples of Work, and a statement of qualifications headed Qualification Requirements or Desirable Qualifications, depending on the policy adopted.[20]

The general statement is an over-all introductory description of the work falling in the class, including both duties and responsibilities. The statement of distinguishing features of work, interpretative in nature, highlights the factors which necessitated the establishment of the class and indicates in what respects the work of the class distinguishes it from the work of other classes, particularly those next higher and next lower in the same series. The illustrative examples of work are selected illustrations of tasks performed and responsibilities borne singly or in combination. The qualification requirements or desirable qualifications are in terms of knowledge, ability, aptitudes, and personal qualities as well as experience, education, or other evidence of the possession of the required qualities.

General Statement

The first part of the text of a class specification, following the class title (which serves as a general heading for the whole specification), is the general statement of duties and responsibilities. This is a brief over-all identification of the kind and level of work included

[18] Although a uniform format is desirable for class specifications, no specification should needlessly repeat material merely to conform to a uniform structure, nor should essential information be omitted even if an additional heading is called for.
[19] For a discussion of class titles, see pp. 214–20.
[20] Pp. 269–74.

in the class. Its principal purpose is to describe the kind of work involved and show broadly its level of difficulty and responsibility.[21]

In form and content the general statement is broadly constructed and is expressed as simply as possible, without repetition of material appearing elsewhere in the specification. It is designed primarily as an introduction to the rest of the text. When the general statements of all class specifications are brought together they serve as a brief descriptive summary. Such summary frequently serves a useful purpose in providing information where the inquirer's interest is casual, where he is not directly concerned with general management or personnel administration, or where succinct abstracts of class specifications are needed for budget or legislative purposes.

The general statement is usually composed of a few declarative clauses, phrased in the present tense. General functional verbs or expressions such as the following may be used to introduce such clauses: performs; supervises; has immediate supervision over a group of . . . engaged in . . .; directs; administers; plans, organizes, directs, supervises, and controls; plans, organizes, directs, supervises, interprets, and reports upon (researches); has responsible administrative and professional charge of . . .; serves as responsible administrative and professional head of . . .; etc. For a good many classes, more precise terms can be employed, such as: types; investigates; inspects; audits; examines; guards; patrols; operates (a machine or office device); etc. Care should be exercised to avoid stereotyped terms where more significant ones can be used.[22]

The clauses of the general statement are usually cumulative; that is, the duties and responsibilities described in each are involved in all positions in the class. Sometimes, however, they are alternative clauses, each of the clauses applying to some, but not all, of the positions in the class. This is the case when the class contains positions entailing different uses of the same subject matter, different approaches to similar problems, or different but equivalent aspects of responsibility. For example:

Serves as a responsible supervisory assistant to a Chief Accountant, having charge of an important phase of the work, and acting for the chief in all matters during his absence; or has responsible supervision over a group of accountants engaged in analytical work in accounting involving difficult and important questions.

[21] The general statement should clearly reflect the differences in *kind* of work among the various "series of classes." See p. 194.
[22] See Riegel, *Salary Determination*, p. 86, footnote 1.

In the general statement, broad adjectives are frequently employed to indicate degree or extent of importance, difficulty, or responsibility. This is necessary where the distinction between two successive classes in the same series cannot be brought out without lengthening the general statement unduly.

These adjectives do not have definite meanings to the reader until they are adequately explained and illustrated by the content of the remainder of the class specification. As a matter of fact, they have no meaning except in relation to other specifications, particularly in the same series of classes. They must, therefore, be consistent with similar expressions of lower or higher degree used in other closely associated class specifications, in order that proper gradation and coordination may be indicated. Sometimes it is convenient to decide beforehand on the rank order of such adjectives as may be used in different specifications. For example, the following may be established as an ascending series of adjectives to indicate difficulty of work: simplest routine; of less than average difficulty; of average difficulty; of more than average difficulty; very difficult; exceptionally difficult. Similar expressions may be used in describing importance or responsibility. Here again, stereotyped phrases should not be used where more significant ones are available.

For purposes of allocating positions to classes, these adjectives taken by themselves are the least useful expressions in the class specification. Their principal value is that they show at the very beginning of the class specification that one of the factors differentiating the class from higher or lower classes is the degree or extent of the importance, difficulty, or responsibility of the work; and this leads the reader or interpreter of the specifications to a consideration of these allocation factors and the bearing the information given in the rest of the specification has upon each of them.

The general statement ends with the clause, "and performs related work as assigned," or one similarly worded. The purpose of this is twofold. It emphasizes that only the preponderant and characteristic duties and responsibilities have been described and that there is no effort to cover all the minute and varied duties involved. It also emphasizes that the employee may be subject to assignments other than those expressly mentioned.

Distinguishing Features of Work

The statement of distinguishing features of work is a very important part of the specification. Written in a direct, "report" style, its function is to emphasize those characteristics of the work of the class that distinguish it from other classes.[23] It must be specific enough to establish the boundaries of the class. Distinctions as to kind of work are brought out by details about its essential nature. Distinctions as to level, that is, differentiations between the class being described and those next above and next below in the same series, are shown by information about the difficulty and complexity of the work, the kind and weight of supervision received, and the nature and extent of specific nonsupervisory, supervisory, or administrative responsibilities. As a whole, this statement covers the essential differentiating factors of classification analysis as they are involved in the work of positions falling in the class.[24]

As a rule no effort is made to subdivide the statement of distinguishing features of work into subheads such as difficulty and complexity, supervision received, supervision exercised, and so on, unless the class is so uniform or so small in its position-content to make this a logical arrangement. In most instances the statement is written as a unit, so that the combinations of allocation factors, as well as the allocation factors themselves, may be better presented.

Difficulty and complexity may be indicated in terms of kind and extent of supervision received, flow of work before and after it reaches the employee, type of assignments, procedure followed, methods used, decisions made, or action taken, control of employee's work by advisers or reviewers, and its variety and scope.[25] Responsibility may be either nonsupervisory or supervisory. A nonsupervisory responsibility, for example, may be shown as a responsibility for reviewing or inspecting the work of others; for independence of action or decision; for recommendations or decisions determining, applying, or affecting plans, policies, methods, operations, or regulations; for negotiation with the public or with other agencies; for the safety

[23] One form of occupational definition for Typist (Grade B) (private industry) has a separate section entitled: "Distinctions between this and other work that might be confused with it." Under this head appears the following: "1. Titles of similar work: (a) Typist (Grade A); (b) Typist-clerk. 2. How may these be distinguished from Item A (payroll title)? (a) The work of the Typist (Grade A) includes the selection of suitable form paragraphs, whereas that of the Typist (Grade B) does not. (b) The work of the Typist-clerk includes adding machine and comptometer operation and the checking of figures, whereas that of the Typist (Grade B) does not. The reports copied by the former contain extensive tabulations; those copied by the latter do not." C. C. Balderston, *Salary and Wage Setting*, Institute of Management Series No. 17 (American Management Association, 1938).

[24] See Chapter V.

[25] Pp. 94–105.

or lives of others; or as any other operating responsibility. Its weight may also be indicated by a clause describing the normal consequence of error.[26] Generally, it is convenient to describe difficulty and responsibility together. For example:

The work of an Electrical Inspector entails responsibility toward the public for seeing that all fire and other hazards of electrical equipment are avoided in building construction. It requires thorough familiarity with electrical machinery, electrical theory, all applicable laws, rules, and ordinances, and exceptional ability to deal effectively with the public.

The work of a Senior Chemical Aid involves scientific and manipulative techniques of a considerable degree of difficulty, although the methods to be used are previously prescribed by professional supervisors. Results are carefully checked at various stages of operation. The worker has no authority to exercise initiative on his own account in deviating from instructions.

The work of a Junior Computer involves a knowledge of the long-established and commonly-known computing methods of higher mathematics. It requires no analysis of mathematical problems, but only the substitution of numerical quantities for the symbols in given formulas and the accurate performance of the mathematical operations indicated in such formulas, e.g., integration, differentiation, and the ordinary trigonometric, algebraic, logarithmic, and arithmetical operations.

One work-characteristic bearing on both difficulty and responsibility is the manner and the respects in which the employee's work is controlled by his supervisor. In some instances, the pattern of supervision received will be fairly uniform for each position in the class. In other instances it will vary. Consequently, clauses describing supervision received will cover either a single condition or several alternative conditions, or will appear separately or in combination with clauses describing other factors of difficulty or responsibility, depending on the facts. As indicated in Chapter V, for purposes of clear analysis, supervision from above is regarded as distinct from difficulty of work although it may affect it. One may encounter in the same class positions involving close supervision on difficult tasks or remote supervision on easier tasks, or degrees of supervision and difficulty in various combinations. Supervision from above, moreover, is interlaced similarly with the individual responsibility of the person supervised. Hence, unless a given class of positions embraces only a few positions or is entirely homogeneous, the quality and degree of supervision received may vary among the positions within

[26] Pp. 105–15.

the class and can be covered only in combination with other factors.

As a factor entering into the analysis and classification of positions, supervision has previously been discussed.[27] In particular, commonly encountered kinds and degrees of supervision have been broadly described, and reference may be made to those descriptions as indicative of the normal variations in supervision received or exercised.[28] These should be expressed as precisely as possible in the statement of distinguishing features of the work. Examples are as follows:

> Choice of problem to be undertaken is decided by supervisor in conference with worker, who then determines method of attack independently and is free from direction or supervision during the progress of the work except as to conformance with administrative policies and the necessity of achieving productive results.

> Receives close guidance and specific, detailed, and frequent instructions as to work-programs, methods, and purposes; has little opportunity for independent or unreviewed action or decision except as to the simpler processes.

> Is assigned to inspection districts and specific inspection jobs by the Chief Building Inspector. Work is subject to general plans, policies, and objectives of the Building Department. Work is checked on completion through review of inspection reports by the Chief Building Inspector, or through the review of exceptions taken by builders or owners.

> Instructions on any new type of assignment are given the Junior Clerk in detail. The work is checked by his supervisor upon completion, either by another step in the procedure or by a physical check for accuracy.

> Consults with Director of Highways and receives instructions concerning general departmental policies, objectives and plans.

For a class composed of supervisory or administrative positions, the statement of distinguishing features of work sets forth the degree, magnitude, and scope of supervisory responsibility involved, that is, the amount and kind of supervision an employee in the class is called upon to provide for subordinates. In this respect, reference may be made to the discussion of the factors pertinent to the evaluation of supervisory responsibility.[29]

Statements of supervision exercised over subordinates are most informative when they indicate the "size" of the supervisory responsibility in terms of the number and kind of staff supervised, the variety and complexity of the functions directed, and the specific ways in

[27] Pp. 115–27.
[28] Pp. 123–24.
[29] Pp. 115–27.

which supervision is actually exercised. Examples are as follows:

As supervisory head of an instrument shop, directs the work of a small group of instrument makers, and estimates for, plans, assigns, lays out, follows through, and inspects jobs involved in the construction, repair, or adjustment of precision instruments and apparatus of standard and special design.

As a working supervisor of a small group of junior audit clerks, assigns work to the group; gives advice and instruction; individually decides more difficult or unusual cases; reviews the work of the group and takes responsibility for its correctness.

Supervises all engineering work in the Highway Department by the assignment of general projects, the interpretation of departmental policies, objectives and plans, and the review of decisions concerning work methods, coordination, production and results obtained. Work involves professional administrative engineering problems of the highest order in the field of highway designing, construction and maintenance; responsibility for formulating, initiating and judging the effectiveness of changes in methods and procedures.

Illustrative Examples of Work

By "illustrative examples of work" are meant characteristic illustrations of tasks performed or responsibilities exercised in positions embraced in the class. The broad purposes of including such examples are to amplify and clarify the general statement, to sharpen and energize the whole specification, and to aid in indicating the boundaries of the class.

Illustrative examples of work should, therefore, be selected, described, and arranged with considerable care. The statement of actual tasks or operations is referred to frequently by administrative officers, employees, and the general public, who rely heavily upon this portion of the specification for their understanding of what kind of work is in a given class.[30] Thus any effort toward making the statement of illustrative examples of work more realistic, reliable, and specific is well spent. Furthermore, classification technicians themselves rely upon this part of the class specification for illustrations of what some of its more general parts mean. They look to the examples of work as bases of comparison with which the tasks involved in a position to be allocated are likened or contrasted. They study the examples to observe the "range" or "breadth" of the class.

[30] Some of this emphasis will undoubtedly be shifted to the distinguishing features statement in specifications of the style here discussed. This in itself is a desirable result.

Consequently, specific illustrations of all the factors pertinent for allocation purposes should be included.

The problem of selecting tasks for inclusion in the specification arises out of the fact that it would be neither feasible nor useful to make the examples a mere catalog of all tasks, from the most simple to the most difficult, performed in all positions in the class. The examples, being illustrative merely, are not intended to constitute a complete list. Unless the class contains only a few positions each single position in the class cannot be represented by some task in the list; and some positions, accordingly, may fall in the class in spite of the fact that none of their tasks is specifically selected for the statement of illustrative data. Further, some tasks may be part of the regular work of more than one class of positions and hence not peculiar to any one class.

From the standpoint of the classification technician, the emphasis in past practice has been on the purposeful, although not exclusive, selection of those tasks which are most characteristic and most useful in showing lines of demarcation—those that have a definite bearing in determining whether a position belongs in the class being described rather than in some other class. Under this principle, examples of typical tasks are selected with these questions in mind: Why do the tasks described fall in this class rather than in some other class? Why are they characteristic of this class and no other? What factors of difficulty, scope, or responsibility distinguish them from somewhat similar tasks which fall in other classes, particularly the class next above and the class next below in the same series or occupational group?

From the standpoint of making the statement of typical tasks genuinely useful to administrative officers, employees, and the general public, more attention might well be paid to describing tasks that frequently occur in positions of the class rather than placing exclusive emphasis upon the value of the typical task as a reference item in the allocation process.

The selection and description of illustrative examples of work would then rest on the recognition (1) that tasks occur *in positions,* not as separate entities isolated from the positions themselves, and (2) that tasks occur as a rule in combination with other tasks, reference to which is necessary for a complete picture of a position or group of positions and to understand why the position or group of positions falls in a given class. Hence, the statement of examples of work should show typical combinations of tasks as they occur in positions in the class—a significant item of information, especially where variety and scope of work are important characteristics of positions in the class. In addition, effort should be made to present an adequate picture of frequent tasks occurring in a majority of the positions in the class, so that administrators and employees may readily see the content of *typical positions* in the class. Furthermore, the meaning of the phrase "related work as required," used in the general statement, is thus illustrated.

While this method of expressing typical examples of work would make the specification more easily understood by employees and administrative officials, a word of caution is in order. To go too far in this direction and incorporate too many details, means that initial specifications may be written which would become out of date and nondescriptive of actual assignments more quickly than otherwise. The *combinations* of tasks, at one time characteristic, may be affected by changes in work methods and size of organization. In many of these instances, however, the position as a whole would not be sufficiently affected to require a change in its class allocation. This means that certain tasks may remain highly characteristic of the class and of the positions it contains, even though they may be combined with other tasks in different ways and even though such combinations will vary from time to time without necessitating a change in the fundamental concept of the class or the allocations of positions. To attempt to keep the specifications up to date as changes in assignments occur which do not affect classes or allocations to classes would, in a sizable jurisdiction, involve considerable work and be of little significance in personnel processes. One public personnel agency uses a separate section of the specification for tasks that are frequent and yet not discriminative of a single class, under the head of "Other examples." It says: "The use of this subsection permits an employee or prospective employee to secure a picture of all the work he must be able to do and occasionally must do and yet at the same time clarifies the statement of factors important for allocation purposes."[31]

After tasks have been selected for inclusion in the class specification, the problem arises as to the precision and completeness to be observed in describing them.

[31] Detroit Civil Service Commission, *The Classification Plan for the City of Detroit* (1935), p. xii.

Naturally, illustrative examples may be described in more precise and concrete language than is usually employed in the general statement. The general statement is intended to cover all positions in the class. Hence broad terms are employed. No one example of typical tasks, however, need be comprehensive. On the contrary, each example may apply to only a limited number of the positions in the class, and it is possible therefore to describe each example in concrete and precise terms. For example, if the general statement contains such broad adjectives as "simple," "elementary," "difficult," "responsible," "important," "considerable," "major," or "minor," the examples should illustrate the standards or levels represented by these terms, and show as precisely as possible their significance in terms of the particular tasks being described. The examples help in showing the lines of demarcation among the classes by minimizing the possibility of confusion latent in any general language appearing in other parts of the specification. To this end, the examples illustrate not only the actual operation or activity involved in the task, but also other factors—such as difficulty of work, independence of action, degree of supervision under which the task is performed, or responsibility for directing the work of others—that differentiate such operation or activity from tasks in other classes which are approximately similar but of greater or lesser difficulty and responsibility. This is especially important where, on account of the large number of slightly varied positions in the class, the statement of distinguishing features of the work cannot be drawn so as to be precise and comprehensive at the same time.

Accordingly, where mere repetition of the distinguishing features statement does not result, it is desirable to bring out, in each example of work performed, the factors relating to the importance, difficulty, and responsibility of the work as specifically as the factors that show the *kind* of work. Two examples follow:

Develops details of supercharges for airplanes, where the design and general layout have already been established and the computations made, except for standard parts and fittings.

Prepares water-color paintings of insects, where many of the specimens are of small size and exhibit a great amount of detail and a wide range of color, and the paintings are required to be scientifically accurate both as to size and color.

In a class-specification writing project of the Detroit Civil Service Commission this point has been emphasized by reference to the task of "filing" papers, the relative difficulty and responsibility of which are uncertain unless the circumstances under which it is done are fully and adequately described. The Commission set forth the following statements as illustrations of the use of "limiting factors" in describing examples of typical tasks:

In a large filing storage unit where material filed consists exclusively of single cards arranged in numerical order with a supervisor in direct charge frequently inspecting work for a small section of such files, arranging cards to be filed in numerical order, filing such cards in their proper place, and occasionally, from a written request for specific card numbers, removing such cards from the files.

As the sole file clerk in a moderately large organization unit, with general filing methods prescribed by superiors, but with full responsibility for accuracy of filing and for securing needed material from files, filing a variety of largely nontechnical materials such as purchase orders in numerical order, requisitions in chronological order according to requisitioning department, standard commodity specifications, trade catalogs and laboratory reports on tests in accordance with a somewhat flexible subject classification scheme, general correspondence arranged alphabetically by vendors' names; securing materials from files which occasionally includes searching files for matter relating to particular commodities.

In the reference unit of a scientific or technical organization, where material filed consists of a variety of documents, reports, manuscripts, pamphlets, and other material in English and several foreign languages dealing exclusively with technical subjects such as a variety of medical specialties as neuro-psychiatry, pediatrics, orthopedics, and roentgenology, with opportunity to occasionally consult superiors on meaning of obscure passages in foreign languages and as to most useful arrangement of material in files: reading new or incoming material to determine subject or subjects with which it deals, classifying such material in accordance with a standard plan, preparing index or catalog cards on subjects dealt with, filing catalog cards and material in files, binders and shelves in accordance with the classification scheme; upon requests for specific material or material dealing with a general subject, searching files for pertinent material, occasionally making abstracts from bulky material and assembling such material for use of specialist making request.

These illustrations, said the Detroit Commission, convey a considerably better picture of the relative difficulty of the three types of work than if only the following statements were made:

Filing cards.
Filing a variety of material including purchase orders, commodity specifications, and general correspondence.
Filing technical material and searching files for such material.[32]

[32] *Ibid.*, pp. xiv–xv.

The delineation of such qualifying or limiting factors in the description of examples of work becomes essential when, as in large jurisdictions, positions which vary somewhat in the weight of one allocation factor, such as supervision received or difficulty of work, belong nevertheless in the same class when the combined effect of all the factors is considered. If this condition exists, the class specification calls for illustrations of typical tasks that set forth all the work factors.

Accordingly, in describing the illustrative examples of work, it should be recognized: (1) that tasks occur under conditions affecting their difficulty and responsibility; (2) that frequently these conditions govern position allocations to a greater extent than the task itself would if considered apart from the conditions; (3) that the same tasks might occur in different positions under such varying circumstances as to cause the positions to fall in different classes; (4) that the crucial elements for allocation purposes in such instances would not be shown by a bare description of the task itself; and that, therefore; (5) wherever selected tasks, the bare descriptions of which would be similar, would fall in several different classes because of factors derived from circumstances under which the tasks are performed, these factors and circumstances should be set forth in detail in the descriptions of each of the tasks.[33]

It is advantageous to present in logical order the material to be contained in the statement of illustrative examples of work. In some instances, examples of work may be given in the sequence in which they are normally performed; in others, a significant order would be to begin with the more important or frequent tasks and continue with other tasks in the order of their importance or frequency. The statement of illustrative examples should not be an unorganized list of seemingly unrelated tasks. Cohesion and the avoidance of misleading emphasis should be the goal. Where minor features are described, they should not be overemphasized either by their place in the statement or by their description.

Qualifications Statement

To make the class specification of maximum usefulness, information is included as to the qualifications necessary or desirable for the duties and the responsibilities involved in positions in the class being described. Such information, of course, should be consistent

[33] See also the discussion of the interpretation of the statement of illustrative examples of work, pp. 282–83.

with and derived from the duties, responsibilities, and other data previously set forth in the specification.[34]

The statements of qualifications in class specifications are, of course, subject to as much revision as any other part of the specification. They will be amended and changed from time to time, probably to a considerable extent at first, as opportunities for their improvement are presented. They are also subject to revision in order to capture the results of recruiting practices, to indicate more clearly the fields from which qualified applicants may be drawn, to prevent misunderstanding on the part of applicants and administrative officials, or to serve generally as a better guide in recruiting, testing, and selection.[35]

The information given about qualifications is designed to make the whole class specification definitely useful as a guide in preparing and announcing tests, rating papers, evaluating experience, making investigations of suitability for employment, conducting oral interviews, and generally determining eligibility for appointment, transfer, or promotion. The very close connection between the writing of statements of qualifications in class specifications and recruiting and testing activities is apparent.

Statements of qualifications cover: (a) knowledges, abilities, and other qualities; (b) experience, training, and education; (c) physical standards; and (d) other qualification requirements, such as licenses or other certificates of qualification required by public law.

Knowledges, abilities, and other qualities. Under this sub-heading are set forth the knowledges, abilities, skills, aptitudes, personal attributes, and other qualities that the work of the class demands. These are qualities employees must possess to perform effectively the work of positions in the class.[36]

[34] "Examination of the present classification plan discloses the absence of statements of minimum qualifications in the specifications. . . . Granted that minimum qualifications cannot in many instances be determined with absolute precision, yet by dispensing with them entirely it appears more difficult to grasp the full significance of the classification plan because of their absence. Certainly in fixing salaries one does not tend to think so much in terms of the specific duties as in terms of the qualifications that are required for the satisfactory performance of such duties. Furthermore, there should be available to both the public and the recruiting agency a statement as to the nature of the qualifications required for the different classes of positions." *Report of the Special Commission on Taxation and Public Expenditures of the Commonwealth of Massachusetts* (prepared by Public Administration Service): Part XV, *The Civil Service System of the Commonwealth*, Sec. II, Problems of Organization and Administration. [House document, 1716], April 13, 1938, p. 63.

[35] Pp. 308–09.

[36] "In defining the qualifications necessary for the successful performance of the job, we leave the realm of fact and are starting the rating procedure, because, for the present at least, any question of qualifications or requirements must to a

This listing of essential work-requirements covers primary qualifications. The possession of the knowledge and ability described may be ascertained in various ways and by deduction from various types of evidence: the applicant's educational and employment record, written tests, performance tests, the submission of exhibits showing past accomplishments, personal investigation, or oral examination. However, the statement of knowledges and abilities does not indicate the method by which those qualifications may be determined or measured. It does not state what employment, educational, or training record or other evidence applicants may be required to present in support of such qualifications.

The knowledge and ability pattern of each class of positions is important as a basis for personnel operations and transactions concerning the class and employees occupying positions within it. Hence, it should cover all knowledge and ability qualities which the duties and responsibilities of the class call for, notwithstanding that in some instances test techniques to measure them reliably and validly have not yet been developed.[37]

Opportunities will be many, however, for indicating knowledges and abilities in terms sufficiently precise to aid in making up test items or questions. For example, the phrase "ability to edit statistical schedules, lay out statistical tables, design box heads, and write simple text explaining what the tables show" is significant, but the expression "statistical ability" is not.

First in order are given phrases which show the subjects, topics, or things that the employee must know. The degree or amount of knowledge is also indicated, because in many instances the depth

considerable extent be a matter of opinion. . . . It is exceedingly difficult if at all possible to arrive at any common agreement as to average qualifications, and especially to define maximum qualifications. It is our opinion (and our experience has borne out this belief) that most satisfactory results are obtained if the appraisal is limited to the minimum qualifications that are necessary for an individual to perform satisfactorily after a minimum learning period." Samuel L. H. Burk, *A Case History in Salary and Wage Administration* (American Management Association, 1939), pp. 14–15.

[37] "The job analysis should uncover information that can be used as criteria of occupational achievement against which measuring devices can be checked and, further, should discover the apparent kinds of abilities, aptitudes, and other potentialities required for proficiency in the occupation. This latter information gives clues to the kinds of items which should be included in the experimental measure or battery of items." William H. Stead *et al.*, *Occupational Counseling Techniques* (American Book Co., 1940), p. 23. See also Morris S. Viteles, "The Human Factor in Substation Operation," *Personnel Journal*, August 1929, pp. 81–113; and the same author's "Job Specifications and Diagnostic Tests of Job Competency Designed for the Auditing Division of a Street Railway Company," *The Psychological Clinic*, May-June 1922, pp. 83–105.

or breadth of the knowledge required correlates with the level of the class. For example, "some knowledge of" or "familiarity with" a given subject matter might be sufficient for a beginning class in a certain series, but "comprehensive and detailed specialized knowledge" of such subject matter might be a suitable requirement for the most advanced class in the series. In other words, the depth and breadth of knowledge required advance in proportion to the importance, difficulty, and responsibility of the work of the classes in the series. Four examples of statements of knowledge required, which will show general form and content, follow: [38]

Good working knowledge of the care, operation, and ordinary adjustments of the graphotype machine.

Thorough and comprehensive knowledge of the use of law books in searching for statutes and authorities.

Comprehensive and detailed specialized knowledge of veterinary science as applied to the eradication and control of diseases of livestock.

General knowledge of the fundamental principles of landscape design, the theory and practice of landscape design as applied to the lesser landscape problems, the planning of city parks or squares, and playgrounds.

After the statement of what an employee must know will come statements of what he must be able to do. These phrases are usually expressed in terms of ability to; capacity to; proficiency in; skill in; technique in; etc., and sometimes modified by a suitable adjective, such as "demonstrated," "marked," "outstanding," etc., to show gradation. Examples follow: [39]

Ability to understand and follow instructions.

Good command of English.

Proficiency in the use of drafting instruments, instruments of precision, slide rule, calculating machines, and trigonometric and logarithmic tables.

Skill with simple hand tools.

Demonstrated ability to plan, lay out, supervise, and direct the work of skilled mechanics, helpers, laborers, enginemen, or others.

Marked capacity in analyzing and appraising facts, evidence, and precedents, in developing legal issues, and in applying legal principles and decided cases to difficult problems.

Ability to analyze conditions and recognize fundamental economic needs and trends involved in the preparation of plans for the management of the various resources of a national forest.

Capacity to determine fruitful lines of scientific research, to organize scientific work, and to direct large staffs of investigators and professional workers.

[38] For other examples, see the specifications in Appendix C.
[39] For other examples, see the specifications in Appendix C.

Following the clauses relating to abilities, there are recorded those personal traits which are especially required of applicants in order to qualify for the class of position concerned. Personal attributes should be stated only when they are particularly in point. Qualities such as honesty, integrity, and industry, obviously desirable for all classes of positions, are usually taken for granted as being required even though they are not expressly stated.

It is, however, desirable to include those personal attributes that have a direct bearing on the duties of the positions in the class, such as integrity for cashiers and law enforcement officers, manual dexterity for card punch machine operators, social intelligence for positions involving much public contact, and so on.

In setting up personal attributes as well as in setting up knowledge and ability, it is well to define the attribute as specifically as possible; for example, it is better to specify for a statistical clerk "accuracy in arithmetic computation" than merely "accuracy"; for a proofreader "alertness in detecting typographical errors" instead of just "alertness." Such qualities as these, when significantly expressed, may well serve as the key points to be determined in oral tests.[40] Several examples follow:

Accuracy and rapidity in arithmetical computation and verification and in recording items and preparing bills, statements, and schedules.

Personal fitness and good address for conferring with professional and business representatives.

Judicial temperament and poise in the conduct of public hearings.

Ability to gain cooperation and to cooperate with others.

Ability to weigh impartially and accurately evidence concerning conflicting interests and make decisions promptly.

Resourcefulness, ingenuity, and sound judgment in gathering material, in planning techniques, and in the solution of economic problems.

Experience, training, and education. Through experience, training, and education persons acquire knowledge, sharpen their skills and abilities, develop work habits and improve their judgment. Experience, education, and training standards, as contrasted with knowledge and ability requirements, are therefore evidentiary or administrative, rather than fundamental or definitive. Taken by themselves, they are evidence—partial or complete—on the question

[40] See W. V. Bingham, *Oral Examinations in Civil Service Recruitment* (Civil Service Assembly . . . , 1939), Pamphlet No. 13; Samuel H. Ordway, Jr., and James C. O'Brien, *An Approach to More Objective Oral Tests* (Society for Personnel Administration, 1939), Pamphlet No. 2; *ibid.*, "New Method of Interview Hiring," *Personnel Journal*, October 1939, pp. 128–35.

of the possession of the kind and extent of knowledge, ability, and other direct qualities the work of positions in the class demands.[41]

As a matter of fact, in preparing statements of qualification standards, the analyst should first make a thorough study of the duties and responsibilities of the class of positions. He should then immediately proceed to a consideration of what knowledges, skills, and abilities are necessary for the performance of those duties and the discharge of those responsibilities. Only then is he in a position to decide on educational or experience standards. In other words, the educational and experience standards come as an answer to the question, "what education and experience backgrounds are most likely to produce these knowledges, skills, and abilities?"

Thus, educational and experiential qualifications are significant to the extent that they evidence or indicate the presence, absence, or degree of possession of the basic attributes of knowledges, abilities, aptitudes, and personal qualities set forth previously in the specification. When well developed, the statements as to education and experience also are useful in that they indicate the likeliest sources of supply from which qualified candidates can be drawn. Thus they serve as guides to examiners in evaluating the educational and experience record of candidates and in explaining such evaluations; to administrative and personnel officers in carrying out vocational guidance functions; to employees as a tool for self guidance; and to recruiting officers in preparing mailing lists for the distribution of examination announcements.

In preparing statements of experience or education, the fact must be considered that in most instances the actual enforcement or use of qualifications standards does not rest upon the basic authority for a position-classification plan, but stems from legal provisions authorizing a personnel agency to hold tests and determine the eligibility of applicants and employees. Usually, in the absence of such provisions qualifications statements in class specifications have only an advisory effect upon the selection and appointment of personnel. Consequently, statutory stipulations governing recruiting, testing,

---

[41] "It should be pointed out that education and experience have little or no value in and of themselves, but only as they result in the acquisition of knowledge, ability, or skill, and work habits and attitudes. In the testing procedure, the possession of certain educational and experience qualifications is considered as a rough indication of the possession of knowledge, ability, and so on, but an effort has been made in the specifications to show these other factors in detail, rather than to rely on mere statements of education and experience." Detroit Civil Service Commission, *op. cit.*, p. xviii.

and in-service transactions may have an important bearing on the content of qualifications statements to be included in class specifications. For example, in some jurisdictions, such as the state of Massachusetts, and the cities of Detroit and Seattle, statutory or charter provisions prohibit or restrict the use of formal educational requirements as prerequisites for admission to tests. On the other hand, definite education and/or experience may be required by law for the exercise of duties having a public interest, such as those of a physician, lawyer, registered pharmacist, or registered nurse.

It is clear, also, that statements of experience, education, and training need to be realistic in the light of administrative policies as to recruiting, testing, in-service transactions, and public relations. Hence, experiential and educational standards should be drawn up with due regard to the effect of (a) general personnel laws or rules, (b) other laws governing the employment or the exercise of duties by employees of certain classes, and (c) administrative considerations such as good public relations, funds available, availability and potential number of applicants, volume of work, delay in establishing eligible lists, administrative feasibility of giving written tests to all who apply, size of eligible list actually needed to fill existing and contemplated vacancies, and the existence of written tests which actually test for and measure relatively the knowledges and abilities required.[42] It has been suggested that at the present stage of development in personnel work, precise educational or experience prerequisites for entrance to tests are usually based (a) on the expediency of limiting competition to those persons who, by reason of their training and experience, are considered most likely to succeed in the work of a particular class and (b) on the necessity of producing enough eligibles to fill the positions. Also, the setting of educational and experience prerequisites is influenced by the necessity of receiving the greatest return from each dollar spent in the recruiting processes.

These factors must be taken into consideration in the writing of requirements as to experience, education, or physical attributes, in the setting of any absolute standard of degree, length, or magnitude, or in the establishment of any prerequisite for entrance to a written test or for the acceptance of applications. They have a significance

[42] See Thomas C. Murray, *Prerequisite Qualification Requirements*, New York City Civil Service Commission (New York, 1922); also appears in *Proceedings, 15th Annual Meeting of National Assembly of Civil Service Commissions*, June 1922, pp. 87–93.

going beyond the content of the statements as to qualifications; they may determine the status of these statements as a whole. On the one hand, the qualifications stated may be established as absolute prerequisites for the acceptance of applications, i.e., no further test will be given the applicant and he will not be considered for employment in positions of the particular class if he does not possess the education, training, or experience described. On the other hand, they may be set up as desirable qualifications, rather than as absolute prerequisites, no applicant being barred from the remainder of the test, although his educational and employment record may be rated against the desirable standard.

In some instances, the law underlying the position-classification plan and the merit system is regarded as requiring the classifying agency to establish for each class specific minimum qualifications, including experience and education, which candidates must possess. Such a legal provision results in a close scrutiny of qualification standards by interested officials, employees, and groups. Experience in utilizing minimum or prerequisite educational or experience qualification statements in recruiting and the consistent questioning and criticism of them eventually lead to greater refinement and precision. Also, in such jurisdictions, there are sometimes indicated in the specification itself the substitutions which will govern in crediting education for experience, or vice versa. Consequently, class specifications in such jurisdictions will necessarily differ, so far as wording of qualification statements is concerned, from those where the emphasis is on required knowledges, skills, and abilities, and the applicant is permitted to enter a test under standards of experience which need not be applied with exactness.

The question whether or not standards as to experience, training, and education are to be described in class specifications as (a) absolute prerequisites or (b) desirable standards, is an important item of recruiting or testing policy to be decided by recruiting and testing authorities in collaboration with the classification staff before such standards are written into the class specifications.

In several recent projects, as indicated by the exhibits in Appendix C, there has been a marked loosening of the definiteness with which educational and experience qualifications have been described in class specifications. For example, most of the specifications prepared for the State of Alabama end, under the heading "Acceptable Experience and Training," with the clause, "or any equivalent combination of experience and training sufficient to demonstrate ability to do the work." In the Rhode Island specifications, under the heading "Minimum Qualifications," the statements of experience and training are worded as if they were examples: e.g., "experience such as may have been gained through extended employment in a responsible administrative capacity in highway and structural engineering; training such as may have been gained through graduation from a recognized college with specialization in civil engineering." In the Los Angeles City specifications, the qualifications are set forth under the heading "Desirable Qualifications," but it has been suggested that this procedure would not preclude the use of minimum prerequisites, strictly applied, in advertising, holding, and rating tests.

Whether formal educational requirements should be incorporated in class specifications depends (a) on the class being described and (b) on the recruiting policy of the jurisdiction. Ordinarily, higher education is not established as a prerequisite except for professional or scientific classes. The question of educational standards, however, has an important public relations aspect. On the one hand, candidates and employees are apt to feel that they can do professional or scientific work efficiently by reason of knowledge and ability acquired by experience or by training outside of academic walls; that they should not, by the enforcement of a mandatory standard calling for a college degree, be barred from an opportunity to demonstrate the possession of such knowledge and ability by written or other direct tests; and that there should be equal opportunity for qualified persons to serve, whether or not they possess a diploma from an educational institution.[43] On the other hand, professional associations, educational institutions, administrative officers, and others frequently stress the necessity for formal educational standards in the public service.[44]

[43] On the value of collegiate educational records, see William S. Learned and Ben D. Wood, *The Student and His Knowledge* (Carnegie Foundation for the Advancement of Teaching, 1938) Bull. No. 29, reviewed by M. W. Richardson in *News Letter* of Civil Service Assembly . . . , July 1938.
[44] A criticism of the Massachusetts law (Sec. 6-A, Chap. 31, Laws of 1935) restricting the use of educational standards in the state service appears in *Report . . . on Taxation and Public Expenditures of . . . Massachusetts* (Public Administration Service), pp. 23–24. See also pertinent discussions in Alice Campbell Klein, *Civil Service in Public Welfare* (Russell Sage Foundation, 1940), pp. 118–20; Wallace S. Sayre and Milton Mandell, *Education and the Civil Service in New York City*, U. S. Office of Education Bulletin, 1937, No. 20, pp. 10–18; American Public Health Association, Committee on Professional Education, *Educational Qualifications of Public Health Statisticians* (1938); William Brownrigg, "The

Attempts to satisfy conflicting views as to the use of educational standards have frequently taken the form of providing substitutions, particularly substitutions of experience for formal college education.

Under such a policy, educational statements in class specifications may be phrased in broad language, e.g., "training equivalent to that represented by graduation from a college or university of recognized standing" or "training such as may have been gained through a four-year college course in. . . ."[45]

The purpose of using the expression, "training equivalent to," etc., is to indicate that, in using the class specification as a guide in recruiting and testing processes, substitutions for formal education are allowable. In actual practice, these substitutions may be additional experience of suitable character, or educational training of a variety different from that mentioned in the specification, or a certain score in a written test.

Of course, where qualifications statements are not prerequisites, but are given as descriptions of desirable backgrounds for the work of the respective classes, the fact that substitutions will be accepted for any stated formal educational requirements will be plain on the face of the class specification.[46] In civil-service jurisdictions, in any event, the problem of evaluating the various combinations of experience, education, and training still remains as one to be met in the course of rating tests and establishing eligible lists.

In preparing a statement of experience required, it will be helpful for the class-specification writer to consider at the outset the

---

Use of Standards in Civil Service," *The Compass*, December 1938, pp. 5–7; Virginia Advisory Legislative Council, "A Growing Intimacy Between Education and Public Service," in *State Personnel Administration*, Report to the Governor of Virginia (Richmond, 1939), p. 13.

[45] ". . . In no case has the Commission recommended that the possession of a degree or a certificate from an educational institution be made an absolute requirement. In every case it has specified educational qualifications 'equivalent to' the education represented by a formal certificate or degree. This has been with the definite view that the employee who through general reading or private study has acquired the equivalent of the education measured by formal certificates or degrees is just as much desired for the Government service as any other. It is left to the employing authorities to apply these terms of equivalents, under the limitations of the proposed bill reading as follows: 'Whenever the possession of a university or college degree or a high-school diploma, or the equivalent of such degree or diploma, is prescribed as a qualification for a class, the Commission shall prescribe as such equivalent a standard, or standards, based on experience or demonstrated ability in the performance of duties similar to those prescribed for such class, which will be accepted as such equivalent.' " *Report of Congressional Joint Commission on Reclassification of Salaries*, H.Doc. 686, 66th Cong., 2d sess. (1920), pp. 77–78.

[46] See Appendix C, Los Angeles City specifications.

various sources of supply or the occupational groups from which qualified candidates may be recruited. After these fields have been determined they can be covered either by a general description or by a series of alternative specific descriptions for each such field. It is not desirable to incorporate in the statement of experience such uninformative expressions as "similar experience of equal value." The temptation to use such phrases will disappear under an analysis of what is intended to be covered by them, and as a result of such analysis a much more informative statement can be prepared.

Experience statements should be informative as to both kind and level. For example:[47]

At least five years' training and experience in research, educational, editorial, or original writing activities in agriculture or one of its major fields, which has involved the editing and criticism of agricultural manuscripts and the successful discharge of substantive responsibility for review of their scientific accuracy and the enforcement of high literary standards, and which has included either meritorious contributions to scientific literature, or noteworthy success as an editor of publications of excellence, or other evidence of recognized scientific maturity and standing.

In describing experience, emphasis should be laid primarily on the success, character, and progressive nature of the experience to be required, rather than on its mere length. For example, for an administrative position it would not be advisable to require "fifteen years' experience in supervisory or administrative work." It would be better to go a little deeper and indicate at least a few of the factors that are intended to be evidenced by such experience. Instead of the experience requirement just mentioned, the following is preferable:

At least five years' experience in administrative work which has demonstrated initiative and resourcefulness, the meeting of substantive responsibilities with marked success, and the ability to direct and manage large and important projects.

As a matter of fact, as has been said, a person's experience or employment record is merely evidence of his other qualifications—such as his knowledge and ability and his capacity to apply them successfully. After stating the amount and kind of experience to be required, it is frequently desirable, therefore, to indicate expressly that this experience is expected to have been such as to demonstrate the knowledges, attainments, and abilities previously set forth in the specification.[48]

[47] For other examples, see the specifications in Appendix C.
[48] "The assumption that the value of experience is directly proportional to its duration or length is a fallacy. Experience of three, five or ten years in some line

It may be questioned whether an exact number of years or months of experience should be established for every class of positions, even if the experience statement is intended as a prerequisite.[49] Those who favor such precision of statement cite (1) the necessity of definitely marking off, for the understanding of the public, such prerequisites as are used for admission to examinations and (2) the necessity of a definite base, for the guidance and control of examining staffs, in evaluating employment records. They also are influenced by the fact that it is easier to measure quantity than quality. Others criticize this approach as "mechanistic" rather than qualitative. They prefer to indicate length of experience by such terms as "some," "short," "reasonable," "considerable," "extended" or "extensive," defining these terms for administrative purposes.[50] They emphasize the quality of experience and what it means in terms of knowledge and ability, and point out that the actual time required to acquire skills, abilities, and knowledges under the same conditions varies with the individual. Resolving this conflict of view involves the procedures of test administration, including the development of reliable and valid tests, and application forms which will elicit adequate and precise information about the kind, quality, difficulty, and responsibility of work in previous employments. It has also been suggested that this conflict of view may be at least partially resolved if length of experience is specifically set out as determinative of a passing grade on this item, with a lower rating scale applying to experience of lesser quantity and/or quality.

---

of work is, in itself, no guarantee of a corresponding increase in knowledge, skill, or in ability to do the work in hand. Indeed, long, unvaried experience may be a liability rather than an asset. It tends to develop habits of thought and action which eventually becomes routines in which flexibility and adaptability undergo atrophy. Duration cannot measure the true value of experience. It must be appraised in respect to knowledge gained." Warner W. Stockberger, *As I See It* (G. P. O., 1940), p. 34.

[49] See State of Rhode Island . . . , *First Annual Report* (1939), p. 3; also Appendix to that Report, Exhibit C.

[50] For example, the Detroit Civil Service Commission has used such terms with the following meanings:

" 'Some' means a relatively brief period, sufficient to give a general idea of the work, but not sufficient to give 'journeyman' skill; 'reasonable' indicates a longer experience, sufficient to give 'journeyman' skill and a reasonable knowledge of the work processes and equipment. This implies that the learning period, particularly as related to methods, principles and acquisition of skills has been completed. 'Considerable' indicates such a length of experience as will make a person an expert in a given line and as will bring thorough familiarity with the work, principles and methods. 'Extended' is used to indicate outstanding or unusual experience."

Physical standards. Physical requirements include bodily conditions, height and weight, muscular development, and condition of health. Sometimes they are regarded as including age limits.

Ordinarily, physical standards applicable to all classes in the service, such as good health and freedom from contagious diseases, would be covered by general rule, and not repeated in each class specification. However, where certain physical qualities or attributes are significant or distinctive work requirements of the class being described, they should be expressly included. For example, in class specifications for penitentiary guards or fire fighters, it is evident that physical standards deserve specific mention.

Physical requirements are especially significant when they bear directly upon (a) ability to operate the machinery, use the tools, or otherwise perform the work of the class of positions; (b) ability to withstand unusual working conditions or environment; (c) ability to avoid hazards or accident risks to which the employee and his co-workers may be subjected, including the possibility that the employee's physical defect may be such as to make him an unusual accident risk; or (d) the application of disability retirement laws, employee-injury compensation statutes, or federal, state, and municipal regulations.

Physical standards should be described as informatively as possible. "Ability to read fine print for continuous periods without fatigue" is better than "good eyesight," because it indicates the reason for the requirement. "Freedom from susceptibility to dermatitis, which sometimes develops from handling printed work" is a similarly informative item in a specification for printer's assistant.

Other qualification requirements. For some classes, requirements of a type other than those previously discussed are germane. For example, admission to practice medicine or law requires a public certificate. Similarly, trade licenses or certificates may be required, as in the case of chauffeurs or operating engineers. In such instances, the license or certificate requirements are set forth under pertinent headings as "Licenses Required" or "Certificates Required."

OTHER ELEMENTS OF CLASS SPECIFICATIONS

In addition to the basic elements described above, a class specification may include information on such other points as will assist in delineating the scope of the class, or in making the specification more useful as an administrative tool.

For example, if the class specification sets forth minimum qualification requirements, representing the lowest hurdles to be cleared by applicants for positions in the class, it is sometimes desirable to add to certain specifications a statement of additional qualifications desired. It is of little or no value to state these simply as more education and/or experience of the same kind as that previously given. Additional desirable qualifications are significant only when they are education, experience, knowledge, and ability of a kind different from those indicated as work requirements or prerequisites. The statement of additional qualifications desired adds to the picture of the positions in the class as shown in the specification, assists the examiners of the testing agency in appraising the potential value of applicants, and in practice in civil service jurisdictions often serves as a foil against the use of statements of minimum qualifications that are so restrictive as to stifle proper competition. It also preserves to the fullest extent the result of the job analysis made at the time of the development of the classification plan which might not be repeated at the time an examination is in prospect. Consequently, where especially significant information of this sort becomes available during the classification process, it would seem useful to make a record of it for later use.[51]

Sometimes there is included in each class specification a statement of the lines of promotion into and from positions in the class, naming the class titles of the positions from which qualified employees may be drawn for promotion into positions in the class covered by the specification, and the class titles of the positions to which promotions may be made.

Experience indicates that unless lines of promotion can be fairly completely outlined, misunderstandings and difficulties tend to arise. Only in the smaller jurisdictions would it generally be feasible to cover all lines and directions of promotion and to define comprehensively in that manner the recruiting field from which candidates for promotion may be selected.[52]

[51] On the other hand, additional desirable qualifications statements have sometimes led to misunderstanding in contacts with operating officials incident to the selective process. Such misunderstanding is caused by a tendency on the part of operating officials to regard additional desirable qualifications as being of equal weight to minimum prerequisite qualifications and to insist, therefore, that they be given the same effect in the certification of eligibles from employment lists and in the selection of employees from such certificates.

[52] Although normal and natural lines of promotion should be pointed out, "there is danger that the lines of promotion may on the one hand fail to point out the real opportunities for advancement, or on the other hand specify so many

It should be remembered that the information in a class specification about lines of promotion is developed by study of the characteristics of classes of positions, not the characteristics of employees occupying those positions. Thus these lines of promotion do not take into consideration the qualifications acquired by the employee before entering the position in question or before entering the service, or the qualifications he may have acquired outside the service since he entered it. Seemingly there is a formality about lines of promotion when stated in class specifications that makes it easy to conclude that promotional examinations for a particular class of positions should be open only to those occupying positions in the next lower classification. This conclusion would ignore the possibility that other employees in the same department may possess the qualification requirements to a very much greater degree, even though they do not happen to be occupying positions on the next lower rung or in the same series of classes at the time the promotional examinations are held. Consideration of employees' personnel records should result in a policy of opening promotional examinations to all employees in any lower level, either in the same series or in any other series of classes, in other words, opening them to any employee able to meet the qualifications for the class to which he is to be promoted. Anything in a class specification seeming to limit this principle or to decide upon the promotional area in advance should be omitted, since this is not a function of position-classification. Defining the area from which competition is to be drawn for promotional examinations should be left to the development of promotional regulations.

It is not customary to append to each specification the applicable salary scale. Salary scales belong to a pay plan and are not parts of a position-classification plan. If printed on each specification they tend to become a source of distraction from the main objectives of the class specification when used for the allocation of individual positions to classes. Also, it should be foreseen that changes in pay scales alone should not require reprinting or reduplication of class specifications. On the other hand, where the position-classification

---

adventitious opportunities to forge ahead that the broad, normal lines are obscured." Fred Telford, "The Theory and Practice of Classification," *Proceedings, Fourteenth Annual Meeting, Assembly of Civil Service Commissions,* June 21, 1921, p. 27. For a procedure of developing and charting lines of promotion after a classification survey, see Robert C. Clothier, "Organization for an Occupational Survey," *The Journal of Personnel Research,* February 1923, pp. 444–46.

plan and the pay plan are controlled and administered by the same agency, it has been found advantageous and convenient to indicate the applicable pay scale on each class specification.

Frequently, certain informational data are given in connection with each specification, such as the accounting or statistical symbol corresponding to the class title.

SPECIFICATION OF A "GROUP OF CLASSES"

Ordinarily, a separate class specification is written for each class. However, in some instances, several class specifications may be usefully combined in one statement.

One convenient editorial device recognizes what is known as a "group of classes," which consists of two or more classes whose characteristics are almost exactly the same except for a difference in one well defined phase of their duties and qualifications, for example, the subject matter of specialization.[53] Two translating classes may be alike except that one requires a knowledge of French and the other a knowledge of Spanish. Two chemist classes involving work of equal difficulty and responsibility may differ primarily in the branch of chemistry represented, such as inorganic, analytical, organic, or physical. Since in such cases there is a difference in the nature of specialization of subject matter—a point essential for recognition in recruiting and selection—each class is distinctive. But for the purpose of avoiding the needless repetition of the same language in writing specifications of the classes, we may set up together in the position-classification plan, all the several Senior Translator classes, such as Senior Translator (Romance Languages), Senior Translator (Teutonic Languages), etc. Similarly, we may set up all Junior Chemist classes together, listing them as Junior Chemist (Inorganic), Junior Chemist (Organic), and so on.

This plan eliminates monotonous repetitions and is designed to facilitate the holding of tests for the whole group of similar classes together, the subjects in the tests that are directed toward ascertaining the common qualifications required in any or all positions of the several classes being obligatory on persons tested but they being allowed to elect those relating to the various specialties covered. It should be borne in mind in the use of titles on payrolls, certificates, reports of changes, and other personnel reports and records that the generic title is incomplete by itself and the qualifying

[53] The expression "group of classes," as used here, should not be confused with the term "occupational group," discussed in Chapter VII as a subdivision of a classification service.

word or words in addition are necessary to complete the title and indicate the class.[54]

In developing a specification of a group of classes, the class specification writer should caution himself against overlooking essential differences. He should be certain that the one difference lies in the special field of work concerned and that the same level of knowledges and abilities is required. Upon close examination of classes apparently lending themselves to a common description, it may be found that each of the classes requires one or more specialized knowledges or skills which are not paralleled in the other classes.

At the head of the combined specifications, the titles of the classes are listed, and at the appropriate points in the body of the statement each of the specializations corresponding to the classes listed is expressly described, or, if convenient, simply referred to as the specialization, subject matter, or function "indicated by the title of the class." Previous practice has involved the listing of a title for the group of classes as such. For example, Senior Translator or Junior Chemist would be the titles of the groups of classes referred to in the text. It is suggested that a formal title for the group may be unnecessary if all the class titles are listed, that its presence at the head of the combined specification might influence some persons to regard the group of classes as though it were a single class, and that its prominence might result in the frequent failure of such persons to use the class titles themselves in personnel reports and transactions.

A somewhat similar editorial convenience may be used in very large jurisdictions for those classes of positions of a supervisory or administrative nature that involve the same subject matter, general authority and functions, but differ according to the size and specific problems or difficulties of the organization over which the incumbents have charge. In such cases the problem resolves itself into one of classifying of various offices, districts, projects, regions, etc., on the basis of predetermined factors and listing these units as Class 1, Class 2, etc.[55] The resulting classes may then be characterized, for example, as Irrigation Manager (Class 1 project), Irrigation Mana-

[54] "The Classification Plan for the Massachusetts State Service," *Public Personnel Studies*, January 1927, p. 16. See also Griffenhagen, "The Principles and Technique of Preparing an Occupational Classification of Positions in the Public Service," *Public Personnel Studies*, November 1924, p. 250; and Griffenhagen & Associates, *Report on Classification and Compensation of Positions, Milwaukee County* (1928) p. 107.

[55] See p. 127.

ger (Class 2 project), etc., or as Chief Customs Inspector (Class 1 division), Chief Customs Inspector (Class 2 division), etc. A combined specification is written for the various classes of irrigation managers or chief customs inspectors, setting forth in the distinguishing features statement the factors and standards upon which the classes are based. Other references, in the qualifications statements and elsewhere, will be necessary to show the differences among the classes being described in the common statement.

INTERPRETATION OF CLASS SPECIFICATIONS

An accurate understanding of class specifications, their purposes, and their limitations is essential for their full use in personnel and administrative transactions. Judgment and interpretation are necessary in using class specifications to determine the class in which a given position should be allocated. Each specification must be interpreted in its entirety and in its proper relation to other specifications.

The position-content of a class is seldom so simple or uniform as to permit the writing of a specification that will identify and describe each single position in the class in precise and express language. Hence, in preparing class specifications, it is not feasible or practicable to restrict the scope of each specification to positions which are perfectly identical, without variation or exception. Of course, the definition and concept of a "class of positions" does not require this exactitude. Slight differences in positions, which are not such as to prevent treating them alike, do not lead to differences in classification. All positions that belong in a class are not therefore precisely identified; and the system of class specifications is not a catalog in which every single position can be found through a routine process of following an index. On the contrary, to identify a position as belonging in a given class, a comparison of the characteristics of the position with the characteristics of the class—sometimes several classes—has to be made.[56] Hence arises the necessity of a definite understanding of how class specifications are to be read and interpreted.

Furthermore, experience has shown that it is necessary, particularly in the developmental and installation stages of a position-classification plan, to explain fully to administrative officers and to employees what the specification is intended to include and exclude. Especially must the purposes and the limitations of each part of the

[56] See pp. 137–41.

specification be indicated. Misunderstandings on the part of department officials of the effect of class specifications may become so prevalent as to give rise to reluctance or even agitation against the adoption or the continued use of a classification plan. Again, class specifications are frequently misinterpreted as a whole or in part. Such misunderstandings and misinterpretations are difficult to eradicate when they are once established. It is desirable, accordingly, to incorporate in formal rules a statement of the interpretation and effect of class specifications.

Frequently, these misunderstandings center around the presumed future restrictive effect of class specifications upon the authority which administrative officers currently possess over (a) assigning duties and delegating responsibilities to employees, or (b) the creation, alteration, or abolition of positions, or (c) the direction and supervision of work. This has been discussed in a previous chapter.[57]

Sometimes misinterpretation occurs because the specification has not been read and construed as a whole; some phrase or clause, or the mere absence of some item is high-lighted to the exclusion of the rest of the text. This is evidenced by a tendency to regard the illustrative examples of work as though they constituted the whole specification. To avoid this tendency, it must always be emphasized that the examples of work cited in a class specification are not complete and exhaustive. In relation to the entire class specification, the examples are only illustrative of the duties outlined by the general statement. They are not intended to be either complete or exclusive. The fact that the actual tasks performed in a single position are not listed in the examples which illustrate a class of positions does not mean that the position is necessarily excluded from that class, provided that the tasks constituting the main work or employment are covered by the general statement and the distinguishing features statement. Similarly, any single example of work, taken without relation to the general statement of duties, other examples of work, and all other parts of the specification, is not construed as determining whether a position should be included within the class.[58]

It is especially important, too, to explain the effect of the statements of qualifications in their relation (a) to present incumbents, (b) to future tests for entrance to the service, and (c) to future tests for in-service changes, such as promotions and transfers. This ef-

[57] See pp. 49-50.
[58] See the preceding discussion (pp. 260-61) on the desirability of describing tasks in the combinations in which they occur in typical positions in the class.

fect, as has already been indicated, depends on the recruiting and testing policies of the jurisdiction.[59]

If lines of promotion are shown in a class specification, it should be understood that they are only typical lines of promotion. They should not be interpreted as limiting or restricting but merely as indicating the natural relation of positions of the class to other positions of higher and lower classes in the same general line of work. The fact that certain classes are named in such lines of promotion is not intended to restrict promotions from or to positions of such classes, and consequently the naming of such classes should not interfere with the establishment of wider latitude in eligibility for promotion from class to class.

The points usually covered in rules for interpreting class specifications may be briefly summarized as follows:[60]

1. Definitions of "class," "class title," and "class specification."

2. Class specifications as descriptive and explanatory of duties and responsibilities, not as restrictive or prescriptive instruments.

3. The character of each specification as an integrated whole.

4. The relationship of each specification to other specifications.

5. Relation of class specifications to the creation of positions, or changes in the duties-content of positions, or the abolition of positions.

6. Explanation of the purposes of certain parts of the specification, particularly the class title and the statement of qualification standards.[61]

PUBLICATION OF CLASS SPECIFICATIONS

The central classification agency should maintain in its own office an up-to-date complete set of class specifications arranged in a form convenient for reference. These should be designated as the official copies and bear appropriate notations as to original adoption and changes. The official copies should be open to inspection by any one under reasonable conditions during business hours.

In order that the class specifications may serve all the purposes for which they are intended, they should be published and distributed so as to be readily available to the operating departments and interested employees. The same is true of subsequent additions or revisions. This means that a record needs to be kept of the original distribution of the class specifications so that those who are using

[59] See pp. 268–74.

[60] See Appendix C, where typical rules covering these points are shown.

[61] In some codes of rules, the interpretation and effect of each part of the class specification have been covered by a separate rule. It is suggested, however, that this practice tends to encourage the habit of interpreting a class specification in segments, rather than as an integrated whole, and therefore is disadvantageous.

them for official purposes may be furnished with copies of new or revised specifications and notified of those that are eliminated.[62]

The book of specifications should contain a suitable general introduction explaining (1) what the specifications are, (2) how they were prepared and on what basis, (3) how they will be kept up to date and on what basis, and (4) how they are to be interpreted and used. In addition, if the classification plan is arranged internally in services, occupational groups, classification-grades, or series of classes, this arrangement should be skeletonized and described so that the whole classification structure and the place of a class within it may be clearly understood.

The specifications should be published in a form which makes each one readily accessible. Two methods of arrangement have been used. One method arranges the specifications in purely alphabetical sequence. The other arranges them in what is known as schematic order based on the successively smaller occupational areas in which the service is broken down. In schematic order, the classification services or occupational groups constitute the major subdivisions of the arrangement. Within these subdivisions the class specifications are arranged in ascending order of series of classes. Since both arrangements are useful for particular purposes, it is essential that whichever form is used indexes in both forms be provided.[63]

The manner of publishing, duplicating, and assembling class specifications for purposes of publication and distribution should, of course, offer no hindrance to the substitution of revised specifications, the addition of new ones at any time in their proper order, or the elimination of obsolete or superseded specifications. This, of course, calls for a loose-leaf system.[64]

[62] It should be recognized, of course, that out of the wide publication of class specifications arise certain difficulties of administration. Among these are (1) the common tendency of operating officials to decide upon a desired classification and to proceed to justify their request by supplying the classification agency with statements taken directly from the class specification instead of proceeding directly from the facts about the duties and responsibilities of the individual position; (2) the tendency of the classification agency to avoid or delay the making of improvements in specifications which would mean their reprinting and redistribution; (3) the work and expense of maintaining a follow-up distribution of amended specifications; (4) confusion in some instances where an operating official or employee or applicant unknowingly uses an out-of-date specification.

[63] See Fred Telford, "The Content, Form, and Arrangement of the Printed Classification and Compensation Plans," *Public Personnel Studies*, February 1925, pp. 47–51.

[64] The substitution of revised specifications is facilitated by beginning each specification on a new sheet and using backs of sheets only where the specification is too long to fit on one side.

Chapter X

Continuous Administration of the Plan

THE establishment of classes of positions, the writing of class specifications, and the allocation of positions to classes are not the short-lived tasks of a period of transition. On the contrary, they are constantly recurring tasks which are important parts of the continuous administration of a position-classification plan, as long as the plan is in effect.[1]

NEED FOR KEEPING THE PLAN CURRENT

The position-content of government services and the duties-content of individual positions are not static and immutable. Both change with time, sometimes rapidly, sometimes slowly. In a large jurisdiction, formal changes affecting positions are continually occurring. The government may engage in new functions calling for the establishment of positions of a type not contemplated when the classification plan was first adopted. Existing activities may be terminated, diminished, or modified. Reorganizations, revisions of methods and processes, alterations in flow of work, or redistributions of authority may take place as a result of improved administrative management. Thus, additional and new positions are created, and existing ones are abolished, merged, subdivided, or materially altered. Changes of this sort are normal in a government as well as in any other organization.[2]

In addition to alteration through formal action, positions may change informally.[3] The capable or incapable employee is con-

---

[1] The function of "administering" a position-classification plan means the maintenance of the plan itself and its continued application to positions in the jurisdiction, after the period of development and installation has ended. It does not refer to other administrative and personnel functions in the performance of which a position-classification plan and its records and results are useful. See Chapter IV.

[2] See California State Personnel Board, *Thirteenth Biennial Report* (1936–38), p. 14. See also Robert I. Marshall, "A Salary Plan in Operation," *Personnel*, February 1938, pp. 110–12.

[3] Experience indicates the necessity, particularly in large jurisdictions, of a formal approval by the higher authorities in the operating departments of material changes in the duties or responsibilities of positions to insure that such changes are not made by subordinate officials merely to change classifications,

stantly exercising an influence on his job. Responsibilities ultimately are delegated to the person who can best shoulder them. As an employee increases in experience, knowledge, and ability, more difficult and specialized assignments become his daily tasks.[4] If he proves incapable or otherwise does not meet expectations, the more difficult or important assignments originally planned for him are gradually shifted to other employees whose own positions are also changed to that extent. Positions within the same organization are closely interlocked by lines of authority and flow of work, and a change in one may give rise to changes in others. The creation of a new position may change the duties and responsibilities of other positions, and the abolition of one position may likewise affect the duties and responsibilities of the remaining positions. The duties and responsibilities of positions, which are the determining factors in classification, are thus in a fluid state, rather than in a fixed mold.[5]

As previously indicated, any position-classification plan, in order to be properly characterized as a plan at all, should contain within itself the seeds for its continued life and growth, and for the adaptation to change that is so vital to its effective administration.[6]

No position-classification plan is at all times a perfect match of the service it is intended to cover. As painstakingly as it may be

---

regardless of whether such changes are at the expense of good organization or efficient methods. If, without the addition of new activities to the functions of a given organization or the subtraction of existing activities, changes or redistributions of duties or responsibilities are allowed to go on promiscuously for any length of time, the structure of what was once a well set up organization may be seriously affected. Furthermore, changes of assignment that have the ultimate result of obligating appropriations should be formally approved. That this situation is not peculiar to the public service is indicated by the following remark: "Employees have a delightful way of making over instructions and procedures to suit their convenience and desires, and an executive plan may gradually be changed radically without the executive being aware of the transformation." Farris L. Morton, in "How to be Your Own Systems Expert," *The Office Economist,* March-April 1934.

[4] This assumes a degree of administrative discretion in changing employees' assignments that does not always exist. In some jurisdictions under the merit system, where competitive plans are in effect for selecting employees for promotion, a reassignment to the work of a higher class is proper only after the employee has qualified therefor through appropriate tests. In other jurisdictions, where employees are not placed in formal competition for advancement, their eligibility for promotion can be definitely ascertained by reference only to their own status, and the act of assigning a particular employee to higher grade work is simply the initial step looking toward his promotion. In any event, nevertheless, a change of assignment is a starting point for the classification process.

[5] See Oliver C. Short, *The Merit System* (Baltimore, 1928), p. 33.

[6] Pp. 47–49.

prepared, its administration will disclose errors requiring correction. As comprehensive and prompt as the procedures may be for securing information about changes in positions, the position-classification plan will still necessarily lag somewhat behind the administrative action of departments in authorizing those changes, in reorganizing working units, in distributing tasks differently among a group of employees, or in creating new positions.

The frequency and the nature of changes in a position-classification plan or in its application to individual positions in any particular jurisdiction depend upon a number of factors. These include (1) the completeness and adequacy of the classes and the class specifications originally adopted, (2) the number of positions covered by the plan, (3) the variety of activities, functions, departments, and agencies concerned, (4) the ease or the frequency with which new or changed activities or positions may be authorized, (5) whether existing activities must be legislatively or may be administratively altered, and (6) whether the duties and responsibilities of positions may be created or changed at the will of administrative officers, or whether definite numbers of positions of specific classes that may exist within a given organization unit are periodically fixed by the legislative body through appropriation measures or other statute or ordinance.

Everyone with experience in administering a position-classification plan appreciates that one of the major problems is the maintenance of equity of classification while material changes are being made in the service and in individual positions. Corresponding changes in the position-classification plan, or in the allocations of positions to classes, must be made as nearly as possible concurrently with the alterations in organization or in the duties and responsibilities of positions which gave rise to them. When they are made, furthermore, they should conform to the general pattern of the classification plan and the policies and principles upon which it is founded. This means that such changes must be accomplished through a constantly operating executive agency, charged with the duty of keeping the classification plan current and of applying it currently to all existing positions. They cannot be accomplished through legislative action with sufficient promptness to meet administrative needs, because legislative action is not continuously available or geared for the handling of the limitless details involved.

It should be recognized frankly that unless material changes in organization structure and in individual positions as they occur are recognized in the current allocations of positions to classes and in necessary amendments of the classification plan itself, eventually the main features of the plan will be its obsolescence, its failure to fit positions in the service as they actually exist, and its consequent lack of utility in salary standardization, recruiting, and other personnel functions. Under these circumstances, the conditions it was designed to correct—unequal pay scales for equal work, lack of logical relation between work and pay scales, misleading position-titles, confusion and wasted effort in recruiting, testing, and certification processes, necessity for inquiring time and time again into the duties of individual positions, absence of an intelligible basis for payrolls, service records, budget estimates, personnel statistics and reports—all will gradually restore themselves to their original vigor.[7]

To prevent this, it is essential to arrange for day-by-day continuity in keeping a position-classification plan up to date and currently applied to the changing position-content of the service.[8]

NEED FOR CENTRAL CLASSIFICATION AGENCY

To carry out the functions involved in the continuous administration of a position-classification plan, it is necessary that a staff agency be designated or created as the central classification agency of the jurisdiction to exercise a coordinative control over the classification plan and its application to individual positions. Such an agency would be charged with the responsibility of equitable appraisal and classification of all positions under the plan. It would be faced every day with the problem of keeping informed of the current duties and responsibilities of positions, determining what changes have taken place, and deciding to what extent these changes affect the classifications of positions, the class specifications, or the classes themselves. It should be given responsibility and authority

[7] See Virginia Advisory Legislative Council, *State Personnel Administration*, Report to the Governor of Virginia (Richmond, 1939), p. 13.

[8] Note the following words of caution: "A program of continuous classification review and revision, although necessary to the adequate maintenance of the classification plan, is easily subject to abuse. There is a constant temptation to reclassify or reallocate positions for the purpose of rewarding superior performance when basic duties have not changed, long service however good or bad, or service the supervisory officer deems 'invaluable' for any reason. Permitting such action will soon render the classification plan useless, if it does not convert it into an actual hindrance to good administration." Public Administration Service, *Personnel Administration and Procedure as Installed in the Indiana Department of Public Welfare and Unemployment Compensation Division* (Chicago, 1938), p. 10.

to enforce and administer the position-classification plan and its code of rules; to recommend or promulgate amendments from time to time; to prepare and issue procedural regulations; to keep the plan and the allocation of positions to classes matched with the actual duties and responsibilities of those positions; to make final decisions on the classification of individual positions; and to keep class specifications current.[9]

From the standpoint both of the effective organization of the administrative functions of government and of the need to secure fairness and equity in personnel administration, there are strong reasons for establishing and supporting such a central agency.

Personnel administration, of course, involves the regulation and control of human relations and therefore requires, in the interests of fairness and equity, uniformity of policy and action under like conditions. This impels us to emphasize the view that a government —whether national, state, or local—should consistently be regarded, not as an aggregation of unrelated departments and agencies, but as one entity in relation to the personnel it employs. If we so regard government, it necessarily follows that when uniformity of policy and action is desired among the various departments and agencies of a public jurisdiction there must be established and maintained a central agency with authority to secure uniformity.[10]

The essence of position-classification is uniformity of treatment of like positions throughout the jurisdiction. The basis of position-classification is what the work of each position is, not where it is performed. However, the probability of accomplishing uniform results throughout the jurisdiction is inversely proportionate to the number of persons who have the power to make uncontrolled decisions. No one operating department has all the information necessary to coordinate the classification of positions in all departments.[11]

[9] A summary of the activities involved in maintaining the position-classification plan of the State of California is given in California State Personnel Board, *Thirteenth Biennial Report*, pp. 14–15.

[10] "It is obvious that if the prime requirements of uniformity and relative equity in the pay for service are to be secured some central independent agency must have the authority—the final authority in every case and in all departments —as to the proper classification of each position. It must ascertain, as the impartial appraiser for the Government and the taxpayer, what the duties of each position are, what responsibilities are involved, what qualifications are required, and into what class and compensation schedule it falls." *Report of Congressional Joint Commission on Reclassification of Salaries*, H.Doc. 686, 66th Cong. 2d sess. (1920), pp. 67, 68.

[11] It is common, however, for an operating official in a department or an employee affected to regard himself as the best judge of what the classification of a given position should be. "The actual facts of the matter are that a given set of

Few departments have the government-wide viewpoint necessary to adhere to common standards when operating considerations seem to them to justify exceptions and divergences; generally they see the problem from the point of view of their own operations; the departments collectively cannot act unanimously or consistently because they have no machinery for agreeing among themselves; and they have no power to bind the inevitable minority of nonconformists within their own ranks.

Hence, the final authority for classifying positions in a public jurisdiction should not be distributed among numerous administrative and operating officials, each acting independently of the others and with responsibility toward only his own department.[12] Instead, it should be vested in one central agency with a government-wide viewpoint and with a responsibility toward all operating departments alike for equalizing and coordinating allocations of positions to classes and for maintaining a unified point of view from division to division, bureau to bureau, and department to department. The objective is to keep the position-classification structure currently consistent with the duties and responsibilities of positions compared across organizational or departmental lines.[13]

From the broad standpoint of effective organization for public

---

duties and responsibilities have significance only on a relative basis, when considered together with similar duties and responsibilities of many other employees scattered throughout the service. A far better perspective can be obtained from a central and detached point of view than is ever possible when a position is regarded either by the supervising officer or by the employee himself, either of whom must inevitably be influenced by many personal factors which, while important in themselves, have no place in a determination of the classification of a position. . . . The individual operating agency is no better prepared to classify positions than the personnel agency is prepared to build highways, administer the unemployment insurance laws, combat epidemics, or carry on any other operating activity." California State Personnel Board, *op. cit.,* p. 17.

[12] See Griffenhagen & Associates, *Report on Classification and Compensation of Positions in the Service of the Commonwealth of Virginia* (Richmond, 1937), pp. 28–29.

[13] "Thirdly, in large organizations, whether public or private, authority is likely to become decentralized and diverse employment policies may be followed in the different administrative units. Almost unbelievable inconsistencies in salaries, sick leaves and annual leaves, working hours, and other conditions of employment may be found within the same department and particularly as between different departments. This is a most fruitful cause of dissatisfaction among the workers in any given jurisdiction, for it is clear that the employees do not draw departmental lines in making comparison of such fundamental matters of employment. To them the firm or the city or state is the common employer. Justice demands that as such it shall adopt a uniform policy, irrespective of departmental or bureau lines. Uniformity of policy obviously calls for the establishment of a central agency." Governmental Research Conference of the United States and Canada, *The Character and Functioning of Municipal Civil Service Commissions in the United States,* Report of the Committee on Civil Service, June 1922, p. 56.

·administration, students have occasionally raised this question: Is there a danger that central control over the classification of positions overcentralizes authority? Sometimes, too, officials regard such concentration of authority in a single agency as an undue "interference" with their operating responsibilities.

Position-classification, being a part of personnel administration, is an institutional function of government rather than a line function. The centralization of other institutional functions, such as budgeting and purchasing, has resulted in increased effectiveness and the avoidance of duplicating and conflicting effort.

In some fields there may be a danger of separating too widely the responsibility for functional operation and the responsibility for administrative management. It is essential, however, that certain phases of personnel administration, by reason of their very nature and objectives, should be planned and conducted under policies and practices applicable to the entire jurisdiction. Position-classification is one of these phases. In this area of activity, the benefits of centralization of authority in terms of effective and equitable personnel management outweigh the importance of the problems that such centralization may occasionally present.

Whether in fact the activities of a central classifying agency constitute an "interference" with what line officials may regard as their prerogatives, or whether they constitute a useful service, depends partly on the manner and the administrative intelligence with which they are carried out.

Realistically, it should be recognized from experience that brakes on the freedom of administrative officers have been legislatively set in personnel, fiscal, and other lines to correct the abuses of free discretion, to avoid duplication of expenditures, or to assure that certain things shall be done by officials whose duty it is to regard the government as a whole rather than as an aggregation of departments, boards, and commissions. Certain actions affecting personnel administration simply have to be taken by agencies having a government-wide, rather than an insular, viewpoint and responsibility. In the administration of a position-classification plan, the integrated government interest is paramount, rather than the interests of maintaining complete individual departmental discretion.

SELECTION OF ADMINISTERING AGENCY

What agency should be selected or created to administer the position-classification plan? This is a question that is scarcely susceptible of an answer applicable to all jurisdictions under all circumstances.[14] In general, it may be said that in the larger jurisdictions it is the prevailing practice, with few exceptions, to designate the civil service commission or central personnel agency as the administrative agency. In the smaller jurisdictions, technical advice and service may be secured from the state personnel agency or from a personnel organization cooperatively organized by several jurisdictions.

A position-classification plan, as has been indicated, touches personnel and fiscal administration at so many points that the objectives and activities of several types of agencies are affected by the manner of its administration.[15] In a sizable jurisdiction, the operating departments, the legislative body and its finance committees, the fiscal control agency, the budget agency, and the personnel agency will be separate entities. All of them need information furnished by a classification plan and upon which such a plan is based. Their own methods and procedures, furthermore, must be consistent with classification structure, terminology, and practices, in order that coordinated fiscal and personnel administration may be achieved and forward-looking action may not be handicapped by conflicts of authority.

In considering an existing unit as the central classification agency, the operating or line departments may be eliminated as possibilities.[16] Also, the everyday activities involved in the continuous administration of a position-classification plan are not of the type for which legislatures or legislative committees are geared and are, of course, administrative and not legislative in nature. The objectives of classification administration and its relation to each operating department require, accordingly, that the choice be confined to agencies in the executive branch of the jurisdiction having an independent, authoritative relationship to other organization units. The personnel agency, the budget agency, and the fiscal control agency are of this type.[17] However, the fiscal control agency, if confined in its activities

---

[14] A helpful analysis of this problem in a specific jurisdiction appears in Griffenhagen & Associates, *Report Proposing and Describing Classification and Compensation Plans for the Service of the City of Detroit*, November 17, 1924, Common Council Proceedings, December 2, 1924, pp. 2807–10. A pertinent extract from this report appears in Fred Telford and Frank O. Everett, "The Detroit Classification and Salary Standardization Study of 1924," *Public Personnel Studies*, March 1925, pp. 90–91.

[15] See Chapter IV.

[16] See pp. 288–91.

[17] It is interesting to note that in one private company, the fact-finding process of job analysis is the responsibility of a research division which also conducts office planning and methods work. The evaluation recommendations

to the enforcement of laws, ordinances, or regulations as to expenditures, the verification and audit of accounts, vouchers, and financial reports, the keeping or audit of financial records, and like functions, has not a sufficient relation to personnel administration to warrant its designation as the central classification agency.

Thus, the question most frequently to be decided has been whether classification administration is to be assigned to (a) the budget agency of the jurisdiction, or (b) the personnel agency.[18] As between these two types of agencies, both general factors based on principle and specific factors based on conditions in the particular jurisdiction have their effect. The principal general factors for consideration are these:

1. The current information needed and the procedures employed by a budget agency in passing upon the number and kinds of positions needed, preparing budget estimates for personal services, assisting legislative finance committees, determining or controlling appropriation allotments, and enforcing a standard system of appropriation accounts and uniform nomenclature for estimates, appropriations, and supporting schedules for personal services are similar to those required in the administration of a classification plan and a pay plan.

2. The current information needed by a central personnel agency in advertising, preparing, and rating tests, certifying qualified persons to fill positions, conducting various in-service transactions, and the procedures employed in securing such information are similar to those required for classification administration. Further, the basis for a sound and comprehensive personnel program is a position-classification plan.

---

of the job analyst are reviewed by a committee on personnel. For a statement of advantages and procedure in this respect, see Marshall, "A Salary Plan in Operation," *Personnel*, February 1938, pp. 110–11.

[18] Another possibility, that of joint control by a board composed of representatives of several independent agencies may be mentioned. This, however, would complicate the over-all organization of a government and would, in addition, give rise to new and difficult relationships among existing agencies. Ordinarily, although there are exceptions, such a plan is not favored. This was the plan of administration provided for in the original Federal Classification Act of 1923. Representatives of the Bureau of the Budget, the U. S. Bureau of Efficiency, and the U. S. Civil Service Commission were constituted as the Personnel Classification Board, 42 Stat. 1488. This arrangement did not work out well until a Director of Classification was charged with everyday operations. Sec. 6, Act of July 3, 1930, 46 Stat. 1003. On October 1, 1932, the Personnel Classification Board was abolished and its powers and functions transferred to the U. S. Civil Service Commission. Secs. 505–509, Act of June 30, 1932, 47 Stat. 416.

It may be observed, however, that in most jurisdictions the interests of a budget agency in the structure and administration of a position-classification plan are less than its concern with the levels, structure, and administration of a pay plan. Necessarily, prime responsibilities of a budget agency are control over total expenditures for personal services and budgeting of the jurisdiction's financial resources. These responsibilities may perhaps influence the selection of the administering agency when the problem is to select an executive agency to administer *both* a classification plan and a pay plan, or a pay plan alone. They should have little weight if a pay plan has not been adopted or if it is to be administered or specifically controlled by a legislative body. On the other hand, the responsibilities of a central personnel agency for keeping informed about the duties of positions which it may be called upon to fill and for which it formulates qualification standards definitely require its selection as the central classification agency if a pay plan has not been adopted or if it is to be administered or specifically controlled by a legislative body.[19]

Such reasoning has led to the conclusion that, on an ideal basis, the personnel agency should administer the position-classification plan and the budget agency, with the advice of the personnel agency, be charged with the administration of the pay plan.[20]

However, there is much to be said in favor of selecting the central personnel agency as the administrative unit for both classification and pay.[21] This is the situation in some jurisdictions.

[19] "Control of the classification plan is vital to the work of the personnel agency, but control of the compensation plan is not. On the other hand, control of the compensation plan is vital to the work of the budget agency, but control of the classification plan is not. This is true even though both plans are important in the work of each agency." *Classification and Compensation Plans, Their Development, Adoption, and Administration* (Civil Service Assembly . . . , 1928), Technical Bull. No. 1, p. 19.

[20] "There has been some difference of opinion as to whether classification work should be undertaken by the personnel agency or the central finance office. . . . In the writer's opinion, the analysis of duties and responsibilities and the classification of positions can be handled best by the personnel agency; there are financial implications in the results of classification but they should not be put in a dominating position. The psychology of budget examiners is to avoid expenditures, a point of view which is important but which ought not to govern allocations of positions. The determination of salary scales stands on a different footing, however; it is primarily a fiscal problem." Leonard D. White, *Introduction to the Study of Public Administration* (Macmillan, 1939), pp. 328–29. For similar conclusions, see also *Classification and Compensation Plans, Their Development, Adoption, and Administration*, pp. 19–20; and Griffenhagen and Associates, *op. cit.*, p. 2809.

[21] See *Report . . . on Reclassification of Salaries*, p. 68; Mosher and Kingsley, *Public Personnel Administration* (New York, 1936), pp. 407–08; and the sym-

From a practical standpoint, local factors may have sufficient weight to turn a close question into a definite recommendation or decision. These include the relative facilities and effectiveness of the personnel and the budget agency[22]; the position-coverage of the laws under which each works, compared with the coverage of the position-classification plan[23]; and the existence or absence of authorization to the personnel agency to check payrolls.

Experience shows that a position-classification plan is best administered by a personnel agency. Under other plans of organization the relations that should exist between the position-classification plan, the pay plan, recruiting, testing, and placement activities, and other phases of personnel administration, as well as the contributions position-classification activities can make to good organization, may not be fully secured.

In Massachusetts the state position-classification plan is administered by the Division of Personnel and Standardization of the Commission on Administration and Finance and the provisions of the civil service law are administered by another agency, the Division of Civil Service. The Special Commission on Taxation and Public Expenditures in its 1938 report emphasized the necessity of coordination between classification and examination activities with relation to positions and employees in the state service:[24]

Perhaps the most important problem is that of administratively coordinating the classification plan with the requirements of the civil service

posium: "Should Rates of Pay of Public Employees in the Classified Service be Fixed by the Budgetary or by the Central Personnel Agency or by an Agency Integrating Budget and Personnel Activities?" *Public Personnel Quarterly*, Fall 1940, pp. 181–85. This matter will be discussed in the report of the Committee on Pay Plans in the Public Service, a companion volume in this series.

[22] In Connecticut, this factor, among others, influenced a recent reorganization commission to recommend that the Division of Personnel of the state be made responsible for the administration of the classification and pay plan and that any conflicting powers and duties of the Board of Finance and Control be repealed. *Report of the Connecticut Commission Concerning the Reorganization of the State Departments* (Hartford, 1937), submitted to the Governor, January 25, 1937. At present, classification work in Connecticut is an initial responsibility of the Personnel Department, which is a division of the Department of Finance and Control.

[23] A unique situation exists in one city jurisdiction. The personnel agency establishes and approves the position-classification plan (classes, class specifications, and rules) and amends it from time to time. The budget agency, which has sole control of salary matters, allocates positions to classes. Apparently, this unusual division of responsibility was developed because of existing charter provisions limiting the coverage of the merit system in the jurisdiction.

[24] The Commonwealth of Massachusetts, *Report of the Special Commission on Taxation and Public Expenditures*, April 13, 1938, Part XV, Sec. II, p. 62; Part XV, Sec. I, p. 39 (Public Administration Service).

unit. Administered by a separate agency as it is at present, there could easily be a tendency for the classification plan to develop without proper reference to the needs of the agency responsible for the selection of employees.

To achieve a more specific coordination in this respect, the Special Commission proposed a legally required liaison as follows:

The Director of Personnel and Standardization shall, before establishing any new classification of positions and employment or compensation schedules of persons filling appointive offices or positions in the classified civil service of the government of the Commonwealth, submit such classifications and schedules to the Civil Service Board, which shall examine them and within fifteen days of their receipt return the same to said Director with its approval certified thereon or, in case of non-approval, its reason therefor in writing. The Director may, notwithstanding the lack of approval of said Board establish such classification and schedules.

In the small jurisdictions the problem of allocating responsibility for classification administration is different. Separate agencies for the various phases of administration may or may not exist. The volume of such activities may or may not warrant the employment of a full-time personnel assistant in the mayor's or city manager's office. Where at least one full-time personnel worker, trained in position-classification, is not available, recourse may be had to (a) periodic audits or resurveys by consultants outside the service; (b) arrangements with the state or some other public personnel agency for technical aid on a contractual or other basis; or (c) arrangements with a personnel service organization, such as the Municipal Personnel Service, established by the Michigan Municipal League, organized cooperatively by the smaller jurisdictions in the area for mutual assistance.[25]

In some jurisdictions, such as New Jersey, municipalities and counties adopting a merit system under the state civil service law are entitled to the aid of the state personnel agency in developing and administering a position-classification plan.[26] Legislation designed for a similar purpose has recently been recommended in Massachusetts.[27] In some instances the state personnel agency is

[25] Public Administration Service, *Personnel Programs for Smaller Cities* (1940), esp. pp. 3–5, 16–17; Civil Service Assembly . . . , *Civil Service Agencies in the United States—A 1940 Census*, Pamphlet No. 16, July 1940, pp. 25–27.

[26] "The Organization and Work of the New Jersey State Civil Service Commission," *Public Personnel Studies*, June 1927, pp. 113–14. Similar authority exists in Maryland, Sec. 22, State Merit System Law of February 1, 1921.

[27] Although the Commission on Administration and Finance administers the classification plan for state positions.

authorized by express law to do such work for local jurisdictions under informal agreements or on a contractual basis.[28] In New York and Ohio, the state civil commission has some general supervisory authority over local personnel programs.[29]

Where a state civil service commission has jurisdiction over the application of the merit system in cities or towns, it should also have control over the manner in which the position-classification plans for such cities or towns are developed and maintained. Without such plans available, the state civil service commission would have to give examinations for local positions without a complete understanding of the nature of the positions in terms of duties and responsibilities. Furthermore, the absence of classification plans where locally applicable would burden the state commission with a multiplicity of job titles, non-uniform across jurisdictional lines and probably in many respects meaningless or misleading. The lack of local classification plans also would impair the development of any plan for the transfer of employees between different services. A state civil service commission should not be expected to handle or assist in local recruiting problems without having at its disposal the necessary tools for doing the work. Of course, local classification plans should be worked out in cooperation with local officials.

TECHNICAL STAFF AND BUDGET

Qualifications of Staff

The composite and individual qualifications needed by a staff engaged in the continuous administration of a position-classification plan are substantially the same as those necessary for a developmental staff. Such qualifications have already been discussed.[30]

One of the principal differences, however, especially in an intermediate-sized service, is that the volume and frequency of classification work on technical positions may not warrant the continuous employment of occupational specialists. To the extent that specialized professional or technical knowledge is required in the smaller jurisdictions, advisory service may conveniently be available. In some personnel departments this advisory service may be rendered

[28] California, Minnesota, New Mexico, Rhode Island, Tennessee, and Wisconsin. See, for example, the discussion of "cooperative personnel administration" in California State Personnel Board, *Thirteenth Biennial Report* (1936–38), pp. 78–80.

[29] See H. Eliot Kaplan, "A Personnel Program for the County Service," *National Municipal Review*, October 1936.

[30] Pp. 153–60.

by other divisions, such as the examining division; it may be secured from outside the service, as from a professional society; sometimes the operating services may be tapped; but in other cases it may be necessary to bring in outside consultants. Through experience, of course, the general classifiers will acquire familiarity with professional and technical positions and will make contacts which will enable them to classify a good many technical positions without assistance.

However, in the larger jurisdictions or in the better equipped classification staffs, there is a strong argument for organizing some of the classification activities functionally. Since the main purpose of the classification process is to see that positions involving similar work are allocated to the same class, it would be natural to desire occupational specialists, through whom classifications of positions in the same occupational field would be coordinated. They would become advisers or reviewers of the allocations of positions in selected occupational series. The familiar advantages of specialists in functions would apply, and consistency in allocations would be better maintained. At the same time it is equally true that since any given position in a work unit is integrated with other positions in the same unit, the work of all members of the classification staff should usually be assigned on the basis of organizational segments. These considerations call for both occupational specialists and general practitioners on the classification staff.

In sharp contrast to smaller jurisdictions having one or a few classification investigators, this composition of the classification staff presents the problem of coordinating the viewpoints and actions of the two groups of classifiers. The preferable procedure seems to be to emphasize the direct contact work of those classifiers whose assignments are made on an organizational basis and to regard the reviewing and consulting service of the occupational specialists as advisory to them.

The members of the classification staff should be qualified to accept as much authority and responsibility as possible consistent with the maintenance of control by the official primarily responsible for classification operations. By delegating authority, higher officials free themselves from too much detail. This permits the classification staff to serve operating officials more effectively, for they are in a position to give prompt, initial answers to classification questions—a circumstance which furthers confidence in the classification staff.

Moreover, if higher classification officials have not participated in the initial discussion of an individual allocation, they can function as the first level of appeal when differences of judgment arise.

Wherever possible, it is desirable that the staff for the administration of the plan shall have had experience in its development and installation. Such experience will provide a broad understanding of the service which otherwise may require a long period to develop.

Size of Staff

The size of the staff required will be influenced to some extent by the same factors which affect the size of the staff required to develop the plan initially.[31] Another very important factor which bears on this point is the relative stability of the structure of the organizations and hence the stability of the duties and responsibilities of the positions in the service. This may be the most important of all factors.[32] Another factor for consideration, of course, is the intensiveness and extensiveness of service to be provided by the classification staff. If, for example, the maintenance of the position-classification plan is limited to occasional spot checks or taking advantage of such events as the holding of tests or the filling of requisitions for certification, the service rendered is apt to be rather inadequate. It has been estimated that under such circumstances, in a relatively stable service of intermediate size, the time of one staff member for each 2,500 to 5,000 employees would be required. However, if more intensive service is to be rendered, including periodic audits, a ratio of one staff member to each 1,000 or 1,500 employees would ordinarily suffice in intermediate-sized jurisdictions. In the largest jurisdictions, the volume of everyday work is apt to be heavy, and these estimates will not apply. Also, the estimates in any case may be materially affected by the characteristics of the classification plan. Fineness of classification according to difficulty and responsibility levels calls for a relatively larger maintenance staff.

Something also depends on the extensiveness of the functions with which classification staff members are charged. Assistance in the administration of service rating systems is frequently one of their functions. They are also called upon for assistance in administering reduction of force programs, in preparing qualification standards in

[31] See pp. 156–58.
[32] See pp. 285–88.

open competitive or other tests, in deciding upon the appropriateness of eligible lists,[33] and in establishing or analyzing and improving organization structures and work methods. To the extent that other functions of personnel or general administration are combined with those involved in administering the position-classification plan, due allowance will have to be made in estimating the size of staff required.

Of course, in the smaller services involving perhaps 1,500 to 2,000 positions, the administration of the position-classification plan may be handled well by the same staff which prepares, conducts, and rates tests, such a staff being given training in both classification and testing techniques.

As in any other undertaking, the size of the total operations determines the degree of division of labor. In large personnel departments, classification work tends to be assigned to a distinct staff group. As the operations become smaller in volume, the tendency is to combine personnel functions in the same individual or unit.

Budget

Depending on how the classification agency is financed and staffed, and the degree to which it is therefore able to keep current the plan and the allocations of positions, the classification system will maintain its role as a beneficial tool in personnel administration or it will become obsolescent and, to a larger and larger degree, useless.

The budget required will of course depend upon the number of employees, their rates of pay, and the expense of office supplies and equipment. In some jurisdictions, transportation costs may be a sizable item. There is the same difficulty in estimating costs for maintenance of the classification plan as in estimating the size of staff required. However, if it is necessary to establish a budget for the proposed new personnel agency, the annual cost of this service might be estimated at from $1 to $2 per position for the less intensive type of maintenance service and $4 to $6 for the more intensive.

PUBLIC AND OTHER WORKING RELATIONSHIPS

Much of what has been already said concerning the importance of and opportunity for good public relations in the developmental

---

[33] For a case study of such an activity, see Committee on Public Administration of the Social Science Research Council, *Case Reports in Public Administration*, No. 24 (Chicago: Public Administration Service, 1940).

period applies to the task of continuous administration.[34] Every investigation, every classification-audit, every hearing or conference, every published form, report, or other document constitutes an opportunity for explaining to others the basis, principles, and procedures of position-classification and for avoiding or correcting misunderstandings.

In particular, the central classification agency should establish and maintain effective working relationships with legislative and executive units of the jurisdiction. Precisely what these working relationships will or should be depends upon the place of the classification agency in the organization structure. Especially important are the relationships with officials and employees of the operating departments, staffs engaged in other phases of personnel work, legislative finance committees, fiscal and budgetary units, and management and procedure agencies.

Necessarily, in the administration of a position-classification plan, members of the staff will maintain close contact with operating and personnel officials in line departments. They will keep well informed of the work program, activities, and future plans of units within their assignments, and currently familiar with the special conditions or circumstances under which the work of such units is carried on and the nature of the problems encountered in day-to-day operations. Every effort should be made to establish and maintain cordial and cooperative relationships. The purpose of these contacts is twofold. First, they place the staff in a position to anticipate changes in organization or in the duties and responsibilities of individual positions so that any necessary changes in the classification plan or in allocations may be promptly initiated. The second and equally important purpose is to make it possible for the classifier to render helpful service to operating officials. His responsibility includes not only the up-to-date maintenance of the position-classification plan, but also touches the various administrative uses and purposes for which the plan exists.

The central classification agency should receive all departmental announcements, bulletins, and instructions that may have a bearing on the distribution of functions between organization units and be-

[34] Pp. 163–68. See also "Public Relations of Personnel Agencies," *Proceedings, Thirtieth Annual Meeting of the Civil Service Assembly . . . ,* October 1938, pp. 60–61; William E. Mosher and Stuart VanDyke, "Public Relations for Personnel Agencies," *Public Personnel Review,* October 1940, pp. 18–29; Maxwell A. DeVoe, "Administrative Relationships of Public Personnel Agencies," *ibid.,* January 1941, pp. 24–27.

tween individual positions. Changes in the distribution of functions between units, or the addition or elimination of functions may have an important effect on a number of key positions, and these effects may be felt downward in other positions. It is equally important for the classification agency to study the detailed written instructions, memoranda, or manuals which many bureaus and work units issue in order to standardize their procedures, and to maintain a current file of them. Where these instructions are carefully prepared, they are presumably authentic statements not only of what is to be done, but of how it is to be done. Thus they are invaluable source material for the classification agency and at the same time indicate changes requiring attention from a classification standpoint.

In a good many jurisdictions, responsible members of the classification staff will have opportunity for frequent contacts with representatives of employee groups. The problems presented in such conferences may be varied. A more advantageous classification may be sought for one employee or a group of employees, a consolidation or subdivision of existing classes may be requested, or changes in qualification standards may be desired. In these and other problems, a classification staff is most frequently the initial point of contact between the personnel department and representatives of employee groups. It is worth remembering that in many instances a classification interview affords the only opportunity for an official or employee to become familiar with the elements of position-classification and to discuss his work or operating problems with some one in a responsible position outside his own department. Depending on the nature and importance of the problem presented, the classification staff member may need to discuss the matter with his supervisors, with officials of the personnel and fiscal departments of the jurisdiction, or may be required to make classification surveys of the positions involved and present a recommendation as to the action to be taken, with the reasons therefor. In many of these contacts the matters presented may be disposed of on an informal basis. In other instances, where far-reaching consequences may be involved, considerable care and thought are required before a decision is reached.

The areas of mutual interest between position-classification and other personnel functions have previously been indicated.[35] These areas include recruiting and testing activities in which class specifications serve as a useful tool of the testing technician. During the

[35] Chapter IV.

course of investigation and analysis incident to the maintenance of the classification plan, members of the classification staff may find out how well the plan is serving its purposes in this respect. They may be called upon to interpret for the benefit of their supervisors and technical associates the relative satisfactoriness of the classification plan and the degree to which qualification standards and recruitment and testing practices meet operating needs.[36]

These various relationships make it desirable for members of the classification staff to cooperate with their associates in the personnel department or in the line agencies so as to forward in every way possible the whole personnel program of the jurisdiction.

Occasionally in some jurisdictions, or periodically in others, there will be direct relationships between the legislative branch and the agency responsible for administering the position-classification plan. Sometimes the contacts will be with individual members and sometimes with committees. Such contacts afford a valuable opportunity to explain the connection between the proper maintenance of a position-classification plan and the administrative, fiscal, and personnel operations of the executive departments and agencies of the jurisdiction.

Ordinarily, only through active cooperation among the central classification agency and the organization units and legislative committees concerned in the administrative preparation of budgets and the passage of statutes or ordinances authorizing funds for personal services can the benefits of a position-classification plan in budgetary and fiscal administration be secured.[37] The intimate relationship between a position-classification plan, a pay plan, and an annual budget must consciously be translated into action through the mutual endeavors of these groups.[38] Involved are the acceptance of such principles as the utilization of the position-classification plan

---

[36] "Furthermore, since the Division of Personnel and Standardization has authority to reclassify positions, it can in reality play an important part in the determination of matters that would otherwise seem to come within the jurisdiction of the civil service unit. . . . There seems to be required a staff not only for making classification field studies involving local as well as state personnel but also for picking up such departmental data as may be required for other phases of personnel administration." The Commonwealth of Massachusetts, *Report of the Special Commission on Taxation and Public Expenditures*, pp. 62–63.

[37] Pp. 61–70.

[38] It should be recognized that line-item budgets and appropriation ordinances in which each position is listed by title and salary, afford a vehicle for either supporting or wrecking a good classification plan. If a city council includes new titles without reference to the classification plan and new rates of pay without reference to the pay plan, both the classification and the pay plan may quickly be broken down.

as a basis for the pay plan and for budgets based on it; the clearance with the classification agency of new positions requested by operating departments or old positions under new titles for the purpose of getting the positions properly classified and named before their administrative need is passed upon; the insistence by all concerned upon adherence to the uniform system of nomenclature which a position-classification plan furnishes; and where a pay plan exists, clearances as to adherence of proposed salary adjustments or rates of pay in the budget with the pay scales and rules of the pay plan itself.[39]

The central classification agency is frequently not the only unit studying distribution of responsibilities, flow of work, and related matters. Administrative and procedure analysts and representatives of an accounting department or budget or fiscal office are frequently assembling data which are of interest to the classification agency. It should, therefore, keep in close touch with these and other offices, both to make use of their data and to avoid duplication of effort. Procedural investigations often are concerned with the precise duties of a group of positions, and there is obviously no need for both units to assemble the same data. Accordingly, it is desirable for the classification agency to develop cooperative relationships with each of the management agencies, so that their staffs may be in mutual contact with the classification staff during the consideration of their particular problems. Frequently the classification staff can make a definite contribution, and in any event is always able to advise on the position-classification results of a proposed administrative action.[40]

There should be a similar effective working relationship between the classification staff and the agency or subdivision that actually audits payrolls in order to assure compliance with laws and regulations.[41]

[39] See Charles P. Messick, Discussion, Proceedings, Fourteenth Annual Meeting of the Assembly of Civil Service Commissions, 1921, pp. 35–36. See also: Griffenhagen, "The Origin of the Modern Occupational Classification in Personnel Administration," *Public Personnel Studies*, September 1924, pp. 191–92; Clay Morris Ross, *A Survey of Public Personnel Legislation and Administrative Regulations*, Bureau of Public Administration, University of Virginia (1939), Report No. 5, Series B, pp. 21–23.

[40] See Griffenhagen, *The Administrative Organization of the Administrative Functions of a State Government*, presented before the American Political Science Association, December 28, 1928, pp. 19–20; Bernard L. Gladieux, *Administrative Planning in the Federal Government*, presented before the Governmental Research Association, September 8, 1939, pp. 21–23.

[41] See Joseph M. Lowery, "Public Budgeting," *Civic Affairs*, October 1939, p. 2.

KEEPING ALLOCATIONS OF POSITIONS CURRENT

The occasion for making initial allocations or reviewing existing ones may be (1) the creation of one or more positions additional to those in existence when the classification plan was installed; (2) a material change in the duties and responsibilities of a position; (3) a request of a supervisor or an employee for a review of the allocation of one or more positions; or (4) a survey or "classification-audit" conducted by the classification agency to improve the accuracy of allocations to classes. Such occasions are intended to be covered by direct techniques or procedures.[42]

In addition, there are other occasions, particularly in civil-service jurisdictions, when a check of existing classifications is desirable. For example, opportunity for checking allocations is afforded where follow-up interviews with new employees are conducted during the probationary period; in personnel transactions such as certifications, promotions, salary adjustments, transfers, or demotions; in cases of separations from the service or from a particular organization unit; in the preparation of competitive tests; or in the preparation of budgets for personal services.

Frequently, more is involved than is at once apparent. The creation of additional positions or changes in the duties and responsibilities of existing positions may make it necessary to determine whether other allocations are thereby affected. There may have been a division of responsibilities among several positions which has modified the responsibility delegated to each, or it may be that duties have been redistributed in such a way as to alter the difficulty of work in one or more positions. The creation of new supervisory positions also requires the careful examination of any resulting modifications of responsibilities of subordinate positions. The creation of a group of new positions forming a unit in itself may alter the duties and responsibilities of existing units and their component positions. Requests for the review of the existing allocations of certain positions may indicate a general need for reviewing all positions. A reduction in the number of positions in a unit may also give rise to changes in the remaining positions.

After the facts about the duties and responsibilities of a position

---

[42] The continuous administration of a position-classification plan includes two major objectives: keeping the allocations of positions to classes up to date, and keeping the position-classification plan itself current. Procedures designed to accomplish these objectives are described later.

have been ascertained, they must be studied, analyzed, and evaluated. They must be measured against the duties and responsibilities falling respectively within the already established classes, as described in the class specifications and as illustrated by the classifications of similar and related positions in the jurisdiction. In the case of a changed position, comparison must be made between its present duties and responsibilities and those it involved when last classified. Many positions will fall readily into appropriate classes, chiefly because they are easily associated with other positions which have already received sufficient study to establish lines of demarcation. In other cases the problem of classification analysis becomes complicated.

As the result of study and analysis, several different kinds of situations may develop when new or changed positions are presented to the classifying agency for classification. A newly created position may be like others already placed in class, as, for example, where another food inspector position is added to a staff of ten food inspectors whose positions have already been classified. The additional position is, of course, allocated to the same class as the others. Or, it may be found that a position originally placed in a certain class has taken on a new character because of the addition, subtraction, complication, or simplification of certain duties or responsibilities. For example, a stenographic position originally involving the taking and transcribing of ordinary letters and reports and therefore classified as Junior Stenographer now is found to comprise the taking and transcribing of verbatim reports of hearings and conferences, which is covered in another class, Hearings Reporter. In that event a change in classification is required. The position is taken out of one existing class, Junior Stenographer, and reclassified by placing it in another existing class, Hearings Reporter. In these two instances, it will be observed, the positions being classified are adequately covered by classes already established.

KEEPING THE PLAN CURRENT

Establishing or Changing Classes

Occasionally, however, and frequently in large and developing public services, it is disclosed upon a study of the facts that newly created positions or changed positions are so different from any previously encountered that the existing classification plan does not cover them. It is then necessary to amend the plan itself either by adding new classes or by realigning, dividing, or merging existing classes. Typical examples of this situation occur when the jurisdiction or one of its departments engages in a new and distinct activity, when a department consolidates in one position distinct phases of work previously performed in different positions, or when it separates for performance in different positions several phases of work previously performed in one position.

Also, revisions of the classes themselves are occasioned by difficulties encountered in using them in recruiting and testing activities and in conducting in-service personnel transactions. Classes, particularly at levels at which entrance to the service is normally gained, may be combined to facilitate the holding of entrance examinations. Conversely, one class may sometimes be subdivided into two or more separate classes, where it is found that more than one type of test or qualification standard is necessary to fill the positions in the class as it exists.

The technical problems involved in establishing new classes, or dividing, combining, or abolishing existing classes are substantially the same as those encountered in determining classes during the process of developing the classification plan originally. Reference, accordingly, should be made to that discussion.[43]

Proposed revisions of the class structure of the classification plan deserve careful analysis. Operating officials, employees, or others may suggest the creation of new classes or changes in existing classes without too much regard for the principles and purposes of position-classification or the difficulties and equities of administration. Sometimes, for example, the establishment of a separate class, only slightly differentiated from an existing class, is requested, merely in order to limit competition to a favored group, to avoid the use of an existing employment list, to secure an increased pay scale for a relatively few employees, or to single out certain employees for distinctive treatment in promotions or lay-offs.[44]

It should be mentioned that in the event of a material change in the classification plan, or in the classification of an existing position, there should be, as a practical matter, some definite time at which the change takes effect for pay purposes or otherwise. Generally such

[43] Pp. 195–205.
[44] See "Suggested Cooperative Attack on Certain Personnel Problems," *Public Personnel Studies*, February 1926, p. 51.

revisions or amendments have no retroactive effect, but date from some time fixed officially by regulation, statute, or legal decision.[45]

Revising Class Specifications

Since the content of class specifications depends on facts about the duties and responsibilities of the positions, they constitute a current record, needing constant revision. As these facts change because new positions are created, duties are altered, or positions are abolished, the class specifications must be changed.

The value of class specifications depends to a large extent upon how well and how currently they describe the duties and responsibilities of existing classes of positions and indicate the decisions of the classification agency as to the differentiating characteristics among classes. When classes change, or are created,' abolished, divided, or merged, the class specifications should promptly follow suit. Similarly, class specifications viewed as technical products or as administrative tools are always susceptible of improvement to make them as clear-cut and as faithful a record as possible of the various classes and their characteristics.

The principal circumstances which call for revision of the class specifications arise: (1) when new classes of positions are established, either to cover additional positions different from those already in existence, or to cover changes in existing positions; (2) when existing classes of positions are abolished, divided, or merged; (3) when revision is desirable in order to reflect the decisions of the classification agency; (4) when positions which are allocated to a certain class are, without any change in their duties or responsibilities, reappraised and reallocated; (5) when the duties and responsibilities of positions allocated to a certain class are so changed as to necessitate a revision of the specifications, even though their class allocation is not altered; and (6) when recruiting processes indicate the desirability of changing the qualifications standards (which serve as a definition of the recruiting field) to show more clearly the various fields of activity from which the applicants may be drawn, to prevent misunderstanding on the part of applicants and administrative officials, and to serve as a better guide in processes of selection.

With respect to revisions of qualification standards, a good gen-

[45] In the federal departmental service payments of increased salaries due to reallocations of positions can be retroactive only to the beginning of the pay period within which the U. S. Civil Service Commission's certification of its action is received in the administrative office of the department. 4 Comp. Gen. 280 (September 8, 1924); 5 Comp. Gen. 202 (September 16, 1925); 11 Comp. Gen. 395 (April 18, 1932).

eral policy would be to require more or less constant review by joint action of the classification and testing staffs, thus permitting revision of these statements, if necessary, before test plans are approved for the class of positions concerned, or before personnel transactions are completed. In this way, statements of qualifications can be amended from time to time to keep pace with advances in testing methods and progress in developing measures of qualifications, as well as to recognize the results of practical recruiting experience.

The California State Personnel Board has developed a form for this purpose called an "Examination-Classification Experience Data Sheet." Entries on this form begin with the initiation of each new examination and are continued in sequence until the eligible list is established. In particular, the examiner who reviewed the applications gives his comments on the ease or difficulty of interpreting and applying the entrance qualifications. The examiner who prepared the written test comments on the knowledges, skills, and abilities. The examiner appraising educational and experience qualifications of applicants comments on that portion of the qualification standards. The form also calls for recording the number of applications received and the proportion of applicants remaining for consideration after each step in the examining process. A disproportion at any point may lead to a reexamination of any part of the qualifications standards deemed to be responsible. After appointments have been made and performance ratings of probationers are available, further comparison of this information with the qualifications standards is made.

An up-to-date copy of the specification for each class should be available in the office of the classification agency. In addition, the specifications should be printed and distributed in loose-leaf form to all who need them in the various departments and agencies, and a list of the persons or agencies to whom they are distributed should be maintained. As amendments or revisions are decided upon, the official set of specifications should at once be brought up to date, and new or revised specifications issued to the persons or agencies on the distribution list. In this way all copies being used for current administrative purposes are kept current.

Amending the Rules

From time to time it may be necessary to change or add to the rules for the administration of the classification plan. Adopted originally before or during the installation period, they may need amendment as the result of operating experience, new legislation, or changes in employment conditions. The procedure of amendment is generally the same as that required in adopting the rules in the first instance. Usually this involves the preparation of a recommendation by the head of the classification staff, director of personnel, or other official of the central classification or personnel agency, the holding of an open hearing on the proposed amendment, and the adoption, rejection, or modification of the amendment by the official head of the agency. In some instances, such action is not effective until approved by higher officials of the jurisdiction, such as a governor, county board of supervisors, mayor, or common council.

ADMINISTRATIVE PROCEDURES

Classification work can be no more accurate than the information on which it is based. The duties and responsibilities of positions are the basis upon which positions are classified, and hence current classifications should conform to duties currently performed and responsibilities currently exercised. The administrative value of a position-classification plan can be measured largely by the closeness with which it is kept fitted to the positions in the jurisdiction. It follows, therefore, that one of the most important functions of a classifying agency is that of constantly securing accurate and adequate information about new positions, changes in the work or responsibilities of positions, or changes in organization or work-methods affecting positions.

It is frequently difficult for the classification agency to learn of such changes promptly.[46] This may be due to a number of causes. The central classification agency may be handicapped by lack of funds and staff, in comparison with the volume of work to be covered. Operating supervisors may not appreciate the nature and effect of gradual changes in their organization units, and some changes may simply escape their notice. Officials and employees are naturally reluctant to bring up any matter that might result in lowering the classification of any position. Positions are presented for higher classifications on the ground of increased duties and responsibilities, but changes in the positions from which these duties and responsibilities have been taken to build up the position presented are frequently not reported.

[46] That this situation is not peculiar to the public service is indicated in Riegel, *Salary Determination*, p. 242.

Experience shows that no single type of procedure is adequate to keep the classification agency currently informed. A combination of procedures is necessary. Information is gathered from reports submitted by the departments to the classifying agency, through investigations by the agency's staff, through cooperative relations with the departments, through examination of budget documents, and annual or other reports, through hearings and conferences held in connection with appeals or requests for reconsideration, and through periodic surveys or "classification-audits."

Reports by Operating Departments

By law or regulation, and in addition to such other reports as may be required in connection with personnel transactions, prompt reports from the various departments of the jurisdiction to the central classifying agency should be required (1) whenever new positions have been or are to be created or additional employees appointed, (2) whenever existing positions have been or are to be abolished or employees separated, and (3) whenever material and permanent changes have been or are to be made in the duties or responsibilities of any position or employee or in the form of organization or work-methods of any unit.

Good practice should encourage the reporting of all material changes in work-assignments, except those definitely known to be of a transient character. Whether such a change requires a change in the classification of a position or an amendment to the classification plan is for the central classification agency to determine. In this way a record of the current duties and responsibilities of positions is maintained. To avoid a tendency to regard assignments as temporary, which actually last over an inordinate period, reports should also be required of all changes in assignments that have continued for some definite period, say 120 days. Investigation by the classification agency will then serve as a basis for decision as to the action to be taken.[47]

These reports are descriptive and informative in nature, not merely lists of positions or changes. A standard, specially designed

[47] See Griffenhagen & Associates, *Report on Classification and Compensation of Positions to the Board of Supervisors of Milwaukee County*, November 10, 1928, pp. 123–24. See also: the discussion of temporary or fluctuating work-assignments in Chapter V, pp. 132–33; the discussion of "wages of employees temporarily reassigned" in Riegel, *Wage Determination*, p. 113; and the discussion of "trial period" in Robert I. Marshall, "A Salary Plan in Operation," *Personnel*, February 1938, p. 113.

form, known generally as a "classification sheet" or as a "job analysis sheet," is usually provided for a description of the current duties and responsibilities of the position reported. This may be the same, or virtually the same, as the position-questionnaire form used in the development of the position-classification plan.[48] Ordinarily it would call for the same information and be filled out in the same way. In some instances, however, it may be simplified by eliminating items originally required for developmental purposes only; or on the basis of the knowledge acquired by the general survey, special questions or items may be introduced, or specialized questionnaires for particular occupational groups may be developed.[49] Because of the close bearing of position-classification on organization structure, delegations of authority and responsibility, work-methods, the creation and filling of new or vacant positions, and fiscal obligations, the position-description form used initially in reporting the creation of new positions or changes of duties or responsibilities is in some cases an official document, executed by supervisors or administrators. In any event, the employee or appointee should be required to familiarize himself with this current description of his duties, tasks, and responsibilities. Also, of course, he should be encouraged to discuss with his supervisor his own conception of the work he is employed to do, current job descriptions being excellent administrative vehicles for conferences of this nature.[50] The form itself or a separate statement should show whether the report is to cover a newly created position, a new incumbent in a previously classified position, a material change in an existing position, or some other situation. In a given case, the report to the central classification agency would consist of the executed form and such supplemental material as may be deemed appropriate, such as explanatory memoranda, organization charts, or exhibits of work. This presentation then provides an initial basis for action by the central classifying agency.

As previously indicated, the central classification agency is frequently able to secure information indicating the necessity for formal department reports of changes in the duties or responsibilities of positions or indicating the need for conference and investigation if such reports have not been received.

[48] See pp. 169–81, and Appendix A. For reproductions of the "classification sheets" currently used by the U. S. Civil Service Commission and by the California State Personnel Board, see John M. Pfiffner, *Research Methods in Public Administration* (Ronald Press, 1940), pp. 346–47, 352.

[49] See pp. 328–29.

[50] See also pp. 79–80.

A difficulty frequently encountered in passing on the classification of new positions or changed positions arises out of the character of the position descriptions presented. Completeness and precision of position descriptions are just as necessary during the continuous administration of a position-classification plan as during its original development. Sometimes the descriptions are vague, generalized, or stereotyped. Sometimes where class specifications are widely circu-̇lated, position descriptions are presented which are merely copies of class specifications or portions of them. In such cases the employee or supervisor may be following the line of least resistance or may be motivated simply by a desire to obtain a specific classification. Only continuous insistence and education by the classification agency for accurate and complete descriptions can make employees and supervisors conscious of their proper responsibilities in this respect.

In some jurisdictions the department head who presents the report to the central classification agency is required or requested to make a recommendation as to the classification of the position.[51] This procedure has the advantage of bringing concretely to the attention of operating executives the use of classification procedures in management matters and the necessity for coordinating classifications within each department.[52] Where they objectively accept initial responsibilities for consistency of classification as among the various subdivisions of the department, the classification agency is aided. Where, however, they simply desire to secure more pay for a particular employee, or regard classification as a process for rewarding efficiency or long service, they are apt to take the viewpoint of advocates for the results they desire. This, however, is inconsistent with that of the impartial classification specialist who must keep his attention focused on all positions.

Classification recommendations of operating officials are apt to

[51] "In companies employing factory, office, technical and supervisory employees every effort should be made toward uniform and comparative handling of all classes without removal of immediate control from those most closely in touch with the various types but centralizing ultimate control in some one person or group." Samuel L. H. Burk, "Salary and Wage Administration," *Personnel Journal*, September 1936, p. 114.

[52] "The participation of department heads in position analysis not only improves their ability to deal with salary questions, but it has other benefits. It frequently reveals better methods of doing work; and it indicates how duties could be delegated more advantageously within departments. It clearly outlines for each executive his task of supervising, training, and rating employees, and thus reveals to him new ways to reduce costs through better management of personnel." Riegel, *Salary Determination*, p. 74.

be sound and helpful only to the extent that the officials have analyzed and evaluated the positions according to recognized principles and have ignored those influences which interfere with impartial judgment. Furthermore, to discharge even an initial responsibility for consistency of classifications within a department, fact-finding and analysis are called for. This means that cooperative relations should be worked out between operating officials and the classification staff of the central agency for the consideration of classification problems at their inception, before formal recommendations are decided upon.[53]

Investigations or Work-Audits

Investigations or work-audits by members of the staff of the central classifying agency should be an everyday part of its work, both to supplement or clarify the information furnished in departmental reports and to secure the facts about new or changed positions in case they are not reported on or reports are unduly delayed.[54]

Inquiries made by members of the classification staff necessarily vary in scope. In their simplest form they may amount to no more than a telephone call to obtain additional data. Such inquiries are frequent where the classifier has a good knowledge of the particular work unit and has already established cooperative contacts. On the other hand, an inquiry may be a comprehensive survey of a large group of positions, the technique for which is discussed below. Between these extremes lies the form of inquiry in which the classifier is initially concerned with one or a few positions, personally interviews supervisors and employees affected, analyzes other positions which are a part of the work-pattern in which the positions in question fit, and may study comparable positions in other units.

Every inquiry or work-audit pays dividends in more detailed information and more accurate classifications. In practice, the fre-

---

[53] In the federal service, or in other jurisdictions which have operating departments large enough to warrant a fully equipped subdivision devoted entirely to matters of personnel administration, the head of department may have one or more classification specialists on his administrative staff to do the preliminary work on which his official recommendation is based. See U. S. Civil Service Commission, *Fifty-fifth Annual Report* (1938), pp. 8–9; Roy F. Hendrickson, *The Personnel Program of the United States Department of Agriculture* (Civil Service Assembly . . . , October 1939), Pamphlet No. 15, pp. 11–12; Stanley T. Orear, "Classification in an Operating Agency," *Personnel Administration*, October 1939, p. 6.

[54] Reference should be made to the discussion of work-audits in Chapter VII, pp. 222–25.

quency with which work-audits are made will depend on the size of the jurisdiction, the relative size of the classification staff, and the nature and volume of changes in positions and organizations. Work-audits are vital when the classifier is endeavoring to set landmarks in a new or reorganized unit.

In conducting a work-audit of a position already occupied, a member of the classification staff interviews the employee at his place of work. He interviews any others who have a firsthand knowledge of the employee's work, such as the employee's supervisor or division chief. He makes personal observations, where practicable, of the work flowing across the employee's desk, or of his tasks during their actual performance in a laboratory or workshop. He also secures any organization or function charts, exhibits, or supplemental statements which seem necessary or helpful.

Experience in classification administration has shown the necessity for a thorough search of the facts by the classifier. The central classifying agency, in passing upon departments' recommendations and in arriving at its own decision as to the proper classification of a position, has to have full information from which inferences can be drawn as to the difficulty, complexity, importance, responsibility, and general character of the work of that position. This is not so simple as it might at first appear. Some of the factors which frequently prove to be controlling elements in evaluating a position are intangible ones which would not be disclosed merely by direct observation of the work of the employee. Frequently it is only after a thorough investigation of the bonds which tie the position to other positions—such as lines of authority, channels of flow of work, sources of advice, and the existence of checks and reviews—that an adequate and objective picture of its duties and responsibilities can be drawn.

Accordingly, the classifier inquires into the manner in which the work in question comes to the employee; what has been done with the work before it reaches him; the form in which it comes to him; what his immediate and specific tasks are; the methods, processes, or practices by which he performs them; whether these are definitely prescribed or depend upon his initiative; what laws or policies he is required to observe in doing his work; what action he takes; what the essential purpose of his work is; the matters on which he has to exercise judgment or discretion; what qualifications would be required of anybody in order to carry out that work; what review his work receives and for what purpose; what the final disposition of his work is; what the importance, the subject matter, and the relative finality of his recommendations or decisions are; and the extent to which the position involves the responsibility of initiating or taking action with or without consultation with others. He also analyzes especially the relationship of the position to other positions in the unit or section, disclosing the kind and extent of supervision flowing toward the position and the kind and extent of supervision exercised by the incumbent over any subordinates.

The classifier, of course, should be thoroughly familiar with the basis and principles of position-classification and with the personnel procedures of the jurisdiction. In addition, he must be skilled in interviewing in order that he may bring out facts bearing on the allocation factors in the field of work of the position, without creating misunderstanding or friction and without consuming unnecessary time or burdening employees and officials.

The classification interview is intrinsically a part of the classification technique. At first thought it might appear that the interview is simply an effort to get the facts about what the employee in question does; but, except in the most routine positions, the facts about what the employee does are almost innumerable. There is a high degree of selectivity involved, and obviously this selection must be made on the basis of a knowledge of what is important for classification purposes. Many questions are possible that seem to be relevant to the work-audit and in fact seem relevant to the employee but which in fact have no bearing on the question of what class the position falls in. In order to interview for the purpose of classifying a given position, it is necessary for the interviewer to have a good knowledge of what are the characteristic and differentiating duties of the various classes in the series or occupational group represented by that position. This leads up to the point that the free type of interview is not the best type for work-audits.

Hence, in order to conserve the time of the interviewer and the interviewee and to aim the interview at a definite target, it is well for the classifier, on the basis of advance office study, to prepare beforehand a list of factors to be discussed and covered or points upon which specific clarification is needed. In some instances it has been of value to write out at least the basic questions to be asked. In other instances, general or specific check lists have been provided for the use of classifiers in order that their interviews may be at least partially guided rather than entirely unguided. These check lists are intended to cover individual items in important factual areas.[55] Time spent in preparing for interviews is well repaid.

It is always desirable to record the facts obtained in a work-audit. In some cases they can be noted on the job description form. However, where the facts to be recorded are too numerous, where controversial questions between the classification agency and the department are involved, where classification standards are discussed and interpreted, or where the results have a precedent value, a separate memorandum or formal report is in order.[56]

In this case, the classifier prepares a descriptive and analytical report with his recommendation for official action. This report is based not only upon a consideration of the immediate information regarding the position, but also upon the classification of similar positions; the specifications of classes and the distinctions among them; the classification policies of the classifying agency; the comparison of the position with others in the same field of work in higher or lower classes or in the same class; and an analysis of the duties and responsibilities of these comparative examples in the light of a similar analysis of the duties and responsibilities of the position

[55] For example, factors common to many types of positions are supervision received and supervision exercised. Among different investigators there should be a reasonably uniform concept of the different types of supervision received and exercised in order that the investigation itself may bring out which type exists in a given case. See, in this connection, the so-called "evaluation" items used in some developmental questionnaires (Appendix A). The mechanical trades afford numerous examples of pertinent factors, such as the fineness of the work to be done, reflecting the degree of skill to be exercised; the variety of work to be done, reflecting the breadth of the knowledge and adaptability required; and the definiteness of the instructions, plans, or specifications by which the worker is guided. Examples of check lists for guidance in interviews for job analysis and position-classification purposes are given in Appendix E and F. Other examples are: "Data Sheet," in Robert C. Clothier, "Organization for an Occupational Survey," *The Journal of Personnel Research*, February 1923, pp. 436–39; "Desk Audit Check List," developed by Public Administration Service (1937, mimeographed), a sample page of which is reproduced in Pfiffner, *Research Methods in Public Administration*, p. 89; "Job Analysis Outline for Collecting Data and Writing Job Specifications," in J. O. Hopwood, *Salaries, Wages and Labor Relations* (New York, 1937), pp. 41–47; Life Office Management Association, Clerical Salary Study Committee, *Job Evaluation for the Establishment of Salary Standards*, Report No. 1 (1938), Appendix, pp. 11–14; "Interviewer's Rough Note Sheet" and "Interviewer's Data Sheet," reproduced in Samuel L. H. Burk, *A Case History in Salary and Wage Administration* (American Management Association, 1939), pp. 9, 11; "Position Classification Analysis—CL1," in Stanley T. Orear, "Classification in an Operating Agency," *Personnel Administration*, October 1939, p. 4; exhibits of forms in N. D. Hubbell, *Salary Administration Plan for Factory Supervision and Staff* (American Management Association, 1939), pp. 28–40. See also the discussion of the use of specialized questionnaires in surveys, p. 91 and footnote.

[56] In addition, where new facts completely change the picture originally presented on the job description, a new report by the department is desirable.

which has been investigated. Where a change of duties or responsibilities has occurred, calling for a change in classification, it is important also for the classifier to record clearly the nature of the change, to what extent the previous duties and responsibilities have continued, and whether the change is of sufficient significance to bring the position into another class.

The comprehensiveness with which classifiers' reports may be prepared depends, of course, on a number of conditions, including time limits, availability of stenographic or typing assistance, the fullness or meagerness of existing records, the relative importance of items included or excluded, and the precedent value of the reports.

Reconsiderations or "Appeals"

Giving the department and the employee the right to request a review of the allocation of a position is fundamental to good classification administration. The way should be open for officials, supervisors, or employees affected to ask the central classification agency to review existing classifications in the light of current facts, with a view to the correction of any errors that may have come about through omissions in reporting changes of duties or responsibilities, through failure to secure adequate and complete facts, or through errors in judgment. Such requests may concern an individual position or a group of positions.

Not only are the interests of employees and supervisors thus served, but advantages accrue also to the central classifying agency. Through requests for review it may uncover unreported changes of duties or responsibilities and find out about and correct its own errors. Also, the existence of a review procedure tends to improve the quality of initial action.

No fixed formula can be laid down for the establishment of a review or appeal procedure. The details will have to be worked out in the light of legal provisions as to final authority and responsibility for classification, the size and occupational complexity of the jurisdiction, the volume and frequency of requests for review in relation to the size of the technical classification staff, finances available, and the attitudes of personnel officials, operating officials, employees, and employee groups.

In general, however, it may be said that certain factors deserve primary consideration. In the first place, the interests of the official or employee must be recognized. He, his immediate supervisor, and others interested in the outcome of the review should be given adequate opportunity to state the facts, both orally and in writing, about the duties and responsibilities of his position, to explain why they believe it to be erroneously allocated, and to cite other positions which they believe are equally difficult or responsible, or the class specification which they believe to be applicable. The employee, as a matter of course, is also entitled to have his complaint or request reviewed objectively and impartially, by qualified persons.

Further, whatever the details of the appeal procedure, it must constitute an effective method of ascertaining facts. This involves (a) the presentation in writing of each request for reconsideration, accompanied by signed statements of the employee, his immediate supervisor, and other official supervisors as to what the employee's duties and responsibilities are; (b) recording of the revelant facts and considerations discussed in the oral hearing or conference; and (c) supplemental work-audit, if necessary, to amplify or check the facts brought out in the written statements or in the conference.[57]

Naturally, employees and operating officers in requesting a higher classification for a given position in perfectly good faith emphasize those features of the position that would point toward raising the allocation. Sometimes this interest in obtaining a higher allocation results in their failure to present all the facts bearing upon the kind, difficulty, importance, and value of the position, whether favorable to their contentions or not. At a hearing, favorable items tend to be emphasized and unfavorable items to be ignored or minimized. Conflicts and inconsistencies are difficult to resolve without making a work-audit. Accordingly, any procedure for hearing complaints and requests for the reallocation of positions works best when it is regarded as only one of several procedures, each contributing to the same end, and when the classifying agency is ready to supplement that procedure—particularly in those cases where its inadequacies are apparent—by other methods of securing information.

[57] In some jurisdictions, distinctive forms are provided for filing requests for reconsideration of allocations. Such forms are in general similar to other position-description questionnaires, but include specifically a short statement of the procedure to be followed, a request for reasons why it is believed the position is erroneously allocated, and space for recommendation of the department. For example, Form 1395 of the Bridgeport Civil Service Commission includes the following item: "Give reasons why it is believed the position has been erroneously allocated. Cite class specification which it is believed applies; also cite other positions, preferably in the same department or division, which are considered comparable, if any." Form CL100 used by the New York State Civil Service Department, and P. C. B. Form 13 used by the U. S. Civil Service Commission are similar.

320 Position-Classification in the Public Service

Also, in an appeal or review procedure, the integrity of the classification plan and correct classification standards affecting the employee requesting the review and other employees must be maintained. The analysis of the position presented for review, its evaluation as to kind and level of work, the applicability of class specifications, the comparative analysis of other positions, the allocation of the position to its proper class, the propriety of establishing a new or changing an existing class, the determination of the characteristics of a new or changed class in relation to existing classes—are all technical questions which are embraced in deciding the action to be taken.

It goes without saying that classification decisions, whether rendered initially or on a request for review, should be made impartially with no regard for considerations other than the merits of the case as a problem in position-classification. Also, the review of a classification requires the same accuracy and completeness of facts, the same broad knowledge of the classes and their differentiating factors, and the same technical knowledge of position-analysis and position-classification as an original allocation. Hence, those who decide classification "appeals" should be as resistant to pressures, have the same responsibility toward the position-classification plan, law, and rules, and be technically as well qualified as those who make original allocations. A single decision may have far-reaching implications which may not always be appreciated by reviewers concerned primarily with the case before them. One of the first and most important lessons that any classification staff has to learn is that a classification plan is an integrated structure, all the parts of which are connected and deserve attention when a change is contemplated in any one of them. To the extent that this lesson is offset by a lowering of operating standards in an appeals procedure, the integrity of the whole plan may be seriously affected.

The appeals procedure, of course, should not be exclusively relied upon as a means of discovering the need for and making classification corrections. Frequently, only one position is presented for review, and unless other positions in the organization are likewise analyzed as to their places in the line of authority and the course of the flow of work, there is danger that through action upon one position the general balance of positions will be disturbed and that dissatisfaction on the part of others will result. Errors that would seriously disturb existing correct relationships may inadvertently be made because these relationships are not always discoverable through the interrogation of the employee and one or two witnesses who have a definite proposition on which they come prepared to convince the examiner.

In addition to these considerations, there is the important administrative item of time and expense. Emphasis on this point would seem to call for an avoidance of the techniques of formal judicial procedures. A mutual conference or informal hearing is preferable, in order to secure full and open discussion of pertinent facts and issues and correct unbiased decisions at a minimum of expense. In the larger jurisdictions, for example, a suitable procedure would resemble that described for adjusting allocation disagreements during the process of installing a position-classification plan.[58] In the smaller jurisdictions, an even less formal process should work as well.

CLASSIFICATION SURVEYS OR AUDITS

A procedure for periodic classification-audits is of prime importance in any extensive program of classification administration.

Experience has indicated that the classification agency should not rely exclusively upon the procedures previously outlined, in which the initiative rests with the operating departments or the employees.

Accordingly, in the endeavor to keep allocations of positions to classes correctly adjusted one to another, a classification agency should adopt as a major activity the making of follow-up surveys or classification-audits of all the positions in a predetermined group so as to determine the facts currently and make necessary classification adjustments. There is a general and an increasing appreciation of the soundness and satisfactoriness of this procedure. Administrative officials and groups of employees seem to prefer that, as far as is feasible, classification of positions be kept current by general surveys rather than by intermittent or sporadic reviews of individual positions. The classification-audit procedure is, in fact, fundamentally an organized and coordinated series of work-audits in which individual positions are studied at the same time, instead of intermittently at different times.

There are two kinds of classification-audits which are distinguished by their scope and nature; one is known as an "organiza-

[58] See pp. 237–39.

tional classification-audit" and the other as an "occupational classification-audit." An organizational classification-audit is one extending to every position, regardless of class or type, in a division, in a small or large bureau, or in an entire department or establishment. An occupational classification-audit, which is not confined necessarily within the organizational lines of one department or an independent establishment, covers all the positions in a given class, series of classes, or occupational group, in whatever departments or establishments they may be located.

The general purposes and objectives of a classification survey or audit are to study all the positions as they currently exist in a given organizational unit (i.e., division, bureau, department, or independent establishment) or in a given occupational class or group; to discover and correct any errors or inconsistencies in their allocations; to disclose any unreported changes of duties or responsibilities; and to provide a basis for any corrections or adjustments that may be found to be necessary in the classes, the class specifications, or the allocations of individual positions.

As contrasted with a procedure of dealing with positions one at a time at segregated intervals, there are decided advantages in the classification-audit. It is the most reliable method of obtaining all the facts. Difficulty is frequently encountered in securing comprehensive and accurate information about changes when departmental reports on individual positions are made at different times, because such reports seldom take into account the total effect of a given change. For example, an increase in the responsibilities of one position at the expense of other positions may be reported without indicating the positions from which those responsibilities have been taken.

Further, the classification-audit makes it possible more effectively to secure uniformity and correctness of relationships within and across departmental lines, because a simultaneous survey of related positions tends to avoid disturbing unknowingly the general balance of classification in a particular organization—a possibility which is always present when individual positions are dealt with at widely separated intervals.

The classification-audit tends to cure sources of trouble and friction by tackling problems whole and not piecemeal; and it is economical because it permits the classifier to handle at the same time problems which otherwise might come before the classifying agency one at a time and would necessitate going over the same ground more than once. Furthermore, a classification-audit frequently brings to light material changes in the duties and responsibilities of positions which have developed so gradually that the department itself was not aware of them.

Through classification-audits, the classification agency more effectively secures uniformity and coordination of classifications within and across departmental lines. There is developed a definiteness of knowledge on the part of the operating agencies, the employees, and the classification agency alike as to the proper relative classifications of all the positions in a given unit or in a given field of work. There are built up some thoroughly considered and deliberate classification precedents and standards, together with a background of facts that permits their use in other cases. By its very nature, the classification-audit serves as a valuable basis for maintaining classification standards and revising them when they are found to be in error. In particular, the occupational classification-audit furnishes the significant information required for the maintenance of intelligible and useful class specifications. These are important advantages accruing from the standpoint of classification administration. From the standpoint of the department as an operating agency, there oftentimes is another advantage that is being more and more appreciated. Sooner or later in a classification survey, every position is explored. When this occurs, and the findings of the investigator are made known to administrative officials, they frequently have unfolded before them evidence of duplication of work, overlapping of responsibility, or lack of coordination between functions, of which they had been unaware. These can be promptly corrected, but they might have continued indefinitely had not the organization been surveyed for classification purposes.[59]

Procedure for an Organizational Classification-Audit

While variations are sometimes necessary or desirable, the following procedure may be generally observed in conducting a large-scale organizational classification-audit:

1. The proper administrative officers are contacted as a preliminary to the survey, for the following purposes:
    a. To explain the purposes and methods of the survey so as to obtain their cooperation and understanding.

[59] See pp. 74–78.

b. To request them to distribute a notice (over the signature of the appropriate official) to all supervisors and employees, explaining the methods and objectives of the survey, and indicating their approval and desire for cooperation.

c. To make arrangements for preliminary group meetings of supervisors and employees, if convenient and desirable.

d. To discuss any special problems involved and especially any difficulties which the survey is expected to overcome.

e. To afford the department an opportunity to participate actively in the survey by assigning a qualified employee from its personnel office or elsewhere to work with the classification agency's representative.

f. To ascertain the most convenient sources of information regarding the development of the organization, its current functions and lines of authority, its organizational structure, the laws and regulations under which it operates, its appropriations and expenditures, and any other useful bibliographic information which is easily available.

g. To secure office space in the department's building as work and conference rooms.

2. Organization and function charts and schedules are then secured or prepared, indicating the specific activities of the various subdivisions of the organization, the number and classifications of existing positions, and the names of present incumbents.

3. After a brief study of organization charts and the flow of work through the various divisions, and after conferences with administrative officials, if necessary, the classifier decides upon the order in which the divisions can best be surveyed. Where feasible, the order usually adopted is that which follows the flow of work through the organization. As a general rule the survey begins with the positions in the lower brackets working toward the supervisory and administrative positions and those in the higher brackets in a given section or other subdivision of a division. Until the final study looking especially toward coordination of classifications is under way, work is concentrated on one subdivision at a time, and the classifier goes into other subdivisions concurrently only when inquiries as to lines of authority or flow of work make that necessary or when unforeseen delays in one subdivision require a temporary postponement.

4. In beginning active work, a foundation is laid as follows: It is explained to each supervisor that as a basis for interviews an informal questionnaire is to be distributed to himself and to each of his employees, and that this questionnaire is to be executed by the employee himself without consultation with his supervisor, who will later be given full opportunity to state and discuss the duties and responsibilities of each employee under his supervision. Further, it is explained to each person who is to execute such a questionnaire that he will be expected to deliver it directly to the classifier.

5. After laying the foundation so as to assure, as far as possible, freely expressed descriptions of duties, tasks, and responsibilities, the individual

questionnaires are distributed by the classifier, immediately after he explains their purpose to the individual employee concerned. On one typical questionnaire of this sort, the employee is requested to state in his own words:

  a. The different duties and tasks he performs and the proportion of time devoted to each, naming each task and describing it in detail.
  b. Any supervisory responsibility he bears, showing its character and extent, and the number of employees supervised and the classifications of their positions.
  c. Who his immediate supervisor is; who assigns work to him; who reviews his work, if anyone; and whose work he himself reviews, if anyone's.
  d. Whether he performs or reviews any work which is not approved or further reviewed by anyone else, describing any such work involved and the extent of his responsibility.
  e. Whether he receives advice and counsel from others in the course of his work, and, if so, from whom, the extent thereof, and to what features of his work it applies.
  f. How long he has been in his present assignment without material change of duties.
  g. Any positions he may know of which are similar or comparable to his own.

These questionnaires are made up by the classifier himself purely for his own convenience and will vary to suit the particular circumstances or positions under consideration. They are work-papers and are not given any official status other than that of a communication passing from the employee to the classifier.

6. After the employees turn in the questionnaires, the classifier compares them with the descriptions of the positions as contained in the classification agency's files and as supplemented by reports, and notes for study any differences either of changes in assignment or of changes in methods of performing work or in responsibility assumed. This is, of course, the principal method of discovering unreported changes in assignments or unreported advances or depreciations in duties and responsibilities.

7. The questionnaires submitted by employees in a given subdivision or division are further examined to determine continuity or flow of work, or similarity of assignments, for the purpose of determining the order in which the positions will be taken up and discussed in the classifier's report.

8. An employee is then interviewed at his desk or place of work where the performance of his work is observed and where typical samples or exhibits of his work are obtained. Other employees holding related positions are usually then interviewed and exhibits of their work are obtained before any analysis of the positions is undertaken. If exaggerations, inconsistencies, misunderstanding of facts, disparagements or disputes as to work performed or extent of responsibility arise or exist, the classifier usually first discusses the matter with the employees concerned and then with their

supervisors, at which latter interviews the employees concerned are also present. These discussions are for the purpose of definitely determining the duties and responsibilities of the particular positions.

9. After the classifier has determined the facts, he prepares a statement in his own words describing, in as understandable a fashion as possible, the employee's duties and responsibilities. He discusses this statement with the employee concerned, who is requested to sign it if it meets with his approval as a true statement of fact, or to suggest changes if it does not. After it is signed by the employee, it is submitted to the supervisor for approval and signature. If the employee or his supervisor differs radically with the classifier, or desires changes to be made which the classifier knows are not in accordance with the facts as he has found them, he proceeds to reconcile such differences through higher administrative channels, chiefly because the disputed points involve for the most part either matters of delegation of responsibility or the form of organization.

In most cases, as a result of discussions across the table participated in by the classifier, the employee, and his supervisor, necessary revisions are made and a mutually satisfactory statement of the employee's duties and responsibilities is finally agreed to in writing.

Up to this point the effort of the classifier has been confined to getting all the facts, and he has refrained, as far as possible, from discussing what the proper classification of the position is to be.

10. These statements of duties and responsibilities, after being agreed to as a statement of fact, are, if necessary, referred to the official whose duty it is to prepare official position-description forms, and to make for the department the official recommendation as to the classification of the position. Almost invariably he uses this material verbatim in preparing the official position-description. *

11. The classifier now proceeds to make an analytical study of the various positions with a view to recommending the proper classification of each one in respect to these relationships:

    a. The relation of its duties and responsibilities to the functions and the structure of the organization in which it is located.

    b. The relation of its duties and responsibilities to those of other positions in the same organization.

    c. Its similarity to or divergence from other positions in the same field of work in the same or another organization.

These aspects of relationship are, of course, extremely important.

12. After the classifier completes this study, and before submitting his report, he conducts conferences with the officials of the organization, at which time they are informed of his tentative conclusions as to the proper classification of the various positions and are given an opportunity to present their views as to their concurrence or disagreement with such conclusions.[60]

---

[60] It is always good practice, during either a classification survey or the work-audit of an individual position, to give the department and the employee an opportunity to discuss the matter and be heard in case a change of classification seems to be called for. This is important in the case of a contemplated lowering of the allocation of the position of the employee, for it gives ample notice of the

13. The classifier then prepares his official survey report, with appropriate introductory and background information; organization charts; descriptions of the functions of organization units; the statements of duties and responsibilities of individual positions as mutually agreed to by the department, the employee, and the classifier; analysis of these duties and responsibilities; comparisons of positions; comments and application of class specifications and classification principles; and appropriate recommendations made by the classifier to the head of the classifying agency with regard to each position, showing whether in his judgment the existing classification of the position is correct or whether it should be changed. This is done in sufficient detail and the whole report sufficiently indexed so that a permanent record of the material facts will be available and so that a thorough review of the classifier's findings and recommendations can be made.

Procedure for an Occupational Classification-Audit

As previously indicated, an occupational classification-audit is selective as to types of work. It covers all positions in a given class, series of classes, or occupational group, in whatever departments or agencies they may be located.

The distinctive additional advantages of this type of survey are (a) the unusual opportunity it affords for reviewing the characteristics and differentiating factors of classes of positions across organizational lines; (b) the consequent improvement of class specifications that should result; and (c) the relative ease with which, in such surveys, the classification agency can secure the cooperation of employee or other groups the members of which have a common professional technical or occupational interest.

In conducting an audit of this type, much of the procedure for organizational classification-audits previously set forth will be applicable. The chief differences are that contacts and arrangements are made with administrative and supervisory officials and with employees usually in more than one department; only those supervisors or employees are interviewed who supervise or perform work in the occupational area to be covered; and generally a specialized form of position-description questionnaire may be employed.

The scope of an occupational classification-audit, therefore, is not automatically determined by organizational lines, as in the case

---

action to be taken and enables him to offer facts in rebuttal. If that is not successful, time still remains for the department, if otherwise desirable and possible, to assign him to a position of the same classification as his present position, or one of equal classification. For a case study of this situation, see Committee on Public Administration of the Social Science Research Council, *Case Reports in Public Administration*, No. 29 (Chicago: Public Administration Service, 1940).

of an organizational classification-audit, but it is a question for the classification agency to decide. In reaching this decision, it is well to include all series of classes having analogous problems or whose lines of separation may be difficult to apply in some individual cases.[61]

After decision has been reached as to the occupational scope to be covered, a master control list is prepared from the allocation records showing the coverage of the proposed survey in terms of names of employees and current classifications of their positions. For convenience, this list is broken down into subsidiary control lists, one for each organization and subdivision. Through such lists the classifier will be guided in arranging for and conducting interviews and in the distribution of special or other questionnaires.

The practical difficulty of using specialized questionnaires in original surveys has been mentioned.[62] However, the conditions surrounding the continuous administration of a position-classification plan stand in sharp contrast to the situation in which an original developmental survey is usually conducted in that the factors permitting the intelligent preparation and effective use of such questionnaires are usually present. The occupational area to be covered by an audit or resurvey of an occupationally homogeneous group of positions can be administratively determined. Facts about the duties and responsibilities of the positions in this area are already a matter of record. Some or much work has already been done by the classification staff in establishing allocation factors of the occupations involved.

Although specialized questionnaires are not common, the use of such questionnaires can be developed into a valuable technique where the number of positions and the difficulties encountered warrant the work of devising a suitable form.[63]

---

[61] For example, if stenographic classes are to be covered, typists classes should also be included. In general, it should be recognized that since the series of classes covered in an occupational classification-audit is not usually wide, special attention has to be paid in the final analysis to the relationship between the classes in the occupational area covered and the classes in occupational areas not covered by the survey.

[62] Pp. 172–73.

[63] Questionnaires of this type have been used, for example, in a survey of library positions by the American Library Association in cooperation with the Bureau of Public Personnel Administration (1924); in a survey of the U. S. Immigration and Naturalization Service by the Department of Labor (1938); and in a survey of Post Office Inspector positions made by the U. S. Civil Service Commission in cooperation with the Post Office Department (Form 546, January 1936).

Some of the advantages of the use of properly constructed specialized position-description questionnaires are as follows:

1. In comparison with a general questionnaire fitting all kinds of positions, the information secured would be more complete and pertinent. The questionnaire itself helps the employee to know what kinds of facts are significant. This partly compensates for the usual inability of the employee to pick out the significant things about his position as well as skilled analysts can do. The employee's task in executing the questionnaire is that of reporting rather than one of analysis.

2. The information obtained is channelized along certain definite lines needed for the allocation of positions, the determination of classes, and the writing of class specifications. It is presented in a form which is more readily analyzed by the classifier.

3. To the extent that definite and complete information is obtained, there is less necessity for interviews with employees, and even in such interviews the time required is materially shortened.

4. A specialized form also has advantages from an employee relations and educational standpoint. It is a uniform approach which recognizes the distinctive character of the group. Designed in terms of the duties and responsibilities of the positions to be covered, it appeals to employees more than does a generally worded form. They naturally would have a greater sense of confidence that they will be able to furnish the kind of detailed information that is necessary. It also helps to convince them that there is full appreciation of the technical aspects of their positions and hence that their duties are susceptible to the classification process.

5. Where, on the specialized questionnaire, the questions lead from the most elementary to the most difficult work, employees become quickly appreciative of the range of difficulty and responsibility in their occupation, which is a distinct aid to them in understanding the classification factors and problems involved. Further, the arrangement of items should tend to show employees at various levels that there is even more difficult or responsible work in their fields. This aids employees in appreciating that more is involved in a survey than the allocations of their own positions.[64]

[64] "Such questions demonstrate to employees that even in engineering positions there are tangible tasks of such nature as to permit appropriate grading. They also demonstrate that in the preparation of the form there was an intimate knowledge of what is, in general, actually involved in these engineering positions. Enough specific questions can be included so that the employee need not feel apprehension from uncertainty and misunderstanding of the nature of informa-

CIVIL-SERVICE PROBLEMS OF CLASSIFICATION ADMINISTRATION

In the administration of a position-classification plan one of the troublesome matters upon which classification activities and testing laws and rules need to be smoothly correlated has to do with the status of an employee whose position is reallocated from a class for which he has qualified to a class for which he has not qualified.[65] Such matters are particularly perplexing where formal competitive promotion tests are required by basic law. In some cases the employee may have actually, although gradually, caused the change of allocation through his influence upon the duties and responsibilities of his position. In others it may have been the demonstration of ability in the service that has led naturally to higher assignments. In the eyes of the employee and his supervisor, it is unreasonable to make retention of the employee in the position of the new class dependent upon the passing of formal competitive tests, particularly when the actual facts in the case are that the employee has been performing the duties of the position satisfactorily for some time.[66]

It has been previously pointed out that in personnel administration the concept of a position is distinct from the concept of an employee. The process of classification is a classification of positions, and not a classification of the employees occupying them. Hence, when positions are created or changed, it is the function of the classification agency to allocate or reallocate them to their appropriate classes. However, the question of who shall occupy or continue to occupy the position, and the question of whether the employee occupying it, or about to occupy it, is qualified to perform the duties and exercise the responsibilities of the position are matters for the

---

tion desired. The use of such a form relieves the engineer from the necessity of preparing a descriptive composition at which he may not feel particularly adept. These factors create in the minds of the employees a greater degree of receptiveness to the proposition of grading their jobs." Robert H. Kirkwood, Associate AIEE, Tennessee Valley Authority, *Grading the Engineer's Job* (New York: American Institute of Electrical Engineers, 1938), p. 6.

[65] This problem is an excellent illustration of the necessity of regarding position-classification as a tool for the accomplishment of personnel transactions, and not as a personnel transaction itself. It emphasizes that the classification process does not carry the whole burden of personnel administration as applied to the advancement of employees, and that the reallocation of positions is no substitute for the important personnel transaction of promotion.

[66] Of course, the operating department has the alternative of reassigning the employees to duties and responsibilities falling within classes for which they already possess an appropriate civil service status, but this is generally unsatisfactory from the operating officers' and the employees' standpoints.

consideration of the operating department and the testing unit of the personnel agency, under the law and rules governing such matters.

The situation with respect to the civil service status of incumbents at the time of putting a classification plan initially into effect has previously been discussed.[67] This should be distinguished from that which exists afterwards, during the course of administration of the classification plan, when it is found that an occupied position has been reallocated to a class for which the incumbent, according to testing rules, has never qualified. The time of installation is a transition from an unstandardized and unsystematic condition to a controlled, standardized classification. However, when the transition period is ended, it is to be expected that tests and the service status of employees shall correspond to what is required in the positions held; and that therefore changes of employees from a position in one class to a position in another class shall be made only in accordance with testing requirements based on the classification plan.

After the classification plan has been placed in operation, reallocations may be divided into the following categories for the purpose of determining the status of an employee whose position is reallocated to a class higher than any class for which he has qualified:

1. A reallocation to correct an error which was made when the classification plan was installed.

2. A reallocation to correct an error or to conform to a changed standard on the part of the classifying agency, the original allocation having been made at some time subsequent to the installation, the employee having been appointed to the position or promoted or transferred to it after the classification plan had been put into effect, no change in duties or responsibilities having been involved.

3. A reallocation based on new or additional duties and responsibilities which may have developed gradually or may have been more formally assigned to the employee by his supervisor as a part of a definite work-plan.

In the first type of case it is equitable that, since the reallocation was for the purpose of correcting an error in the original installation, the employee should have the same status as if his position had been correctly allocated initially and should, therefore, be subject

[67] Pp. 241–44.

to the procedure (preferably continuance in the position without formal test) which would have been applied at the time of installation.

In the second type of case, the employee was placed in the position in accordance with test requirements based on an allocation deemed at the time to be correct. The fact that this allocation later turned out to be incorrect or was changed to conform to a change of allocation standards, should not, when the allocation is corrected or adjusted to new standards, result in the employee's taking formal tests again, especially in competition with others. Equity demands, too, that his existing status be continued in the reallocated position.

The situation is different, however, in the third type of case. Here a reallocation becomes necessary because of the assignment to an employee of additional or new duties and responsibilities calling for a higher allocation of the position. In such case, what has in fact happened is that a new position has been created in a different class and that the employee has been placed in such new position without the approval of the personnel agency, and usually without its knowledge. Such procedure, if allowed to. persist uncontrolled, would encourage unreported changes of duties, followed by reallocations, as a procedure for circumventing promotional regulations. Consequently, it is essential for the personnel agency to maintain control.[68]

Initially, the status of an employee who is found to be occupying a position which warrants a reallocation to a different class, and who has not qualified therefor according to the rules of the personnel agency, may be regarded as no different from that of an employee occupying a position in a certain class and proposed for promotion to a vacant position in a different class. Depending on the reason for the reallocation, the sudden or gradual character of the change of duties, the nature and extent of such change, or other factors, the personnel agency should be authorized, in its discretion, either (a) to require the employee to qualify formally in accordance with existing promotional procedures and tests, or (b) to modify the

[68] The pertinent observation has been made that the seriousness of this problem in a given jurisdiction could be lessened (a) by furnishing the central classification agency with adequate staff facilities so that through current scrutiny of changes of duties and responsibilities the effect of such changes on the civil service status of the individual can be made a matter of prompt attention; and (b) by the intelligent and prompt cooperation of appointing powers and employees in reporting to the personnel agency all major changes in assignment which are likely to extend over a period of time. California State Personnel Board, *Thirteenth Biennial Report* (1936–38), p. 17.

formalities of such procedure where the equities of the situation warrant. Such authority would permit noncompetitive promotion procedures in proper cases.

It should be recognized, of course, that the possibility of placing a policy like this into effect depends not only upon the current rules of the personnel agency and the possibility of amending them, but also upon the basic law governing its activities. In some jurisdictions the civil service law will, in promotion cases, permit the personnel agency to substitute other methods for competitive promotion examinations. In this event, the agency may, through the adoption of a special rule approved by appropriate authority, utilize investigations, hearings, noncompetitive tests, or the submission of written evidence in adjusting an employee's status to that required for his position as reallocated. A special rule of this type is particularly appropriate when there is nothing in the facts to indicate that there was any deliberate effort to avoid or violate a civil service rule, and when the reallocation is due to a correction of a classification error, a change in classification standards, or a change in the duties or responsibilities of a position representing a perfectly natural growth over a long period.

In other jurisdictions, formal tests, frequently competitive, are always required if the class to which the position is reallocated has a higher maximum salary rate than the class to which the position existed before it was reallocated, regardless of whether the reallocation was made to correct an error or to recognize a change in assignment.

There are, in fact, some jurisdictions in which the basic personnel law requires the orderly processes of promotional examinations in cases where positions have been reallocated because of a change in duties and responsibilities, leaving little, if any, discretion to the personnel agency to follow any other course.[69] Obviously, if it desires such discretion, the remedy is to change the basic law. This may be a matter of considerable difficulty, particularly where the merit system is founded on a charter or constitutional provision requiring that promotions, as well as appointments, shall be based upon merit and fitness as ascertained by competitive examination.

In the State of California in a recent case a group of employees appealed to the courts from the decision of the State Personnel Board

[69] Note also that in some jurisdictions the civil service rules prohibit reallocations when they would directly or indirectly result in a promotion contrary to statutory or charter provisions.

denying an appropriate civil service status without examination to employees whose positions had been reallocated on the basis of different and higher duties assigned after appointment. The court said:[70]

> It cannot be held that the sections on classification above referred to [sections 63 and 64 of the Act] were placed in the Civil Service Act for the purpose of giving civil service employees status in positions higher than those for which they were examined. If the appointing power could, by assigning duties of a higher nature to an employee, and the State Personnel Board could, by classifying those duties to a higher class than that of the employee's original position, give to an employee a permanent civil service status, the entire fabric of the civil service system would fail. Promotions and appointments in civil service would then no longer be made exclusively under a general system based on merit, efficiency, and fitness, as ascertained by competitive examination.

Equally troublesome, if not more so, are instances in which an employee's position is reallocated downward. Where this is attributable to his own deficiencies or his inability to perform work or discharge responsibilities assigned to him, the procedure relating to demotions for inefficiency is applicable. In other instances, the employee's status may be preserved by promoting or transferring him to another position conforming to his civil service status and equaling in rank that held before reallocation. For this purpose he may be placed on a preferred list to fill appropriate vacancies as they occur. Every effort to preserve his status by transfer or promotion is warranted where the reallocation is to correct an error on the part of the classification agency or is caused by a redistribution of work or responsibility in an organization unit.[71]

One of the latest rules governing the status of incumbents when their positions are reallocated is as follows:[72]

> Whenever new positions are authorized and created, when the duties and responsibilities of existing positions change, or when the classification plan is amended, the Director shall allocate or reallocate the affected positions in the same manner as the original allocations are made. When the classification or allocation of a position is changed in accordance with this Rule and the new status of the position is approximately equal to its former status, the Director may approve the transfer of the incumbent of the posi-

[70] *Elsie Pinion et al* v. *State Personnel Board,* 29 Cal. App. 2d, 314, cited in California State Personnel Board, *Thirteenth Biennial Report,* p. 16.

[71] The pay plan may in such cases justifiably authorize continuation of the employee's salary in the meantime.

[72] State of Rhode Island . . . , Section 6 of Rule IV, Rules Approved by the Governor, December 20, 1939.

tion in its former status to the position in its new status. When the new status of such a position is higher than the former status, the Director may, in his discretion, approve the reallocation of the incumbent of the position in its former status to the position in its new status after such investigation as the Director deems necessary, which may include a noncompetitive examination of the same degree of difficulty as an open competitive examination for the same class.

Appendix A

Position—Description Questionnaire Forms and Instructions

Suggestions and Instructions to Employees for Filling Out Item No. 23 of the Field Questionnaire (P. C. B. Form No. 14)[1]

PERSONNEL CLASSIFICATION BOARD,

Washington, July 2, 1928.

The act of May 28, 1928, requires the Personnel Classification Board to make a survey of positions in the field services, excluding certain groups, and to make a report to Congress at its next session which shall contain, among other things, adequate descriptions of all the classes of positions within the scope of this act, including a statement of the characteristic duties and responsibilities of each such class, illustrated where desirable by examples of typical tasks or of typical positions included in the class.

It is essential therefore that the board be furnished with adequate, accurate, and detailed information as to the duties and responsibilities of your position.

To write a good description of one's work is oftentimes rather difficult. For this reason it is suggested that you compose your statement on a separate sheet of paper and review it critically in the light of these instructions before typing it on the questionnaire.

Certain viewpoints and suggestions are offered below to help you in preparing a good statement of your duties and responsibilities.

1. Item 23 of the questionnaire asks you to describe in detail the work you do. It is a most important item. Go into detail. If you have not space enough on the questionnaire for all your answer type it on a separate sheet, label it "Item 23," and paste it to the upper edge of the questionnaire at the back.

2. Do not use broad general terms without explanation; they are not definite. Try to give a specific and concrete picture of your work, so that one unacquainted with it may from your description visualize it truly and accurately; or if it is one that requires professional, scientific, or technical training, describe it so that another medical officer, another chemist, or another engineer will be able to understand the characteristics of the position. Imagine that you are "breaking-in" a new man of adequate qualifications and that you are giving him his first information concerning the duties of the job.

3. Make your statement plain. What is wanted is a description, not an appraisal through the use of such purely relative adjectives as difficult, important, complex, etc. The use of these adjectives is of no value to the board. It is more essential to set forth what you do that you regard as a difficult, important, or complex task or duty.

4. USE YOUR OWN WORDS; MAKE AN ORIGINAL AND INDEPENDENT STATEMENT. Do not copy expressions from the classification act or from the act of May 28, 1928, or from class specifications issued by the board. Descriptions of individual positions must necessarily be more specific and definite

---

[1] *Personnel Classification Board Form No. 15, prepared to accompany P. C. B. Form No. 14, shown in Figure 1, following page 342.*

than descriptions of grades or classes of positions which are given in broad terms so as to include many individual positions. Do not collaborate with others in your office or station doing similar work in the effort to present uniform descriptions under the belief that this assists the board. On the contrary, several original descriptions taken together generally give a better picture of the position than one description prepared by one person or by several in conference.

5. Here are suggestions for certain kinds of work. Read them, even if you do not do that kind of work, because they may help to suggest the points you should cover in describing your own work.

(*a*) For example, if you are a stenographer, it is not sufficient for you to state: "I take dictation and transcribe my notes." What kind of dictation—correspondence, reports, informal conferences, formal hearings? What subject matter—general administrative, medical, engineering, legal, or what? What is the official position of such officers or employees as dictate to you? Do you have occasion to compose your own letters? How often? In what kinds of cases? Do you do any clerical or secretarial work? Exactly what are these clerical or secretarial tasks? How much of your working time is devoted thereto? Describe them in as much detail as your stenographic duties. If your position requires you to have unusual speed and accuracy as a stenographer, so state and tell why.

(*b*) If you are an inspector it is not sufficient to say: "I assist in the enforcement of the —— act (whatever it may be) by making inspections and reports." Where do you go to make an inspection? Whom do you make contact with? What do you inspect? What precise tasks constitute an inspection? What is the purpose of your inspection? What do you look for? What points are you supposed to cover in your report? Do you make a report on a prescribed form by filling in blanks or in a prescribed manner, or do you organize and prepare your material on your own initiative and dictate it to a stenographer? To whom do you present your report? What happens to it after that? If your report establishes the existence of some violation or the absence of some requirement, what steps are taken on the basis thereof? Do you have anything to do with these subsequent steps? If so, precisely what?

(*c*) If you are engaged on part of a regular method or process, others being engaged on prior and subsequent steps of the same flow of work, your description of duties should be such that the board will gain therefrom a clear idea of (1) the relationship of your job to the entire method or process, (2) the type of material or data you work with or from, (3) the procedure you follow in the performance of your work, and (4) what the work is like when it leaves your hands.

(*d*) If you are an administrative official, the description of your work will naturally be broader than otherwise. In such cases a satisfactory answer to item 23 can be prepared by considering replies to such questions as the following:

(1) What functions do you direct, supervise, and control?

(2) What part do you play in the formulation and development of operating plans, programs, methods, and policies?

(3) Upon what types of problems do you make decisions that do not require higher approval and that generally are unreviewed?

(4) Upon what matters do you generally have only recommendatory authority?

(5) Over what geographical territory do you have administrative jurisdiction?

(6) Give some indication of the size of your establishment by showing such facts as the number of your assistants and subordinates, the annual amount of receipts, disbursements, collections, or other figure or figures that will serve as an index.

(7) With what other administrators, public or private, do you make contact in carrying out your work? For what purposes?

6. Do not use such rather loose and indefinite expressions as "I assist in ———" or "I handle correspondence in connection with ———," without explaining just what you do when you assist and just what you do when you handle correspondence. The fact that you assist in doing a certain thing shows the purpose of your work, but it does not show exactly what you do. Obviously there are a great many ways of assisting in a given project. Similarly, an executive, a stenographer, a typist, a messenger, a mailing clerk, a file clerk may all "handle correspondence" each in his own way. In the case of an employee who dictates, or writes rough drafts for, or types correspondence, it is essential to show what the class of correspondence is, what the employee does in order to get the information required to answer the letter, what sort of review or approval the letter requires, and other facts that will indicate the degree of independence with which the letter is composed and the subsequent review or check to which it is subjected.

7. Sometimes the best way to make the duties statement clear is to use typical tasks as illustrations. Avoid the unusual or exceptional task that occurs once in a lifetime as it can not serve as the basis for classification. The tasks used as illustrations should be such as are typical of the duties occurring time and time again. Do not be reluctant to give specific tasks merely because you believe that it is common knowledge that they are part of the duties of your position. For example, a graduate nurse in describing her work ought to specify that she takes and records temperatures, administers prescribed medicines, changes dressings, makes beds, etc.

8. Sometimes it is helpful to think of your work as requiring you to accomplish certain major objectives or tasks. In all but the simplest jobs, these major objectives are accomplished through lesser or contributing tasks. This process of dividing each task into its contributing tasks can obviously be carried out to a ridiculous point; for example, the opening and closing of a file case are tasks which contribute to the objective of filing a paper. Naturally, the board is not interested in such minute tasks as those; but it suggests that in writing your description you consider all the contributing tasks that go to make up a given objective, and if these tasks are the sort of work that you would include in describing your work to a fellow employee or an employee in the same line of activity, incorporate descriptions of them in your statement, showing their relation to the major objective to which they contribute.

9. In the column at the left of the space provided on the questionnaire for item 23 you are asked to show the percentage of your time given to your different duties. Everyone understands that ordinarily you can not distribute your time exactly. Give your best estimate.

10. Your answer to item 23 should be typewritten.

11. Try to put on paper the best possible picture of your job. Your co-operation in preparing a carefully and thoroughly considered statement will be appreciated.

Suggestions and Instructions to Supervisory or Administrative Officers for Filling Out the Field Questionnaire (P. C. B. Form No. 14)[2]

PERSONNEL CLASSIFICATION BOARD,
Washington, July 2, 1928.

NOTE.—Suggestions and instructions to employees for filling out question 23 of P. C. B. Form No. 14 are given in a separate circular designated as P. C. B. Form No. 15.

The act of May 28, 1928, requires the Personnel Classification Board to make a survey of classes of positions in the field services of the Government (with certain exclusions) and to make a report to Congress at its next regular session, containing compensation schedules covering such classes; adequate descriptions of such classes, including the title of each class established by the board, a statement of its characteristic duties and responsibilities, and a statement of the minimum qualifications as to education, experience, knowledge, and ability required; allocation lists; recommendations as to principles and procedures for the administration of the classification and compensation plans; and such statistical or other information as may be necessary or desirable in exposition of the board's findings and recommendations.

In order to carry out this task, it is essential that the board secure definite and reliable information concerning the duties and responsibilities of positions and certain data for statistical purposes. The items upon which information is desired are stated on the field questionnaire, P. C. B. Form No. 14.

EMPLOYEES TO BE REPORTED

Personnel Classification Board Form No. 14 will be filled out for all civilian officers and employees in the various field services of the Government, except the following:

A. Officers and employees of the Postal Service.

B. Officers and employees of the Foreign Service of the State Department.

C. Employees in mechanical or manual groups whose wages are now or

[2] *Personnel Classification Board Form No. 16, prepared to accompany P. C. B. Form No. 14, shown in Figure 1, following page 342.*

have heretofore been adjusted from time to time by wage boards or other administrative authority serving the same purpose, after an investigation and application of rates for like service prevailing in the locality, including—

(*a*) Employees holding positions the duties of which are to perform or assist in apprentice, helper, or journeyman work in a recognized trade or craft, when such employees are paid at hourly or daily rates adjusted from time to time in accordance with commercial or trade scales and practices prevailing in the locality.

(*b*) Laborers, whether skilled or unskilled, paid at hourly or daily rates adjusted from time to time in accordance with commercial or trade scales and practices prevailing in the locality.

(*c*) Emergency or seasonal employees hired on a temporary basis at rates adjusted from time to time in accordance with industrial rates prevailing in the locality.

D. Employees in drafting groups whose wages are now or have heretofore been adjusted from time to time by wage boards or other administrative authority serving the same purpose, after an investigation and application of rates for like service prevailing in the locality.

Questionnaires will be submitted for all civilian positions not specifically and expressly excepted above.

Questionnaires will likewise be submitted for regular positions temporarily vacant. See instructions herein under item 1.

PREPARATION OF THE QUESTIONNAIRES

All items, except those allotted to signatures, are to be filled in by typewriting. The signatures on the white (original) copy of the questionnaire should be made in ink. Those on the buff and pink copies may be made in ink or in typewriting, whichever is found more convenient. The questionnaire requires four signatures—that of the employee (item 24), that of the preparing officer (item 27), that of the head of the field office or station (item 28), and that of the head of the bureau or his representative (item 29).

The items on the questionnaire, except Nos. 1–11, 23, 24, 28, and 29, are intended to be answered by supervisory officers or employees, spoken of as "preparing officers," to be designated by the head of the field office or establishment. Nos. 1–11 are more conveniently filled in by the administrative and pay-roll office of the field station (or in a few instances by the department in Washington). No. 23 is to be answered by the employee. Nos. 24, 28, and 29 are certificates to be signed, respectively, by the employee, by the head of the field office or station, and by the head of the bureau or his representative.

Some items require reference to official personnel records. Others—particularly those relating to the duties and responsibilities of the position (especially items 17, 18, 19, and 25)—are to be answered from the personal knowledge of the preparing officer.

Accordingly, in any individual instance, the preparing officer should be one who has intimate knowledge of the work of the employee, and therefore preferably should be the employee's immediate superior. There will thus be several preparing officers in any sizable field establishment.

Employees should be consulted for information personal to them which is not officially of record.

The questionnaire will be printed in three colors—white (original), buff (first carbon copy), and pink (subsequent carbon copies). The white and buff copies are to be submitted to the board. The pink copy or copies are intended for the files of the field office or station and the department. Invoices are also to be made as directed later herein, corresponding in number to the number of sets of questionnaires.

The following suggestion of a method of distributing or routing the questionnaires is offered:

1. The administrative and pay-roll office, upon receipt of the blank questionnaires, will number them in series, separate series of numbers, beginning with 1, being used for each substation, large office section, or other separate administrative subdivision under the jurisdiction of the field office or station. So far as possible, it is desired that this numbering correspond to the form of organization of the field office or station. It is suggested that this end can be accomplished by preparing a preliminary control list of the personnel and regular vacant positions in organization order. The sheet numbers may be entered on this control list and transferred to the questionnaires. This list will then serve as a check upon the distribution and return of the questionnaires within the field establishment, and also as a basic draft for the invoice which the board requests shall accompany the completed questionnaires. (See instructions and sample invoice given later herein under the heading, "Transmission of completed questionnaires," etc.) These numbers should be entered on the line designated "Sheet No. ——." The space for a "Bureau No." is provided for the convenience of the department.

2. The administrative and pay-roll office should fill out items 1 to 11, inclusive. (In case of doubt, items 5 (*b*) and 7 may be left to the preparing officers.)

3. The questionnaire then may be routed to the employee, together with a copy of P. C. B. Form No. 15, for preparing the statement of his duties asked for in item 23. After this is typed on the questionnaire, the employee will sign item 24. If the official records do not contain adequate information as to the employee's education and experience, or if it will expedite matters, he should also be requested to fill out items 21 and 22. *It is essential that the employee be furnished with P. C. B. Form No. 15, and that he be requested to digest it thoroughly before composing his answer to item 23.*

4. The questionnaire then should go to the appropriate preparing officer, who should fill out all the remaining items except Nos. 28 and 29.

5. The head of the field office or station will then examine the questionnaires and execute the certificate contained in item No. 28. He will then direct the preparation of invoices in accordance with the instructions given later herein, and forward questionnaires and invoices through customary channels to the appropriate departmental office in Washington.

6. When the questionnaires and invoices are received in Washington, the head of the bureau or a representative designated by him will examine the questionnaires, sign the certificate contained in item No. 29, and forward the original copy (white) and first carbon copy (buff) of the questionnaires, together with invoices in duplicate, through customary departmental channels to the board.

DETAILED INSTRUCTIONS FOR GIVING THE INFORMATION CALLED FOR BY
THE NUMBERED ITEMS ON FORM NO. 14

Item 1.—Give the name of the employee as it appears on the pay roll, with the surname first, then the given name, and then the middle initial or initials, if any.

If the position in question is temporarily vacant, submit a questionnaire for it with the word "Vacant" given in answer to item 1, provided that it is a regularly authorized position and that steps are being taken to fill it in the near future. Do not submit questionnaires at this time for positions that have not as yet been officially created.

Item 2.—Give the name of the executive department or independent establishment, as Agriculture, Interior, Veterans' Bureau, Interstate Commerce Commission.

Item 3.—Give the name of the bureau or corresponding unit of the department, as Animal Industry, Mint, Internal Revenue, Aeronautics, Quartermaster General.

Item 4.—Give the name of the particular branch of the bureau or of the particular field subdivision of the department, as Immigration Service, Indian Service, Steamboat Inspection Service, Quartermaster Corps.

Item 5.—Under (*a*) give the name of the particular local unit or field office having jurisdiction of the employee's work, as Veterans' Bureau Hospital No. 23, Pine Ridge Indian School, Office of Collector of Internal Revenue, Arlington Experimental Farm, Headquarters Ninth Corps Area.

Under (*b*) give the name of the suboffice, section, division, or other subdivision of the field station to which the employee is assigned, as supply depot, office of chief field deputy, inspection division, administrative subdivision.

Under (*c*) give the location of the employee's official station or headquarters.

Item 6.—Give the employee's title as it appears on the pay roll.

Item 7.—Give the customary descriptive, occupational, or organizational name of the position in which the employee is actually working, as stenographer, file clerk, chief of land section, supervising field clerk, engineer in charge. This designation will not necessarily correspond with the employee's pay-roll title.

Item 8.—If, in carrying out the provisions of section 3 of the act of May 28, 1928, or in its general administration of personnel matters, the department has made a record of the present administrative allocation of the position to a compensation range, give the range, as $1,440–$1,740.

This item, it will be observed, presupposes an administrative allocation and a record thereof. Its purpose is to elicit such record as exists of the present administrative allocation of the position, and the item should not be understood to call for a recommendation. (Cf. items 28 and 29.)

Item 9.—Give the employee's gross compensation, including the value of any allowances, whether per day, per month, or per year. The term "allowances" refers to such items as are given in item 12. It does not include traveling expenses or per diem in lieu of subsistence while in a travel status.

Item 10.—Give the total amount of any allowances, which is deducted from the employee's gross compensation in computing his net cash salary.

Item 11.—Give the rate of compensation paid to the employee in cash, after deducting the total value of allowances from his gross compensation.

Items 9, 10, and 11 should, of course, be arithmetically consistent.

Item 12.—Make the proper indication of allowances, if any. Do not report per diem in lieu of subsistence or actual expenses incurred and reimbursed while in a travel status.

Item 13.—Indicate the kind and estimated annual value of any allowance not specifically covered in item 12.

Item 14.—Indicate whether the employee is required to furnish a bond at his own expense, and, if so, the annual amount of the premium.

Also indicate such special equipment as the employee is required by law or by regulation to furnish at his own expense, as automobile, horse, motor cycle, uniform, etc. Where the life of such equipment is longer than one year, distribute the initial cost over the life of the equipment and give an approximate annual maintenance cost, which should include a reasonable allowance for depreciation as well as the actual expense for maintenance.

Item 15.—Under (a) give the time fixed by regulation for beginning and ending work on the ordinary week day.

Under (b) give the total number of hours per week required by regulation, exclusive of unusual or irregular overtime work, during the summer and during the winter.

If the position is a part-time position, or if it does not require duty all the year round—i. e., if the employee is required to work less than the regular number of hours per day or per week or less than 12 months in the year—state the number of hours per day and the number of days per week, month, or year, whichever most clearly shows the part-time or seasonal character of the position, striking out two of the words "week," "month," "year," which are not applicable.

If in addition to regular hours of work as given in 15 (a), the employee is required to remain on duty, subject to call, for a prescribed overtime period, state the time of beginning and ending such overtime availability, and the type of duty, as driving ambulance, making blood counts, etc.

Item 16.—If the employee is paid for overtime, state the overtime rate under (a). Under (b) give the approximate amount of overtime pay earned by the employee during the last 12 months.

Item 17.—Under (a) show whether the employee directs or supervises others. Do not answer "Yes" to this question if the employee is *merely* a reviewer or checker of the work of others. The question contemplates such duties as involve a degree of control of subordinates and responsibility for the results or products of their work.

If the answer to (a) is "Yes," explain in answer to (b) in just what way and to what degree the employee directs or supervises others; and state in answer to (c) how many persons are under the supervision of the employee.

The answer to item 17 (b) should be a statement of the principal tasks the employee performs which are of a supervisory or administrative nature and which show his official relationship and responsibility with respect to the work of the persons he or she supervises. The following supervisory tasks which are often encountered are given as illustrations:

(a) Assigns regular work (or special tasks).

(b) Reviews work for accuracy (or for compliance with instructions).

(c) Preserves order and application to work through personal presence.

(d) Instructs others in details of work according to plans or rules laid down by a superior.

(e) Instructs and guides others only in general features and purposes of work.

(f) Plans methods to be followed by subordinates.

(g) Plans programs and flow of work.

(h) Reviews work for compliance with policies.

(i) Makes recommendations on major matters of policy affecting work of subordinates.

(j) Makes decisions on major matters of policy; reviews plans and decisions of assistants and subordinates.

(k) Makes decisions on important matters affecting the work of subordinates, which decisions do not generally or regularly require the review or approval of a superior.

A supervisory employee generally performs several of these tasks or similar ones. A description of all the principal supervisory tasks performed should be given in answer to item 17 (b). If space is lacking, it is suggested that the rest of the supervisory tasks be incorporated in the answer to item 25.

The tasks given above are only suggestions or illustrations. If some of them fit the work, use them. If some would do with some changes, make those changes. If none seems to fit, compose an independent statement.

Item 18.—Give the sheet numbers of the questionnaires representing the positions supervised by the employee, if any, through immediate contact, and the names of the incumbents. If the employee supervises enlisted men for whom, of course, no questionnaires are submitted, state the number and kinds of positions occupied by such enlisted men, grouped by descriptive or occupational titles—e. g., six file clerks, three correspondence clerks. Follow a similar procedure in case the employee supervises other persons not covered in this survey.

If the employee exercises supervision over a good-sized organization which is subdivided into divisions or sections, show the names of the subdivisions and the names and sheet numbers of their chiefs.

The purpose of item 18 is to elicit information that will identify all subordinate positions under the employee's supervision and the questionnaires representing them. For example, if this item is correctly executed on all the questionnaires for a given office, the questionnaire for the head of the field office or station will show the names and sheet numbers of those in his immediate office and the names and sheet numbers of all his assistants through whom he manages the various divisions of his office. The questionnaires of such assistants will show the names and sheet numbers of persons in their immediate offices and also of others in lower administrative positions through whom these assistants direct their organization units, and so on until the point is reached where all the employees named as being supervised are individual workers. In this way the organization scheme is spread out on the questionnaires.

Item 19.—Under (a) state whether the employee is in any way directed, supervised, or instructed, or whether his work or the product of his work is reviewed. In practically every instance the answer to this question will be "Yes," since even the highest administrative officials in the field are required to conform with administrative policies laid down by the head of the service or the head of the department, or are required to submit the more important plans or programs to the department for review and approval.

Under (b) explain in what way and to what degree the employee is directed or instructed or his work controlled or supervised. This item is the converse of item 17 (b) and the suggestions given with reference to that item may prove helpful here. It is important to bear in mind that this item does not aim to draw out information as to how well the particular employee performs his work or as to how much confidence his superiors have in his ability. It is aimed at developing the characteristics of the position as a primary unit in the organization and the relationship of the duties performed to the functions of the field office or field service as a whole, whether such position is occupied or such duties are performed by the present or some future incumbent.

In addition to the converse of the phrases suggested under 17 (b), the following are given as illustrations of control of the employee's work that are met with frequently:

(a) Works under close observation and is expected to confer with superior frequently.

(b) Each task (or the result of each task) is inspected or reviewed.

(c) Follows detailed directions as to methods and purposes.

(d) Follows prescribed plans, programs, or general instructions, but executes details virtually on own responsibility, with only occasional (or infrequent) reference to a superior for advice and instructions.

(e) Subject to general administrative policies only, not otherwise controlled as to the administration of his office. Accountability is primarily for results.

These expressions are only suggestions or illustrations. If one of them fits the work, use it. If one would do with some changes, make those changes. If none seems to fit, compose an independent statement.

Item 20.—Give the name, official position, and sheet number of the questionnaire of the employee's immediate superior. By the term "immediate superior" is meant the man or woman who occupies the next position in authority above that of the employee in the plan of organization, who is closest in personal contact with the employee in allotting tasks or assignments, giving instructions or advice, or laying down methods, plans, programs, or policies to follow, and who, next to the employee himself, is generally considered most directly responsible for the employee's work. The term is not intended to apply to one who merely inspects, verifies, or checks the employee's work and who has no further authority. The use of the modifier "immediate" emphasizes that it is the employee's closest superior whose name is called for, not one more or less remote.

In case the employee's immediate superior is a person whose position is not covered by this survey, and for whom therefore there is no "sheet number," give his name and the title of his official position. If he is a military or naval officer, give his name, his rank, and the title of his official assignment, as Capt. John H. Smith, Chief of Materials Branch.

Item 21.—Information as to the employee's education may be taken from the official personnel records or the preparing officer may refer the question to the employee for answer. In the latter case the employee should write on the margin of the questionnaire, "Composed and certified by ————," and sign his name to show that he, and not the preparing officer, has composed it and is vouching for its correctness.

The information is to be given by typing an "X" on top of the number representing the highest grade or year completed in each type of school attended. In the case of postgraduate or professional study show briefly the field involved, such as medicine and surgery, law, chemistry, plant pathology, etc.

Education not covered by the tabular arrangement may be described on the last line of item 21.

Item 22.—Information as to the length and kind of experience or other training which the employee possessed upon original entrance into the position now held that was most qualifying or pertinent may likewise be deduced from the official personnel records, or the preparing officer may refer the question to the employee for answer. In the latter case the employee should write on the margin of the questionnaire, "Composed and certified by ————," and sign his name to show that he, and not the preparing officer, has composed it and is vouching for its correctness.

For practical purposes the time of "original entrance" may be taken as that to be indicated in item 26.

Item 23.—This item is to be answered by the employee. Instructions and suggestions for composing the required statement are given in P. C. B. Form No. 15. Preparing officers should see that each employee is given a copy of this form when the questionnaires are distributed; otherwise the employee's statement will probably not prove of maximum assistance to the board.

Where it is impracticable, by reason of the extended absence, illness, or inaccessibility of the employee or vacancy in the position or other reason, to secure his signature, the preparing officer will answer the question and will state the reason for the omission of the employee's signature in item No. 24.

Item 24.—The employee is required to certify to the correctness of the statement of his duties. Note that he is required to certify that he himself composed the statement and that he composed it after reading P. C. B.

Form No. 15. It is thus essential that the employee compose an original and independent statement and that he be furnished in advance with a copy of P. C. B. Form No. 15.

Item 25.—In this space the preparing officer is to write his own description of the employee's work. The board desires that a separate, independent description be written. To be of maximum value to the board, the preparing officer's statement should be something more than mere concurrence in the employee's description as given in item 23.

If the space provided is insufficient for the preparing officer's statement, he may paste a separate sheet, labeled "Item 25," to the upper edge of the back of the questionnaire.

The preparing officer should read the employee's statement in item 23 and the instructions given to the employee in P. C. B. Form No. 15; see in what respects, if any, the employee's statement is deficient or inadequate; and endeavor in his statement in item 25 to correct such deficiencies or inadequacies. In no case should the preparing officer erase or strike out any part of the employee's statement.

If the preparing officer, in fact, concurs in the employee's statement and believes he can not make an appreciably clearer or more adequate statement of the facts, he may write, "I concur in the above." But in this event he should utilize the rest of the space by describing some of the general characteristics of the position which the employee may not have covered, or give facts—not adequately brought out elsewhere on the questionnaire—which he believes the board should know concerning the duties and responsibilities of the position, its place in the organization, the purpose of the work performed, the working conditions of the position, the next process, method, duty, or responsibility both below and above the employee's position in the normal flow of work, etc.

Item 26.—Give the approximate period of time (or the date since when) the employee has been performing the work described in items 23 and 25, not the total length of time in the service.

Item 27.—The preparing officer will date and sign the certificate on the white copy and affix his title. The signature on the buff and pink copies may be typed.

Item 28.—The head of the field office or station will examine the questionnaire, and date and sign the certificate on the white copy. The signature on the buff and pink copies may be typed. If he wishes to except any item or part thereof from his certificate, he may do so by explaining his exception and the reason therefor in a separate memorandum, securely pasted to the upper edge of the back of the questionnaire, and labeled with a letter for identification purposes, which letter is to be given in the space provided therefor in the language of the certificate.

In stating the range of compensation which in his judgment would be proper for the position described on the questionnaire, he should state as the minimum salary of the range the lowest rate which should ever be paid to an employee acceptably performing the duties of the position. The maximum rate should be the highest salary allowable to the most efficient employee.

Item 29.—The head of the bureau or of the corresponding departmental subdivision or a representative designated by him will date and sign the certificate on the white copy. The signature on the buff and pink copies may be typed. (See the suggestions under item 28.)

There follows a list of the salary ranges applying to the departmental service in the District of Columbia under the terms of the classification act of 1923 as amended by the act of May 28, 1928. These will serve as a guide to field officers and bureau representatives in the preparation of the certificate required.

$600 to $840	$1,620 to $1,920	$3,200 to $3,700
$1,020 to $1,320	$1,680 to $1,980	$3,500 to $4,000
$1,080 to $1,380	$1,800 to $2,100	$3,800 to $4,400
$1,200 to $1,500	$1,860 to $2,200	$4,600 to $5,200
$1,260 to $1,560	$2,000 to $2,500	$5,600 to $6,400
$1,320 to $1,620	$2,300 to $2,800	$6,500 to $7,500
$1,440 to $1,740	$2,600 to $3,100	$8,000 to $9,000
$1,500 to $1,800	$2,900 to $3,400	

TRANSMISSION OF COMPLETED QUESTIONNAIRES FROM FIELD OFFICE OR STATION TO APPROPRIATE DEPARTMENTAL OFFICE AT WASHINGTON

The completed questionnaires will be assembled separately by substations or other subordinate organization units. Invoices will then be prepared, as follows:

As many copies of the invoices are needed as there are sets of questionnaires.

The questionnaires will be listed in detail on plain letter-size paper. The list will be prepared in form as indicated below and will show for each employee and vacant regular position the following particulars: Serial number of questionnaire; name of employee (in the case of vacant positions the word "vacant" will be inserted in the list in lieu of the employee's name); pay-roll title; and annual gross rate of compensation. In the case of regular employees receiving compensation at other than annual rates, the rate per month, per day, or per hour will be stated, as the case may be, followed by the notation p. m., p. d., or p. h.

In all cases the list should correspond to the serial order of arrangement of the questionnaires themselves, and it should be made to exhibit as clearly as possible the form of the organization of the field office or station as a whole. Generally speaking, the nonsupervisory employees should be listed in the order of their rates of compensation, those receiving the higher salaries being placed at the top in the several sections of the list.

The following specimen invoice is shown for purposes of illustration:

List of employees reported on P. C. B. Form No. 14

Department: Interior.
Bureau: Reclamation.
Field service: Reclamation.
Field office or station: Yakima project.
Location: Yakima, Wash.

Sheet No.	Name	Pay-roll title	Present gross salary
	PROJECT MANAGER'S OFFICE		
	Administrative division		
1	John Smith	Project manager	$4,500
2	J. K. Jones	Chief clerk	3,000
	* * *	* * *	
38	John Doe	Clerk	900
39	Charles Carter	Messenger	¹ 80
	Accounting division		
1	John Smith	Chief accountant	3,500
2	John Doe	Accountant	2,400
	* * *	* * *	
23	J. K. Jones	Clerk	1,000
24	Jennie Carter	do	900
	Engineering division		
1	John Smith	Supervising engineer	4,000
2	John Doe	Office engineer	2,500
3	J. K. Jones	Assistant engineer	2,000
	* * *	* * *	
21	Vacant	Clerk	1,400
	Total, project manager's office, 84.		
	SUNNYSIDE DIVISION		
1	John Smith	Assistant manager	3,000
2	John Doe	Maintenance engineer	2,000
3	J. K. Jones	Powerhouse foreman	¹ 180
	* * *	* * *	
26	Charles Carter	Timekeeper	1,400
	TIETON DIVISION		
1	John Smith	Superintendent of irrigation	3,000
2	John Doe	Maintenance engineer	2,000
	* * *	* * *	
20	J. K. Jones	Clerk	1,200
21	Charles Carter	do	1,000

¹ Per month.

RECAPITULATION

Project manager's office	84
Sunnyside division	26
Tieton division	21
Total	131

The completed questionnaires, with the accompanying invoices, will be transmitted through the customary channels to the appropriate departmental office at Washington, D. C.

Instructions and Suggestions
For Filling Out the Classification Questionnaire[3]

BOARD OF CIVIL SERVICE COMMISSIONERS—CITY OF LOS ANGELES

DO NOT START TO FILL OUT THE QUESTIONNAIRE UNTIL YOU READ THESE
INSTRUCTIONS

What the Classification Survey Is

This survey is being made in order to examine the duties and responsibilities of positions in the city service and to effect a classification plan in accordance with the requirements of the City Charter. This classification plan will consist of the grouping together of all positions which have the same, or nearly the same, duties and responsibilities, and which require like abilities and skills for successful performance. Such standard groups or classes of positions will then be described. The work requirements and responsibilities of each will be carefully expressed, and the qualifications needed by applicants for a position in each class will be defined. Before these position descriptions are finally approved, however, you will be given a chance to read the description of the class in which your job will be placed and to point out whether or not it is a true statement of necessary facts.

The resulting classification plan will be used to prepare examinations for filling vacant positions in the city service and to effect a sound system of promotion and transfer within the service. Consequently, it is important that the plan be accurate. To be accurate and fair, detailed and exact knowledge of the duties and responsibilities of each position in the city service is necessary.

It is believed that you are the best person to present complete information about your own job, and that you should know the exact duties you are performing and responsibilities which you have. For this reason you are being asked to fill in the questionnaire form accompanying this instruction sheet. Great care should be used in doing this so that a *clear and complete understanding of your job* can be obtained by those persons who will study it. The title given your present position and its relation to other positions in the city service will depend largely upon the information you supply. The statements you make are not to be changed by your supervisor. An interviewer from the classification staff of the Civil Service Department may call on you later to discuss your work with you.

Remember that the questions asked are about your *job* and not about you as an individual. This survey is not concerned with how well you perform your work or how well qualified you are. Nor is it concerned with your pay. The Mayor announced in his budget message, "It is not planned by the Civil Service Commission or the present city administration to decrease compensation in any instance where a position is now filled." The kind of

[3] *Public Administration Service. Instructions to accompany the form shown in Figure 2, following page 342.*

work you do, the responsibilities of your position, and the relationship of your work to that of others are the things desired.

Please do not present the words of others in filling out the questionnaire even though the work involved is the same as that of another person. Your own statement of your work is wanted—not the ideas of others about your work. You may ask your supervisor or any member of the classification staff to explain any question you do not understand, but use your own words in answering all questions. If you are certain that a question does not apply to your work, write in "DOES NOT APPLY," but be sure that this is true before saying so.

The following instructions are divided into two sections in order to be as helpful as possible. The first part is for all employees and suggests how each item of the questionnaire may best be answered. *Read these over carefully before attempting to fill out any answers.*

Part 2 is for supervisors only and explains how the classification questionnaires should be distributed and how items 18 to 20 inclusive should be filled out.

PART 1—TO THE EMPLOYEE

Suggestions for Filling Out the Questionnaire

After you have read over the instructions carefully, work out your answers on the work sheet (the yellow copy) and read them over to be sure they are correct and complete. Because of the large number of forms which must be studied, it will be necessary to have three copies typewritten. The white copy should be the original with the blue and pink as carbon copies. You may type your own if you care to. If not, your immediate supervisor will arrange to have your answers typed on these three additional copies. Be sure to return your answers and all the forms to your supervisor *within four days.* Whether you or someone else types your extra copies, be sure to read them over carefully to see that your statements are clear and exactly the way you have intended them. Then sign each copy and hand the three typewritten copies to your supervisor. You may keep the yellow copy (work sheet) for your own use and reference.

The following explanations will help you to understand just what information is wanted. Read the explanation for each item just before filling in that part of the questionnaire. Items 1 to 5 may be filled out in advance by your departmental personnel office. If not, fill it out yourself, being sure to find out your payroll title, and code number, if you have any, from your supervisor or department head.

Item 1—In entering your name be sure to give your last name first, then your full first and middle names, *NOT* just initials.

Item 2—The place where you work should be indicated here by room number and building, or by street address if you do not work in a municipal building. If you work out of doors on general projects, give the district and location where you customarily work.

Item 3—The entry here should be the department, such as POLICE DE-

PARTMENT or FIRE DEPARTMENT and *not* the division, or the district office, or other sub-division.

Item 4—Indicate here the departmental sub-divisions (Bureau, Division and Section or Unit) in which you are employed, giving the larger unit first and the smallest last.

Item 5—Place here the official title and code number of your position at the present time. The title carried on the payroll should be given.

Item 6—Place here the name which you and your fellow workers use for your job (if different from the official title).

Item 7—The hours of each regular working day, and the days of the week or month on which you do not work should be shown here. If you work different shifts, or have one shift one week and another the next, explain, using the margin if necessary.

Item 8—Your work may be for only two hours a day, for three days a week, for two weeks each month, or for four months every year. Or you may have been appointed for only six months, and then your work will end. Or you may be on call and work only when needed. If your work is irregular in any way, explain and, if possible, give the reason.

Item 9—This is one of the most important questions on the form. This is the place where you tell in detail just exactly what you do. Each different kind of work that you are called upon to do should be briefly but carefully explained. The task which you consider most important should be given first, followed by the less important work, until the least important is described. If your work varies very much from season to season or at specific times, duties should be grouped together according to such periods. Be sure to give your complete work assignments over a long enough period of time to picture your job as a whole. If one kind of work takes one-half your time, say so. If another kind takes one day a month, say that. You may prefer to show the time spent on different duties as percentages or fractions, as 75% of your time, or 1/3 of the year. Use whatever method you think will give a clear understanding of how you spend your working time, but be sure to show how much time is used for each type of work. Do not state it is impossible to estimate the time spent on various tasks; you are in a better position to do this than any one else.

If necessary for a full explanation of your job, attach copies of forms which you use, being careful to explain how each is used and what entries you make, but do not attach copies unless you feel they are needed to describe your work. Necessary forms will be collected for the whole office later.

Make your description so clear that anyone who reads your answer, even if he knows nothing about your job, will understand *exactly* what you do. Do not use general phrases; be specific. Examples of the types of statements that would be descriptive of work in several different fields are given below as a guide to the kind of statements wanted. Do not copy any of these examples—*use your own words.* Ordinarily it will take all of the space provided on the questionnaire to tell what you do. If you do not have enough space, attach additional sheets.

EXAMPLES IN THE LABOR FIELD:

2 months:	I dig trenches and post holes with a pick and shovel. Mr. Brown, my straw boss, tells me where to dig and when to stop. After the cable is laid or the pole is set, I fill in the trenches or holes by hand. Sometimes, I use an air hammer on rock cut.
1 month:	I fill wheel barrows with sand or gravel and take it to the concrete mixer. I tamp concrete after it is poured into forms.
1 month: Etc.	I ride a 10-ton flat bed truck and help the truck driver load and unload bags of cement, heavy rock, reinforcing steel and so forth. We generally haul from the N Street yards to jobs in the Western District. I wash the truck . . . etc.

8 months:	(3 days wk:)	I mow fairways with a 5 gang mower pulled by a light tractor.
	(2 days wk:)	I help Mr. Ralph Smith, the gardener at the 90th Street filtration plant. I mow and sprinkle lawns for him.
3 months: Etc.		I spread manure and spade around shrubs. Sometimes, I help ball or box out trees and shrubs. I load . . . etc.

EXAMPLES IN THE MECHANICAL FIELD:

1/3:	I machine iron, steel, brass, or copper parts for pumps, motors, and heavy equipment, according to a blueprint or a sketch which we get from the engineering office. Most of the time I use machine tools—lathes, planers, shapers, and milling machines.
1/3: Etc.	I operate . . . etc.

10%:	Replacing defective field coils and armatures on heavy duty motors.
5%:	Tearing down, cleaning, and reassembling electric motors.
1%:	Making out requisitions, and time and material reports (forms 41, 62, and 63).
2%: Etc.	Assembling . . . etc. (Work in shop one day a week. On call at one of the substations rest of the time.)

	Working from rough drawings and blue prints, I make desks, cabinets, chairs, tables, and other office furniture.
2/10:	Cutting pieces with band saw, planer, shaper, etc.
1/10:	Lathing furniture legs, pedestals, and ornamental pieces.
2/10:	Assembling, gluing, and fitting parts.
1/10:	Sanding off, staining, and polishing.
2/10: Etc.	During slack periods I . . . etc.

	I operate heavy construction equipment.
3 months:	Heavy street grading with a ¾ yard gas shovel.
1 month:	Hoisting work with a two or three drum hoist. (Vacation relief.)
2 months: Etc.	Pile driving for retaining walls, excavations, and foundations. Sometimes I . . . etc.

	I operate a 10-ton diesel cat, doing the following jobs:
15%:	Pull a scarifier regrading streets.
10%:	Cut new grade and regrade dirt and gravel roads with heavy duty tractor-grader.
5%: Etc.	Clear out . . . etc.

	Driving truck.
1 hr:	Spot 8-ton dump truck for load from a power shovel, drag line, or bin.
3 hr:	Haul dirt to fill or dump—or aggregate to job.
1 hr:	Back and dump on high, loose fill so as to build grade without extra hand shoveling.
1 hr: Etc.	Help spread load . . . etc.

	I repair autos, trucks, and gas motors. I specialize in ignition work, but do all kinds of motor repair.
50%:	Testing ignition systems, tracing shorts, timing motors, installing brushes and armatures, putting in new points . . . etc.
10%:	Tearing down motors, fitting bearings, crank shafts, and pistons, and installing rings.
5%:	Grinding valves.
5%: Etc.	Honing cylinders . . . etc.

EXAMPLES IN THE ENGINEERING FIELD:

50%:	I am in charge of a field survey party of four people making preliminary surveys for paving, grading, and grade crossing elimination. We establish center lines, run profiles, stake curves, set grade stakes, and do cross-sectioning. I work from established monuments and bench marks. I personally keep the field notes, etc.
10%: Etc.	Office work consists of . . .etc.

6 months:	I lay out and trace plan-profile sheets for street improvements. I reduce survey notes, balance traverses and plot maps from the field books sent in by the field survey parties, also plot cross-sections and planimeter for cut and fill areas.
2 months: Etc.	I draft . . . etc.

2½ hrs:	I check the design computations of other engineers mainly for mathematical accuracy and proper application of design formulae. I am not responsible for the type of structure.
1½ hrs: Etc.	I figure . . . etc.

2 hrs:	I detail bridges, retaining walls and other structures. I work from design notes and turn my pencil layouts over to Jones for tracing. I also check shop detail drawings furnished by fabricators.
1 hr: Etc.	I check . . . etc.

65%:	I design concrete and steel beam and girder bridges, retaining walls, culverts, and under and over passes. The general type of structure and foundation is determined by Mr. Brown, but I make all computations, determine member types and sizes and otherwise complete the design. Examples of such structures are . . .
10%: Etc.	I also . . . etc.

EXAMPLES IN THE CLERICAL AND RELATED FIELDS:

Average 4 hrs. per day:	I type invoices (form 169) in quadruplicate from pencil order blanks (form 326) after they have been approved by Mr. Jones and extensions checked by Miss Smith.
2 hrs:	I type reports from rough pencil copy.
1 hr: Etc.	I also . . . etc.

2 days:	I file purchase orders chronologically and by department and vendor.
1 day: Etc.	I segregate . . . etc.

10%:	I take dictation from Mr. Brown, including letters, memoranda, and draft of speeches, but Miss White takes all his technical engineering dictation.
5%: Etc.	I file . . . etc.

Posting 80%:	I enter all payments made at the counter in the daily journal by hand, using receipt stubs, and
Balancing 5%:	balance each day's entries with the cashier's records.
Checking 5%:	I check . . . etc.
Etc.	

1 hr:	I classify all correspondence, according to subject and enter the code number for filing.
3 hrs:	I type out an index card, giving names, code number, date, and a summary for each letter, etc.
1 month:	Each year I review the files, pull all old correspondence, and revise the subject code to meet current needs.

EXAMPLES IN THE ACCOUNTING FIELD:

	Supervising three clerks assigned to the cost accounting system for power line construction and maintenance.
5%:	Assembling job record reports (forms 65 and 39) from the field, post to summary sheets, and do other routine work.
10%:	Tabulate and prove material for weekly, monthly, and annual operating reports.
10%:	Compile . . . etc.

10 complete days each month:	Posting tax receipts by posting machine on ledger cards showing levies as debit items and payments as credits. There are about 100,000 active accounts. Payments are posted monthly just after tax receipt period.
Average ½ hr. per day during posting period: Etc.	Proving out account balances by running a journal sheet and checking against blocks of ledger cards, etc.

50% time:	Posting the general ledgers of X department by entering all journal entries to ledger account cards by means of a multiple keyboard bookkeeping machine. There are 16 general ledger accounts including expense control, property, equipment, salaries and wages, etc., etc.
20% time: Etc.	By means of the same machine, posting all expenditure vouchers to the various subsidiary accounts included under expense control, etc.

1/10:	Take off daily, weekly, and monthly trial balances of control accounts, and reconcile the subsidiary ledgers to these balances.
1/10:	Reconcile bank accounts.
1/10: Etc.	Analyze and age accounts receivable, etc.

| 4 hrs: | I pre-audit all vouchers by checking to see that all supporting forms and documents are included and properly signed, that extensions are correct, discounts taken, and everything is in proper form. |
| 1 hr: Etc. | I check to be sure each department's accounts are correctly debited and credited, etc. |

EXAMPLES IN THE POLICE AND FIRE FIELDS:

| 4 hrs: | I regularly patrol the downtown business area in a radio car with another officer, usually from 4 P.M. to 12. I drive. We answer calls and investigate according to instructions. Part of our duty is to question drunks and prowlers, keep a lookout for stolen cars, and warn or give tickets to traffic violators. One of us sometimes leaves the car to inspect commercial premises. When one leaves . . . etc. |
| 2 hrs: Etc. | During the traffic peak, we . . . etc. |

| 6 months: | I investigate crime reports and calls with a fellow officer. We take reports from victims and witnesses and make arrests if evidence so indicates. We look for and preserve evidence, calling on print men, photographers, etc., from headquarters, when necessary. We prepare cases and testify in court, etc. |
| Vacation relief 2 mo.: Etc. | I work on the pawn shop detail, visiting second hand shops . . . etc. |

| 4 days wk: | I specialize in getting latent prints, photographing the scene of the offense and making moulages: I make measurements and drawings to preserve facts, etc. |
| 1 day: Etc. | Each Friday, unless on a case, I inventory stock, etc. |

| 3/8: | I direct traffic at the corner of Broadway and Fifth from 4 to 7 P.M. |
| 2/8: Etc. | During the rest of my shift I am on foot patrol and try all business establishment doors, etc. |

| 3 days wk: Etc. | I receive all callers who want to see Inspector Guinn. I talk to them to find out what division they should see. I decide whether or not they need to see the Inspector, and, if not, try to get them to go directly to the right place. When they . . . etc. |

| 90%: | I am in charge of a ladder company at Y house, during the day shift. I also have charge of the station premises. I conduct roll call, inspect the men, and maintain discipline while I am on duty, etc. |
| 10%: | At a fire I decide . . . etc. |

| 5%: | I drive a pumper to fires. At the fire, I operate the pumper according to orders given, etc. |
| 25%: Etc. | At the house I check and pack pumps, clean . . . etc. |

| Average 2 runs per day: | I connect and lay hose, put up and climb ladders, make openings in burning buildings, remove persons from burning buildings, clean and dry hose, etc. |
| 2 hrs. wk: Etc. | I attend drill and instruction periods, study . . . etc. |

5 days Inspecting:	I inspect theatres, factories, garages, retail stores, etc., for accumulated waste and inflammable material, the condition and location of extinguishers and hose connections, etc. I enforce the fire prevention code and give formal notice as required.
1 day: Etc.	I give talks to school children, etc.

EXAMPLES IN THE MEDICAL FIELD:

	I direct the medical services in the psychiatric ward of the General Hospital.
5%:	Consultations with attending physicians.
5%: Etc.	Instructing and consulting with internes (3 attached to this unit). We have weekly staff conferences at which the prognosis of each case is reviewed . . . etc.

10%:	Personally diagnose all patients on entry and dictate a report prescribing treatment.
5%:	Interpreting case histories, prescribing treatment, etc.
2%: Etc.	Inspecting laboratory and ward facilities, etc.

3 hrs:	I review the diagnoses of six resident physicians when I feel circumstances require, either by going over their reports (forms 69 and 105) or by personal examination of patients. My usual procedure is . . . etc.
2 hrs: Etc.	I perform all appendectomies, tonsillectomies, etc.

	My duties are those of a laboratory technician. My work is distributed as follows:
2 days:	Blood counts, urinalyses, Wassermanns, bacteria counts, etc.
About 2 hrs. daily:	Sectioning, staining, preparing slides, and making microscopic examinations of tissues.
1 day: Etc.	Innoculating, maintaining case histories, noting reactions of experimental animals, etc.

1/5:	Giving talks and demonstrations on prenatal and postnatal care.
2/5:	Instructing 1st to 6th grade children in hygienic self care.
1/5: Etc.	Preparing children for vaccination, etc.

Item 10—List here any equipment, machinery, tools, office appliances or other devices which you use or operate in connection with your work. The time and way in which you use such equipment should have been explained under Item 9.

Item 11—Give the name and title of your immediate supervisor, the person to whom you look for orders, advice, and decisions. If you are not sure who your superior is, or if there is more than one, give explanation so that the persons reading your statement will know whether you work for one person part of the time and for another the rest of the time, or whether you work for two or three persons all the time.

Item 12—Exactly what instructions and directions does your superior give you? What questions does he refer to you? You may have had instructions only when you were new on the job. You may get special instructions with every new task. Give a description of these basic conditions under which you work.

Item 13—This question applies chiefly to those employees whose duties and responsibilities are not clearly defined by regulations, well established office procedures, or the standard practices of a trade or craft. In answering it, summarize as concisely as you can what you consider to be the essential nature and degree of your responsibilities. It may be responsibility for doing what you are told to do in a workman-like manner, for doing journeyman work on assignment, for some highly skilled operations, for some type of technical or professional work or judgment, for all operations of a particular office, for interpreting departmental policy, or whatever it may be. Are your responsibilities for execution, for planning of work, for final decisions, for supervision, or for technical or professional work or judgment?

Your responsibilities may be different with respect to the various duties you have. Tell briefly the difference.

Item 14—Usually more than one person has some responsibilities for completion of a task. You have told what you consider your responsibilities to be—now, explain in a few words what you believe to be the most important ways that you receive help from your supervisor in carrying out your tasks. Do you receive instructions or advice from your supervisor or other employees only on the more difficult or unusual problems? If so, give examples. Use your supervisor's name in your answer.

Item 15—Does anyone check or review your work? If so, who is it and what kind of a check is made: Is it a mathematical check, an inspection of quality, a review of your judgment, or what? Maybe your work is such that there is an automatic continuous check of your actions. If so tell about it. If the check or review is fully explained under Item 14, simply say so.

Item 16—If you have only a few persons under you, give their names. If you have a larger group, give an answer such as "all employees in Westlake Park: Three gardeners, one truck driver, eight laborers, and one clerk." If you have a major division or department give the name of the unit and the total number of employees.

Item 17—Estimate the period of time you have been doing the work described under Item 9.

Part 2—Instructions to the Supervisor

Method for Distributing and Reviewing the Classification Questionnaires

Through departmental channels, sufficient copies of the classification questionnaires will be supplied you so that there will be one complete set for each employee under your supervision. These sets will consist of one white, one blue, one pink, and one yellow form and a copy of printed instructions.

Each employee should be given a yellow form and the instruction sheet with the request that the yellow form be filled out and returned to you within four days. Clerical employees who have access to typewriters may be asked to make out their own typewritten triplicate sheets. At the end of four days, check to see that all forms are returned. Then have the original answers given by the employees typed in triplicate, with the white form as the original and the blue and pink forms as carbon copies. Arrangements should be made to have questionnaires typed either in your own office or some designated office of your department.

As soon as typed, redistribute the four copies to each employee for review, date, and signature. Then collect the three typewritten forms. Go over each carefully to see that they are accurate and complete, and then fill out Items 18 to 21, inclusive. *The immediate supervisor, foreman, or boss should fill out Items 18 to 21,* inclusive, on the questionnaire forms of *only* those employees over whom he exercises direct supervision. A department head should not fill in these items for employees whom he directs through a sub-executive but only for those to whom he assigns work directly. In all instances, however, the *department head,* or a representative designated by him, should look over both the employees' and the supervisors' statements and indicate under *Item 22* any inaccuracies found. If there is a substantial disagreement of opinion between the employee and the supervisor or between the supervisor and the department head, that fact should be noted so that a special analysis of the position can be made. *Neither the supervisor nor the department head, however, should make any alteration or change in the statements made by a subordinate.*

In the event there is a regular position in the department which is temporarily vacant, or the incumbent is not available to fill out a questionnaire, the supervisor or department head should make arrangements to supply a form for that position, made out as accurately as possible. The nature of the situation and the fact that an incumbent did not fill out the form should be clearly indicated and upon the employee's return, the employee should fill out and submit a questionnaire for the position.

Suggestions for filling out Items 18 to 21

Item 18—Do not attempt to change the employee's statement or to influence his answers. Read them through and then give your opinion of their accuracy and completeness. Is it a good description of the position, or has he neglected to give a full picture of his duties and responsibilities; has he overstated or understated them; has he put emphasis on the wrong points? Give either a general evaluation of the statements or refer to specific items.

Item 19—Sum up what you consider to be the distinguishing points of the employee's job. What do you expect of it, what supervision and direction does it get, what check and review is provided? What is the essential nature of the duties and responsibilities? Is it a beginning or is it an advanced job?

The following are examples of the types of statements which will be helpful. "Requires sound judgment and accuracy, but is subject to considerable supervision and decisions by a superior on questions of engineering policy." "A routine stenographic job but courtesy, tact, and discretion toward officials and the public are essential. Not a beginner's job." "This is a beginning job requiring alertness and willingness to learn." "A section chief and key man. Must know all about the unit and its procedure besides being well grounded in accounting theory and practice. I review results only." "A key position in my unit. I tell what results I want and he formulates the work program and assigns the subordinates. It is up to him to get the job done." "Strictly a helper's job, but requires at least a year of experience around electrical work to know tools, materials, and work processes." "A journeyman job. Also requires familiarity with our system." "I lay out the work in detail for this position every time there is any change in the work. I keep in close touch with the work in process and check it carefully when completed." "This position needs little supervision but all work is thoroughly checked by Mr. Black." "This is a repetitive operation and requires little attention after it has been learned."

If you have a number of positions under you which are practically identical, it will be sufficient to answer Items 19 and 21 fully for one such position only, and then refer to such answers on the other questionnaires. You can merely state "Same as John Doe."

Item 20—With full consideration of the duties and responsibilities of this position, tell what kind of person you would choose for the position if it were to become vacant. What must he know?

Of what basic subjects, procedures, principles, laws, or regulations must he have a knowledge?

Must the knowledge be thorough or is a general knowledge or familiarity sufficient?

What abilities or skills must a successful employee possess?

Is formal education necessary? If so, which course or subjects are required? Which are helpful but not essential?

Is previous experience necessary? If so, how much previous experience, and in what type of work?

Please be as specific and complete as you can in answering these questions.

Item 21—If the job involves any *typing or stenography*, even if merely incidental, answer this item. Otherwise simply say NO and pass on.

Item 22—In large departments where the department head is unable to sign the white copies personally, his designated representative should sign his superior's name and place his own name or initial immediately underneath.

Method for Returning the Classification Questionnaires

The white copies bearing the signatures of the supervisor and department head, and the blue copies of the completed questionnaires should be returned to the Civil Service Department, 1100 City Hall, within ten days after original distribution. If this is found to be impossible, communicate immediately with the classification staff of that department (Station 506, City Hall). The pink copy should be retained for departmental files.

Instructions
For Filling Out Position Description Cards[4]

To Each Officer and Employee:

General Explanation and Suggestions: A blank form of "Position Description" has been prepared for the purpose of assembling significant facts about each office and position in the service, for use in an analysis of the organization. It is desired to get at these facts from both the point of view of each individual officer and employee, and that of the official superiors of the several officers and employees.

You should have received a copy of the form, with these instructions, through department channels. If you have not received your copy, you should secure one from your immediate official superior, the person next in line of authority and responsibility above you.

You are urgently requested to fill out the form promptly, and to turn it in to your immediate superior within three days of the time that it reaches you. The work you are expected to do on the form, and how you are expected to do it, are next described.

You are asked to fill in, on the copy of the form furnished you, your answers to the questions that this form contains, down to and including your signature to the certificate at Question 45.

Please read the form through carefully before you try to answer any of the questions. Then go back and prepare your answers. It is suggested that you write your answers first on separate sheets and then compare them with the questions. *After* you have satisfied yourself that all the answers are correct and complete, then copy the answers into the spaces provided, or have them so copied for you.

Please use the typewriter in entering your answers on the form, or have someone else type them for you, if either course is at all practicable. Otherwise, write your answers, as clearly and legibly as you can, in ink. Do not fold or crease the form.

If there is any question that does not seem to you to apply to your position, indicate that fact by the remark "Does not apply," or, where space is limited, such an expression as "None." But please be sure that the question really does not apply, before passing it over in such a way.

If you are in doubt about the answer to any question, ask your immediate superior for any needed explanation or other help. Each officer and employee is requested to give all help he can to others, and to co-operate in every way practicable to effect the prompt completion and return of all the forms. But please remember that your answers are intended to be definitely your own. Others may *help* you in answering the questions, even frame the answers and write them on the form, but the answers should say what *you* want them to say. You accept all answers written by others when you sign the certificate. Do not sign unless you do

---

[4] *Griffenhagen & Associates. Instructions to accompany the form shown in Figure 3, following page 358.*

so accept them. Insist on changing them as necessary to make them acceptable to you, before signing.

How to Answer the Questions: The proper answers will be clear in most cases from the questions. The following additional explanations, numbered to correspond with the questions, should be helpful:.

1 to 9, inclusive. If it is practicable, these will have been filled in before the form reaches you. If that has been done, please check the entries for correctness and completeness, and make any corrections needed. Or if the blanks have not been filled in, please enter the information called for.

10. This is the most important part of the position description form. Please make your answer so clear and complete that anyone reading your description will get a clear idea of the work you actually do.

Think what you work at in the course of a day, a week, a month, or a year. Make your description apply to such period as will provide the best picture. For example, if your duties are just about the same day after day, the year round, a statement of the work done in a single day will give an adequate idea of your job. If there are some tasks that you perform at the end of each week or month, or if there are other variations by weekly or monthly periods, then the week or the month is the best unit. If your work in summer is different from that in winter, or otherwise varies by different months of the year, then the work of a whole year should be described. If you are detailed temporarily to different work from that you ordinarily perform, describe both the temporary and the regular work, and state the conditions of the detail, whose place you are taking, for how long, and any other information that will help to make the situation clear.

Describe each distinct kind of work that you do in a separate paragraph. Make the first paragraph cover the kind of work that takes up the greatest part of your working time; then take up and describe the kind that occupies the next greatest portion; and so on, until you reach special or occasional duties, which should be shown at the end.

Be specific. For example, if you do inspection work, tell what kinds of establishments or premises you visit, what you look for, the purposes of the inspection, and the operations that you carry out. If you do carpenter work, tell the kinds of things that you make or repair, where you work (as in a shop or on projects) and the tools or machines that you use. If you do office work, tell the kinds and purposes of the records you work on, the letters you write, or other matters that you handle, and state plainly the things that you do in connection with them. If you use office machines, such as typewriters, comptometers, bookkeeping machines, etc., indicate which. If you are responsible for certain things in a territorial district, in a ward of a hospital, or in some other division, specify and describe. Indicate as far as you can how many units of work are handled by you, as by stating the number of permits issued, entries posted, letters written, inspections made, people interviewed, or other things done, by kinds and periods.

If your work requires you to hold a license or a certificate to perform it, please state on the line indicated on the form, what the requirements are.

If your position has a title different from the one shown in answer to Question 4 state the title by which it is commonly called. Quite often a position is known, for working purposes, by a different title from its official payroll, civil service, or appropriation title. A junior engineer, for example, may be working as a "chief of party" in the field, or a "squad boss" in the drafting room. A senior clerk may be serving as a "cashier" or "reception clerk." An employee hired as a hospital attendant may actually be working as a "farmhand" or "laboratory assistant." What is your position called by those who work with you?

In the column at the left, indicate, as closely as you can estimate, the portion of your working time given to each of the various kinds of work described. That is, opposite each paragraph describing the work you do, make an entry to show what part of the total time of the period covered by your description is taken up by the kind of work described in that paragraph. You may prefer to show this as a per cent of the total time, such as 75%, 10%, or 2%, or as a fraction of the total time, such as 3–4, 1–8, or 1–100, or by means of the approximate number of hours spent on the work in the period, as 30 hrs., 5 hrs. or 1 hr. Use whatever method you prefer that will indicate as fairly as you can make it do so, the relative amounts of time spent on the different kinds of work described. Do not say that it is impossible for you to estimate the portions of your time spent on different tasks. You are in a better position to estimate the portions than anyone else can be. You know whether certain duties take a very small or very large portion of your time. You can estimate closely enough how large or how small is the portion taken. Give the best idea you can of the distribution, even though it is merely approximate rather than closely accurate.

12 and 13. Give the name and title of the person who is next in line above you in authority and responsibility for the work that you do. This is not the head of the division, institution, or department unless you regularly receive all instructions from such head and are responsible to him alone. If you are a helper or assistant, your immediate superior is the person that you work with. If you are a member of a group, your "straw-boss," sub-foreman, foreman, section head, or other closest supervisor is the one to show here. It does not matter whether or not the person named is definitely recognized by a supervisory title if he is in fact responsible for your work and actually in a position to tell you what to do and how to do it or to control your actions as an employee. But mere inspection or checking of your work, by itself, is not to be taken as involving authority or responsibility.

14. Tell about the kind of supervision your work receives from your immediate superior. Some officers and employees, of executive type, make their own plans and programs and are held responsible only for results. Others lay out general plans and programs, which are approved from above and proceed to carry them out in their own ways with but a limited degree of general direction. Others carry out plans and programs prescribed for them, in some cases with very little instruction or oversight, and in others subject to more or less close and frequent checks and control. Still others follow rather definite procedures, or work under close and constant oversight. Make your statement show as clearly as you can where your position fits into this outline from the standpoint of the kind and extent of supervision.

15. Indicate what other employees, if any, are under your own control or supervision, for whose work you are responsible; and explain just what your supervision consists of. Be sure, as to those you mention, that you actually do have authority to tell them what to do and how to do it, and are held responsible for their work or conduct, or both. If no employees are supervised, write "None"; if five or fewer, list them by titles and names; if more than five, group them by titles, showing how many of each title, and omit the names. Show the kind and extent of supervision over the work of each employee or group listed. If you share supervisory responsibility over some employees with other supervisors, so indicate, mentioning the other supervisors.

16. It should not be difficult for you to indicate the tenure of your position, and whether it is of full-time or part-time character, in the manner provided.

If you render only part-time service, do not say that you are unable to estimate the time put in. Even though your hours of service are uncertain and vary widely from period to period, you know better than anyone else how much time you actually do work. It is important to know whether you work one or two hours a week or month, or practically full time every working day, or an amount of time somewhere between these extremes.

17a and 17b. Indicate whether or not your position is in the classified civil service. If it is in the classified civil service, indicate the nature of your appointment, that is, whether it is permanent, transitory, temporary or emergency.

18. Please give your regular rate of pay in money for the normal service required of you, not counting extras or deductions, and indicate the period to which such rate applies, for example, $1,200 a year, or $2,400 for 10 months, or $4.00 a day.

19. If there is any provision for payment for overtime service in your position, show the rate of pay therefor. Otherwise write "None." Also give your best estimate of the total amount of overtime pay you received in the year just past, if any.

20. This question is intended to bring out the facts regarding any other money you receive for services rendered in connection with your position, that has not been mentioned in answer to any of the preceding questions. For example, if you receive additional pay, pension, or other allowance (beyond that already mentioned) from some other government (U. S., State, county, city), or from a different account or fund of the same government, so indicate. Or if you hold some other public office or employment, which you carry on in conjunction with, or in addition to, the position covered by this form, and for which you receive compensation, state the facts as to the amount. Show both the sources and the total amount from each, as nearly as you can estimate, received in the year just past. Employees regularly employed only during certain months of the year, as is often the case with firemen and teachers, for example, should include any extra pay for special services during the off months. A doctor or a dentist who serves two different institutions should show the second source and amount of payment here, unless he has combined the two in his previous answers. In any such case, the work as a whole should be described under Question 10.

21 to 24 inclusive. These questions are intended to bring out the facts regarding any items furnished you for your personal use and that of any dependents, for which you would have to pay if they were not so supplied. Give your own best estimates of what the allowances would cost you if you had to pay for them yourself. Do not include as allowances any supplies furnished you for use in carrying on your work, such as gasoline for travel on official business, though you should count such part of gasoline or other supplies furnished you, as you use for your own purposes, including travel to and from your place of work.

25. If you receive any money payments in lieu of board, lodging, or other allowance commonly pertaining to such positions as your own, indicate the total amount, as nearly as you can estimate, so received in the year just past. Do not include expense allowances or reimbursements for expenses incurred by reason of the work.

26. This question refers to such expense as that of a watchman required to furnish his own uniform or a carpenter required to furnish his own tools. Also, if your work requires automobile transportation (not counting transportation between your home and your place of work) and you furnish your own car without reimbursement, or receive back less than it costs you, the cost to you of the use of the car for your work should be included.

27 and 28. Show losses of pay on account of lost time, fines or other penalties, and other causes, and contributions, as indicated.

29 to 32 inclusive. Give the facts, as indicated, as to your normal working hours, that is, the amount of working time you are expected to put in for the regular rate of pay specified in answer to Question 18. If you work longer hours than are regularly required in such a position as your own, the extra time should be shown, as nearly as you can estimate, divided among the overtime hours for which you receive pay, those rendered without pay, and those offset by time you have had off during regular working hours. Explain any variations, as by different shifts, in your hours of work and any other special conditions or circumstances. If you have no regular hours, and your time worked is variable and uncertain, so state and give your best estimate of the average hours you do work.

33 to 35 inclusive. The days of absence with pay during the course of a year are to be indicated according to the divisions shown. Where you do not have exact figures, use your own best estimates. Include all losses of time during working hours not compensated for by overtime work or loss of pay. Do not overlook losses from absences for days or parts of days not treated as on formal leave, including losses from late arrivals, early departures, and extra time taken for luncheon periods.

36 to 44 inclusive. The information asked for by these questions relates to you as an individual rather than to the position as such, but is desired for use in its bearing on the position. It is intended primarily for statistical use in determining, for example, how many employees of different age and sex groups there are in the service, and how they are distributed by departments and kinds of employment. Some of this information is already on record elsewhere, but your help in assembling it on these forms will save a lot of searching and compiling that would otherwise be necessary to bring the desired information together.

45. Do not sign the certificate until you have checked all the answers on the form and are certain that you can honestly certify to them according to the terms of the certificate. Only when fully satisfied that you have made your answers correct and complete, should you date and sign the certificate. As soon as you have signed the certificate, deliver the card to your immediate superior, without delay.

To Supervisory Officers and Employees below the Department Head:

As the description forms of employees under your supervision are handed to you, please examine each carefully to see that all spaces through Question 45 are filled in correctly and completely, insofar as it is practicable to do so. First see that the headings, Questions 1 to 9, inclusive, are filled in properly, and supply any omissions and correct any errors therein. Then examine the entries in the blanks to be filled by the employees (10 to 45 inclusive) and try to get the employees to make any changes or additions necessary to make this portion correct and complete.

Proceed to fill in your answers to Questions 46 to 49 in the cases of all employees who are directly subordinate to you and of whom you are, consequently, the immediate superior.

Be sure that you are, in fact, the immediate superior of an employee before you undertake to fill in the entries as such. In this connection, pay particular attention to the employee's answers to Questions 12 and 13. If you are not the officer or employee indicated by him in his answers to these questions, you should pass the form to the person so indicated, unless you are *sure* that the employee is wrong and that you are, in fact, the one next above him in the line of authority and responsibility. In that case, see whether you can get him to agree with you and to change his answers. If not, your comments under Question 46 should show why you think that the employee is wrong and that you are the person to fill this portion of the form instead of the person named by the employee.

On the cards that you do sign as immediate superior, do not make any corrections or additions to the entries of the employees, but make note of any that you think ought to be made, by means of comments under Question 46. Explain each comment fully. Then fill in your answers to Questions 47 and 48. Please read these questions carefully and be sure that you understand them before you attempt to answer them. Very commonly, the immediate superiors describe the qualifications of the present employees in the positions. That is not what is wanted, as the questions themselves will show on a careful reading.

After you have finished your entries, as just described, on each of the forms of your immediate subordinates, you should turn the form over to your own immediate superior, to whom also should go your own position description, and those of any other employees under you whose immediate superiors are also under your supervision. In the case of any of these latter, since there is no space provided for comments by you, attach a slip calling attention to any corrections or additions that you think ought to be made, to go along with the form until it reaches the head of the department, as a suggestion to him to cover the point in his comments.

You are urgently requested to do all you can to expedite the completion and delivery to your own immediate superior, of the position descriptions of all of the employees under you, and your own.

To the Head of the Department:

Please examine all the position descriptions of employees under your control, or have this done under your direction by someone on whose judgment you rely. So far as practicable, please secure such corrections and additions to the answers of employees and their immediate superiors as you think are necessary to make all these answers correct and complete, and as the employees themselves are willing to make. But please do not require any employee under you to make any change or addition that he does not desire to make of his own volition. The answers should be definitely the answers of the employees, not what they are told to say.

If you disagree with any statement of any employee, which he does not wish to change, or wish to add anything to the statements that any employee is willing to make, or if you have a correction or addition to any statement of an employee which is not practicable to take up with the employee, please indicate the correction or addition you desire to make in the blank for Question 50.

You are invited to include here also any further observations, comments, or suggestions that you may wish to supply relative to the position, or its work, or the adequacy or inadequacy of the existing rate or method of pay and what you consider a more appropriate rate or method, or any other matter that you deem pertinent.

When you are satisfied with any position description, as executed down through Question 50, with or without comments of your own, please fill in the blanks for Question 51.

You are urged to read the answers on the form with care and not to pass them with perfunctory inspection.

Your earnest cooperation in effecting prompt completion and return of the forms will be greatly appreciated.

Appendix B

Letter Accompanying Questionnaire and Instructions

 I N a recent classification survey conducted by Public Administration Service for the State of Minnesota each employee received with his questionnaire forms the following letter:

To: All Employees in the Classified Service
Subject: Classification Survey

We attach to this bulletin the Employee and Classification questionnaires which will be used in the classification of positions in the state service. This is the only questionnaire which will be submitted to you for filling out.

We ask that you do not fill in the questionnaire without previously making sure that you know what is wanted and have in mind what you are going to write.

The questionnaires are extremely important to us. The Employee questionnaire will form the basis for our service records. The Classification questionnaire will be reviewed and will form the basis for further analysis of your position in the development of the classification plan. A classification plan groups together under single titles those positions which have similar duties and responsibilities, which require similar basic training and experience, and to which similar salary ranges may be assigned with equity. The classification survey is in no way concerned with an evaluation of your qualifications or efficiency. Its sole objective is to determine the duties and responsibilities of each *position* in the service.

The care and attention you give to these questionnaires will determine in a large measure the speed with which the classification plan can be established. We ask that you take not more than three working days in returning these questionnaires to your immediate supervisor. If you are a supervisor, we ask that you submit your own questionnaire and the questionnaires of employees under you, with requested notations by you, to the department head within five additional days.

You may be contacted by the classification staff at a later date. Personal visits will be made wherever necessary to secure additional information, or to clarify information on the questionnaires.

If you have any questions about the questionnaire or the objectives of the survey, please contact the Civil Service Board by letter or telephone and the survey staff will be glad to assist you.

Yours very truly,
CIVIL SERVICE BOARD

Appendix C

Class Specifications

JUNIOR STENOGRAPHER [1]

Duties

Under immediate supervision, to take notes by hand or machine from simple dictation and transcribe them on a typewriter; to do general typing and simple clerical work; and to perform related work as required.

Typical Tasks

Taking shorthand notes from dictation and transcribing them; maintaining files and records; typing form letters, bills, reports, or licenses; figuring and typing purchase requisitions; issuing routine permits; giving out information or answering telephones; typing payrolls; assisting in the preparation of statistics, reports, or financial statements; keeping time records; cutting stencils; having charge of X-ray files and records; requisitioning and caring for office supplies; distributing courses of study and other publications; opening and distributing mail.

Minimum Qualifications

Common school education, and preferably some high school training; completion of a standard course in stenography and typewriting; preferably six months of experience in stenographic and clerical work; good command of English and spelling; ability to take simple dictation at a speed of not less than seventy-five net words a minute and accurately to transcribe the notes on a typewriter at not less than twenty-five net words a minute; ability to typewrite at not less than forty-five net words a minute from clear manuscript or from printed or typewritten matter; clerical aptitude; neatness; and alertness.

SENIOR STENOGRAPHER [2]

Duties

Under supervision, to take notes from dictation and to transcribe them on the typewriter; to do difficult and responsible office work calling for individual judgment in carrying out established procedures or applying law or regulations; in some cases to supervise a small group of others in routine office work; and to do related work as required.

[1] Civil Service Commission of the City of Cleveland, Ohio, *Laws, Rules, and the Classification of the Public Service of the City of Cleveland, the County of Cuyahoga and the Board of Education,* adopted October 25, 1926. Griffenhagen & Associates.

[2] *Report of the Joint Legislative Committee on Classification of Positions in the Civil Service—State of New York.* Legis. Doc. No. 55 (1932), p. 663. Griffenhagen & Associates.

Examples

Taking and transcribing dictation in connection with or in addition to such clerical and typing work as is specified for the class of Senior Typist.

Minimum Qualifications

High school education including or supplemented by a course in stenography and typing and two years of office experience including stenography and typing, or junior high school education and a business course including stenography and typing with three years of such experience, or any equivalent combination of education and experience; abstract intelligence represented by a score of 105 in the army alpha intelligence tests; advanced knowledge of office practices and appliances and skill in their application; ability to take notes from dictation and to transcribe them on the typewriter, and to type neatly and correctly from plain copy, corrected manuscript, and tabular matter; ability to meet the public and to get along well with others; ability to lay out work for others and to get results from their work; mental alertness; neatness; accuracy, and dependability.

Principal Lines of Promotion

From: Assistant Stenographer.
To: Principal Stenographer; Principal Clerk.

ASSISTANT TRAFFIC ENGINEER[3]

Duties Statement

Under direction, to be immediately responsible for the investigation and analysis of traffic and related transportation problems; individually, to perform the more difficult and specialized work involved therein; and to perform related work as required.

Typical Examples of Work Performed

In accordance with established general policies, subject to outlining by superiors of general assignments and procedures, with reports and recommendations subject to review by superiors, but with considerable responsibility for developing plans and technical details and for adequacy of work performed:

Supervising the investigation of traffic conditions and problems through field surveys and study of existing statistical data; developing traffic survey techniques; assigning investigations to subordinates, advising them as to objectives and procedures; analyzing and critically reviewing the reports and recommendations of subordinates as to their adequacy and feasibility; in specific situations, devising methods of control including signals, signs and other control devices; designing or selecting and preparing specifications for such devices and inspecting them for workmanship and suitability

[3] Detroit Civil Service Commission.

both during manufacture and upon delivery; studying the efficacy of existing traffic regulations and formulating and recommending desirable revisions or innovations; assembling traffic and related data in report form and arranging for their dissemination; as aids to traffic studies and control, directing the preparation of maps and layouts of proposed traffic structures with indications as to their general characteristics; generally assisting in the work of the Traffic Engineering Bureau by devising or preparing a wide variety of material for educational purposes on traffic, accident prevention, and related problems.

Minimum Entrance Qualifications

Education equivalent to graduation from a university of recognized standing with specialization in fields relating to traffic engineering; considerable experience in traffic and related engineering activities, particularly in the study and installation of traffic controls in urban areas, including reasonable experience in the statistical analysis and reporting of traffic data, a reasonable amount of which experience must have been in a supervisory capacity; considerable knowledge of problems of traffic control and of the principles, methods and equipment involved in their solution; reasonable familiarity with statistical and graphic principles and methods, including the collection, compilation, analysis and presentation of data in graphic and other forms for technical and popular use; reasonable ability in supervising the investigation and analysis of traffic conditions, in designing methods and in utilizing mechanical and electrical devices for effective traffic control, and in preparing technical and popular reports in textual and graphic form; good powers of observation; physically active; tact in dealing with subordinates, other departmental personnel, and the public; initiative and resourcefulness in solving complicated problems of traffic analysis and control; no disabling impairments of vision, speech, hearing, or members.

Age Limits

Minimum 27 years.

INTERMEDIATE CLERK-STENOGRAPHER (Spec. No. 9)[4]

General Statement

To perform high grade stenographic and typing work and moderately difficult, responsible clerical work; and to perform related work as required.

Evaluation of Duties

The position requires a combination of first-rate stenographic ability, familiarity with office practice and equipment, a knowledge of business and professional terms, good working knowledge of business English and correspondence forms, and mature clerical judgment. It may involve con-

[4] Seattle Civil Service Commission, *Class Specifications of The City of Seattle*, 1938. Public Administration Service.

siderable contact with the public. Employees must be able to take dictation at the rate of one hundred words a minute and transcribe accurately at the rate of twenty-five words a minute, or type from copy at a rate of fifty net words a minute. They should be able to transcribe stenographic notes taken several days before transcription. When solely stenographic, the work is on a production basis. Familiarity with office practice involves knowledge of postal regulations and modern office procedures and appliances, such as filing systems, simple calculating machines, mimeographs, and tabulating machines, and ability to perform common clerical tasks.

Supervision Received

Letters and reports are reviewed before signature, and new clerical work is preceded by general instructions. Detailed instructions as to work methods are received only on unfamiliar assignments of a clerical nature, such as compilation of data, etc.

Supervision Exercised

Normally none, but work may require supervision of junior clerks or distribution of work to clerks.

Desirable Preparation

Experience and education equivalent to at least two years of stenographic work and completion of a standard four-year high school course, with courses in stenography and typing.

Examples of Duties

To:

Take dictation and transcribe letters, legal opinions, financial memoranda, or reports involving medical or scientific terminology;

Perform typing work of all kinds, including the compilation and tabulation of figures, the preparation of statistical tables, and the typing of payrolls;

Compile yearly reports from readily accessible sources, and maintain office files and records;

Interview persons and answer the telephone, taking down information in shorthand;

Take depositions of department trials and investigations and transcribe the same;

Wait on the counter, issuing licenses and handling other routine matters;

Answer routine correspondence, selecting proper form letters;

Act as a law stenographer, taking dictation and transcribing legal documents, ordinances, letters, agreements, and legal opinions, and copying police court transcripts and complaints; and

Do related work as required.

X-Ray Technician[5]

General Statement of Duties

Makes, develops and prints X-ray films; assists in the X-raying process; does related work as required.

Evaluation of Duties

Employees of this class perform scientific processes requiring the technical knowledge of a skilled craftsman. This work entails responsibility for competent performance of technical tasks. However, the work performed involves no special, advanced, or unusual techniques.

Examples of Duties

Makes radiographic exposures; develops and arranges negatives; prepares various developing solutions; develops, fixes, washes, and files X-ray films; is responsible for the general upkeep of the X-ray laboratory; assists in taking photographs of persons and physical lesions; assists in keeping general tuberculosis records; does related work as required.

Supervision Received

Tasks are assigned and laid out by a professional person to whom assistance is given. The work is subject to check at completion.

Required Knowledges, Skills, and Abilities

Good knowledge of the operation of plate and film cameras; ability to develop photographic films and plates; thoroughness; accuracy; good judgment; no serious defects of vision, hearing, or members.

Acceptable Experience and Training

At least one year's experience in making and developing X-ray films; completion of a standard high school course, with training in chemistry desirable;

Or

any equivalent combination of experience and training sufficient to demonstrate ability to do the work.

Head Typist (Grade 5)[6]

Duties and Responsibilities

Under general supervision, to plan and supervise the work of a group of Typists and Senior Typists; to perform personally the most difficult typing; and to do other work as required.

[5] State of Alabama Personnel Department, *Classification Plan*, approved November 29, 1939. Public Administration Service.
[6] *Manual of Class Specifications for Positions in Regional Offices*. Home Owners' Loan Corporation, Washington, D. C., November 1, 1940, p. 17.

Examples of Work Performed

To supervise a moderately large group of Typists engaged in typing forms, letters, and other material from straight copy or rough draft; to select material to be typed; to instruct typists as to methods, procedure, and work to be performed; to maintain performance records and review, verify, and correct the work of subordinates; and to do related work as required.

To serve as working supervisor over a group of Senior Typists engaged in typing difficult tabular matter requiring orderly arrangement of material and use of long carriage machines, or engaged in typing from rough draft in which a knowledge of procedure and terminology is essential; to assign and review work and maintain production records on performance of subordinates.

Minimum Qualifications

Training. Equivalent to that represented by graduation from high school and one year* of experience in positions involving difficult typing duties and the performance of some general clerical duties. The foregoing must have demonstrated:

Knowledge. Of general office methods and procedures and ability to keep simple records; ability to type accurately and rapidly and to arrange and space complicated copy skillfully; ability to plan typing assignments, make proper assignments, maintain flow and output of work, and check the completed work; ability to understand and carry out complex verbal and written instructions; ability to get along well with others.

*An equivalent period of specialized training in typing and commercial subjects may be substituted for any part of the required experience.

GUARD I[7]

Kind of Work

Maintenance of order and supervision of the conduct of inmates at a penal institution on an assigned shift; and related work as required.

Difficulty and Responsibility of Work

Positions vary in scope of activity from wall guard, with no inmate contacts, or night cell house guard, to guards maintaining contact with inmates in or outside the walls. Due to the nature of the institution, guards are necessarily subject to a form of military discipline, and to assignment from one post to another to insure inmate control.

Regulations and oral assignments specify in detail the method and manner of work, and guard work is closely checked by officers.

Essential Requirements of Work

Understanding of the methods and objects of discipline as applied to persons under restraint.

[7] Minnesota State Civil Service Department, April 10, 1940. Public Administration Service.

Ability to control and direct inmates individually and in groups.

Proficiency in the use of firearms.

Agility, strength, and good physical condition.

Freedom from serious defects in vision, hearing, or members.

Exceptionally good physical condition, strength and agility, with measurements of 5 feet 9 inches minimum height, 165 lbs. minimum weight, and freedom from serious diseases and defects.

Examples of Work

(Illustrative only; indicates kinds of work performed in the class outlined above.)

Stands guard or patrols grounds, galleries, corridors, walls or shops.

Inspects trucks, automobiles, and other vehicles entering the institution.

Takes periodic counts of inmates.

Oversees the work of a group of inmates detailed to shop or farm activities.

Supervises the bathing and feeding of inmates.

Accompanies prisoners to and from places of employment, chapel, and meals, and supervises them while there.

Inspects quarters of prisoners and sees that they are sanitary and in an orderly condition.

Issues clothing, shoes, or other supplies or material to inmates, and keeps records of issues.

Escorts inmates on trips outside prison grounds.

Supervises visits to inmates, and ushers visitors through the institution.

Searches inmates and quarters for contraband and weapons, and censors mail.

Reports infractions of rules and regulations.

Desirable Preparation for Work

Graduation from a standard high school.

Necessary Special Qualifications

Minimum age at entrance: 25 years. Maximum age at entrance: 45 years.

SENIOR MATERIALS CHEMIST[8]

General Statement of Duties

To supervise and to participate in physical and chemical analyses of highway materials; and to do related work as required.

Supervision Received

Materials for testing are received through regular work flow channels; testing methods are defined closely by standards selected by superior; test results often are checked against results of duplicate runs done by a senior chemist or by a subordinate; all test results are summarized and reviewed by superior.

[8] Rhode Island Department of Civil Service, *Tentative Class Specifications*, 1940. Public Administration Service.

Supervision Exercised

Exercises rather close supervision over subordinates in chemical laboratory; makes specific assignments to subordinates; checks the work of subordinates while in process and upon completion.

Examples of Duties

To instruct subordinates in various techniques and methods of physical chemistry; to review the methods and the results of subordinates; to obtain samples according to definite specifications; to perform physicochemical tests in order to determine viscosities, specific gravities, penetrations, elongations, and ductilities; to perform distillations and extractions; to gauge material dimensions; to perform quantitative or qualitative examinations on materials to be used in the highway system; to analyze coal and fuel oil according to specifications; and to do related work as required.

Minimum Qualifications

Experience. Such as may have been gained through: employment in a responsible professional position conducting physical and chemical examinations of highway and related materials;
Training. Such as may have been gained through: graduation from a recognized college with specialization in physical chemistry;
Or, any combination of experience and training that shall have resulted in: a thorough knowledge of the principles, practices, materials, and methods of physical and chemical analyses and examinations of fuels and materials used in the construction of roads and bridges; an understanding of the principles, practices, materials and methods of qualitative and quantitative chemistry; a familiarity with the use and care of laboratory equipment; and related capacities and abilities.

Special Characteristics

Ability to plan and arrange work for subordinates; resourcefulness; accuracy; integrity; good physical condition.

AUDITOR, GRADE 1 [9]

Definition

Under direction, to perform the less difficult technical office and field auditing work; and to do other work as required.

Typical Tasks

Assisting in the making of large and complex field audits of the accounts of state departments or political subdivisions, or of persons or business firms subject to taxation or regulation by the state; independently making the less complex and more routine audits; reviewing tax returns and financial statements and noting inconsistencies and irregularities; verifying postings, footings, and vouchers and preparing schedules

[9] California State Personnel Board, May 28, 1940.

in support of reports submitted; dictating routine correspondence in connection with audits made; testifying in court occasionally on matters involving audits completed.

Minimum Qualifications

Experience. One year of experience within the last five years on the staff of a recognized Public Accountant* or in the auditing department of a large commercial or governmental organization in any of the following types of work, or any combination thereof:

a. Analytical and critical examination of financial records or books of accounts.

b. Construction and installation of varied accounting and cost systems.

c. Preparation of comprehensive financial statements.

*Either a Certified Public Accountant or an accountant admitted to practice as agent before the United States Treasury Department.

and

Education. Equivalent to graduation from college with at least fifteen semester hours in accounting.

Alternate education requirement. Graduation from the twelfth grade and completion of the accounting curriculum of a recognized school of accountancy with a certificate showing satisfactory completion of courses in elementary and advanced accounting, commercial law, auditing, and cost accounting. (Note: Courses in bookkeeping not acceptable.)

and

Knowledges

1. Thorough knowledge of accounting and auditing principles, practices, and procedures.

2. General knowledge of commercial law.

3. Some knowledge of:

a. Principles of public finance and taxation.

b. Statistical methods.

c. Financial mathematics.

and

Ability

1. To analyze and verify financial documents and records.

2. To prepare schedules, financial statements, and reports.

3. To make audits of small business firms involving no special difficulties.

4. To analyze provisions of laws and regulations and to apply them to specific cases.

5. To make arithmetical calculations with speed and accuracy.

6. To write clear and concise reports.

7. To follow oral and written directions.

8. To size up situations and people accurately, to adopt an effective course of action, and to get along well with others.

and

Personal characteristics. Willingness to live and work away from headquarters office; neat personal appearance; resourcefulness; initiative; integrity; tact; industry; accuracy; good judgment; and good health and freedom from disabling defects.

Monthly Compensation

$160   170   180   190   200

POLICE PATROLMAN [10]

Kind of Work

Routine police work in protecting life and property and enforcing criminal and traffic laws and local ordinances; and related work as required.

Distinguishing Features of Work

Work involves responsibility for maintaining law and order, for preventing crime, and for protecting life and property within the city. Work methods are of a routine nature and were developed and demonstrated in detail by superior officers. A patrolman must be able to independently exercise quick but sound judgment in applying these methods in emergency situations involving danger to life and property. Work requires good social and general intelligence and involves responsibility for tactful and courteous treatment of the public at all times, and for conscientious and efficient performance of all duties without specific instructions in each case. Work is supervised by a superior officer through personal inspection, through review of daily reports, and through general appraisal of the effectiveness of the police service. Ordinarily no supervision is exercised.

Examples of Work

(Note: The following examples are intended only as illustrations of the various kinds of work performed in the class.)

Patrols a specified beat or district on foot, on motorcycle, or in a radio cruiser; checks doors and windows of business establishments and investigates any suspicious conditions.

Makes arrests for violation of laws and ordinances, escorts prisoners to court, testifies in court.

Watches for and makes investigations of wanted and missing persons, and stolen property.

Enforces traffic laws, directs traffic, assists children at school crossings.

Checks cars for overtime parking, investigates and makes detailed reports concerning traffic accidents, analyzes traffic statistics, escorts funerals and parades.

Operates a police patrol wagon and escorts prisoners from the jail to the prison farm.

Makes criminal investigations when on detective assignment, visits scenes of crimes and searches for evidence, questions suspects, suppresses vice, watches pawn shops for stolen property.

Makes daily reports of all activities.

[10] City of Atlanta, Ga., Public Administration Service survey, December 1940.

Necessary Knowledge, Skills, and Abilities

Good social and general intelligence.
Ability to be courteous but firm with the public.
Ability to understand and carry out complex oral and written directions.
Aptitude for learning police methods.
Ability to drive an automobile or motorcycle.
Good powers of observation.
Courage to perform hazardous duties.

Desirable Preparation for Work

Graduation from a standard senior high school.

Requirements for Acceptance of Applications

Not less than twenty-three and not more than thirty years of age on the final date for receiving applications.

Weight, Height, and Chest Measurements

In accordance with the following table:

Height (without shoes)	Minimum Weight (stripped)	Maximum Weight (stripped)	Chest Measurements	
			Expanded	Minimum Mobility
5 ft. 9 in.	145 lbs.	185 lbs.	38 in.	2½ in.
5 ft. 10 in.	150 lbs.	190 lbs.	38½ in.	3 in.
5 ft. 11 in.	155 lbs.	195 lbs.	39½ in.	3 in.
6 ft.	160 lbs.	205 lbs.	40½ in.	3 in.
6 ft. 1 in.	165 lbs.	210 lbs.	41 in.	3 in.
6 ft. 2 in.	170 lbs.	220 lbs.	42 in.	3 in.
6 ft. 3 in.	180 lbs.	230 lbs.	43 in.	3 in.

SENIOR CLERK [11]

General Statement of Duties

An employee of this class individually performs varied and difficult clerical work of a responsible nature requiring a thorough knowledge of the operation of the agency to which assigned, the work being done without close or regular supervision; may supervise a small group of clerical employees in the performance of routine and repetitive clerical duties; and does related work as required.

Distinguishing Features of the Work

The work of senior clerks is distinguished from that of clerks by the fact that senior clerks are required to make decisions on their own responsibility which require the exercise of independent judgment based upon a good understanding of specific laws and ordinances and of established departmental rules, policies, or activities. Moreover, senior clerks may frequently perform a variety of routine and largely unrelated duties

[11] Los Angeles City Civil Service Commission, *Preliminary Classification Plan,* July 1940. Public Administration Service.

on their own responsibility under conditions which permit little opportunity for direct supervision by superiors. In such cases, these employees are required to exercise initiative in determining the priority of completion of work, the sequence in which tasks are to be performed and the work methods to be employed, and in taking action on unusual problems which arise in the course of a day's business.

Employees of this class meet the public under circumstances which require a thorough knowledge of departmental activities, policies, and administrative precedents. They are expected to be so familiar with sources that they can answer any questions of fact and sometimes even questions involving minor interpretations. They frequently have occasion to accept applications and other forms and examine them for conformity with established regulations and policies and specific laws and ordinances.

Senior clerks may supervise either a small group of subordinate employees engaged in simple, repetitive, clerical and typing work such as filing or checking for accuracy and completeness, or a few subordinates on routine but diversified work. Errors in judgment made by senior clerks may result in duplication of work, loss of time, or inconvenience to outside individuals dealing with the department but they are not of serious consequence to the organization. Senior clerks are usually given detailed instructions upon being assigned to their duties and thereafter, instructions or directions are given on unusual or special problems and review is a matter of spot-checking rather than detailed scrutiny.

Examples of Duties

A senior clerk: personally performs the posting of information from such media as time reports, material consumption reports, performance reports, applications, bills, invoices, requisitions, and demands and many other media, the posting being to control records or statements of various types including rosters, card records, journals, ledgers, permit records, or summary statements, and is made under conditions in which the correct posting is not apparent from the media involved but may be made to any of a number of records and under conditions in which no standardized routine exists, thus requiring a thorough knowledge of the use and purpose of the media worked with in order that the posting may be properly performed;

Makes final checks, usually with the necessity for assuming personal responsibility, of the accuracy of records and reports of many varieties, or reconciles one form of media with another in cases where no guide lines exist in the form of either internal evidences in the media themselves or in the form of standardized procedures, and where such check requires the application of and frequent reference to specific statutes, charter provisions, ordinances, departmental rules, regulations, administrative orders, or precedents;

Receives applications for permits or licenses, petitions or contracts, rolls, or other documents and checks for compliance with requirements as to form and content and for completeness, such checking requiring independent decision as to whether the documents comply with the provisions of applicable statutes, charter provisions, ordinances, rules, regulations, administrative orders, precedents, or tariff and rate schedules, and sometimes involving the study of such sources before judgment can be rendered;

Gives out information at a public counter or over a telephone relative to the filing of or issuance of such permits, licenses, or other documents when judgment and knowledge and study of such sources as those just detailed are involved in answering questions from the public, representatives of other city departments, or other official agencies; answers other questions where judgment and knowledge and interpretation are involved in addition to answering questions of fact;

Handles billing or financial record-keeping operations or serves in a money-handling capacity where such work involved discretion for permitting deviations from standardized routines in accordance with the best judgment of the employee, such as in granting time extensions, or where a knowledge of general principles underlying the record keeping operations as well as knowledge of routine is required;

Supervises a small group of employees operating office appliances; assists in supervising larger groups or personally performs the most difficult and responsible tasks involved in connection with such operations;

Collates a large variety of data from office records for use by a superior; performs restricted library research on non-technical subjects; subject to approval by a superior, devises or revises routine office procedures, usually those relating to filing or record keeping; prepares periodic reports which involve searching out materials from a number of sources and working out the details of presentation;

Supervises a small group of clerical employees engaged in filing, sorting, and miscellaneous record-keeping operations in connection with sorting and filing bills, invoices, requisitions, demands, permits, applications, work orders, purchase orders, and similar documents when such filing and sorting is performed according to some predetermined classification; responsibility amounts essentially to seeing that a proper flow of work is maintained, and when questions raised by employees do not require the authorization of major deviations from established procedures;

And does related work as required.

Desirable Qualifications

A senior clerk should have: a good knowledge of modern office practices including filing, indexing, and cross referencing methods; a good knowledge of correct punctuation, spelling, and grammatical usage together with a good vocabulary; a general knowledge of elementary bookkeeping practice; a general knowledge of commonly used office machines and devices coupled with some skill in their operation; the ability to learn rapidly specific laws and ordinances and office policies, regulations, and procedures coupled with alertness and good judgment in applying them in a variety of cases; the ability to meet and deal tactfully and effectively with the public; the ability to do clerical work and perform arithmetical computations; initiative in organizing work and completing assigned tasks; and some ability in planning, laying out, and directing the work of others.

The knowledges, skills, and abilities normally acquired through completion of four years of high school and at least three years of experience in the performance of varied clerical work, or other training or experience which would provide these knowledges, skills, and abilities to a similar degree, would constitute a desirable background for a person performing the work required.

Appendix D

Basic Rules for the Installation and Administration of a Position-Classification Plan

T<small>HIS</small> illustration of a code of rules assumes the existence of a personnel agency of the form described in the *Draft of a State Civil Service Law* recently prepared by a joint committee of the Civil Service Assembly of the United States and Canada, the National Civil Service Reform League, and the National Municipal League.[1] This draft of law establishes a Department of Civil Service in which there is a Civil Service Commission of three members and a Director of Personnel. The members of the Commission are appointed by the Governor. The Director of Personnel is appointed by the Governor as the result of a competitive test. The Director of Personnel is the executive head of the Department of Civil Service and is responsible for the direction and supervision of its administrative and technical activities. In particular, he is authorized to issue procedural regulations, consistent with the law and rules.[2] The duties of the Commissioners involve rule making, hearing, investigative, public relations, advisory, and reporting activities. The Commissioners are made finally responsible for the position-classification plan and the Director is made finally responsible for the allocations of individual positions in accordance with such plan.

Section 1. Definitions of Terms

The following terms wherever used in these rules shall have the meaning indicated below:

Rule 1. *Position.* The term "position" means a group of current duties and responsibilities, assigned or delegated by competent authority, requiring the full-time or part-time employment of one person.

Rule 2. *Employee.* The term "employee" means a person who is legally an incumbent of a position or who is on authorized leave of absence and whose position is held for him pending his return.

Rule 3. *Class or Class of Positions.* The term "class" or "class of positions" means a group of positions established under the Civil Service Law or these rules sufficiently similar in respect to duties and responsibilities that the same descriptive class title may be used to designate each position allocated to the class, that the same entrance qualifications may be required

---

[1]Published in 1939 by the two last-named organizations. The sample rules given here are to be read in connection with the provisions of that draft. There is, however, some variation between them.

[2]Accordingly, the rules given herein are for the most part fundamental rather than detailed in the procedural sense.

of incumbents of positions in the class, that the same tests of fitness may be used to choose qualified employees, and that the same schedule of pay may be made to apply with equity under the same or substantially the same employment conditions.

Rule 4. *Class Title.* The term "class title" means the designation given under these rules to a class, to each position allocated to the class, and to the incumbent of each such position.

Rule 5. *Allocated.* The term "allocated" means officially placed in a given class and assigned the class title for the class.

Rule 6. *Class Specification.* The term "class specification" means a written statement describing the duties, responsibilities, and entrance qualification standards of a class of positions.

Rule 7. *Position-Classification Plan.* The classes of positions described in the official class specifications, with such amendments as may be made under these rules from time to time, and as interpreted herein, shall, together with these rules, the class specifications, and any amendments thereto, constitute the official "position-classification plan."

SECTION 2. INTERPRETATION OF CLASS SPECIFICATIONS

Rule 8. *Effect of class specifications is to describe duties and responsibilities, not to restrict or prescribe them.* Class specifications are descriptive and explanatory and not restrictive. They are intended to indicate the kinds of positions that should be allocated to the several classes, as determined by their duties and responsibilities, and shall not be construed as prescribing what the duties or responsibilities of any individual position shall be. The use of a particular expression or illustration as to duties or responsibilities shall not be held to exclude others not mentioned that are of similar kind or quality.

Rule 9. *Class specifications do not destroy or create authority over certain operating responsibilities.* The language of class specifications is not to be construed as limiting or modifying the power that department heads may now have or hereafter be given to take from, add to, eliminate entirely, or otherwise change the duties and responsibilities of a position, to assign duties or delegate responsibilities to employees, or to direct and control their work.

Rule 10. *Each specification to be read as a complete unit.* In determining the class to which any position should be allocated, the specification of each class shall be considered as a whole. Consideration shall be given to the general duties, specific tasks, responsibilities, and qualifications standards as together affording a picture of the kind and level of employment that the class is intended to embrace.

Rule 11. *Relationship to other class specifications to be considered.* Each class specification is always to be construed in its proper relationship to other specifications, so as to maintain proper gradations and differentiations among the several classes of the position-classification plan.

Rule 12. *The class title.* The class title is always to be used with the meaning set forth in the remainder of the specification, that is, the text of the specification determines the official meaning of the class title.

Rule 13. *Statements of entrance qualifications standards.* Statements of entrance qualifications standards in a class specification shall constitute the basis for the acceptance or rejection of applications for examinations and provisional appointments, for the tests to be included in examinations, and for the evaluation of the qualifications of applicants.

Rule 14. *Certain qualifications not expressly stated are to be understood.* Qualifications commonly required of all incumbents of positions of different classes, such as acceptable physical condition, freedom from disabling defects, United States citizenship, suitable age, honesty, sobriety, and industry, shall be deemed to be implied as entrance qualification requirements, even though they may not be specifically mentioned in the specifications.

Section 3. Official Copy of the Position-Classification Plan

Rule 15. *Official copy of position-classification plan to be maintained in current, accurate form, available for reference.* The Director of Personnel shall establish and maintain in the Department of Civil Service, in a form convenient for reference, an accurate and complete copy of the position-classification plan to be designated as the official copy. The official copy of these rules and of each class specification shall be endorsed with the date of adoption and the attesting signature of the Director. All amendments or revisions of these rules or the class specifications shall be similarly endorsed. The official copy of the position-classification plan shall be open to inspection by the public under reasonable conditions during business hours. Duplicates of the official copy of any class specification shall be furnished by the Director to appointing officers or department heads upon their request. The Director shall promptly give notice of revisions or changes in the position-classification plan to the departments, the budget or fiscal agency, and all other agencies dealing with personnel or pay.

Section 4. Installation of the Classification Plan

Rule 16. *Initial allocations of positions.* As promptly as practicable after the adoption of the position-classification plan, and after consultation with appointing authorities and principal supervisory officials, the Director shall allocate each position to the appropriate class on the basis of its duties and responsibilities.

Rule 17. *Notification of initial allocations.* The Director shall promptly give notice of such allocations to the departments and employees affected.

Rule 18. *Certification of initial allocations.* After affording department officials and employees affected a reasonable opportunity to be heard on controverted allocations, the Director shall certify official lists to the respective departments showing the allocations of positions to the appropriate classes.

Rule 19. *Effect of initial allocations.* Such certified allocations shall constitute the official allocations in force at the time the position-classification plan takes effect, and they shall continue in force until changed by the Director under the provisions of these rules.

Rule 20. *Official adoption of class titles.* Upon the certification of these allocations the title of the class to which each position is allocated shall forthwith become the title of each such position, and shall henceforth be used in all records, communications, documents, reports, and processes relating to personnel matters, including the recruiting, testing, selection, appointment, transfer, promotion, reemployment, demotion, or dismissal of employees, the preparation and audit of payrolls, and all budget and fiscal processes dealing with the appropriation and expenditure of funds for personal services. When approved by the Director, other titles may be used for purposes of internal administration, public convenience, or in connections other than personnel, budgetary, or fiscal.

SECTION 5. THE ALLOCATION OF POSITIONS DURING THE CONTINUOUS
ADMINISTRATION OF THE POSITION-CLASSIFICATION PLAN

Rule 21. *All positions to be allocated.* Every position existing when these rules take effect, or hereafter authorized or created, shall be allocated by the Director to the appropriate class. No person shall be appointed to a position until such allocation has been determined.

Rule 22. *Allocation of new, additional, or changed positions.* Whenever a new or additional position is, or is intended to be, authorized or created, or the duties or responsibilities of an existing position are, or are intended to be, substantially changed, and such change is of indeterminate duration, the head of the department shall report such fact to the Director and shall transmit to him such information, and in such manner and form, as he may, by regulation or otherwise, request. After such inquiry or conference as he may deem necessary, the Director shall allocate or reallocate the position to the appropriate class and shall certify such allocation to the department.

Rule 23. *Abolition of positions.* Whenever an existing position is abolished, the head of department shall report such fact to the Director and shall transmit to him such information, and in such manner and form, as he may, by regulation or otherwise, request. Whenever an existing position is reallocated to a different class, a new position shall be deemed to have been created in lieu of the one previously existing, and the latter shall be considered to have been abolished.

Rule 24. *Reallocation on the initiative of the Director.* On his own motion, the Director may at any time make investigations or classification audits of organization units or groups of positions, and may, in accordance with these rules, reallocate positions whenever the facts, in his judgment, warrant such action, and shall certify such reallocations to the head of department. No reallocation of any position shall be made under this section, however, until the administrative officials concerned and the employee holding the position shall have had a reasonable opportunity to be heard.

Rule 25. *Requests for review of the allocations of positions.* The head of the department in which the position is located or the employee occupying the position shall have the right to request and obtain a review by the Director of the correctness of the existing allocation of such position. The Director shall prescribe regulations not inconsistent with these rules for the form, content, and filing of requests for review of allocations, for the conduct of conferences and investigations in connection therewith, and for taking action upon such requests, which regulations shall have the same force as these rules.

Rule 26. *Force and effect of allocations or reallocations.* Whenever, under the provisions of any of these rules, a position shall have been allocated or reallocated to a class, the title of such class shall forthwith become the title of such position and shall henceforth be used in all records, communications, documents, reports, and processes having reference to such position, as set forth more particularly in Rule 20. Such allocation or reallocation shall continue in force until changed by the Director under the provisions of these rules.

SECTION 6. AMENDMENT OF THE POSITION-CLASSIFICATION PLAN

Rule 27. *Authority of Commission to amend and revise classes and class specifications.* Whenever circumstances warrant, upon his own initiative or in connection with the allocation of new positions or the reallocation or abolition of existing positions, or otherwise, the Director may, after affording the administrative officials and employees affected a reasonable opportunity to be heard, recommend to the Commission changes in the classes or class specifications of the position-classification plan, such as the amendment or revision of the specification for any class, the merger, division, alteration or abolition of existing classes and the corresponding class specifications, or the establishment of new classes and new class specifications to cover existing and newly created positions. Any such change recommended by the Director shall take effect when approved by the Commission or on the thirtieth day after it is recommended to the Commission if prior thereto, after a reasonable opportunity for the administrative officials and employees affected to be heard, the Commission shall not have disapproved it.

Rule 28. *Procedure in amendment where reallocations of positions are involved.* When any change is made in the position-classification plan by which a class of positions is divided, altered, or abolished, or classes are combined, or when amendments or revisions of the position-classification plan require changes in the existing allocation of one or more positions, the Director shall forthwith reallocate the positions affected to their appropriate classes in the amended position-classification plan, following the procedure of Section 4 of these rules.

Rule 29. *Force and effect of amendments and revisions.* Amendments, revisions, and changes in the classes and the class specifications made under the provisions of these rules shall have the same force and effect as the classes and class specifications originally adopted.

Rule 30. *Amendment of these rules.* These rules may be amended in the manner provided for their original adoption.

Appendix E

General Check List of Questions Involved in Analyzing the Difficulty and Responsibility of a Position for Classification Purposes

A. DIFFICULTY AND COMPLEXITY OF DUTIES

1. *Status of work or stage of development of problem when first presented to the employee*

What place does the employee's position occupy in the flow of work? What preparatory or previous steps have been taken which increase or lessen the complexity or difficulty of his tasks? Which, if any, of the operations necessary to dispose of the matter or problem have already been performed? Which of the necessary decisions have already been made?

2. *Segregation or selection of assignments for the employee*

a. Does the employee's work cover the "mine-run" of questions, cases, or tasks, or are they segregated according to their difficulty, and assignments made to different employees on that basis? If a segregation is made, to what employees are the more difficult (or less difficult) tasks customarily assigned?

b. Is there a segregation of cases on some basis other than difficulty, for example, source of origin, amount of money involved, and the like? If so, what is the general average of difficulty of the cases in one group as compared with those in another? What would be a sound standard of comparison to employ in determining the relative general average of difficulty among the several groups?

c. Especially in research positions, what is the present state of knowledge on the particular subject? Has the particular field of data been previously organized and classified?

3. *Procedure followed, processes performed, plans or action initiated or developed, or decisions made by the employee*

a. Exactly by what method, process, or procedure is the work done? What special skill or technique is employed in the performance of it? What sequence of steps is involved? What does the employee do at each step of the sequence and how does he do it? Is the procedure repetitive or varied? Reducible to a mechanical routine?

b. Is the action to be taken obvious? Is it defined by regulations, well-established office policy, or the standard technique of the occupation? Are guide lines and sources of information easily available and easily used?

Do ways and means have to be developed by the employee? If the work requires deliberation and study, what steps and mental processes are involved? To what extent and along what lines is the employee required to exercise original judgment, discrimination and independent thought?

c. What are the problems inherent in or peculiar to the type of work performed that have to be solved by the employee himself? Are the problems easy to apprehend and to decide? What particular types of obstacles are met, or complications found in his work? From a functional or subject-matter standpoint, what is the scope of the problems dealt with?

4. *Control of employee's work by others*

a. Does the employee receive instructions, advice, or counsel from his superior or another authorized person before and/or during the performance of his tasks, regarding what is to be done and how it is to be done? Along what lines and how far-reaching?

b. Is there another employee or a group of employees within the establishment (or possibly elsewhere) whose authority it is to render decisions and advice on the more difficult or unprecedented problems? If so, what connection do they have with the employee's work?

c. Is supervisory control confined to administrative matters or does it extend to functional or technical matters?

d. Is the employee's work free from technical control by others except for final review after completion? Is it reviewed purely from the standpoint of administrative considerations or is critical review given to it from a functional or technical viewpoint?

5. *Variety and scope*

a. Do the problems or tasks vary materially in character? If so, do they vary also in difficulty? What is the difficulty of each item making up the variety? Are there one or more outstanding tasks involved among a number of relatively simple duties; if so what proportion of time is spent upon them? Does the work consist of a mass of detailed tasks, complex in the sense that many different actions have to be taken by the employee, but not complex as to any one item?

b. To what extent and with what frequency do the problems or tasks of varying types occur (occasionally, intermittently, repetitively, periodically, frequently, rarely, etc.)? Is the position constituted of a recurring series of varied tasks, or does it involve a non-repetitive series of new demands to be met, new tasks to be performed, new problems to be solved?

c. From a functional or subject-matter standpoint how distinctive are the various tasks and problems? Are they intimately related to or part of, the same occupation, function, or field of work, or are they mutually distinct? Do they lead toward the accomplishment of the same objective, each forming a part of a continuous process within a limited field, or do they signify a succession of assignments or problems presented for interpretation and decision wherein each involves a new or different objective, body of rules, technique, or approach? What is the total scope of the various tasks and problems? What is the scope and comprehensiveness of qualifications needed to perform such tasks and solve such problems?

B. Nonsupervisory Responsibilities

1. *Responsibility for reviewing the work, actions, or decisions of others*

a. Of what processes, steps, or procedures does the review consist?

b. What is the purpose of the review—
   i. To determine accuracy of copy?
   ii. To determine the propriety of conclusions only?
   iii. To rework or otherwise verify prior operations or actions? What prior processes or actions are verified?
   iv. To obtain information for purposes of coordination or to make recommendations?

c. What is the scope of the review? Does it cover the merits or the formalities of the cases, or both? The technical or administrative aspects, or both? Is it a partial or complete review? If partial, what part of the work is reviewed? If presumably complete, does it cover all the aspects of the matter that were dealt with by the employee doing the work initially?

d. Does the review carry with it a specific responsibility (authority to change results) on each matter or case reviewed, or does the reviewer act in an advisory capacity without specific responsibility in a particular case?

e. Does review in borderline supervision give substantive responsibility to the reviewer to change details?

2. *Responsibility for independence of action or decision*

a. To what degree and subject to what check or control does the position involve the responsibility for independently initiating or taking action under certain circumstances?

b. Consider control of employee's work by others. Broadly considered, is the supervision over the employee close or general? Direct or indirect? Administrative or technical? Of what precise elements does such supervision consist? What are its outward manifestations?

c. To what degree does such supervision include (and to what degree does it not include):
   i. Assignment of tasks? How much initiative has the employee in deciding (1) what he shall do, (2) when he shall do it?
   ii. Instruction and guidance as to purposes, plans, or policies of work? How far is the employee's work controlled by plans or policies laid down by higher authority?
   iii. Instruction and guidance as to methods and technique of doing work? How much initiative has the employee in deciding how he shall accomplish a given task or objective? Is such initiative confined to simple, routine operations, or does it regularly extend, for example, to planning details to carry a given broad program into effect?
   iv. Overseeing to determine whether work is being done according to instructions. Is the employee actually guided or controlled during the progress of his work? How far is he permitted to go with a given assignment before the results of his work are examined and reviewed?
   v. Inspection, checking, or review of final product as to accuracy or other qualities, or as to compliance with plans and policies? What is the nature of such review as tested by the questions in "B-1" above?

d. What is the place of the position within the organizational structure?

e. What is the scope of the employee's authority? To what extent does the employee make decisions that do not require higher approval and that generally are unreviewed? Upon what types of questions or problems? What is the importance of those questions or problems?

f. How final is the employee's authority? Is it final with respect to the organization to which he is attached? Is it final with respect to the completion of the work? Does the work pass through any other processes before completion, and if so, who is responsible for these further processes?

g. Are the specific responsibilities attaching to the position lodged in this position exclusively? Or is there a divided responsibility and are these responsibilities shared by other employees? In the latter case, what are the places and the extent of distribution?

h. What are the importance and purpose of the final products or results of the work of the position? To what use are these products or results put?

i. What would be the effect of errors, inadequacies, etc.?

j. What is the relation between the work of the position and the functions of the organization unit, section, division, bureau, or department, taken as a whole?

3. *Responsibility for recommendations or decisions determining or affecting plans, programs, methods or policies*

a. What is the importance or consequence of such plans, programs, methods, or policies?

b. What is their relative degree of finality; how close do they come to the final executive action of putting them into effect?

c. To what extent is this responsibility shared by others?

4. *Responsibility for safety or lives of others*

a. In what way is such a responsibility manifest in the position?

b. Is safety present only to a limited degree or in a very indirect form? Does it refer only to activity in which the major burden of responsibility for physical safety falls upon mechanical safeguards and those who install and inspect them? What specific mechanical safeguards exist?

c. To what degree are human lives dependent upon the incumbent of the position?

5. *Responsibility for the custody of money, securities, or other things of special value*

a. What are the operations in which such responsibility is contended to be present?

b. Is this responsibility merely one of honesty and trustworthiness on the job?

c. Is there involved real responsibility for extreme care in the oversight or safeguarding of things of special value? In what way?

d. What control exists over the complex official tasks, acts, or decisions in positions involving responsibility for the custody of money, securities, and other things of special value?

6. *Responsibility for accuracy or for freedom from errors*

a. To what extent is the necessity for accuracy present in the position? What is the standard of accuracy involved in the nature of the work, either perfection or reasonable approximation of some objective?

b. To what degree is long or unusual experience essential to produce accuracy?

c. Is the accuracy mathematically or mechanically measurable, or is it but a matter of freedom from misapprehensions, misconstructions, or misapplications of judgment?

d. How difficult is it to achieve the desired standard of accuracy? Is it a matter of carefulness, alertness, or other quality that any satisfactory employee should possess or can acquire on the job in a reasonable time, or must the employee initially bring to the job special skill or special knowledge of a particular method, or advanced training or experience in that field when compared to the requirements for like or associated positions generally?

e. How responsible is the work in the light of the necessity of that degree of accuracy? What is the purpose of the work? To what use is the result of the work put? What happens when the desired standard of accuracy is not met? What is the effect of errors usually? What might be an unusual effect of an error? What provision is there for the discovery of errors and for review, inspection, or correction of the employee's work by others?

7. *Responsibility for public contacts*

a. To what extent is public contact involved in the position?

b. What classes of persons are dealt with?

c. Is the subject matter of the contact simple or complex, narrow or broad in scope, controversial or commonly accepted?

d. Is the purpose of the contact the giving of information, official negotiation, obtaining support and cooperation, or otherwise? To what extent does the purpose involve influencing others toward a course of action?

e. What degree of authority has the employee to make official commitments?

C. Supervisory and Administrative Responsibilities

1. *The "supervisory pattern"—number and types of supervisory action present*

Which of the following phases of supervisory or administrative control are present in the position concerned:

a. Control over policies (broad principles of law interpretation, management, or ethics governing the conduct of the work);

b. Control over objectives (purposes of the work; the characteristics of the completed product);

c. Plans (ways and means for accomplishing the objectives);

d. Flow of work (organizational and functional course which a given piece of work takes from inception to completion);

e. General management (matters of personnel, discipline, leave, expenditures, supplies, equipment, space, etc.) ;

f. Assignments (what the employees supervised are to do and the order in which they are to do it; selection of employees for particular assignments; determination of the priority of activities) ;

g. Work-methods (the technique of doing the work; the sequence of steps by which the employee, using the appropriate technique, accomplishes the prescribed objectives) ;

h. Coordination (development and operation of mechanisms for proper consistency and gearing of varied functions and tasks) ;

i. Production (amount of work done; promptness with which it is accomplished) ;

j. Results (the accuracy, adequacy, propriety, etc., of the work in the light of established policies, objectives, and work methods) ?

2. *Extent to which the initiative and judgment of those supervised is limited and the results of their work passed upon*

a. On what matters and to what degree does each of the various phases of supervisory and administrative control exercised by the employee actually limit the initiative and judgment of his subordinates?

b. What are the mechanics by which supervisory or administrative control is exercised over individual workers? (For example, direct personal and oral contact; written instructions; guiding precedents; intermediate supervisors; or a combination of these methods?)

c. In comparison with the examples given in Chapter V, is the control of the type describable as "immediate supervision," "general supervision," "general direction," or "executive direction," either on administrative or technical matters or both?

d. On what activities, within which segments of the "supervisory pattern," and to what degree have responsibilities been delegated to individual workers or intermediate supervisors? To what extent do they exercise initiative and judgment virtually independently of the supervisor? Which, if any, of the procedures followed, processes performed, actions initiated or developed, or decisions made by the employees supervised are virtually unreviewed?

3. *Size of the organization supervised*

a. How many employees are supervised—directly and through intermediate or subordinate supervisors?

b. What are the levels of employees supervised?

c. What special problems of supervision or administration arise by reason of the size of the organization?

d. What is the effect of mere magnitude when considered in the light of other factors affecting difficulty, supervisory or administrative responsibility, and/or qualifications needed? On the basis of a suitable class or group of positions for purposes of comparison, do differences in these factors offset differences in magnitude?

4. *Importance and variety of functions and the complexity of the organization supervised*

a. Selecting one or more pertinent viewpoints, what is the relative importance of the work of the organization supervised? Examples of viewpoints that may be taken are:

    i. Importance to the department, considered as an operating organization.

    ii. Importance to the government, considered as an operating organization.

    iii. Importance in respect to government finance, industry and commerce, agriculture, public health and safety, or other general economic or sociological factors.

    iv. Importance from the standpoint of effect or significance to the jurisdiction.

b. What is the structure of the organization supervised? In what successively smaller organization units are the employees grouped? What are the functions of each unit? How are these units connected by lines of authority?

c. What kinds of work are performed by the employees supervised? In what classes and grades do their positions fall? Are they all engaged on one process, function, or activity or are they engaged on a variety of activities? In what way, if at all, are these various activities functionally related? How are the employees distributed, by number and grade, among these activities?

d. How are the organization units and the employees supervised geographically distributed?

D. QUALIFICATIONS STANDARDS OF THE POSITION

For the proper and efficient performance of the work involved in the position—

a. What must the employee know? Of what subjects, processes, principles or applications of principles, laws, rules, regulations, etc., is knowledge necessary? To what extent—familiarity, general or working knowledge, or thorough and detailed knowledge?

b. What particular skills, abilities, or proficiencies (physical, manual, or mental) does the work demand?

c. To what extent and along what lines of study is formal educational training a necessity?

d. To what extent and along what lines is previous experience a prerequisite? Is a training period on the job necessary and, if so, to what extent?

e. To what extent and for what purpose does the work require contact with the public or with other employees in the same or a different organization? To what extent is social intelligence necessary?

f. Is the work unusually arduous requiring special physical aptitudes?

Appendix F

Classification Allocation Check Lists

I. Type of machine

a. Non-writing accounting and posting machine. No typewriter keyboard although it may have keys with whole words on them used for writing.

b. Typewriter accounting or billing machine. Has typewriter keyboard with ten numerical keys below space bar in case of accounting machines and some billing machines, or twenty numerical keys on billing machines where multiplication is possible. Without twenty keys, machine can add only.

This group will include typewriter accounting and billing machines of following makes: Burroughs, Burroughs-Moon Hopkins, Elliott Fisher, Remington, and Sunstrand. Note: In case of Ellis Typewriter Billing Machine (National Cash Register), typewriter keyboard is below full adding machine type of numerical keyboard. There is no school in the operation of this machine, and typist will have to be trained on the job.

II. Type of application

a. What accounts do you post?
b. Is posting operation identical in each operation?
　1. How many variations? How indicated on media?
c. Who assembles posting media?
d. How many entries do you make?
e. What closing or adjusting entries do you make? From what media?
f. Volume of funds for which you maintain accounts?
g. What balancing operations do you make?
　1. How do you check if accounts don't balance?
h. What figures do you draw off for statements?
　1. What statements? Who prepares?
　2. How are your figures checked?
i. Do you post control accounts?
　1. What posting media?
　2. If not, who keeps control?
j. How many documents do you post each entry? List. Single operation or separate operation each document?
k. What billing are you doing?
l. What are media for writing bills? Who prepares?
m. Describe billing operations. What calculations do you make on billing machine? What other calculations?

[1] Prepared by Public Administration Service.

ACCOUNTING POSITIONS[2]

I. Do you classify vouchers, invoices, etc., according to account classification for posting?

If the answer is yes:
a. How many such accounts are involved?
b. Is there any further check on your work?
c. What is the nature of such check?
d. How much of your time is spent on this work?

II. Do you keep books of record?

If the answer is yes:
a. What journalizing do you do? What are the funds and accounts affected?
b. What review do you have of journal entries made by others?
c. To what books do you post?
d. How many entries do you make?
e. What closing or adjusting entries do you make?
f. What other departmental or state accounts are affected by your closing entries?
g. Volume of funds for which you maintain books of accounts?

III. Are financial statements prepared by you?

If the answer is yes:
a. What is the form and subject matter?
b. Are the form and content prescribed or are they developed by you?
c. What is the scope—a picture of the entire financial position or of a portion?
d. What are the sources of data?
e. Is special analysis needed to prepare statements or do they flow from the totals of ledger and register accounts?

IV. Is auditing a part of your work?

If the answer is yes:
a. How large a firm or political subdivision do you examine? Variety of assignments?
b. How complete is the scope of the audit?
c. Detailed or spot audit of accounts within the scope indicated?
d. Do you work by yourself or in a crew?
e. What phases do you handle?
f. Who lays out the work and assigns it to you?
g. Is your work checked? Nature?

V. Have you anything to do with the installation and revision of accounting procedures?

If the answer is yes:
a. Are the forms, books, and statements and classification of accounts prescribed by other departments or units?

[2] Prepared by Public Administration Service.

b. Is it possible to change the forms and procedures? Which ones? To what extent?

c. Are you responsible for the operation of accounting procedure in the department or unit?

d. Do you advise department and unit heads as to account problems? Setting up books, etc.?

VI. Do your activities include cost accounting?

If the answer is yes:

a. Are costs in terms of work units, irrespective of projects, or individual projects?

b. Do you determine work units to be used?

c. Do you develop forms and procedures to secure desired data?

d. Do your books close to the general accounts? Details.

e. Is special analysis needed to prepare statements or do they flow from the unit breakdowns of operations?

VII. Are you exercising any supervisory power?

If the answer is yes:

a. Responsible for the work of accountants and account clerks under you? (The number of positions and type.) How close check is made of their work?

b. Are your decisions final or are they approved by someone else?

Translator Positions[3]

I. Translating into English

1. From what source and through what channels is the material to be translated received?

a. Who makes the assignment? What instructions are given?

b. Who selects the material to be translated?

i. Is the material selected by a superior officer?

ii. Is the subject of translation assigned but selection of actual material left to the translator?

iii. Is the selection of material left to the discretion of the translator?

c. To what extent is research necessary (e.g., in the compilation of material, covering a definite subject matter to be used for scientific research)?

i. Of what does the research work consist?

ii. How much time is devoted to such assignments?

d. Has this material received any preliminary treatment by others prior to assignment which would have a bearing upon the duties of the position? Describe.

[3] Personnel Classification Division, U. S. Civil Service Commission. Prepared by Robert S. Hare.

2. From what languages are translations made?

    a. Regularly

    b. Occasionally

      i. How often are such translations made?

3. From what language groups* are translations made?

    a. Regularly

      i. What is the relative difficulty of these language groups?*

    b. Occasionally

      i. What is the relative difficulty of these language groups?*

    *See pages 16–20 inclusive, relative to the question of language difficulty and difficulty groups. Romance and Teutonic languages are considered the less difficult, the Slavic, and Asiatic, and Eastern European being considered the more difficult.

4. What kind of material (not subject matter) is translated (i.e., the vehicle of expression, such as ordinary newspaper articles, correspondence, technical journals, reports of scientific experiments, certificates, etc.)?

    a. Is there a variety of kinds of material? (If there is a variety, and it is pertinent to the investigation, describe the distribution or frequency of different kinds of material by percentages if possible, otherwise in general terms.)

5. What is the subject matter of the material translated (i.e., aviation, ordnance, photography, metallurgy, soil science, economic, political, etc.)?

    a. Is there a variety of subject matter? (If there is a variety, and it is pertinent to the investigation, describe the distribution or frequency of different subject matters by percentages if possible, otherwise in general terms.)

    b. Is the subject matter scientific or technical, or non-technical? (Give percentages if possible.)

    c. If not previously covered, describe the difficulty of the subject matter.

    d. To what extent is knowledge of the subject matter *absolutely* necessary for the successful performance of the duties of the position? (e.g., familiarity, general or working knowledge.)

      i. If a knowledge of the subject matter is absolutely necessary *how* was this knowledge acquired? (i.e., by college work, home study, as a part of the duties of the job.)

      ii. Was this knowledge acquired prior to or during the incumbency of this position?

      iii. Is knowledge of the subject matter required for consideration for this position (original appointment)?

6. What degree of accuracy is required in making translations (i.e., must it be a faithful, close translation or may it be a literal or free translation as for administrative or for informational purposes)?

7. What is the importance of the translations?

    a. For what is the translated material used?
    Examples:
        i. Intra-office information
        ii. Inter-office information
        iii. Publication or public information
        iv. Regulatory purposes or as a basis of court action
        v. Preparation of statistics
        vi. Classifying or cataloging library or other material
        vii. Basis of money payment
        viii. Basis of awarding or bidding on contracts
        ix. Handling problems of international scope
    b. What would be the consequence of errors in translating?
    Examples:
        i. Would errors result in intra-office confusion, misfiling, etc.?
        ii. Would errors result in loss of money to the Government or to a claimant of the Government?
        iii. Would errors result in possible international complications?

8. What responsibility, other than accuracy, attaches to the making of translations?

9. To what extent are translations reviewed by a superior? Of what does the review consist?

10. Is any other person in this unit, or other unit of the bureau, charged with the *regular* translation from the languages from which the incumbent of this position *occasionally* translates?

11. What proportion of time is devoted to work described under I., i.e., translating into English?

II. Translating from English

    1 to 11 (Same as for translating into English, under I).

III. Interpreting

    1. From and into what languages are interpretations made?

    2. What language groups are involved in interpreting?

    3. On what occasions is interpreting work performed (e.g., at court hearings or formal or informal conferences) ?

    4. For whom is the interpreting done?

    5. What subject matter is interpreted?

    6. How many times in the past year has interpreting been done?

        a. What were the occasions?

7. Does any other person in this unit, or other unit in the bureau, do interpreting?

a. Is any other person in this unit, or other unit of the bureau, charged with interpreting which involves the same language or languages used by the incumbent of this position in his work?

8. What proportion of time is devoted to work described under III, i.e., interpreting?

IV. Duties other than translating and interpreting (excluding supervisory)

1. Does the incumbent of this position perform stenographic work?

a. Stenographic work in foreign languages?
   i. What are the languages?
b. What proportion of time is devoted to these duties?

2. What duties other than stenographic are performed by the incumbent of this position in addition to the work previously described?

a. What proportion of time is devoted to these duties?

V. Supervisory duties

1. How many persons are supervised?

a. What are their grades?

2. What work is performed by the persons supervised?

3. To what extent does the supervision include—

a. Assignment of work
b. Instruction and guidance during the process of work
c. Checking and review of final product

4. What proportion of time is devoted to supervisory duties?

VI. General considerations

1. Who reviews the work of the incumbent of this position?

a. Is he engaged primarily in translating or in the supervision of translating work, or in other activities?
   i. If he is not engaged primarily in translating or in the supervision thereof, does he have sufficient knowledge of languages to closely check or review the work of the incumbent?

2. What other positions in the immediate unit or in the bureau are comparable to this one?

a. Give names and grades

3. Are work records kept? (If so obtain sufficient information therefrom to verify incumbent's statements as indicated in I, II, and III.)

4. Is this position permanent or temporary? Full-time or part-time?